I0121068

FAITH
OF OUR FATHERS

A HISTORY
OF THE GERK FAMILY

EDWARD ROY GERK

Faith of Our Fathers: A History of the Gerk Family

Copyright © 2018 by Edward Roy Gerk

All rights reserved. No part of this publication may be reproduced in any form except for the inclusion of brief quotations in review, without permission of the author.

Printed in the United States of America

Third Printing: March 2020

ISBN-13 978-0-9878149-1-3

DEDICATED TO

My Parents: John & Margaret Gerk
My Beginnings

And

My Children: Elissa, Rebecca, Natalie, Andrew, David, Stephanie, Kristina,
Kimberly, Steven, Josiah & Ashley.
Our Future.

Psalm 100:5
For the Lord is good and his love endures forever;
His faithfulness continues through all generations.

Faith of Our Fathers

Text: Frederick W. Faber, 1814-1863

Faith of our fathers, living still,
in spite of dungeon, fire, and sword;
O how our hearts beat high
with joy whene'er we hear that glorious word!

Refrain:
Faith of our fathers, holy faith!
We will be true to thee till death.

Faith of our fathers, we will love
both friend and foe in all our strife;
and preach thee, too, as love knows
how by kindly words and virtuous life.
(Refrain)

Faith of our fathers! Days of old
Within our hearts speak gallantly.
Long ages hast Thou stood by us,
Dear Faith, and now we'll stand by Thee.
Faith of our fathers! Holy Faith!
We will be true to Thee till death.
(Refrain)

Table of Contents

Chapter 1:   Foreword: A Modern Gerk Detective Story

Chapter 2:   A 10 minute History of the Volga Germans...1

Chapter 3:   Our Family Gerk: German Origins...7

Chapter 4:   Sebastian Gerk & the Gerk's of Koehler, Russia...21

Chapter 5:   The Gerk's of Josefstal...33

Chapter 6:   The Gerk's of Marienfeld...45

Chapter 7:   The Gerk's of Pfeifer...53

Chapter 8:   Johann Georg Gerk & Family...57

Chapter 9:   Paul Gerk...71

Chapter 10:   The Russian Revolution & Uprising of 1918...73

Chapter 11:   The Turbulent Years: Civil War & Famine...83

Chapter 12:   Paul Gerk: Volga German Refugee from Minsk...87

Chapter 13:   The Johannes Dieser Family of Josefstal...103

Chapter 14:   Elisabeth (Dieser) Gerk...111

Chapter 15:   Last Letters & the Great Silence ...117

Chapter 16:   Deportation to Siberia...125

Chapter 17:   Lost in the Gulag...129

Chapter 18:   Left Behind: My Memories about our Gerk Family...139

Chapter 19:   A Russian Gerk Photo Album...147

Chapter 20:   The Life of Paul & Elisabeth Gerk in Photographs...153

Chapter 21:   The Gerk Family of Alberta...173

Chapter 22:   The Gerk Family of Colorado...179

Chapter 23:   The Gerk Family of Iowa...189

Chapter 24:   The Gerk Family of South Dakota...195

Chapter 25:   The Gerk Family of Wisconsin...203

Chapter 25:   The Joseph Gerk Family of Missouri...205

Chapter 26:   The Gerk Family of Kassel...207

Chapter 27:   The Gerk Family of Brazil...209

Chapter 28:   The Martin Gerk Family of Santa Maria, Argentina...213

Chapter 29:   The Peter Gerk Family of Crespo, Argentina...215

Chapter 30:   The Peter Alois Gerk Family of Crespo, Argentina...219

Chapter 31:   The Johann Adam Gerk Family of San Miguel Arcángel, Argentina...221

Chapter 32:   The Joseph Gerk Family of San Miguel Arcángel, Argentina...223

Chapter 33:   The Georg Gerk Family of Santa Anita, Argentina ...225

Chapter 34:   The Peter Gerk Family of Santa Anita, Argentina...227

Chapter 36:   The Descendants of Sebastian & Magdalena Gerk...237

THE DANGERS OF WRITING A FAMILY HISTORY

An amateur genealogical researcher discovered that his great-great uncle, Remus Starr, a fellow lacking in character, was hanged for horse stealing and train robbery in Montana in 1889. The only known photograph of Remus shows him standing on the gallows. On the back of the picture is this inscription:

"Remus Starr; horse thief; sent to Montana Territorial Prison 1885, escaped 1887; robbed the Montana Flyer six times. Caught by Pinkerton detectives. +Convicted and hanged 1889."

In a Family History subsequently written by the researcher, Remus's picture is cropped so that all that's seen is a head shot. The accompanying biographical sketch is as follows:

"Remus Starr was a famous cowboy in the Montana Territory. His business empire grew to include acquisition of valuable equestrian assets and intimate dealings with the Montana railroad. Beginning in 1885, he devoted several years of his life to service at a government facility, finally taking leave to resume his dealings with the railroad. In 1887, he was a key player in a vital investigation run by the renowned Pinkerton Detective Agency. In 1889, Remus passed away during an important civic function held in his honor when the platform upon which he was standing collapsed."

-Author Unknown.

After over 30 years of searching and collecting information, in 2012, I was happy to finally print the first edition of this History book.

I thought it would be the final word.

Happily, though, new information arrived that necessitated revising some important elements of this history.

Because of the hard work of Helmut Gerk, and his important new history, *"Chronik Müs"*, we now are pretty certain who our Sebastian Gerk is!

That is no small feat. Archival documents show a variety of variations for names and ages, which have added a lot of confusion to finding out the truth.

Through the diligence of William Gerk, Helmut Gerk, and Brigitte Kilian-Gerk, we are now closer to the truth.

New documentation from the Bistumsarchiv in Fulda, sheds new light on the family of Sebastian, the first Gerk to Russia.

Also added was a new chapter dealing with the Gerk family of Missouri, in the USA, and their ties to the Fulda area Gerk's.

There are small typo corrections and some new documentation on some individuals as well.

Those make up the bulk of the changes in this revised edition.

I want to thank again Dr. Igor Pleve, William Gerk, Helmut Gerk, Brigitte Kilian-Gerk and Dr. Christina Reiche for their research assistance.

Thank you to everyone who has made comments and suggestions. I appreciate your care and concern.

I hope that this will be the catalyst for other Gerk's to research and publish their own story!

Enjoy!

-Edward Roy (Ted) Gerk, May 2018

Finding one's family can be a difficult task. And when you add the equation that you have not heard from them for 60 years, and they live in an "Iron Curtain" country, it can be well-nigh impossible.

It took many years and a lot of hard work to be able to write these words. I remember well the conversation I had with my brother Bill in 1978, when he made the suggestion to me that it would be great if he and I could find some relatives still alive for our grandmother, Elisabeth (Dieser) Gerk.

Our grandmother, whom we affectionately called "Granny", was 76 years old. She often talked to us about her life as a youth in Russia. I had remembered seeing her photographs from the old country, carefully wrapped in wax paper.

I was to look carefully on those photos many times over the years...treasuring them when she gave them to me...thinking about those same pictures when Granny spent many patient hours with me talking about the "old country".

I agreed with Bill. It would indeed be cool if we could find some relative for Granny.

But where to start? My brother Bill was a true leader in this regard.

He assigned the task to me.

Bill assured his involvement by allowing me to "use" his post-office box for any correspondence that might be generated as a result of our quest. But Bill's idea was really the catalyst for this work you hold in your hands. In the great scheme of things, it only took about 6 years to finally track down the living remnants of the Gerk and Dieser family in Russia. But it quickly became a labour of love for me...as it set me on a path in which much of my future was mapped out. The family history bug can be a nasty disease. But in my case, I was stricken wonderfully. I was able to meet my beautiful wife Marina, all in the interest of interviewing people from Russia, as my detective work grew.

I was able to meet my great uncle, the younger brother of my grandfather. He visited Canada in 1989.

I was able to stand at the remains of our ancestral village of Josefstal in Russia. It's German identity bulldozed into oblivion. All that remained was the cemetery...where hundreds of graves lie unmarked. Iron crosses lie strewn about, the names ripped from them as if to hide some dark secret.

I interviewed Granny Gerk many times for the project. Two of those many interviews are on tape, now transferred to a CD where they are preserved.

Granny talked about her home near the Volga River in Russia, and her home village of Josefstal. She talked about a neighboring village named "Mariental", also Catholic.

It was time to set to work. My Uncle Ed and Aunt Sharon in Edmonton heard about my project and mentioned a book about the German villages in Russia: "*Paradise on the Steppe*", by Dr. Joseph Height. Aunt Sharon provided me with the details in tracking down the book, and I set off.

Immediately I was stymied. The book talked about a Josefstal, and indeed talked about a village named "Mariental", but they were in the wrong area of Russia. The villages featured in this book were in the Ukraine, near the Black Sea.

I quickly learned that there were other colonies, other such German villages... right near Granny had said. All near the Volga River in Russia.

Granny's old German dialect made it sound like "Mariental". The Mariental she stated was actually "Marienfeld", and it was right near her home village of Josefstal. In fact, all the villages she mentioned were there. Josefstal, Marienfeld, Semenovka, Koehler, Kamenka, and the cities of Saratov and Kamyshin.

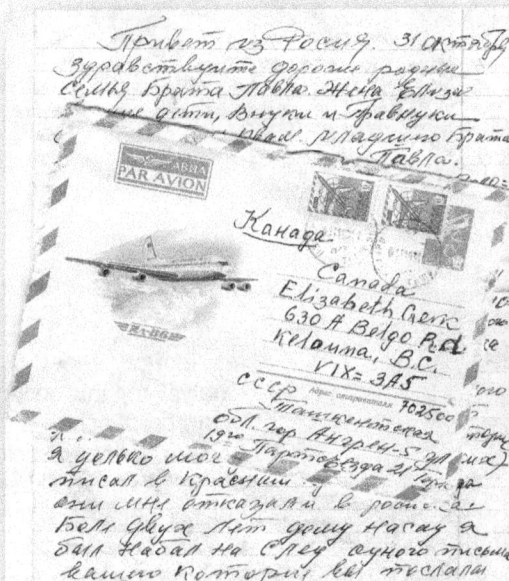

The first letter of many from Johannes Gerk (Uncle Vanya) of Angren, Uzbekistan, former U.S.S.R

Going further in my research, I joined the *American Historical Society of Germans from Russia*, based in Lincoln, Nebraska and was able to purchase old maps of the area.

I started writing to any and every Russian address I could get my hands on. Granny had some Kelowna-area friends who were also from Russia, so I interviewed them, in hopes they might assist me.

Letters were written to the Canadian and International Red Cross. But to no avail. "No such person" was the constant response.

A story was told to me that my grandfather, Paul Gerk, had sat in on a newsreel movie in a theatre, and was shocked at a report on the civil war in Spain (1936 – 1939). He was sure he saw his younger brother Johannes being taken prisoner! He immediately wrote the Red Cross for help, but also received no assistance.

Brick wall after brick wall.

Meanwhile, as my list of people interviewed grew, in 1978 I was given the opportunity to meet and interview a 17-year old girl attending Kelowna Secondary School. She was born and raised in the USSR, only immigrating to Canada 3 years earlier.

And so would add another exciting chapter to my life...the girl I interviewed not only helped me with the family history, she became part of it, as I married Marina Loewen on August 1, 1981.

Together we worked writing people all over Russia, with the kind help of Marina's Tante Agnes.

I subscribed to *"Neues Leben"*, a Soviet newspaper for Germans living in the USSR, hoping I might come across some clues. Carefully, I noted any reference to the family names of Gerk and Dieser.

One name appeared regularly in a "greeting" section of the paper, that of Johannes Gerk and his wife Barbara.

This was, I now suspected, the younger brother of my grandfather, Paul Gerk. He had married his childhood sweetheart, Barbara Dieser, and the chances were good that if anyone survived, he would have.

Shortly after I came across the numerous references to Johannes, I again contacted the Red Cross in hoped of finding some link.

In September of 1984 I received a letter from them (it took a year to reach me) that they had success, and that they had located Johannes Gerk, Paul Gerk's youngest brother. They also added they had found a nephew of Granny, Josef Dieser, who was interested in renewing contact with our family.

We immediately compiled letters and sent them away to the addresses given.

On Nov. 12, 1984, our family received a strange looking envelope with Russian stamps. I had seen enough Russian to know the name Gerk on the return address.

It was a letter from Johannes Gerk, the youngest brother of Paul Gerk.

He stated: *"I wrote a lot to find you. For 9 years I wrote to any Canadian address I could get my hands on. I wrote to the Red Cross in Canada too. All could not find you! More than 2 years ago I was on the trail from one of your letters which you wrote and found out you were looking for me..."*

Indeed we were!

СССР
ИСПОЛНИТЕЛЬНЫЙ КОМИТЕТ ОРДЕНА ЛЕНИНА
СОЮЗА ОБЩЕСТВ
КРАСНОГО КРЕСТА И КРАСНОГО ПОЛУМЕСЯЦА
Телефон 221-71-75

№ 478025/12   При ответе ссылайтесь на наш номер   Москва «29» апреля 1983г.

Канадское общество Красного Креста
г. Торонто

Уважаемые господа!

Просим передать м-ру Тед Герк (Mr. Ted GERK of 2375 Rhondda Rd., Kelowna B.C. Canada), что в результате большой, кропотливой работы установлено следующее:

Дизер Иван Иванович умер в 1972 г., его сын, Дизер Иосиф Иванович, 1941 г.р., проживает по адресу:
638710 Павлодарская обл., Экибастузский р-н, совхоз Степной;

Дизер Адам Иванович умер 7 июля 1976 г.;
Герк Готфрид Георгиевич, 1908 г.р. умер 19.II. 1980 г.;
Герк Иван Георгиевич, 1910 г.р., проживает:
702500 Ташкентская область,
г. Ангрен, ул. XIX Партсъезда, угольный разрез, д.21.

Надеемся, что в ближайшее время переписка между родственниками восстановится и члены семьи Герк из Канады узнают о судьбе родных.

Рады были помочь.

С уважением,

Фатюхина В.П.

Начальник Управления по розыску

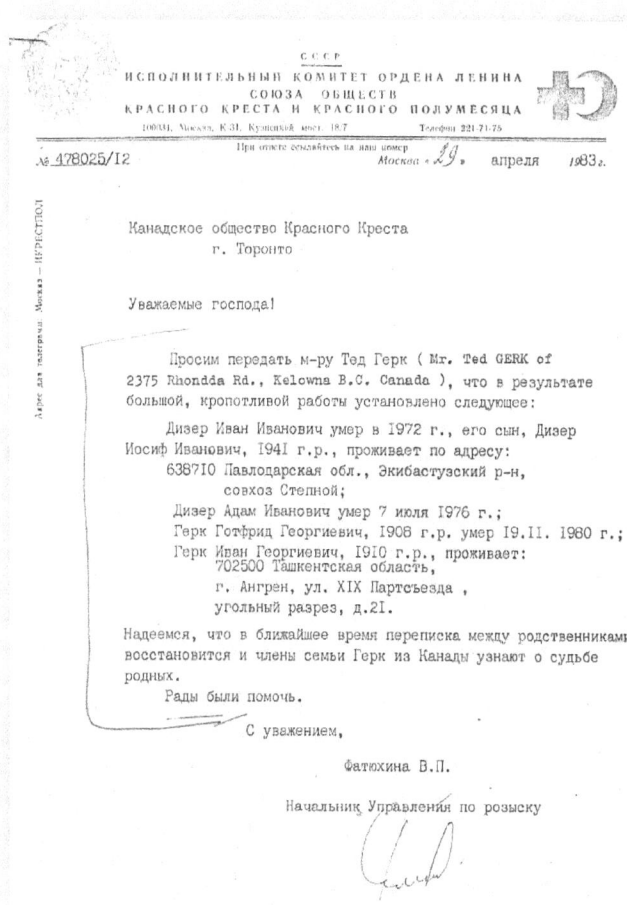

After numerous inquiries through the years, the USSR Red Cross finally responded positively! In a letter dated April 29, 1983, they confirmed the whereabouts of members of the Gerk and Dieser families. The letter took a year to reach us.

ACKNOWLEDGMENTS

To tell you that there are many people responsible for the work you hold in your hands, would be an understatement.

Not that I want to pass the blame around, I want to make clear that any errors or omissions are mine and mine alone. But there were so many people that helped in this labour of love, for so long, where can I even start?

I think of the many hours I spent with my grandmother, Elisabeth Gerk. Granny told me the stories, and then she told me again when I asked her. My deepest prize is the two taped interviews I have of her and I talking about the old country. From a historian's perspective, Granny was bang on, on so many accounts that I am still amazed!

With mixed emotions I want to thank my Mom and Dad – who always believed in what I was doing. Dad especially encouraged me in my quest, because I think I asked all the questions he wished he had asked when his Dad was alive. I should have recorded our talks together too...but we never thought he would leave us so soon. I miss you Dad!

Marina was perhaps the biggest gift to me. Not just because of her help finding family in the former USSR. Her translation abilities allowed our family to reconnect with lost loved ones that no one had heard from in over 60 years. The added benefit in all of this is she became a Gerk, being very patient with me as I worked on all of this.

Mrs. Ellen Buehler was also a big help to my work. Her translation of German documents, letters and articles also enabled this work to continue. And oy, her potato pancakes were the best in the world. Sadly, she never got to see the finished work. She passed away in 2000.

Others who assisted and deserve thanks are

Henry and Paula Raschke, for their help in translating letters from Germany. Carlos Alberto Schwab, a native of Brazil, whom I have never met in person, translated my ever growing Spanish correspondence, and without his kind help I would have never been able to renew the link between North and South America. Thanks Carlos!

Others who were of great assistance, especially with the new-found Argentina connection were: Daniel and Norma Pagliero of Buenos Aires, Maria Alicia Gerk, Carina Kerke, Cristian Gerk, Maria Luisa Gerk and Sergio Keiner. These wonderful people were responsible for taking photographs of old gravestones, sending me information and data on their families, and just about anything I needed to find...they were willing to help a complete stranger from another world away! Thank you my dear friends!

Donald Gerk, Barry Dieser, Geoff Gerk and Charmaine Gerk Moeller were also some of the folks that allowed me into their lives to document some of this. Thank you again for your help - it's fun having you as relatives!

"I wrote a lot to find you. For 9 years I wrote to any Canadian address I could get my hands on. I wrote to the Red Cross in Canada too. All could not find you! More than 2 years ago I was on the trail from one of your letters which you wrote and found out you were looking for me..." Johannes Gerk (Brother of Paul Gerk) 31 October 1984

In Germany, I need to mention the kind and generous help of Eva Gerk, husband Joerg and Eva's dear Mother, Mrs. Karol Gerk. It was Karol Gerk who told me as they welcomed me into their Fulda, Germany home: *"Gerk's are always at home for other Gerk's!"*

Of course, I need to also mention Rick Rye, for his advice and Russian proficiency...he is an honourable man! Thanks also to Lee for help with the cover design - and thank you to my daughter Stephanie for helping with translations of Spanish documents!

The folks at the Saratov State archive (acknowledged on these pages with the acronym GASO) deserve thanks for their assistance – and allowing a foreigner to ask lots of questions and peruse old Church books in their office. Dr. Igor Pleve of Saratov State University was also responsible for help in acquiring numerous old documents.

The staff at the State Archive of Volgograd Oblast (acknowledged on these pages with the acronym GAVO) went beyond the call of duty – allowing me to copy literally anything I wanted. This institution carries the Josefstal fond (files). A special thank you to Nadezhda and the rest of the archive staff. Also thanks to our dear Russian friends Len & Olga Stolyarchuk, for all our Russian adventures!! The fields of Volgogradskaya Oblast will never be the same!

How can I describe the feeling one gets when you stand in an old deserted cemetery in Russia, knowing that so many of your ancestors lie buried there? I also remembered my family...and what they went through to give my family a new start...and freedom. It's a story I wanted to tell my children.

I think of these words: *"We will not hide them from their children, but tell to the coming generation the glorious deeds of the Lord, and his might, and the wonders that he has done"* (Psalm 78:4)

This work is by no means complete. The detective work goes on. Other family members moved to Argentina, Brazil, and the United States. There are Gerk's in Slovenia and Hungary. Who and why did they move? Some appear to be from the Fulda area of Germany, the area of Sebastian's birth.

This could never be an exhaustive look at all Gerk families. But it should provide a catalyst for many seeking their Gerk origins. What started as just a history of my grandparents, soon branched out to include chapters on the origins of other Gerk's.

And yes, most of this history is compiled based on the life and families of Paul and Elisabeth (Dieser) Gerk....and all of us who are the descendants of that first Gerk to Russia, Sebastian Gerk.

So here it is. I hope it was worth the wait!

Ted Gerk – July 2012

"A teenager has breakfast, then goes to the store to buy the latest CD of a new band. The kid thinks he lives in a modern moment. But who has defined what a 'band' is? Who defined a 'store'? Who defined a 'teenager'? Or 'breakfast'? To say nothing of all the rest, the kid's entire social setting - family, school, clothing, transportation and government.

"None of this has been decided in the present. Most of it was decided hundreds of years ago. Five hundred years, a thousand years. This kid is sitting on top of a mountain that is the past. And he never notices it. He is ruled by what he never sees, never thinks about, doesn't know. It is a form of coercion that is accepted without question. This same kid is skeptical of other forms of control - parental restrictions, commercial messages, government laws. But the invisible rule of the past, which decides nearly everything in his life, goes unquestioned."

-Michael Crichton, "Timeline"

"I wonder what sort of tale we've fallen into?"

-J.R.R. Tolkien, "Lord of the Rings: The Two Towers."

Mein Wolgavolk

Mein Wolgavolk, du hast aus deinen Tiefen
gehoben deinen Sohn ans Licht empor;
die Kräfte, die in meinem Herzen schliefen,
du riefest sie zu frohem Tun hervor.

Mein Wolgavolk, ich habe stets in Treue
mit dir geteilt die Freude und das Leid,
dir weihe jeden Tag ich mich aufs neue
in stillem, ernstem Wirken allezeit.

Mein Herz schlug bebend dir in trüben Tagen,
und wenn die Sonne schien, hat's dir gelacht;
so soll es je und je in Treu' dir schlagen.

Wenn zu den Vätern ich versammelt werde,
mein letzter Mahnruf sei's vor Grabesnacht:
„Bleib treu, mein Wolgavolk, der Heimaterde!"

P. Sinner

My Volga folk, you have from the depths
lifted your son to the light on high.
The forces which slept in my heart,
you called forth to blessed deeds.

My Volga folk, I have always truly
with you shared joy and pain.
To you every day is offered
in stillness, bringing silence.

My heart shook in your dark day,
and when the sun shone, rejoiced with you,
so shall it beat ever and ever in faith to you.

When to the fathers I shall be gathered,
my last request before the grave's night:
Remain true, my Volga folk, to your
homeland!

"Meir Wolgavolk", by Peter Sinner, translated by Samuel Sinner.

A 10 minute History of the Volga Germans

Soon after coming to power in a bloodless coup, Catherine II (later "The Great"), herself German, extended an invitation to Germans to colonize portions of the lower Volga, to improve farming in the region [colonization by Russians was not deemed feasible, because serfs were tied to the land they worked]. The offer included free land for all colonists, payment of passage to Russia, freedom of religion, freedom from military servitude, freedom from taxes for 30 years and self-government of national groups. Needless to say, this was an enticing proposal to German peasants who had little chance of owning land in Germany and who had suffered mightily under the Seven Years War (1756- 63).

The German colonists flocked to the Volga region from 1764 on, establishing over 100 colonies between Saratov and Kamyshin and coming to be known as "Volga-Germans (Nemtsy povolzhe). The majority of Volga-Germans came from the Southwest portion of Germany. Large numbers of Germans also settled along the Black Sea coast.

The Germans lived largely in isolation from the surrounding Russian population and, not limited by the ties of serfdom, were able to develop much better local economic conditions. But, toward the end of the 19th century, with the Russifying policies of Tsars Alexander II and Alexander III, the advantageous conditions and self-government extended the Germans was curtailed. This led to massive German emigration (over 100,000 to the US alone) and, with other reforms at the turn of this century, to internal emigration - to the southern Urals, Kazakstan and Siberia, where new lands were being opened up for settlers. The 1897 census showed some 1.8 million persons of German ancestry living in Russia, in over 2000 settlements.

The First World War brought certain repressive measures for Russians of German ancestry. Germans living near the front lines were relocated; limits were imposed on property ownership and the use of the German language. The revolution brought respite and, in 1918, with the establishment of the Workers' Commune of the Volga Germans, the Nemtsy povolzhe became the first ethnic minority to receive local autonomy in the new USSR (largely because this was one of the first areas the Bolsheviks controlled). The Autonomous Republic of Volga Germans, centered on the city of Engels (formerly Pokrovsk), superseded the Commune in 1924.

The period between the wars saw huge emigrations of Germans from Russia - some 400,000 Germans left different parts of Russia, mainly for Germany. But the most notorious migration was yet to come. With the onset of WWII, in 1941, Stalin ordered the forced migration of some 800,000 Germans from European portions of Russia to Kazakstan and Siberia (the emigrants were not told this was a permanent evacuation and expected to return after the war was over). Half of these were from the Volga region, as, in 1939, there were 392,500 Germans living along the Volga, comprising over 60% of the population of the autonomous republic. With the forced emigration, the Autonomous Republic of Volga- - Germans ceased to exist.

A decade after the war there were 1.6 million Russians of German ancestry living in the USSR, roughly half in Russia and half in Kazakstan. By 1979, the number was close to 2 million.

Needless to say, with the forced migrations and the related social pressures of this and the war, ties to a German cultural heritage began to unravel. By 1989, less than half of Germans in the USSR considered German to be their first language, and only 45% spoke German fluently.

Still, in the period after the war, some Germans did make their way back to the Volga (the Volga-Germans were not officially "rehabilitated" until August 1964). There are an estimated 17,000 Russians with German ancestry living in the region. This represents about 0.6% of the population, ranking the population of ethnic Germans in the region between Belarusians and Azeris. Russians now comprise 85% of the region's population.

Igor Plehve, professor of history at Saratov State University and a noted authority on the Volga-Germans, said that the autonomy movement began as early as the 1960s, but until 1972, it was virtually impossible to get a propiska to settle in the region. And, after the onset of perestroika, the movement began to pick up speed. But "local authorities were very scared by that. Very scared." So opposition, Plehve said, was "created" by party apparatchiks, "who knew they would lose all their power... if other bodies of power, new German structures, could be created." The publication of a USSR Supreme Soviet Resolution in 1989 on the resurrection of the Volga-German Autonomous Republic incited further action.

In early 1991, there was even talk of resettling 200-300,000 Germans from Kazakstan and Siberia back to the Volga. Seven raions in Saratov oblast and five in Volgograd oblast were marked out for recreation of an autonomous German republic. The Volga-German movement picked up speed over the course of the year, but was sidetracked by the dissolution of the USSR.

The turning point, Plehve said, came in January 1992, when President Yeltsin visited the region and declared that there will be no autonomy until Germans comprise 90% of the local population.

"From that point on," Plehve said, "the idea of German autonomy began fading away ... a de

facto mass exodus began ... Now there is no one to create autonomy for ..." Since 1991, Germans from Russia were allowed to freely emigrate and resettle in Germany and some 200,000 have done so each year.

(SOURCE: Anonymous, The Volga-Germans. Vol. 41, Russian Life, 06-01-1998, pp 24.)

Manifesto of the Empress Catherine II issued July 22, 1763

By the Grace of God!

We, Catherine the second, Empress and Autocrat of all the Russians at Moscow, Kiev, Vladimir, Novgorod, Czarina of Kasan, Czarina of Astrachan, Czarina of Siberia, Lady of Pleskow and Grand Duchess of Smolensko, Duchess of Esthonia and Livland, Carelial, Twer, Yugoria, Permia, Viatka and Bulgaria and others; Lady and Grand Duchess of Novgorod in the Netherland of Chernigov, Resan, Rostov, Yaroslav, Beloosrial, Udoria, Obdoria, Condinia, and Ruler of the entire North region and Lady of the Yurish, of the Cartalinian and Grusinian czars and the Cabardinian land, of the Cherkessian and Gorsian princes and the lady of the manor and sovereign of many others. As We are sufficiently aware of the vast extent of the lands within Our Empire, We perceive, among other things, that a considerable number of regions are still uncultivated which could easily and advantageously be made available for productive use of population and settlement. Most of the lands hold hidden in their depth an inexhaustible wealth of all kinds of precious ores and metals, and because they are well provided with forests, rivers and lakes, and located close to the sea for purpose of trade, they are also most convenient for the development and growth of many kinds of manufacturing, plants, and various installations. This induced Us to issue the manifesto which was published last Dec. 4, 1762, for the benefit of all Our loyal subjects. However, inasmuch as We made only a summary announcement of Our pleasure to the foreigners who would like to settle in Our Empire, we now issue for a better understanding of Our intention the following decree which We hereby solemnly establish and order to be carried out to the full.

. *"The foreigners who have settled in Russia shall not be drafted against their will into the military or the civil service during their entire stay here."*

1.

We permit all foreigners to come into Our Empire, in order to settle in all the governments, just as each one may desire.

2.

After arrival, such foreigners can report for this purpose not only to the Guardianship Chancellery established for foreigners in Our residence, but also, if more convenient, to the governor or commanding officer in one of the border-towns of the Empire.

3.

Since those foreigners who would like to settle in Russia will also include some who do not have sufficient means to pay the required travel costs, they can report to our ministers in foreign courts, who will not only transport them to Russia at Our expense, but also provide them with travel money.

4.

As soon as these foreigners arrive in Our residence and report at the Guardianship Chancellery or in a border-town, they shall be required to state their true decision whether their real desire is to be enrolled in the guild of merchants or artisans, and become citizens, and in what city; or if they wish to settle on free, productive land in colonies and rural areas, to take up agriculture or some other useful occupation. Without delay, these people will be

Copy of the Manifest of Catherine the Great, dated July 22, 1763, inviting Germans to settle in Russia. Source: "Die Geschichte Der Wolgaedutschen"

assigned to their destination, according to their own wishes and desires. From the following register* it can be seen in which regions of Our Empire free and suitable lands are still available. However, besides those listed, there are many more regions and all kinds of land where We will likewise permit people to settle, just as each one chooses for his best advantage. (*The register lists the areas where the immigrants can be settled.)

5.

Upon arrival in Our Empire, each foreigner who intends to become a settler and has reported to the Guardianship Chancellery or in other border-towns of Our Empire and, as already prescribed in # 4, has declared his decision, must take the oath of allegiance in accordance with his religious rite.

6.

In order that the foreigners who desire to settle in Our Empire may realize the extent of Our benevolence to their benefit and advantage, this is Our will -- :

1. We grant to all foreigners coming into Our Empire the free and unrestricted practice of their religion according to the precepts and usage of their Church. To those, however, who intend to settle not in cities but in colonies and villages on uninhabited lands we grant the freedom to build churches and bell towers, and to maintain the necessary number of priests and church

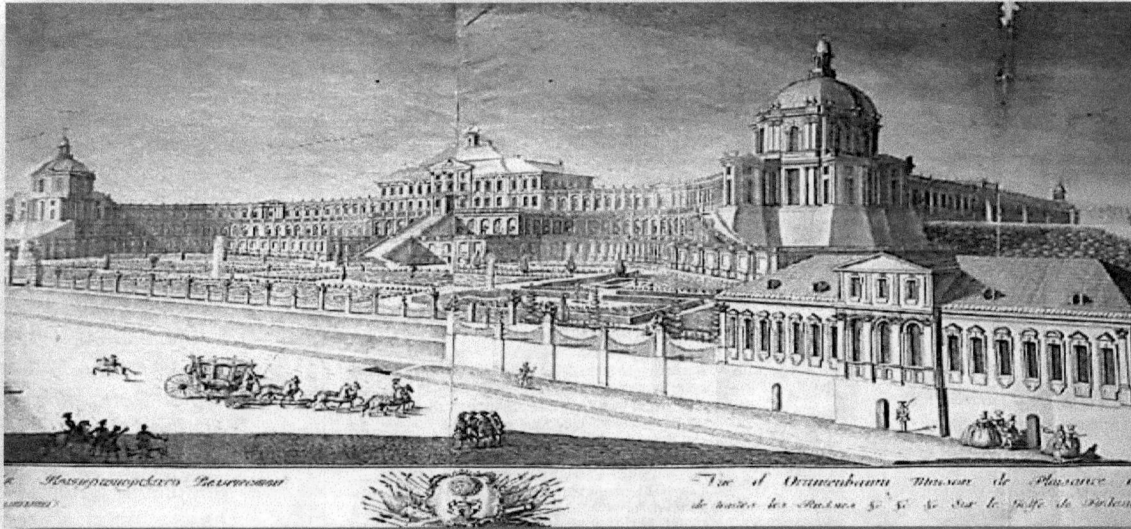

A print by Chelnakov and Knunov after a drawing of the Great Palace in Oranienbaum, Russia by Makhaev. The Great Palace was also known as Catherine II Summer Palace. This is the likely landing spot for the Germans who were arriving in Russia. Source: The Center for Volga German Studies

servants, but not the construction of monasteries. On the other hand, everyone is hereby warned not to persuade or induce any of the Christian co-religionists living in Russia to accept or even assent to his faith or join his religious community, under pain of incurring the severest punishment of Our law. This prohibition does not apply to the various nationalities on the borders of Our Empire who are attached to the Mahometan faith. We permit and allow everyone to win them over and make them subject to the Christian religion in a decent way.

2. None of the foreigners who have come to settle in Russia shall be required to pay the slightest taxes to Our treasury, nor be forced to render regular or extraordinary services, nor to billet troops. Indeed, everybody shall be exempt from all taxes and tribute in the following manner: those who have been settled as colonists with their families in hitherto uninhabited regions will enjoy 30 years of exemption; those who have established themselves, at their own expense, in cities as merchants and tradesmen in Our Residence St. Petersburg or in the neighboring cities of Livland, Esthonia, Ingermanland, Carelia and Finland, as well as in the Residential city of Moscow, shall enjoy 5 years of tax exemption. Moreover, each one who comes to Russia, not just for a short while but to establish permanent domicile, shall be granted free living quarters for half a year.

3. All foreigners who settle in Russia either to engage in agriculture and some trade, or to undertake to build factories and plants will be offered a helping hand and the necessary loans required for the construction of factories useful for the future, especially of such as have not yet been built in Russia.

4. For the building of dwellings, the purchase of livestock needed for the farmstead, the necessary equipment, materials, and tools for agriculture and industry, each settler will receive the necessary money from Our treasury in the form of an advance loan without any interest. The capital sum has to be repaid only after ten years, in equal annual installments in the following three years.

5. We leave to the discretion of the established colonies and village the internal constitution and jurisdiction, in such a way that the persons placed in authority by Us will not interfere with the internal affairs and institutions. In other respects the colonists will be liable to Our civil laws. However, in the event that the people would wish to have a special guardian or even an officer with a detachment of disciplined soldiers for the sake of security and defense, this wish would also be granted.

6. To every foreigner who wants to settle in Russia We grant complete duty-free import of his property, no matter what it is, provided, however, that such property is for personal use and need, and not intended for sale. However, any family

that also brings in unneeded goods for sale will be granted free import on goods valued up to 300 rubles, provided that the family remains in Russia for at least 10 years. Failing which, it be required, upon its departure, to pay the duty both on the incoming and outgoing goods.

7. The foreigners who have settled in Russia shall not be drafted against their will into the military or the civil service during their entire stay here. Only after the lapse of the years of tax-exemption can they be required to provide labor service for the country. Whoever wishes to enter military service will receive, besides his regular pay, a gratuity of 30 rubles at the time he enrolls in the regiment.

8. As soon as the foreigners have reported to the Guardianship Chancellery or to our border towns and declared their decision to travel to the interior of the Empire and establish domicile there, they will forthwith receive food rations and free transportation to their destination.

9. Those among the foreigners in Russia who establish factories, plants, or firms, and produce goods never before manufactured in Russia, will be permitted to sell and export freely for ten years, without paying export duty or excise tax.

10. Foreign capitalists who build factories, plants, and concerns in Russia at their own expense are permitted to purchase serfs and peasants needed for the operation of the factories.

11. We also permit all foreigners who have settled in colonies or villages to establish market days and annual market fairs as they see fit, without having to pay any dues or taxes to Our treasury.

7.
All the afore-mentioned privileges shall be enjoyed not only by those who have come into our country to settle there, but also their children and descendants, even though these are born in Russia, with the provision that their years of exemption will be reckoned from the day their forebears arrived in Russia.

8.
After the lapse of the stipulated years of exemption, all the foreigners who have settled in Russia are required to pay the ordinary moderate contributions and, like our other subjects, provide labor- service for their country.

9.
Finally, in the event that any foreigner who has settled in Our Empire and has become subject to Our authority should desire to leave the country, We shall grant him the liberty to do so, provided, however, that he is obligated to remit to Our treasury a portion of the assets he has gained in this country; that is, those who have been here from one to five years will pay one-fifth, whole those who have been here for five or more years will pay one-tenth. Thereafter each one will be permitted to depart unhindered anywhere he pleases to go.

10.
If any foreigner desiring to settle in Russia wishes for certain reasons to secure other privileges or conditions besides those already stated, he can apply in writing or in person to our Guardianship Chancellery, which will report the petition to Us. After examining the circumstances, We shall not hesitate to resolve the matter in such a way that the petitioner's confidence in Our love of justice will not be disappointed.

Given at the Court of Peter, July 22, 1763 in the Second Year of Our Reign.

The original was signed by Her Imperial Supreme Majesty's own hand.
Printed by the Senate, July 25, 1763

This manifesto was very soon followed by many supplementary stipulations, for instance the enactment of March 19, 1764, concerning the right to own land. In 1874 all privileges were revoked; from then on the Germans became subject to military service.

Image of Catherine the Great on the 1910 Russian 100 Rouble bank note.

Photo take of the Volga German village of Streckerau, gives an example of what most of the Volga Grman villages looked like. Circa 1920
Source: Deutsches Bundesarchiv (German Federal Archive), Bild 137-000471

The Russian city of Kamyshin circa 1900. Kamyshin was a major commercial city for the Volga Germans, including the Gerk family, who would have travelled here often. Kamyshin was about 35 km from Josefstal and surrounding villages. Source: www.kam.su

Gerk

The Gerk Coat of Arms and its History is what is known as a "speculative" history.

Coats of Arms were developed in the Middle Ages as a means of identifying warriors in battle and tournaments. The present function of the Coat of Arms (although still one of identity) serves more to preserve the traditions that arose from its earlier use.

Heraldic artists of old developed their own unique language to describe an individual Coat of Arms. The Coat of Arms illustrated was drawn by a heraldic artist from information recorded in ancient heraldic archives. Research indicates that there are often times a number of different Coats of Arms recorded for a specific surname. The Gerk Coat of Arms illustrated is officially documented in Siebmacher's Wappenbuch. The original description of the Arms (Shield) is as follows:

"Schwarz - R. Getheilt, Oben Wachsender S. Low, Unten S. Rose" When translated the"Divided horizontally: 1) Black, A silver Lion Issuing; 2) Red, A Silver Rose."

Above the shield and helmet is the crest which is described as: "The Silver Lion Issuing".

Now, does this mean the Gerk family had royal blood flowing through their veins? Usually, as is the case with a Coat of Arms, it just means that someone, somewhere, with a name similar to Gerk, had this as their family emblem. As for our "Gerk" Coat of Arms and the constant marketing to Gerk's worldwide? Speculative and based on little data. We may never really know.

Which then brings us to our next task.

What exactly is the origin of the Gerk surname?

For that information we have some historical reference. As far as can be stated, it is indeed a German name, meaning: "descendant of Gerhard, the bold spearman."

Our line of Gerk's certainly come from the area of Fulda, in the former German Province of Hesse.

Documents from Russian archives show us that the first Gerk's to Russia were the Sebastian Gerk family.

Sebastian stated as his place of residence "Shiftfulda" or Shift Fulda. Hochstift Fulda (Princely Abbey of Fulda) was until 1802 a sovereign state.

Fulda was not just a town, it was a major seat of power for the abbey of Fulda. Wikipedia records:

"Fulda Abbey, or the Princely Abbey of Fulda, or the Imperial Abbey of Fulda (German: Fürstabtei Fulda, Hochstift Fulda, Kloster Fulda) was a Benedictine abbey as well as an ecclesiastical principality centered on Fulda, in the present-day German state of Hesse. It was founded in 744 by Saint Sturm, a disciple of Saint Boniface. Through the 8th and 9th centuries, Fulda Abbey became a prominent center of learning and culture in Germany, and a site of religious significance and pilgrimage following the burial of Boniface. The growth in population around Fulda would result in its elevation to a prince-bishopric in the second half of the 18th century.

It later served as a base from which missionaries

Wikipedia: Fulda in 1655. Source: Kupferstich von Fulda von Matthäus Merian (1655)

could accompany Charlemagne's armies in their political and military campaign to fully conquer and convert pagan Saxony.

The initial grant for the abbey was signed by Carloman, the son of Charles Martel. The support of the Mayors of the Palace and later, the early Pippinid and Carolingian rulers, was important to Boniface's success. Fulda also received support from many of the leading families of the Carolingian world. Sturm, whose tenure as abbot lasted from 747 until 779, was most likely related to the Agilolfing dukes of Bavaria. Fulda also received large and constant donations from the Etichonids, a leading family in Alsatia, and the Conradines, predecessors of the Salian Holy Roman Emperors. Under Sturm, the donations Fulda received from these and other important families helped in the establishment of daughter houses Johannesberg and Petersberg near Fulda.

After his martyrdom by the Frisians, the relics of Saint Boniface were brought back to Fulda. Because of the stature this afforded the monastery, the donations increased, and Fulda could establish daughter houses further away, for example in Hamelin. Meanwhile Saint Lullus, successor of Boniface as archbishop of Mainz, tried to absorb the abbey into his archbishopric, but failed. This was one reason that he founded Hersfeld Abbey, to limit the attempts of the enlargement of Fulda.

Between 790 and 819 the community rebuilt the main monastery church to more fittingly house the relics. They based their new basilica on the original 4th-century (since demolished) Old Saint

Peter's Basilica in Rome, using the transept and crypt plan of that great pilgrimage church to frame their own saint as the "Apostle to the Germans". The crypt of the original abbey church still holds those relics, but the church itself has been subsumed into a Baroque renovation. A small, 9th century chapel remains standing within walking distance of the church, as do the foundations of a later women's abbey.

The great scholar Rabanus Maurus was abbot from 822 to 842.

From its foundation, the abbey Fulda and its territory was based on an Imperial grant, and therefore was a sovereign principality subject only to the German emperor. Fulda was made a bishopric in 1752 and the prince-abbots were given the additional title of prince-bishop. The prince-abbots (and later prince-bishops) ruled Fulda and the surrounding region until the bishopric was forcibly dissolved by Napoleon in 1802.

The city went through a baroque building campaign in the 18th century, resulting in the current "Baroque City" status. This included a remodeling of the Dom (Cathedral) of Fulda (1704–1712) and of the Stadtschloss (Castle-Palace, 1707–1712) by Johann Dientzenhofer. The city parish church, St. Blasius, was built between 1771–1785."

So where did Sebastian Gerk come from?

Members of the Gerk family in Germany feel they solved the mystery.

The village of Müs.

Villages such as Kleinlüder, Müs and Grossenlüder are all in the vicinity of Fulda, have had numerous families with the last name of Gerk (sometimes spelled Gerck) and also boys born with the name Jois (Johannes) Sebastian Gerk

First mentions of the name "Gerk" or "Gerck" include a document found in 1498, dealing with Wytzel Gerck of Müs. Additionally, *"Die Türkensteuerliste von 1605"*, taken from the Uffhausener Ortschronik - a list of taxpayers in all the villages....covering the cost of war with the invading Turks, found the name of "Cunz Gerck" from Uffhausen, very close to both Müs and Grossenlüder in the Fulda area. *(See: http://juerschik-busbach-ahnenforschung.jimdo.com/familienverband-gerk/*

But we now know the birth of "Johann Sebastian Gerck", born 1725 in Müs, who was married to a Magdalena Helwig in 1752. Listed also are six children, Anna Catherina Gerck, born around 1758, and Joannes Gerck, born approx. 1761.

Discrepancies in documentation for Russia show a change in possible ages. For example, in the first settler list for Koehler, it states that the son of Sebastian Gerk was Johann Kaspar, and that he was born approx. 1751. In later Russian

documents it suggests his birth as 1754 or 1755.

It is the same for both Sebastian and Magdalena. The original settler list suggests Sebastian was born around 1729. For Magdalena, around 1737. The 1798 Russian census suggests Magdalena was born around 1726, her death in 1810 suggests 1730.

Russian researcher Igor Pleve states that the reasons for the age discrepancies were many: settlers gave incorrect ages in order to pay lower taxes, government clerks heard the ages wrong, etc. Remember, people of the day did not celebrate birthdays like we do today. And if a settler had no document proving a specific baptism or birthdate, then it was often left up to speculation.

We do know that Sebastian Gerk and his family disappear from Germany in the around 1766....the exact time that Germans from Hesse were making their way to Russia. So it fits.

Our Sebastian Gerk has been found.

.

The small town of Müs, located near Fulda, was founded in the 900's.
One of the originating places of the Gerk (Gerck) family.

Various Gerk families still live in Fulda, Germany and the surrounding towns. Here are two examples: Gerk Bakery and Emil Gerk construction.

The Catholic Cathedral in Fulda. Built 1704-1712.

Main altar in Saint Georg's Church in Grossenleuder (Großenlüder), not far from Müs. The original chapel in the church dates from the year 822. Many members of the Gerk family were worshipped here.

COLD CASE FILES:
The Gercks of Müs

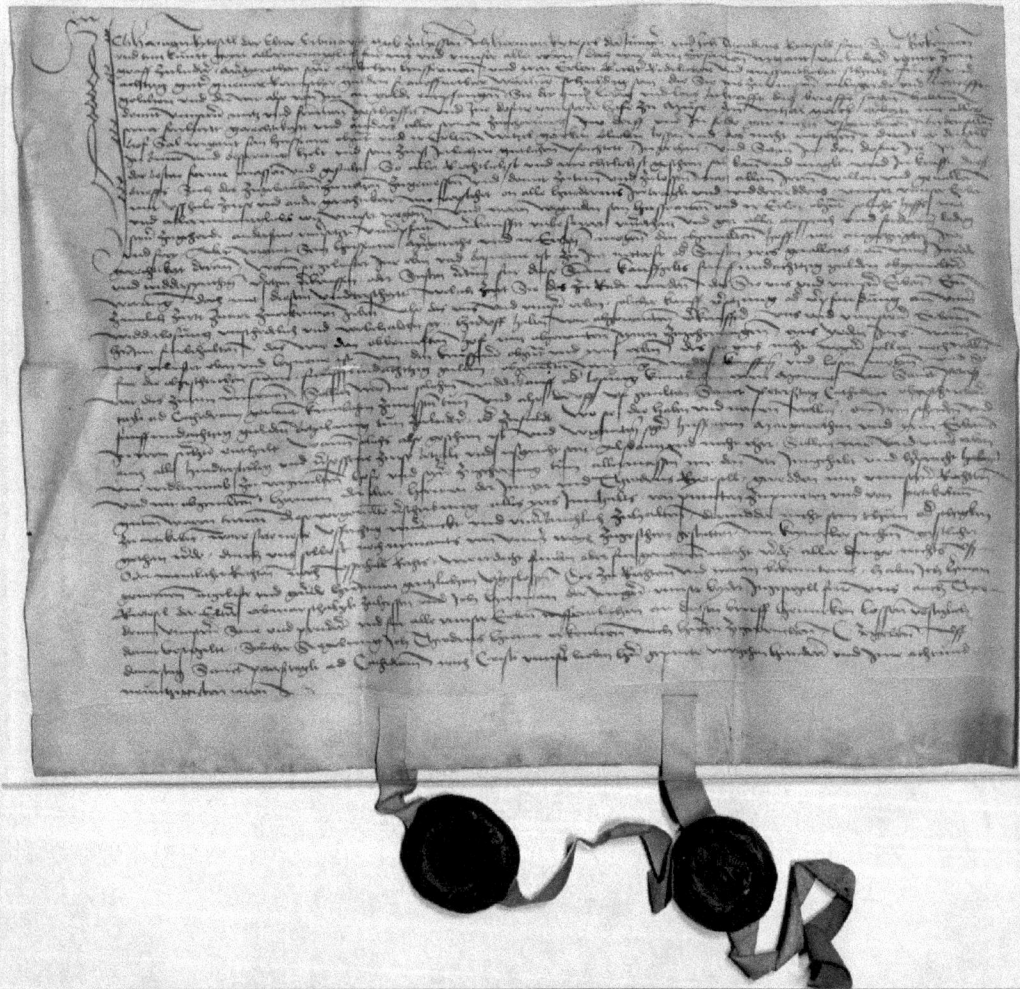

One of the earliest mention of the Gerck family is found in this parchment document from 1498, which mentions Wytzel Gerck of the Müs area, dated February 22, 1498

Wytzel Gerk is mentioned in Lines 6 & 8.

It states, in a loose translation, in part: "Hermann [III.] Riedesel d. Ä., Erbmarschall zu Hessen, as well as his sons Hermann [IV.] Riedesel d. J. and Theodor Riedesel pawn Wigand von Lüder, centurion to Lüder, and his wife Margarethe for the Rhenish gulden of Frankfurt currency their farm at Mües, which is processed by Wytzel Gerck, who can not be dismissed if he does a good job, to redemption…

Source: Hessisches Staatsarchiv Darmstadt: HStAD Fonds B 13 No 406

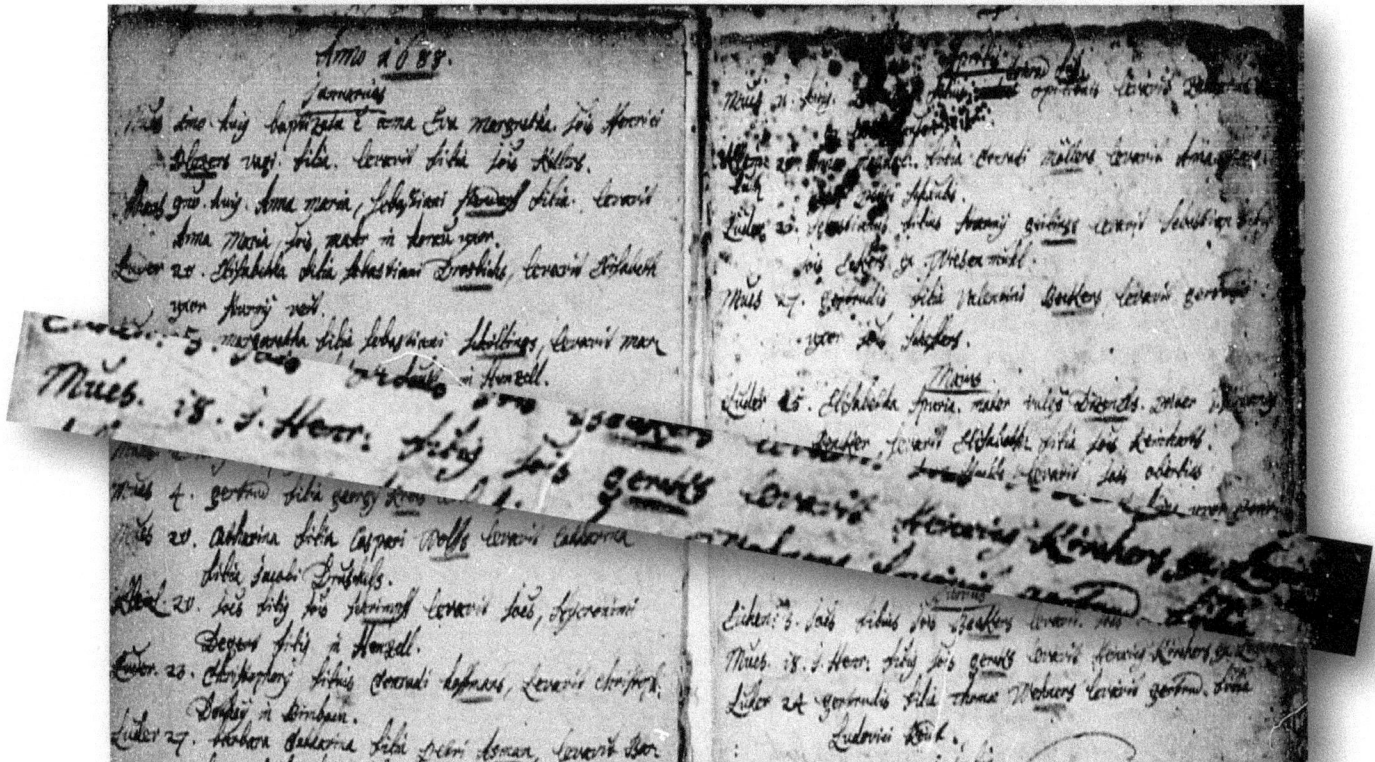

Birth record for J. Heinrich Gerck, born 18 June 1688 in Müs. Father is Johannes Gerck. Johann Heinrich Gerck is the father of Sebastian Gerk.

Courtesy: Dr. Christina Reiche, Bischöfliches Generalvikariat, Bistumsarchiv, Fulda

Birth entry for Sebastian Gerck 30 April 1725 in Müs

In Latin:
Müs   30 hujus legitimus Fl Joannis Henrici Gerck et Catharinae conjugum Joannes Sebastianus, levante viri honesti Heinrici Gerck hospitis in Kleinlüder legitimo filiolo Joanne Sebastiano

Müs   30. April [hujus refers to the month mentioned on the page above] legitimate son of the couple Johann Heinrich Gerck and Catharina: Johann Sebastian, godfather is the little legitimate son [filiolus] Johann Sebastian of the honorable man Heinrich Gerck, landlord in Kleinlüder

Courtesy: Dr. Christina Reiche, Bischöfliches Generalvikariat, Bistumsarchiv, Fulda

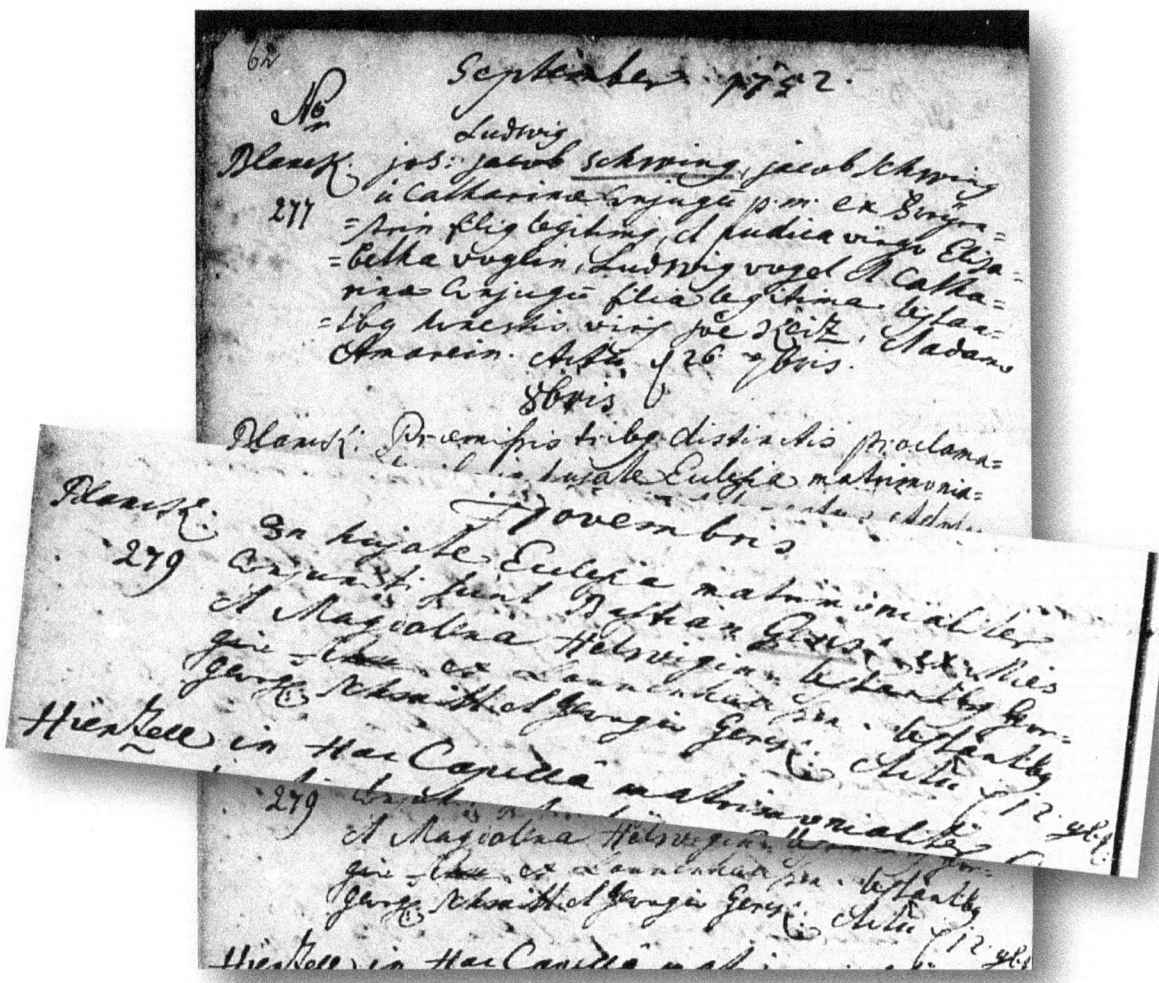

Marriage entry of Bastian Gerck and Magdalena Helwig 12 November 1752 in Blankenau

In Latin:
Blank   In hujate Ecclesia matrimonialiter conjuncti sunt Bastian Gerck ex Müs et Magdalena Helwigin testantibus origine [...] ex Landenhausen, testantibus Georgus Schmitt et Georgus Gerck, Actu d. 12 9bris

Blank   In this church are married Bastian Gerck from Müs and Magdalena Helwig from Landenhausen, witnesses are Georg Schmitt and Georg Gerck, done 12 November

Courtesy: Dr. Christina Reiche, Bischöfliches Generalvikariat, Bistumsarchiv, Fulda

Chronik Müs
von Helmut Gerk

„*Blick auf Müs*" Margarete Schönherr (1999)
Ätzradierung, koloriert

Begonnen: 2006   Dezember 2016

---

2. Ehe

Ww. Johann Henricus Gerek Bauer, u. Melter (Imker)		* 18.06.1688 + ... 1744
Anna Catharina, geb. Hasenau (aus 69) T.d. Georg Hasenau		* 01.05.1697 + 30.04.1772
Cop. 26.05.1716		

Kind Johann P: Joh. Hasenau		* 08.10.1717 + ..
" Dorothea P: Heinr. Gerek's Tochter		* 21.10.1719 + 22.02.1737 (+17)
" Johann Georgius P: J. Georg Hasenau (kauft 41, cop. Elis. Frank, aus 44)		* 09.01.1722
" Anna Maria P: Anna Maria Hasenau (nach 49, cop. Jacobi Pfeil)		* 16.03.1724
" Johann Sebastian P: Heinr. Gerck, Kleinl. **Auswanderer n. Russland**		* 30.04.1725
" Johann P: Joh. Hasenau, Müs (hat 18 gekauft, cop. 1759 A. Cath. Brehler)		* 02.01.1728
" Barbara P: Barbara Gerck, Kleinl. (cop.14.5.1752 Georg Frank)		* 02.01.1728
" Georg Jacob (*in Salzschl.) (nach 19, cop.30.10.1754 Anna Cath. Feldmann)	*	 1730
" Anna Maria P: Anna Maria Keller (in 45, cop. 1750 Joh. Brehler, Salzschl.)	*	16.04.1732

Der Vater v. Anna Cathar. Hasenau in 69: Georgi Hasenau (Ludensis Centurio et Scabini in Müs)

Joh. Sebastian Gerek *1725 + 1798, cop. ..11.1752 in Blankenau mit **Magdalena Helwig** T.d. Georg Helwig, aus Landenhausen, ist 1766 mit Familie nach Russland ausgewandert (Zarin Katharina II.). Ihre Reise ging ab Lübeck mit dem Schiff bis nahe St. Petersburg, von hier auf dem Landwege bis nach Saratow / Köhler an der Wolga. Von diesem Ehepaar ausgehend gibt es heute noch Nachkommen nahezu in der ganzen Welt verstreut (siehe hierzu FAITH OF OUR FATHERS A HISTORY OF THE GERK FAMILY) Der Verfasser ist ein Nachkomme der Familie in Kanada, Edward Roy Gerk, er hat alle Nachkommen der Familie Joh. Sebastian Gerek, aus Müs erforscht und in einer Familien - Chronik festgehalten.

Chronik Müs (2016) by Helmut Gerk holds the key to who Sebastian Gerk was. From his research we learn not only about Sebastian, but his family as well.

The known ancestors of Sebastian Gerck

Johann Gerk (7381)
b. Unknown
at Müs, Fulda, Hesse, Germany
m. Unknown
+Margaretha
d. 24 Jun 1678
at Müs, Fulda, Hesse, Germany

Johannes Gerk (7381)
b. circa 1645
at Müs, Fulda, Hesse, Germany
m. 25 Oct 1671
+Elisabeth Bappert
d. 23 Feb 1694
at Müs, Fulda, Hesse, Germany

Johann Heinrich Gerck(498)
b. 18 Jun 1688
at Müs, Fulda, Hesse, Germany
m. 29 Apr 1708
m. 26 May 1716
+Cunigunde Sclitzer
+Anna Catharina Hasenau
d. 1744
at Müs, Fulda, Hesse, Germany

Sebastian Gerck (496)
b. 30 Apr 1725
at Müs, Fulda, Hesse, Germany
m. 12 Nov 1752
+Magdalena Helwig
d. circa 1797
at Koehler, Saratov, RUS

COLD CASE FILES:
Did Sebastian Gerk hide his plans to move to Russia?

In 1930, there were a series of articles published in the "Buchenblätter", which was a publication of the Fuldaer Zeitung, a newspaper out of Fulda in Germany. This one specific article was entitled: *"Die Auswanderung fuldaischer Landes-Untertanen nach Ungarn 1717-1804"*, which, loosely translated means, *The emigration of Fulda area residents to Hungary, 1717 - 1804.*

The articles document various families applying for and then leaving for Hungary. It's a fascinating account also because emigration to Russia was illegal in those days...so many thought that the people on these lists actually ended up in Russia.

One such family is listed here in May of 1766: Joh. Bast. Gerd (?), which archivists think was Johann Sebastian Gerk with his wife and three children. Leaving from the area of Großenlüder, specifically the village of Kleinlüder, Germany, which was located about 5 miles from the city of Fulda.

Archival officials think that it is possible that Sebastian applied for permission to immigrate to Hungary, but intended on accepting the invitation of Russia's Catherine the Great.

But what of Church records? Although no further information seems to be available about this "Joh. Bast. Gerk", we do find a reference for a Jois Sebastian Gerck born in 1730 in Kleinlüder, married in 1750 to a Anna Maria, born also in 1730 in Kleinlüder. They have listed 3 children: Marie Agnes Gerck born 1754; Joannes Gerck born 1757 and Maria Elisabetha born 1760.

This Jois Sebastian Gerck stayed in Kleinlüder and died there.

So, once again, this entry fits with our Sebastian Gerk.

But it's another of those Gerk Mysteries!

The Gerk family home in Müs. Early records for the village show that this dwelling, on the left, was the house that Sebastian Gerck was born in (1725) constructed in 1710. Photo courtesy Willi Gerk

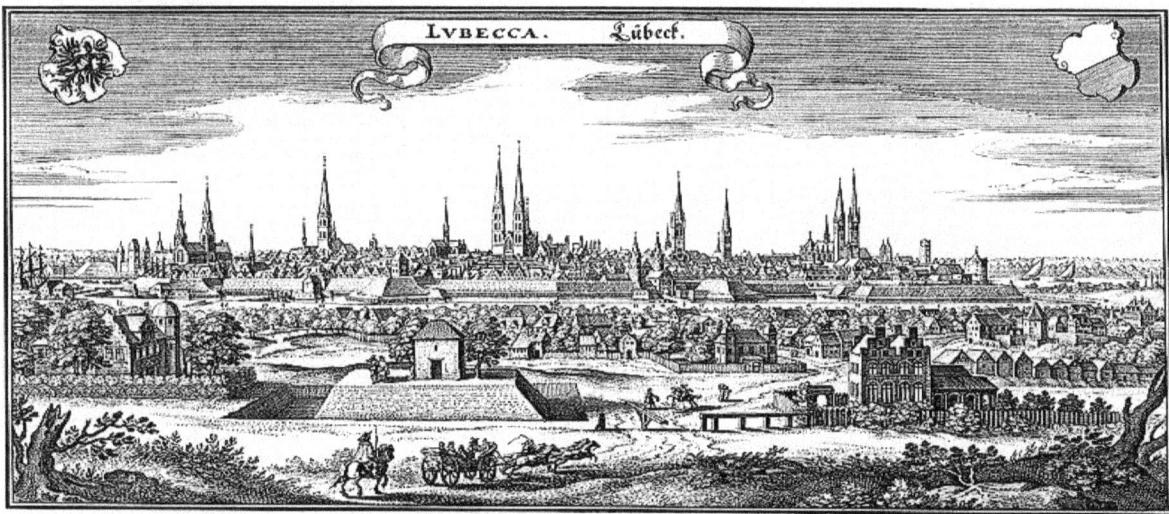

Top inset: Koehler was known as Colony #27 before it received its official name. Above: The Baltic Port of Lübeck, where Sebastian Gerk and Family will leave in the spring of 1766.
Drawing from Wikipedia; Lübeck in 1641

The beginning of **OUR** story takes us from Fulda, Province of Hesse, Germany, where Sebastian Gerk will make the decision to accept the call of Catherine the Great, thus sealing the fate of the Gerk family with that of Russia.

Sebastian and family will travel to Lübeck on the Baltic Sea. The family will leave sometime in the spring of 1766 on the British ship *Catharina Eleanora*. The journey would take, at the very least, several weeks to complete.

They will arrive, according to documentation provided by Special Commissar Ivan Kuhlberg, on May 20, 1766.

After arriving in Oranienbaum, Russia (now Lomonosov, Russia) they will be housed in special barracks. After the formalities of pledging allegiance to Catherine the Great and Russia taking place, they will then start the long trek to the Volga.

Historian Steven Schreiber writes:

"After completing their processing in Oranienbaum, the (colonists) were transported to nearby St. Petersburg where they remained on ship for as long as three weeks. From this point, they were formed into convoys, led by military officers, bound for their settlement sites on the lower Volga near Saratov".

He continues:
"After departing from St. Petersburg, the river rafts proceeded 45 miles up the Neva River

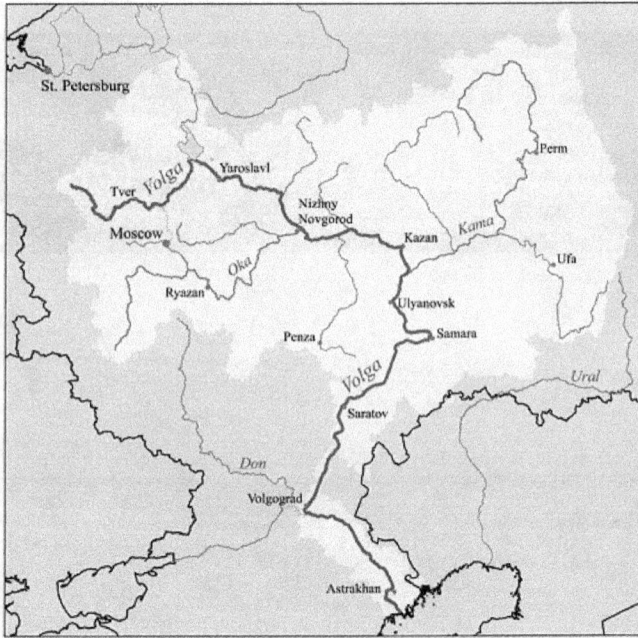

The journey down the Volga River began in Torzhok (west of Tver) and continued to Saratov
(Source: First Christmas in Norka
http://www.volgagermans.net/norka/christmas_1767.html)

through the Schlüsselburg Canal to Lake Lagoda and then to the mouth of the Volkhov River. The rafts then navigated 130 miles southward up the Volkhov River past the ancient city of Novgorod and into Lake Ilmen.

From Novgorod they continued by ship further upriver before disembarking to begin the journey overland to Torzhok (west of Tver). Torzhok was the place where the upper Volga River became navigable at that time. The 200 mile trip overland was by horse drawn wagon. Women, children and baggage were loaded aboard the wagons and the able bodied men walked. Like most of the colonists, it is likely that… spent their first winter and Christmas with a Russian peasant family near Torzhok. In the spring, when the river was again navigable, they continued down the 1,100 meandering miles of the Volga to the frontier town of Saratov. The days on the river must have seemed endless as they drifted day after day. The trip down the Volga was difficult and large numbers of adults and children died along the way. The dead were taken to shore and quickly buried while relatives erected an improvised cross above it. Time was of the essence because they feared the groups of bandits hiding in the forests along the Volga.

Sometime in early August, the transport group reached Saratov…Saratov was established as a frontier fortress in 1590 by Tsar Feodor Ivanovich and would have been an unkempt, ramshackle town of about 10,000 residents in the 1760s."

Our story thus takes us to the place of beginnings for us. The Volga German village of Kohler.

Among its' original settlers, Sebastian Gerk along with his wife Magdalena Helwig, two sons and daughter would arrive in Kohler on August 21, 1767. Just over a year after their arrival in Russia. Even though members of the Gerk family would later settled in other villages, the Gerk family continued to play a prominent role in the life of Koehler)

To know what the family of Sebastian Gerk went through as a new colonist of Russia, we turn to an account of the history of Koehler, written by former resident and historian Edmund Imherr. His chronicle of Kohler, found in his book, *"Verschollene Heimat an der Wolga"* (Stuttgart 2000), documents the birth of the village to its ultimate destruction in the early 1940's.

This chapter on the history of Koehler was translated by Joe Gareis:

As of August 10, 1997, it had been 230 years since Colony Number 27 (see top photo at beginning of chapter) was created out on the Mountainous (West) bank of the Volga. The village was laid out by surveyors under the direction of Captain Johann Reis, an officer from the Vormundschaftskanzlei (government office) in Saratov. He provided guidance on the village plan, and showed the Vorsteher (mayor) where its roads and boundaries lay. The village was called Kohler after the name of its first mayor.

The first settlers came from the German provinces of Hessen, Nordbayern-Franken, and Alsace-Lorraine, seeking their fortunes on this fertile soil. They numbered 95 families and 282 "souls": 151 males and 131 females.

The nearby colonies of Leichtling and Hildmann, only 3 kilometers away, were settled on the 14th of May of that year. The somewhat more distant colony of Kamenka had already been in existence for two years.

The settlers pitched their tents for the first time as close as possible to the river-ford to Leichtling. Huts were thrown-up quickly in preparation for the coming winter. The loamy soil was well suited for building uses. After the earth was dug up, it could be formed into bricks and later whitewashed. Materials for the roof were also near at hand. The colonists came to call these clay-huts "Zimlinka" after the Russian word "semljanka." This was the first of many mixed-language words that the settlers would adopt over the centuries.

The first year was particularly hard, even unbearably so. But the tenacity and unshakable confidence of the colonists, in addition to help from the crown, allowed them to succeed in the face of obstacles.

Right away, in the first year, the apparently quiet stream swelled from the melting mountain snows, and fully flooded its banks, driving the inhabitants from their Zimlinkas. The settlers left their clay-huts, moving to higher ground where they began to build houses.

Building materials were brought in by wagon from Nishnaja Bannowka, about 30 kilometers away along the Volga. Round beams about 4 to 6 meters long were loaded onto extended horse-drawn wagons and driven up the steep banks of the Volga. Not only was this difficult, but also sometimes dangerous since a heavily loaded wagon is not always easy to brake to a stop. About halfway along the route on the return trip to Kohler was Kamenka. There the village leaders allowed the horse trains to rest, and to feed and drink from the river Lawl, which is what they called the Ilowlja. The leader of organized religion in the area, Father Muller, had his seat in Kamenka, where a wooden church was erected and soon surrounded by streets leading to it. Father Muller encouraged the guests from Kohler to hold on, that with patience, diligence and God's speed they would succeed in building their colony.

Log cabins were (initially) built in Kohler. Later, properly milled and squared lumber from spruce became available. And after they became more familiar with the area and began to know their way around, the colonists were able to create "Kreidesteine" (chalk or white - bricks) and "Eisensteine" (metal work) to finish the walls and foundations of their houses. Each year they also discovered how to find and make use of loam, sand and white-earth pits.

1773 map showing village of Koehler and surrounding area. Koehler is listed by its Russian name of Karaulnoi Bujerak (middle left corner). Source: "Karte worauf alle im Saratofschen Gebiet zu beiden Seiten des Wolga Stroms angelegten teutschen Kolonien ange zeigt sind" by Peter Pallas.

Page from the Koehler settlement list. Dated 21 August 1767, the Sebastian Gerk family is number 35, on the list. Source: Saratov State Archive (GASO)

A foundation made of "Eisensteinen" was invariably the best possible and walls made of "Kreidensteinen" enjoyed many advantages. The first houses made of red brick were built about 130 years after the founding of Kohler, in 1897. It was the tradesman Peter Bellendir and the teacher Joseph Gareis who first built red brick houses with decorated facades.

In the northwest side of the village, flowed the stream Karaulny. In snow-rich winters, the stream rushed noisily into the Ilowlja. The colony's Russian name originated from this stream -- Karaulney Bujerak. In one record of the village written in 1923 by an inhabitant of Saratov, named Denger, the village is also referred to as Kassanlai. I have been unable to determine the source of this name. Perhaps one of our readers will know better.

The seed and grazing pasturelands of the community were hilly, traversed here and there by ravines and ditches, deep in parts and with steep cliffs. Approximately 13 kilometers to the West of Kohler rose the "High" or the "Black" hills, and gleamed blue in the setting sun. The surrounding earth was largely fertile humus, but there were also areas of predominantly clay or sand content. In between such stretches of land lay islands of "Weisserdeflachen" (white-earth pastures), in notable contrast to the monotonous gray steppes (Wermutsteppe?). The total landholding of the village ran about 16,600 Desjatinen).

Family Number 35: Sebastian Gerk, age 38, Farmer from "Shift Fulda", and his wife, Magdalena Halbig, age 30, with children Kaspar, age 16, Zacharius, age 1 and Katarina age 14.
Source: Saratov State Archives (GASO)

Over the course of the decades the hard-working farmers built a system of damns, from which many commercial uses sprang, especially in the summer.

The river Ilowlja formed a winding natural boundary with the colonies of Leichtling and Hildmann, to the East of Kohler. To the North to the East of Kohler were other Hildmann properties and those of the village of Pfeifer. To the South, land was shared between Kohler and Hessen colony of Semjonowka (Rothling), 10 kilometers away. Neighboring Kohler to the West was the Russian village Perschtschipnoje; outside the boundary that would come to define the German Volga Republic; beyond that was Crown-owned forest.

Over time, the vocabulary of the settlers evolved to include a mixture of Russian words, reflecting daily life there: Zimlicka, Zau, Wassrschoppa, Schinkgrowa, Strossagrowa, Kerschagrowa, Fuchsagrowa, Kreizgrowa, Krauteck, Genseeck, Kelwerdemmja, Driftadamm, Buschdamm, Lawlberch, 'hoha' or 'schwarza' Berch, Windmihlplatz, Ehlemihl, Feirmihl, Ruh, Unnr, Aspa, Grund, Staatemp, Jablobairak, Warlasalacha, Gelhoh, Peifers, Kopja, amm Gbrennta, Kleeskippl, Kronswald, Klucha Garda, Zarns Garda, Gerka Garda, Filips Garda, Klaa Wassrja, Laamaloch, Gerwershaus.

The emigration of Germans continued through the middle of the nineteenth century. During this time, the population of Germans in the Volga area increased ten-fold. For example, in Kohler by 1864, 2,960 colonists lived and prospered (compared with about 250 original settlers). Conditions continued to improve in the next 50 years and the 1914 census increased to 5,970 souls. The rapid growth to that point occurred even though a significant number of inhabitants (mostly men of working age) emigrated to America in the 20 years preceding the First World War as land became scarce. It was said: "They've gone to earn some money."

The First World War, the civil War, the famine of 1921, and various other misfortunes changed the situation, however, so that by 1926 the number of residents in Kohler had fallen to 3,097. But as was true throughout the Soviet Union, the New Economic Policy then brought sudden, dramatic improvement in conditions. All at once adequate supplies of bread, meat, eggs, butter, milk and other provisions became available to the masses in the villages and cities.

For a few years Kohler prospered. Carpenters received orders to erect new houses, cabinet-makers produced furniture, not just for Kohler but also for neighboring villages, and the "Putzmaschinen" from Kohler were valued throughout the region. Tailors, shoemakers, (Walkers -- mullers?), weavers, dyers, tanners, tinsmiths, clock-makers, masons, stove-fitters and artists were fully occupied. Good times were also had by those who made musical instruments to supply the two brass bands in the village (villages of Bruckman and Habig, or named . . .). Both musical groups were booked steadily in the winter. In the fall they were in demand to play weddings in neighboring villages.

Outside the village there were 7 working windmills owned by Peter Kohler, Georg Kohler, Adam Kohler, Andreas Thuring, Johannes Gerk, Peter Gareis and Johannes Schachtel. Adam Kohler's "Feuermuhle" (fire mill?) burned down in 1926. An "Olmuhle" (oil mill?) owned by Peter Bellendir served all of the residents of Kohler and five forges actively competed to improve the quality of their products. In contrast, merchants and salesmen earlier had been forced to close their businesses. Included in this list were Peter Bellendir, Aloysius Weimann, Jakob Weimann, Peter Gerk, and Jakob Macht.

The availability of medical care services left much to be desired. A midwife lived in neighboring Leichtling and served Kohler as well. Those in need of a "Feldscher" (?) or doctor had to drive 10 kilometers to the village of Gobel.

The decline and ultimate ruin of Kohler began in 1929. During the collectivization, homes of well-to-do farmers were divided and then torn down. Houses were torn down with the lumber in most cases used for firewood: It was so economical! Gaps developed in the rows of houses. Streets were completely neglected.

During the famine of 1932/33 many families abandoned their homes and farms and fled to the cities, especially to Minsk and Baku, in search of safer homes and more secure livelihoods.

Despite this, valuable homes remained standing next to the church and two schoolhouses until the end -- the deportation to Ukas -- August 28, 1941. After the deportation, the entire village with the exception of 13 houses was leveled. The orchards were cut down to the last tree. Today the Ilowlja has dried up, it's channel can no longer be found. No paths or roads remain in Kohler, the landscape there appears desolate and abandoned. The village of Kohler or Karaulny Bujerak is gone. Only the 13 arbitrarily spared houses remain to offer a sad sight. A train line connecting Kamyschin and Saratov was built in 1942, but it bypassed Kohler denying it an opportunity to grow again. Trains will no longer stop where Kohler once lay.

The Layout of the Colony

Kohler was laid out in checkerboard pattern, divided lengthwise by nine parallel avenues and across by seven streets. The separate quarters of the village were formed in squares. Homesteads in the village were bordered on either side by the propertied of two neighbors. The back border of each property was shared with a third neighbor, whose land fronted on the next street over.

The church was placed on a rise in the center of the colony, somewhat removed from the other buildings. With its tall steeple it towered over the village. Near the church stood one of the two schoolhouses; the school was near the outer edge of the village.

The geometric grid of roads conferred an ordered appearance to Kohler. The avenues pointed exactly from East to West and the cross-streets lay on a perpendicular, North-South axis. Those without clocks -- in the early years this included more than a few -- could judge the time reasonably well based on the direction of shadows. It would be another 97 years (1864) before the first clock bells rang in the village, giving accurate times.

Houses in the village had large windows facing the street and were separated from it by a fence, passable through massive ornamental gates. The dome-topped posts were covered with tin plates and oil-based paint. By regulation they were required to match the height of the house roof. The appearance of the gates indicated the status of the household. Those who could not afford a proper gate had to be satisfied with a "sleeper-door."

The first houses were made from wood and were referred to as log houses. Later, Kreidesteine (white-stones? stucco??) were used to cover the outer walls of the homes. This improved the air inside, keeping homes warmer in the winter and cooler in the summer.

The interior yards in Kohler were arranged in a manner typical of farmer houses on the mountainous (West) bank of the Volga. Right next to the home was found the so-called summer kitchen or bake-house, that normally included a bake-oven. Cellars were of widely varying quality. In a well-built cellar, for example, one might find a stepped entry leading to a space with walls and a vaulted ceiling made of cut stone. Next door however might be a very primitive cellar, little more than a dug-out trench, topped with beams supporting layers of earth and accessible by a wooden ladder that would from time to time would rot and need to be replaced. Sometimes the entry to the cellar would be covered by "cell-hut" made of boards.

Grain silos were referred to by the Russian name "Ambar." The silo along with a barn and one or more live-stock stables formed the boundary of the property from the front- to the back-yard. Stables in smaller farms were housed in a single row of livestock stalls. Those in larger farms included two rows. In the wealthiest farms one would find separate stables for each type of livestock: horses, oxen, cows, calves, pigs, and sheep. Stables holding sheep and pigs were built toward the rear of the lot.

In front of the stables one would find the well, usually with a drinking trough for the animals. Now and then neighbors would share a single well, placed along the fence dividing their properties. In the Eastern side of the colony, closer to the river, wells only 1.5 to 2.0 meters deep yielded "soft" water. On the hill where the Church stood, and in parts of the village west of it, wells often reached 20 meters or more. The water from these wells was "hard" and unfit for washing. Well structures were built of oak or larch wood, many with fieldstones formed into a circle. Above that, the super-structure of the wells was solidly-built using wide, closely-fit boards supporting a tight lid. By the brook, above the "ham-trenches" along the avenue there was a community well with good quality water. In contrast to the wells described in previous pages, the community well was equipped with a pump-handle.

Backyard borders were separated by fences, in addition to a barn for storage of dried manure and firewood -- together referred to simply as fuel -- for use in the cold winter seasons. Manure from the livestock was moved back from the stables and stored in a round heap and kept until spring. The manure had to "cook" before being formed into bricks. Despite this, yards were constantly swept clean. Streets were cleaned every Saturday without fail, and this included spreading sand around houses. Only then would the colonists feel comfortable on their Sunday strolls, chatting with neighbors on the streets in front of their houses.

It was not uncommon in Kohler to find a number of families with the same surname in one street. An extreme example is that of the Zieglers with 14 different families living along "Wassrschopp" Street in 1928. Four of the householders in these families were named Johannes, three were named Peter, and two Andreas. The others were Wilhelm, Hans, Valtin, Nikolaus, and Adam. Little wonder the street as commonly known by the name "Zichlersch" Street. Similar concentrations could be found for the Gareis, Kohler, Haspert, Strechmel, and Klug families. Because of this, inhabitants of the village were often identified by nickname.

The parish church building in Kohler was completed in 1864 and constructed of wood in the neo-classical style. It stood on a solid foundation of fieldstone. Because the church site was on an incline, the main entrance to the church, from the North, required additional steps. The double-door main portal lay below an overhanging façade supported by a row of columns on the front face of the building and led to the so-called "Vorhaus" (entry-room or vestibule), formed by the four walls at the base of the steeple. Beyond the vestibule, was the choir (Empore -- in the dialect of the colonists, called "Bor").

Portals were also found on each side of the Church, running lengthwise. These provided two additional entries to the church through identically sized set of double doors. Similar to the main entry on the North face of the church, the two side portals were covered by a gabled roof facade, supported by columns. The sacristy could only be reached through the "Presbyterium."

Although the steeple could have housed them, the church bells were nevertheless placed in a separate tower. This allowed the bells to be heard farther, helpful during noisy storms and so those perhaps blinded by snowstorms could orient themselves by sound from the bells.

Walking through the main entryway into the vestibule, on the left and right one would see holy water vessels. This opened into a wide center aisle flanked by two rows of pews running the length of the church from the vestibule to the middle, and flush against the walls across. The choir loft, occupied in large part by the organ, was shaped like horse-show and rested on ten supporting pillars. The choir had no seats and was only accessible to men and boys.

Both parish priests (called Kerchavorstehr -- dialect for Kirchevorsteher) shared just one seat in the church. Two chairs stood below in the center aisle and two additional chairs in the altar room. These were reserved by the priests for those who passed the collection pouch or maintained order during the Mass or during processions. The benches were only there for married folks. Youths stood in ordered rows: the smallest children right in front and the larger children behind the rows of benches. As a matter of principal, strict separation by gender was enforced with females on the left side and males to the right. In the middle of the right half of the church, three meters above the floor stood the oak-paneled pulpit, accessible by stairs.

The Interior Furnishings of the Church

The richly carved woodwork was coated with gold, sky-blue and white paint. The altars stood on three-step high podiums. The right-side altar was decorated with a statue of Saint Joseph with the Christ child. To the left, stood the Holy

Sepulcher. All other statues to be seen in the beautiful church shone in bright, deep colors.

Along the each of the two church walls from front to back were seven Stations of the Cross, respectively, in natural size figures. The linens and tapestries throughout the church were very impressive, adorned with symbolic pictures. In In the middle of the "Langhauses" hung a stepped candleholder about two meters wide. In the altar room was a lamp that was constantly kept lit. It has always been true of Catholics that they are most impressed by things magnificent and celebratory. So there was always something there in Churches to appeal to the eyes as well as the emotions. Lordly churches, dignified processions, golden implements, jewel-adorned relic shrines, choice paintings, and costly sculpture served as evidence of the community's appreciation of beauty. And with the organ at full volume and the sound of many voices shaking the columned church, worshippers were moved to reverence and fear of the lord.

The interior furnishings of the church were done by Dutch artists. In the final renovation of the church in 1927, the pews, flooring, walls and pulpit were covered with oil paint. I happened to be among those involved in painting the Church then.

The fenced churchyard could be entered from the East, North, and South through three gates. The wood picket fence was painted bluish-gray. Decorative glass globes topped the fence posts at three-meter intervals. The ground of the church square was covered with grass. Along the fence were planted practical flowering trees. Wooden chapels were located at each of the four corners of the churchyard. On Holidays, the chapel exteriors and the altar inside were covered in white cloth, and were richly decorated throughout with green plants and flowers.

The Destruction of the Church

The church was closed in 1929. The crosses and bells were dismantled. The interior furnishings were barbarously ruined. At the time of the deportation (1941) the church building remained standing to be sure but was left abandoned, with no human presence. The church finally was destroyed in 1942 by order of the party authorities in Volgograd. Part of the scrap wood taken from the church was used in the construction of the Saratov - Petrowal railway.

Notes:

1. The church in Kohler was in 1914 served by the parish at Hildmann and its pastor Florian Schulz.
2. Pastor Josef Beilmann returned to his hometown of Vollmer after 1928 and lived in his parents' home with his two sisters until 1932.
3. Pastor Nikolaus Meier from Berlin also became actively involved in advocacy for the Russian German community. He was co-founder of the union of Volga Germans and was a member of the central committee of the Germans from Russia. During the 1921 famine, he traveled to the United States with Bishop Kessler and collected money for bread and provisions for the impoverished people of the land. Even today, Volga Germans remember this assistance to the community with gratitude.
4. From 1922 until 1924, Kohler was held under interdict forbidding the presence of church officials.

Years:	Pastor:	From:
1873-1877	Phillip Dorzweiler	Pfeifer
1877-1880	Georg Riessling	Selz
1887-1892	Andreas Brungardt	Hildmann
1892-1893	Stanislaus Kubik	Polen
1893-1895	Phillip Becker	Selz
1895-1897	Josef Heim	Bessarabien
1897-1901	Adolf Ulrich	Kohler
1901-1905	Ferdinand Hirsch	?
1905-1913	Nikolaus Meier	Berlin
1913	Adam Bellendier	Kohler
1913-1915	Josef Veith	Hildmann
1915-1922	Martin Fix	Sulz
1917-1918	Klemens Weissenburger	Selz
1924-1928	Josef Beilmann	Vollmer
1928-1929	Johannes Beilmann	Vollmer

COLD CASE FILES:
Passenger List Error?

We know that Sebastian Gerk and family settled in the Volga German village of Koehler in August of 1767. Sebastian listed as his original place of residence "ShiftFulda". But on the passenger lists compiled by Ivan Kuhlburg, shown above, documenting the 1766 transports of German colonists to Russia, Sebastian Gerk is listed as coming from Pfalz, Germany. Not only that, but the name of his wife is listed as Anna and there are different names for two of his children…Johann, 15 and Maria, 10.

A historian would look at this and know that both records could not be correct. Were there Gerk's in the German area of Pfalz? We know Gerk is a common family name in the area of Fulda, indeed scores of Gerk families still reside there. Other historians state that the Kuhlburg lists have scores of errors in them, and they often cannot be trusted with the information found.

But, we really don't know. We can document, through Russian census records and some Church books that the names of Sebastian's wife and children are indeed wrong in the Kuhlburg lists, and correct in the Koehler first settler list.

But the confusion is still there. Sebastian did not list his exact birthplace, so while we now know that he was born in the village of Müs, we don't know there is this misleading passenger list. The incorrect Kuhlburg passenger lists thus becomes part of the mystery of Sebastian Gerk.

Source: Dr. Igor Pleve, Saratov State University

The six known children of
Sebastian and Magdalena Gerk

Johann Kaspar Gerk (498)
b. 1753
at Fulda, Hesse, Germany
m. 1776
m. 1790
+Unknown
+Anna Maria Mützig
d. 14 Jan 1830
at Koehler, Saratov, RUS

Ekaterina Gerk (499)
b. 21 Feb 1758
at Müs, Fulda, Hesse, Germany
m. 1777
+Johann Michael Schmidtlein
d. circa 1835
at Koehler, Saratov, RUS

Sebastian Gerk (496)
b. 30 Apr 1725
at Müs, Fulda, Hesse, Germany
m. 12 Nov 1752
d. circa 1797
at Koehler, Saratov, RUS

Johannes Gerk (7381)
b. 7 Feb 1761
at Müs, Fulda, Hesse, Germany
d. 22 Sep 1763
at Müs, Fulda, Hesse, Germany

Johannes Gerk (7832)
b. 4 Nov 1763
at Müs, Fulda, Hesse, Germany
d. circa 1765
at Müs, Fulda, Hesse, Germany

Magdalena Helwig (497)
b. 1726
at Landenhausen, Mainz
Germany
d 24 Nov 1810
at Koehler, Saratov, RUS

Zacharius Gerk (500)
b. 1766
at RUS?
m. 1789
m. 1794
+-?- Hasenauer
+ Anna Maria Brescher
d. 1834
at Koehler, Saratov, RUS

Johann Adam Gerk (501)
b. 1768
at Koehler, Saratov, Russia
m. 1788
+Barbara Schenk
d. 1816
at Koehler, Saratov, RUS

COLD CASE FILES:
So Whatever Happened to Sebastian Gerk?

Excerpt from the Koehler census of October 1798, states that the head of Family Number 7 was Magdalena Gerk, age 72 (born in 1726). It included her son Kaspar, age 44 listed as the son of Sebastian Gerk, and who was "deaf and sees very little", and Kaspar's wife, Anna Maria Lutsig from the village of Goebel. Source: GASO

…We don't know. This first Gerk settler to Russia "disappears" before the 1798 census.

Church Books for the Parish of Semenovka, in which Koehler was a part, do not exist for 1798.

Sebastian is not listed in the October 1798 census. The following census, 1816, in which colonists were listed along with their year of death, also has no listing for Sebastian.

Sebastian must have died before October 1798…shortly before the census was taken. We cannot confirm that theory. His name seems to have vanished into history.

Excerpt from the Koehler census of October 1798, states that the head of Family Number 15 was Zacharius Gerk, age 32 (born in 1766). It included his 2nd wife Anna Maria Brescher age 23, daughters Anna Maria age 3, Elisabetha age 2, sons Adam age 9, and children from his first wife (who was the widow of Nikolaus Hasenhauer: sons Josef age 19 and daughter Anna Maria age 21 Source: GASO

24 November 1810 is the date listed as for the death of Magdalena Gerk, age 80, the wife of Sebastian Gerk. This would mean she was born in 1730, which is different than from the Koehler first settlement list and the 1798 census. This is an excerpt from the Church records for Koehler. Source: Igor Pleve & GASO

Some members of the Gerk family remained in Koehler, while other moved to Josefstal, Marienfeld and Pfeifer.

Our story next takes a turn to a newly formed village located just south of Koehler, Josefstal.

Considered a "daughter: colony, Josefstal was founded by colonists from a number of other Volga German villages, who, for a variety of reasons, wanted to take advantage of the possible prosperity that could be found in a new village.

Gerk's would take advantage of the new situation, and so various lines moved to the villages of Marienfeld and Josefstal. One line of Gerk's even moved to the village of Pfeiffer, also located in the area.

Dr. Igor Pleve, the dean of History at Saratov State University wrote an article documenting the founding of the colony that our Gerk line was to call home: *"From the History of Josefstal"*

The German colony of Josefstal is one of a number of "daughter" colonies founded on the right shore of the Volga River at the beginning of the 50s of the nineteenth century. (1800's)

According to the Josefstal Revision or Census of February 14, 1858, it states that the family of Peter Gerk , family Number 8 and consisting of 8 people, settled there from the village of Koehler. Church records suggest they must have moved to Josefstal in 185, before the village became an official town. Peter Gerk died in 1852, but his son Josef, age 14, Peter's brother Gotlieb, age 15, Gotlieb's son Johannes age 8 ½; and Peter's brother Johann Georg age 31, along with Johann Georg's son Georg, age 4, all were original settlers. Johann Georg Gerk is the grandfather of Paul Gerk. Source: GAVO: Fond 299, Opis 1, No. 375

The first third of the nineteenth century was for the colonists a time of definitive strengthening of their economy. The first uncertain decades after settlement had passed. The well-being of individual families had grown, as it had for the colonies as a whole.

But successful development of the colonies had created a new problem: lack of land. For the period between the fifth revision (census) of 1788 and the eighth revision of 1834, the population of the colonies increased three-fold (1). Such a situation could not but reflect on the stability of the colonial economy. In 1834, each person of the male sex in the colonies on the Bergseite (Hilly side) required from 7 to 8 desyatina of land. And this situation did not go unnoticed by the Office of Immigrant Oversight. Constant appeals to St. Petersburg resulted in the assertion of 12 March 1840 by the First Department of State Property about the situation "On allocation to the colonists of the Saratov Gubernia according to the number of souls in the 8th revision." The land allotment was set at 15 desyatina. The department ordered that certain districts allocate the broadest possible plots (2).

One of these plots was the territory of the so-called Kamyshin city lands, some 20,000 desyatina already set aside by the Saratov Kontora of Immigrant Oversight in 1826, and rented for various periods to the colonists (3) On 17 October

1849, the Kontora allocated these lands to 28 colonies "to facilitate out-migration." (4) But division of these territories into workable plots for new colonies proved complicated. In the course of the spring and fall of 1850, the plot of land was divided into 14 colonial holdings where 2732 persons or 683 families were to settle. But the next spring when the land near Kamyshin was again assessed, it was determined that only 551 families could be settled on it, some 132 fewer than had been initially estimated. So it was determined to establish only 9 new colonies (finally, there were only 8). (5)

After taking all preparatory measures, the Kontora ordered the districts to proceed with the settlement of the newly established plots.

One of the 8 colonies established in 1852 was the colony of Josefstal. In all the documents it is initially noted as colony N 3. It was initially proposed to accommodate 56 families or 336 persons. By 17 October 1852, in Josefstal there were already 206 persons in 34 families (6). Such fast growth of the newly established colonies is explained not only by a desire for land, but also by the close disposition of the mother colonies.

Upon settlement of the colonies, problems arose with those who had already rented this land for several years, even decades, and in spite of prohibition had constructed houses and outbuildings. Tension between the arriving colonists and the "old residents" was high. The Kontora determined that all colonists who did not have permission to settle in the colonies established in 1852 must return to their original colonies.

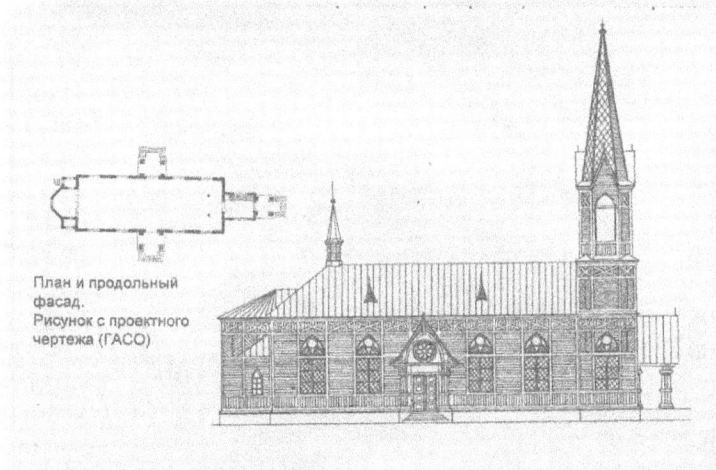

While Josefstal residents built a Catholic Church in 1870, it proved to be too small for the growing village. A new Church was built in 1904. This is a drawing from the blueprints of that Church.
Source: GASO Fond 656, Opis 1 No. 916

One of the "old residents" on the territory of the colony of Josefstal was the colonist Schwab, who established a settlement [khutor] in 1833. Therefore one of the other names of Josefstal was Schwab Khutor. The Russian inhabitants of the region called Josefstal "Skripalevka," because among the population of the colonists were those who played musical instruments. [Translator note: in Russian, a violin is a "skripka."]

By autumn of 1852, the village elder [Vorsteher in German, Starosta in Russian] and his deputy [Beisitzer in German] had been elected. In 1853 Josefstal was listed in the newly established Ilavlya okrug [district].

The colony was formed by colonists from the Kamenka volost (only one family arrived from the Sosnovka volost, from the colony of Kamenny Ovrag [Degott]). According to the census of 1857, 23 families (149 persons), moved from the colony of Kamenka. A smaller number, 21 families (132 persons) came from the colony of Gnilushka. The remainder came from: Karaulny Buyerak - 16 families (111) persons; Ust-Gryaznukha - 11 families (49 persons); Panovka - 7 families (45 persons); Yelshanka - 6 families (39 persons); Ilavlya - 4 families (24 persons); Gryaznovatka - 4 families (23 persons); Kopenka - 4 families (19 persons); Kamenny Ovrag [Degott] - 1 family (6 persons); Marienfeld - 1 family (4 persons); and one family came from an unknown place. It also must be noted that of the 99 families listed in the colony, 15 families (94 persons) did not actually reside in the colony.

The number of inhabitants of the colony in its first years of existence did not change significantly. By

1860 it was practically at the level of 1857: 617 (8). By 1886 that number had increased to 887 persons (9). The low pattern of growth can be attributed to the constant outmigration of the population from Josefstal. In 1864 one family moved to the Kuban oblast. The next year another 55 "census souls" (a "census soul" was a male) moved to the villages of Semenovskoye and Rozhdestvenskoye in the Kuban oblast. A few families moved to other Volga colonies in the 70s and 80s. The migration of inhabitants from Josefstal to America started in 1877. That year 6 families crossed the ocean; and in 1866, four young men of the age of conscription (10).

Most Volga German Churches in Russia had separate belfry's. This belfry, from the village of Merkel, was similar to the belfry in Josefstal. Source: The Center for Volga German Studies at Concordia University.

The relative stabilization of migration processes in the 80s lead to fast growth of the population, and by 1894 there were 1206 inhabitants listed in the colony (11). But this did not mean that they all resided in the colony. According to gubernia statistical data, in Josefstal permanently lived 58 families of the 143 listed in the colony. The remainder went to work in the nearby colonies, 37 males and 12 females were taken as day laborers, 16 males and 2 females were farm laborers, 10 males were shepherds. Some 28 families were so far removed from the colony that in the land re-allocation of 1878, they were deprived of their plots of land (12). The situation is explained not only in terms of insufficient land, but also its poor quality, which would not allow support of the growing colony. By 1912 the number of inhabitants had not only not grown, but it had declined and consisted of 1007 persons (14).

There are several contradictions in the data about the number of craftsmen in Josefstal. According to data from 1886, 12 persons were occupied in boot making, 5 were weavers (14). According to data from 1894, the colony had the following cottage industries: tailor - 1; boot maker - 1; turner - 1; teamsters - 2; blacksmiths - 2; weavers - 2 (15). There was no heavy industry in the colony. There

was only one water mill and three windmills. At the end of the nineteenth century, a small brick factory was constructed. Most of the inhabitants of Josefstal built their homes out of the poorly worked local stone, reinforcing it with clay mixed with straw. Often they used unfired bricks. Straw was also used to cover the roofs. At the beginning of the colony, only the more wealthy inhabitants could afford to construct wood homes. If, in the first years after founding of the colony, there were more than 2/3 of the homes roofed with thatch, then according to data in 1894, only 1/3 had thatched roofs. Because families were large, the homes were likewise. More than half (71 houses) were more than 9 meters in length and no less than 6 meters wide. Only 4 homes in the colony were less than 6 meters long (16). Dung was used to heat the homes.

The basic occupation of the inhabitants of the colony was farming. Ploughed fields, about 4,000 hectares, surrounded the colony in a single plot. The furthest plot of land was located 10 km from the colony. The colonists primarily planted spring wheat, with a smaller quantity of rye and oats. Favorable climatic conditions also permitted the cultivation of watermelons.

From the moment of founding of the colony, Josefstal had a church-parish school, where by law, all children from the ages of 7 to 14 were to study. The school year began on 20 August and concluded on 20 June. Classes were conducted from 8 until 11 am, and from 2 to 4 in the evening. In 1886, there were 87 boys and 55 girls enrolled in the school. By 1890 there were 103 boys and 87 girls. In spite of a fine of 3 kopeks for truancy, many children, especially boys, did not attend school (17). Religious education was extremely weak. Of 887 inhabitants of the colony, in 1886, only 311 persons could read printed letters with difficulty. In reality, there were very few literate people.

2.	37.	Христіанъ Геркъ			50
		Его Сыновья: 1. Якобъ			30
		2. Николаусъ			25
		Его сынъ Георгъ			1½
		Христіана 3ъ Сынъ Петеръ			22
		4. Іоганнесъ			12
		5. Конрадъ			10
		6. Цахаріасъ	умеръ въ 1855 году		"
		7. Іосефъ			5

The additional Gerk family settling in Josefstal in 1852 was the Kristian Gerk family, consisting of 14 people, all from Koehler. Kristian was the Uncle to the Peter Gerk family. Members of the family were: Gerk, Kristian age 50, son Jakob- 30, wife Barbara ?, daughter Magdalena-1 month; son Nikolaus age 25, wife Katarina Margareta - 26, son Georg -1½, daughter Elisabeta 3; son Peter 22, son Johannes 12, son Konrad 10, son Josef 5, daughter Katarina 15   Source: GAVO: Fond 299, Opis 1, No. 375

Dissatisfaction with the system of education in the church school led to the establishment by several wealthy families in 1885 in Josefstal of a trade school. Taught in it were reading and writing of the Russian and German languages, religion, a little geography, and 4 rules of arithmetic. Upon the founding of the school, the zemstvo [local governmental body] allocated an annual sum of 13 rubles. The teacher was paid about 80 kopeks a year per pupil. Each student had his or her own textbooks, but at the beginning, school was conducted in the teacher's house. Interest in the new form of education in the colony was great. The next year following the founding, the trade school enrolled 9 boys. In 1887 there were 12, and by 1890 there were more than 10 students (18).

Notes:

1. Klaus, A. A. "Nashi Kolonii"
2. Complete collected laws of the Russian Empire, St. Petersburg, 1841 Vol. XV, page 138.
3. State Archive of Saratov Oblast (further GASO), fond 180, op. 1, d. 365, page 465.
4. GASO F.180 op.7, d38, I.81
5. same, pages 85 obverse through 87 obverse.
6. same, pages 361 - 361 obverse.
7. GASO f.28, op. 1, d.2187
8. Saratov gubernia, List of populated places, St. Petersburg, 1862, p. 58
9. Collection of Statistical Data about the Saratov Gubernia. Saratov, 1891. Vol. XI., Kamyshin uyezd.p.409.
10. Minkh, A. N. Historical-Geographic Dictionary of the Saratov Guberniya. Saratov, 1903. p. 363
11. Same
12. Historical-Geographical Dictionary, p. 410
13. List of populated Places of the Saratov Gubernia. Kamyshin uyezd. Saratov, 1912. p. 10
14. GASO F.1, op.1, d.2465. I.56
15. Minkh, A. N. Historical-Geographical Dictionary, p. 365.
16. Collection of Statistical Data, p. 147
17. Same
18. Minkh, A. N. Historical-Geographical Dictionary, p. 365

Thanks to Rick Rye for the translation of this article

DID YOU KNOW???

Josefstal was part of the Catholic parish of Marienfeld. The village of Marienfeld was only 10.6 km away from Josefstal. This meant that both villages shared one priest and that Sunday Mass was alternated between villages. The village of Josefstal had a Catholic prayer house at the time of its founding. However, a church was built and dedicated in 1870. It was made of wood but covered with metal. In 1904 the parishioners in Josefstal built a new church, also made of wood. At each corner of the churchyard stood a small chapel, or "Kapelle". These chapels were used on special holy days. The church also had a large belfry in front, detached from the church. It was three tiers high. The church bells would ring to mark the death of a villager, to warn the village of danger, to guide a lost soul through a blizzardy night or to announce to the village that it was time to pray. Josefstal, like other Catholic German villages in Russia, had specific times during the day designated for prayer. The villagers could always decipher what the message was.

On a hill in Josefstal stood the fourteen Stations of the Cross. The villagers would partake in the services at the fourteen Stations on Roman Catholic holy days. These would usually be sung by the local schoolmaster. Some villagers would walk on their knees to the Stations to fulfill their penance after attending confession.

It was the natural custom in those days for the younger members of the congregation to kneel on the floor or to stand during mass. Only the older members could sit, unless one sang in the choir. The congregation was always placed according to age and sex—males on the right and females on the left. There were always four ushers sitting at various points in the church, making sure that the younger members were behaving themselves. It was not uncommon for an offending party to be given a stern look or a "cuff on the ear".

There was a large altar in the church, with a large statue of the Virgin Mary surrounded by roses. There was also a large statue of Saint Joseph in the church. The priests who served the parish were:

- Josef Yakubovski – 1860 – 1867
- Georg Dechant – 1877
- Johannes Weisman -- 1877
- Johannes Knutschko—about the year 1887
- Franz Loran—1897-1901?
- Nickolaus Maier—1901-1905
- Ferdinand Hirsch—? -1909
- Alois Oks-1902-1914
- Franz Rauh—1914-as administrator
- Alois Kappes—1914-1922?

Josefstal became an independent parish in 1919. The Catholic church in Marienfeld had been destroyed by fire shortly before. The priests who served in the new parish of Josefstal were:

- Alois Kappes—1923-1924 (about 10 months)
- Johannes Falkenstein--1925-1931?

Most of these men would be shot under Communism. The Church in Josefstal was destroyed by order of Communist officials in 1937.

**Early Gerk Settlers to Josefstal, Saratov Province &
their ties to the first Gerk settlers of Russia**

Johann Kaspar Gerk (498)
b. 1753
at Fulda, Hesse, Germany
m. circa 1776
m. circa 1790
+unknown
+Anna Marie Mützig
d. 14 Jan 1830
at Koehler, Saratov, RUS

Johann Kaspar Gerk was the 1st child
of Sebastian & Magdalena Gerk

Kristian Gerk (532)
b. 9 Aug 1807
at Koehler, Saratov, RUS
m. 2 Nov 1827
m. 28 Oct 1840
at Koehler, RUS
+Anna Maria Weisheim
+Maria Elisabetha Bisheimer
d. 23 Dec 1877
at Josefstal, Saratov, RUS

Brothers

Zacharius Gerk (512)
b. 1787
at Koehler, Saratov, RUS
m. circa 1809
at Koehler, Saratov, RUS
+Eva Elisabeta Schilling
b. 1790
at Saratov, RUS
d. 2 Feb 1843
at Koehler, Saratov, RUS

Family moved to Josefstal in 1852

Kristian Gerk (532) is the
uncle of Zacharius Peter
Gerk (514), both first settlers
to Josefstal.

Zacharius Peter Gerk (514)
b. 1820
at Koehler, Saratov, RUS
m. 24 Jan 1839
at Koehler, Saratov, RUS
+Katarina Schmidt
d. 2 Sep 1852
at Josefstal, Saratov, RUS

Family moved to Josefstal in 1852

Zacharius Peter Gerk (514)
b. 1820
at Koehler, Saratov, RUS
m. 24 Jan 1839
at Koehler, Saratov, RUS
+Katarina Schmidt
d. 2 Sep 1852
at Josefstal, Saratov, RUS

Zacharius Gerk (512)
b. 1787
at Koehler, Saratov, RUS
m. circa 1809
at Koehler, Saratov, RUS
+Eva Elisabeta Schilling
b. 1790
at Saratov, RUS
d. 2 Feb 1843
at Koehler, Saratov, RUS

Johann Georg Gerk (401)
b. 1826
at Koehler, Saratov, RUS
m. 3 Nov 1852
at Koehler, Saratov, RUS
+Katarina Buss
d. 27 Jul 1886
at Josefstal, Saratov, RUS

Gotlieb Gerk (515)
b. 1822
at Koehler, Saratov, RUS
m. 25 Nov 1846
at Koehler, Saratov, RUS
+Julia Gittlein
d. 1 Jul 1894
at Josefstal, Saratov, RUS

All 3 sons of Zacharius Gerk and their families moved to Josefstal in 1852. Not included in this chart are daughters who also married and moved to Josefstal. See the Sebastian Gerk descendent chart for further information

Jakob Gerk (554)
b. 4 Mar 1828
at Koehler, Saratov, RUS
m. 3 Nov 1852
m. 25 Oct 1854
m. 10 Nov 1859
at Josefstal, Saratov, RUS
+Margareta Erdle
+Barbara Rosenbach
+Anna Maria Loos
d. 4 Sep 1863
at Josefstal, Saratov, RUS

Nikolaus Gerk (555)
b. 21 Nov 1831
at Koehler, Saratov, RUS
m. 24 Nov 1853
at Josefstal, Saratov, RUS
+Katarina Margareta Ziegler
d. Unknown
at Josefstal, Saratov, RUS

Peter Gerk (705)
b. 20 Jan 1836
at Koehler, Saratov, RUS
m. 10 Nov 1859
at Josefstal, Saratov, RUS
+Anna Marie Wagner
d. Unknown
at Josefstal, Saratov, RUS

Kristian Gerk (532)
b. 9 Aug 1807
at Koehler, Saratov, RUS
m. 2 Nov 1827
m. 28 Oct 1840
at Koehler, RUS
+Anna Maria Weisheim
+Maria Elisabetha Bisheimer
d. 23 Dec 1877
at Josefstal, Saratov, RUS

Johannes Gerk (743)
b. 20 Jan 1836
at Koehler, Saratov, RUS
m. 9 Nov 1865
at Josefstal, Saratov, RUS
+Barbara Dittler
d. Unknown
at ARGENTINA?

There were 7 sons of Kristian Gerk
who moved to Josefstal in 1852.
These are the 5 that survived.

Konrad Gerk (705)
b. 26 Apr 1847
at Koehler, Saratov, RUS
m. 9 Nov 1865
at Josefstal, Saratov, RUS
+Elisabetha Lambrecht
d. 26 Dec 1877
at Josefstal, Saratov, RUS

Peter Gerk home in Josefstal circa 1939.

Josefstal Church Choir circa 1929. Photo taken next to Church. The Priest in the photo is Father Johannes Falkenstein. Father Falkenstein was shot by Soviet authorities in 1937. Paul & Elisabeth Gerk were married in this Church.

The Johann Georg Gerk Family circa 1917 in Josefstal.
Standing Left to Right: Margareta (Stremel) Gerk, Unknown Farm worker, Jakob Gerk, Maria Gerk, Paul Gerk.
Sitting Left to Right: Michael Kisser, Piada Kisser, Anna (Gerk) Kisser, Anna Margareta (Rohwein) Gerk, Johannes Gerk, Kristina (Rausch) Gerk, Infant Georg Gerk.

Johann Georg & Margareta (Bauer) Gerk and family in Josefstal circa 1920. Johann Georg is the grandson of Josefstal first settler Kristian Gerk. His son Martin Gerk will settle in the Coronel Suarez area of Argentina. Most of the family pictured here will die of starvation in 1933.
Source: Catharine (Winter) Kern

43

Another Georg Gerk family, circa 1938, taken in the Caucasus area of the USSR
Back Left to Right: Georg Gerk, Maria (Knaub) Gerk, Peter Gerk, Olga Gerk, Ida
Gerk, Adam Gerk
Front Sitting Left to Right: Anna Margareta (Haberkorn) Gerk, Johannes Gerk,
Georg Gerk

Cross marking grave in the abandoned cemetery in Josefstal – 2009
Source: Edward Gerk

For reasons exactly the same as Josefstal, members of the Gerk family would also move to the neighboring village of Marienfeld, located just 11 km away from Josefstal.

The life of the colonists of Josefstal and Marienfeld were intertwined, due to the close proximity with each other, as well as the reality that both villages were part of the same Catholic Parish of Marienfeld, and thus alternated Sunday Church each week.

For now we glimpse at the history of Marienfeld as of the year 1900 from the pages of *"Istoriko-geograficheskii slovar' saratovskoi gubernii"* by Alekandr Nikolaevich Minkh (Saratov: Tipografiia gubernskago zemstva, 1898-1901)

Marienfeld, also known as Spatzenchutor, is a German colony located in Kamyshin County. It is 25 *verst* from the town of Kamyshin and 21 *verst* southwest of the county seat of Rosenfeld. The village is located on the left shore of the river Mokraya Ol'khovka and near the Kamyshin-Tambov Railroad which opened in 1894.

The inhabitants are Germans and all are Catholics. There is a Catholic church in the village and a Catholic school.

About 1828 a settler by the name of Brunner from the village Ustkulalinka [Galka], whose nickname was "Spatz" (Sparrow), founded a farmstead and started farming at this location to raise wheat for bread. Therefore, the village today is called "Spatz' Farmstead" or Spatzen chutor. *[A khutor (English spelling) is a farmstead isolated from the home village. Many such farmsteads eventually grew into new, daughter villages, as did*

Spatzenchutor.-Ed.] It is sometimes called New Avilova since the village of Avilova is nearby. The village is located on the lot which belonged to the Spatz farmstead. After a while some new settlers settled from the Kamensk District. In 1852 a final settlement of this area by colonists from the Catholic villages in the Kamensk and Norka Districts took place.

The official name of Marienfeld, which means "Mother Mary's Field," was given to this village in 1852. The colonist settlers of Marienfeld received from the government a 14.5-dessiatine plot of arable land per man [1 dessiatine = 2.7 acres]. According to the paper in 1852, there was a total of 4339 dessiatines of land. There were 105 families and 55 households. There were 275 males and 301 females for a total of 576 people. In 1862 there were 71 households with 345 males and 319 females, a total of 664 people. In 1865, 17 people resettled in the village of Semenovka, and 29 people resettled in the village of Rozhdestvenskoye in the Kuban District [Caucasus].

In 1871 there were 312 males and 286 females for a total of 598 people. In 1877, 9 families consisting of 20 people left for America and were excluded from the community list. In 1886, 21 more families left for America. Prior to leaving for America, they sold their houses, livestock, and possessions. The community did not help these people.

In 1886 there were 129 households consisting of 585 males and 494 females, totalling 1079 people. In addition to the above, 24 families were permanently absent. They belonged to the community but lived elsewhere.

In 1886, there were 264 literate men and 258 literate women besides the students. There were 129 houses, 87 brick and the rest wooden. Thirty nine houses were covered with metal sheets, and the rest were covered with straw.

There were 123 plows, 16 windrowing machines, 484 horses, 140 oxen, 270 cows, 114 calves, 820 sheep, 302 pigs, and 98 goats.

In 1886 there were 4 carpenters, 15 shoemakers, 4 people who made oil from sunflower seeds, 3 [grain] millers, and 2 bakeries.

In 1890 there were 696 males and 639 females, totaling1335 people, all Catholics: In the village there were 1 liquor store, 1 *butter* or oil mill, 1 windmill, and 1watermill. There were 5862 dessiatines of arable land, 251 dessiatines of meadow, 195.5 dessiatines of forest land, and 2187 dessiatines outside the village area. The land owned by the village totalled 8495.5 dessiatines. The river Mokraya Ol'khovka, which has a bridge across it, crosses through a section of 5862 dessiatines. The distance from the village to the farthest boundary is 10 *verst.* [1 *verst* = .6629 mile].

The hay land is along the river which is southeast of the village; the forest is west of the village. One *verst* from the village, the arable land is partly hilly and slopes in the direction of the river. There are no deep canyons on the land. One-third of the soil is black earth, one-third consists of sand and black earth, and one-third of the soil is clay. The subsoil is red clay.

Prior to 1874 the land was distributed according to the census figure of 510 males. In 1880 the second distribution was made to 590 males. In 1886 the third distribution was made to 650 males. (This includes all men and boys, including infants.) The land was redistributed every six years. The amount of tillable land gradually increased due to the periodical tilling of pasture land.

The forest is cut each fall and is divided among the people. The houses are usually heated by dried manure mixed with grass. The land for potatoes and cabbage is close to the river.

There is no regular rotation of crops grown on the land. The community elders decided that rye would be grown one year and wheat the next two years. They produce watermelons, flax, hemp, rye, wheat, cabbage, potatoes, sunflowers, and garden vegetables. The rye, wheat, and flax are harvested using scythes. The grain is sold in Kamyshin.

In one area to the south of the village, the land had an overpopulation of chipmunks (gophers?). Every owner of land had to deliver to the district authorities 30 chipmunk tails each year. The extermination of the chipmunks was especially difficult because the Russians living in the nearby villages did not pay any attention to the chipmunks.

Many farmers rented land in the area of the Don River for 60 kopecks per dessiatine, but due to the distance away from the village, the farmers discontinued farming that area. (100 kopecks = 1 ruble.) All payments to the government in 1885 totalled 4383 rubbles.

In 1890 there were 115 boys and 96 girls, totalling 211 children. Generally speaking, the Catholics had a much weaker education than did the Lutherans, and that is why so many of the people in Marienfeld could not read or write.

Marienfeld, also known as Spatzenchutor, is on the lower shore of the river Mokraya Ol'khovka, which has a dam. The village was established in 1828 and now has a wooden church covered with a wooden roof, which was dedicated in 1856. The school opened in 1852. The Catholic priest was assigned in 1859.

In 1894 there are 134 households, 4 community buildings, church, priest's residence, school, and a blacksmith forge. All in all, there are 580 buildings, 241 wooden and 339 stone and brick. Most of the buildings are covered with wooden roofs and some with straw. The priest's residence has a metal roof. The village is built according to plan and divided into blocks of 4 households each. There are 29 wells, 1 liquor store, and 1 hardware shop. There are 787 men and 700 women, totalling 1487 people. There are 8 shoemakers, 1 tailor, 2 carpenters, 5 wagon makers, 1 blacksmith, 2 weavers, and 1 leather tanner.

There are 2 windmills and 1 mill for making, butter and oil from sunflowers. Marienfeld has a total of 8495 dessiatines of land, 5161 dessiatines of good land and 3334 dessiatines of fair land. The distance to the county center, Rosenfeld, is 20 *verst;* to the village of Avilova, 3 *verst;* to the village of Baronovka, 7 *verst;* to the colony of Unterdorf, 14 *verst;* to the railroad station of Avilova, 1 *verst;* to the town of Kamyshin, 25 *verst;* and to the city of Saratov, 174 *verst.*

Street view in Marienfeld, now called Novonikolaevka, in August 2003. Source: Edward Gerk

The Kamyshin Railroad crosses the communal land of Marienfeld. There is a communal watermill with the proper equipment and a household for the miller. There are 3 men and 3 women living in the household. The watermill is 2 *verst* from Marienfeld. The colony is located at 50° 12' north (latitude) and 14 ° 46' east (longitude). [1A base line running through Pulkovo, south of St. Petersburg, was used to determine the longitude rather than using the primary meridian of Greenwich. A contemporary gazetteer for the U.S.S.R. gives the latitude and longitude of Marienfeld as 50° 12' north (latitude) and 45° 06' east (longitude). The present-day name for this village is Novo Nikolaevka.-Ed.]

Cemetery in Marienfeld, September 2009
Source: Edward Gerk

DID YOU KNOW??

This photo of the club-house in modern-day Marienfeld (2003) was said to be, according to former Josefstal resident Johannes Gerk (brother of Paul Gerk), constructed from wood taken from their Gerk house in Josefstal. Source: Edward Gerk

Early Gerk Settlers to Marienfeld, Saratov Province & their ties to the first Gerk settlers of Russia

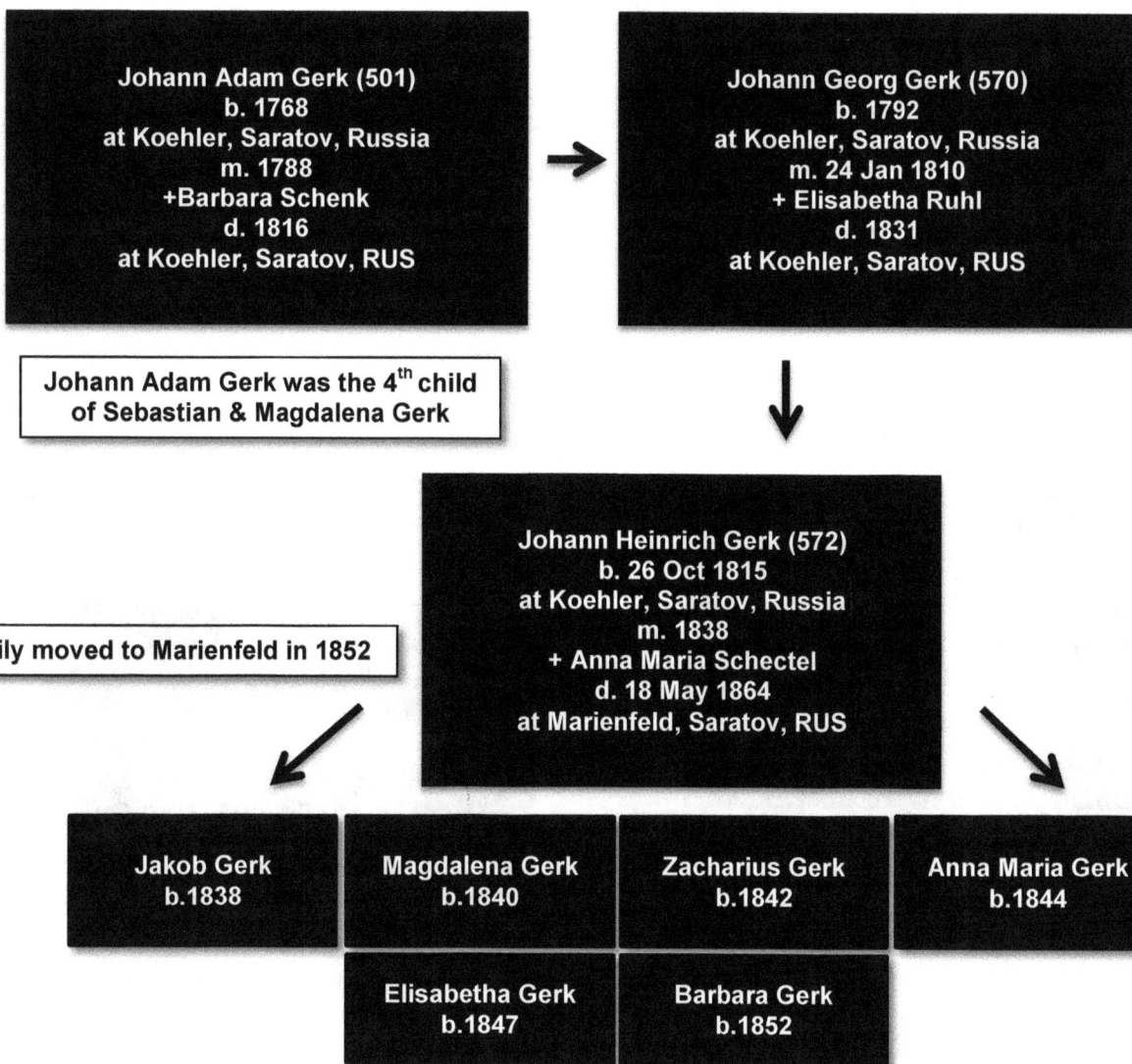

Family #20 to Marienfeld in the February 15, 1858 tax census were from Koehler, consisting of 6 people, were Heinrich Gerk age 42, Heinrich Gerk's daughter Magdalena age 17, 2nd daughter Anna Maria age 13, 3rd daughter Barbara age 9 and 1st son Jakob age 19 and 2nd son Zacharius age 15. They were Family Number 207 in the 1850 tax census of Koehler. The wife of Heinrich was Anna Marie Schectel, born circa 1819, who died circa 1850 in Koehler. Source: GAVO Fond 299, Opis 1, Delo 375

Johann Adam Gerk (501)
b. 1768
at Koehler, Saratov, Russia
m. 1788
+Barbara Schenk
d. 1816
at Koehler, Saratov, RUS

Johann Georg Gerk (570)
b. 1792
at Koehler, Saratov, Russia
m. 24 Jan 1810
+ Elisabetha Ruhl
d. 1831
at Koehler, Saratov, RUS

Johann Adam Gerk was the 4th child of Sebastian & Magdalena Gerk

Johann Heinrich Gerk (572)
b. 26 Oct 1815
at Koehler, Saratov, Russia
m. 1838
+ Anna Maria Schectel
d. 18 May 1864
at Marienfeld, Saratov, RUS

Family moved to Marienfeld in 1852

Jakob Gerk
b.1838

Magdalena Gerk
b.1840

Zacharius Gerk
b.1842

Anna Maria Gerk
b.1844

Elisabetha Gerk
b.1847

Barbara Gerk
b.1852

Excerpt from Family #51 to Marienfeld from Koehler, consisting of 7 people was headed by Peter Gerk (died 1853 – actual date was 1854) Peter Gerk's wife Elisabeta age 60, 1st son Peter (died 1858 – actual date 1857) Peter's wife Anna Maria age 24, 2nd son Johannes age 20, Johannes' wife Marianna age 17. The census will be amended to include Johannes Gerk's wife's illegitimate son: Michael age 1 ½. Michael will head up the branch of the Gerk family that will settle in Colorado. Source: GAVO Fond 299, Opis 1, Delo 375

Johann Adam Gerk (501)
b. 1768
at Koehler, Saratov, Russia
m. 1788
+Barbara Schenk
d. 1816
at Koehler, Saratov, RUS

Johann Adam Gerk was the 4th child of Sebastian & Magdalena Gerk

Peter Gerk (573)
b. 1796
at Koehler, Saratov, Russia
m. 1817
+Anna Elisabeth Leonardt
d. 28 May 1854
at Marienfeld, Saratov, RUS

Family moved to Marienfeld in 1852

Peter Gerk (589)
b. 27 May 1833
at Koehler, Saratov, Russia
m. 20 Nov 1851
+Anna Maria Ringelmann
d. 4 Nov 1857
at Marienfeld, Saratov, RUS

Family moved to Marienfeld in 1852

Family #54 is the Valentin Gerk family from Koehler. The family consists of 12 people that include: Valentin Gerk, age 36, Valentin Gerk's wife Maria Eva, age 29, 1st daughter Elisabeta age 4, 2nd daughter Katarina, age 2, 1st son Peter age 9, 2nd son Jakob age 6 ½, 3rd son Johannes age 8 days, Valentin's brother Johannes age 31, Johannes' wife Katarina age 27, 1st daughter Elisabeta, age 8, 2nd daughter Katarina age 5 and Valentin's 2nd brother Johannes age 17. Valentin's son Jacob, age 6 ½ at the time of this census, will settle in South Dakota. Source: GAVO Fond 299, Opis 1, Delo 375

Johann Adam Gerk (501)
b. 1768
at Koehler, Saratov, Russia
m. 1788
+Barbara Schenk
d. 1816
at Koehler, Saratov, RUS

Johann Adam Gerk was the 4th child of Sebastian & Magdalena Gerk

Family moved to Marienfeld in 1852

Heinrich Gerk (574)
b. 1799
at Koehler, Saratov, Russia
m. 1819
+Kristina Ziegler
d. 10 Sept 1848
at Koehler, Saratov, RUS

Valentin Gerk (591)
b. 1821
at Koehler, Saratov, Russia
m. 1841
m. 26 Nov 1846
+Katarina Mildenberger
+Marie Eva Graf
d. 22 Sept 1868
at Marienfeld, Saratov, RUS

Valentin Gerk (591)
b. 1821
at Koehler, Saratov, Russia
m. 1841
m. 26 Nov 1846
+Katarina Mildenberger
+Marie Eva Graf
d. 22 Sept 1868
at Marienfeld, Saratov, RUS

Family moved to Rozhdestvenskoye, Stavropol Province, Russia, from Marienfeld circa 1865. Son Jakob Gerk will later move with his family to South Dakota

Peter Gerk
b.1842

Anna Maria Gerk
b.1843

Peter Gerk
b.1848

Jakob Gerk
b.1850

Katarina Gerk
b.1852

Elisabetha Gerk
b.1853

Katarina Gerk
b.1856

Johann Gerk
b.1858

Elisabetha Gerk
b.1860

Nikolaus Gerk
b.1862

Phillip Gerk
b.1868

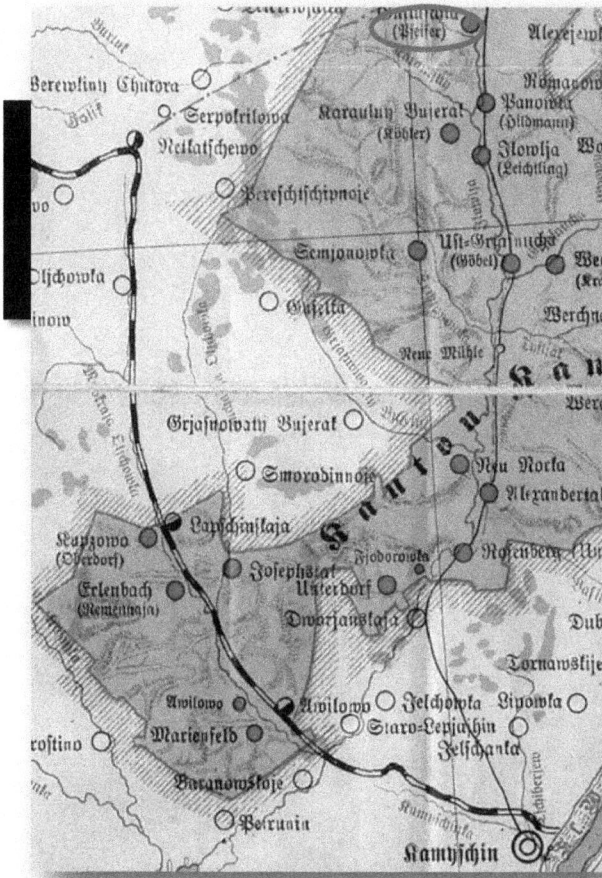

Pfeifer was located north of Koehler, as seen on the above map, and although there was a family of 10 Gerk's that settled there, very little is known about the family and their descendants.

A short history Peifer, provided by Pfeifer historian Rosemary Larson, states:

At the general Russian census of 1788, Pfeifer had 89 families, with 270 males and 237 females. Since the founding, the following have left the colony: in the years 1860-1864, 23 families migrated to the province of Samara (probably Streckerau); in the years 1877-1886, 64 families went to South America; in the years 1868-1876 six persons were expelled from the community for immoral behavior and were banished to Siberia. There are also 90 families, still belonging to this community, who now have their homes elsewhere.

PFEIFER has been an independent Catholic parish since 1871. In the 1798 census the parishioners belonged to St. Mary's Catholic Church in Kamenka where there was a priest as well as a church for worship. The parish church was built of wood in 1846. There is a parochial school where small children are taught reading, writing, and religion by a schoolmaster under the supervision of a priest. Since 1888 there was also a government-supported Russian school. 618 adult males and 524 adult females are able to read and write. Church of St. Francis is no longer standing.

The first priest serving St. Francis of Assisi at Pfeifer was Philipp Dorzweiler. He was followed by Michael Haag 1869 -1877, Sebastian Wolf 1877-1878, [again] Philipp Dorzweiler 1878-1880, Johannes Burgardt 1880 -1894, Peter Mueller in 1887, Josef Paul 1897?-1898, [in 1897 Josef Hein from Koehler attended to the needs of the parish at Pfeifer], in 1904 Alexander Staub of Kamenka served Pfeifer, Joseph Guetlein in 1905, Johannes Fix 1905 -1909/1910, Johannes v. Pauer 1890 - 1905?, Joseph Beilmann 1911-1913, Nikolaus Maier 1914 -1918, Emanuel Simon ?-1921, and Leo Weinmayer 1921 -1928.

The colony has the following artisans: 27 shoemakers, 4 cabinetmakers, 5 wheeelwrights, 2 weavers, 7 carpenters, 4 tailors, 2 oven-builders, 8 blacksmiths and I musician. It also has an oil-mill, 2 wind-driven flour mills, 21 establishments dealing in manufactured goods, 4 small shops and 3 liquor stores.

The land owned by the community has an area of 11,979 dessiatines, of which 8,195 are under cultivation, 150 hayland, 245 are wooded, 265 are pasture, 6 are seeded to hemp, 37 are potato field, 6 are cabbage field, 126 are occupied as village lots and vegetable gardens and 45 are used for threshing-floors. The surface of the land is mostly hilly. Of the total area, 450 dessiatines have good black soil, the rest is mainly clay with sandy subsoil. On the land are seven dams for the watering of livestock. The land is divided among the families according to the number of males.

The colonists sell their produce mainly in Nishnaja-Panovka [Hildmann] on the Volga, less frequently in the district capital, Kamyshin.

1 verst = 2/3 mile. 1 dessiatine = 2.7 acres

Sources:
AHSGR Work Paper #16 (December 1974)
1798 Revision List (Census)
DIE KIRCHE AND DAS RELIGIOSE LEBEN DER RUSSLANDDEUTSCHEN by Joseph Schnurr

Photograph of home in Pfeifer, Russia circa 2001

Source:
http://intermountainchapterahsgr.blogspot.com/

Catholic Church of St. Francis of Assisi in Pfeifer- constructed of wood in 1846

Source: DIE KIRCHE AND DAS RELIGIOSE LEBEN DER RUSSLANDDEUTSCHEN by Joseph Schnurr

Gerk Settlers to Pfeifer, Saratov Province & their ties to the first Gerk settlers of Russia

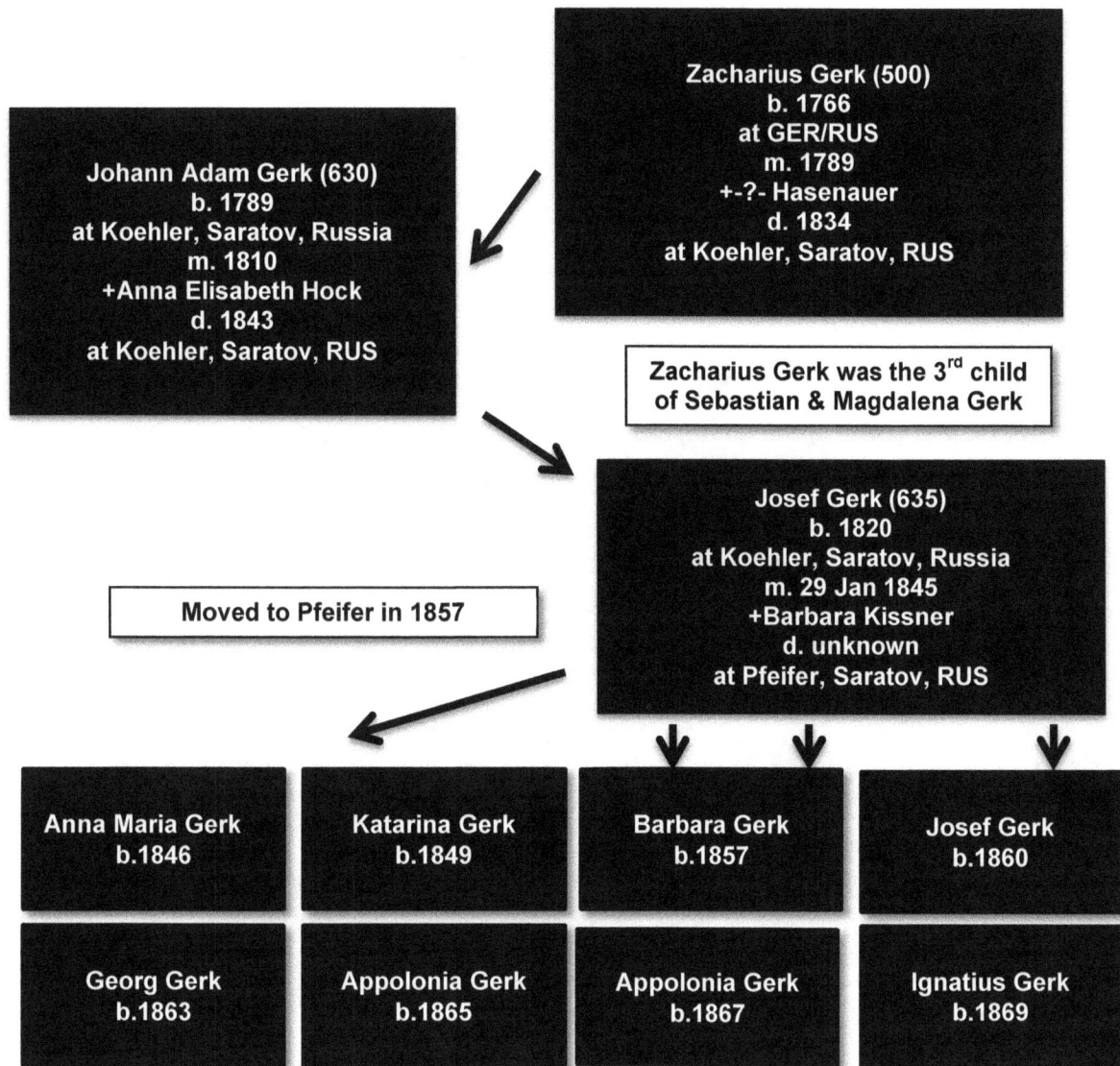

Family #163 in the 10 December 1857 Koehler census is the Josef Gerk family. It states that Josef was 30 years old in 1850 and that in 1857 his family moved to Pfeifer. His brother Johannes, age 26 in 1857, and son Georg, age 1/2 in 1857, stayed in Koehler. Source: GAVO Fond 299.

Zacharius Gerk (500)
b. 1766
at GER/RUS
m. 1789
+-?- Hasenauer
d. 1834
at Koehler, Saratov, RUS

Johann Adam Gerk (630)
b. 1789
at Koehler, Saratov, Russia
m. 1810
+Anna Elisabeth Hock
d. 1843
at Koehler, Saratov, RUS

Zacharius Gerk was the 3rd child of Sebastian & Magdalena Gerk

Josef Gerk (635)
b. 1820
at Koehler, Saratov, Russia
m. 29 Jan 1845
+Barbara Kissner
d. unknown
at Pfeifer, Saratov, RUS

Moved to Pfeifer in 1857

Anna Maria Gerk b.1846	Katarina Gerk b.1849	Barbara Gerk b.1857	Josef Gerk b.1860
Georg Gerk b.1863	Appolonia Gerk b.1865	Appolonia Gerk b.1867	Ignatius Gerk b.1869

DID YOU KNOW??

Jacob & Barbara (Gerk) Schoenfeld circa 1920

The only known Gerk descendent from the village of Pfeifer to make it to the west was Barbara Gerk, born 3 Oct 1857 in Pfeifer, the daughter of Josef Gerk and his wife Barbara Kissner.

Barbara would marry Jacob Schoenfeld on 19 Oct 1874 in Pfeifer. They Arrived in New York USA on S.S. Main 15 July 1876.

They will be among the first settlers of Pfeifer, Kansas. The town of Pfeifer is located 10 miles south of Victoria on the south bank of the Smoky Hill River. It was founded in August 1876.

Barbara and her husband will have 14 children.

Barbara died 10 Oct 1937 in Pfeiffer, Kansas.

Her husband Jacob Schoenfeld will die 19 Sept 1922, also in Pfeiffer, Kansas.

Further information on this line of the Gerk family shown in the Sebastian Gerk descendant chart.

Source: The Golden Jubilee of German-Russian Settlements of Ellis and Rush Counties, Kansas, 1926.

Photo courtesy of Jan Lawler

Johann Georg Gerk & Family

We now look at the father of Paul (Grandpa) Gerk, Johann Georg Gerk.

Johann Georg Gerk was born January 12, 1869 in Josefstal.

He was the ninth and youngest child of First Josefstal settlers Johann Georg Gerk and his wife Ekaterina Buss.

Not much else is known about him. Granny (Elisabeth Dieser) Gerk described him as an extremely "strict" and hard man...with his wife being the love of his life and the only one who could "reason" with him.

This author was told that he never allowed his photograph to be taken...so we have no photo to show what he looked like.

What we know, we collect from recollections and stories passed down by Granny Gerk, and through former Soviet archives, now available to us.

We know that he was youngest of nine children, and only three of those nine survived until adulthood.

Johann Georg's oldest brother was named, wait for it, Johann Georg!

This first Johann Georg Gerk was born October 8, 1853 in Josefstal, and would marry Margareta Magdalena Haberkorn on November 14, 1871 also in Josefstal.

These two brothers would often go by the name of "Georg Gerk"...with the Dad also named Georg Gerk. This brings us to the problem of same names in a family....an ongoing issue among Volga Germans.

The solution to the Volga German problem of same names was simple: "nicknames" or "Beinamen".

In this case, the father of Paul Gerk, Johann Georg Gerk, was simply called "Hanseatic". Now, why he was called this, no one knows. Such names were bestowed for various reasons by either friends or family members.

Another interesting piece of information was the fact that our Gerk family tried to leave Russia in the 1870's.

It was in this decade that the Russian Tsar made the decision to rescind the privileges that Volga Germans had. Historian Steve Schreiber writes:

According to Fred Koch in his book titled "The Volga Germans", when Catherine the Great solicited and recruited German immigrants into her country, the new colonists were well received by the Russian people. Her government's policy of segregating the Germans within demographically closed villages inside the Volga enclave contributed a great deal to harmony between the two peoples for several generations. In later years it contributed to envy and resentment by many Russians.

The primary reasons for emigration from Russia included:

- *Russification movements*
- *Land shortages*
- *Loss of privileges and compulsory military service*
- *Recruitment by New World countries*

Emigration to North America began in 1875.

The immigration of Russian Germans to the United States resulted from several causes. The most significant was Czar Alexander II's revocation, in 1871, of one of the guarantees made to the first Volga colonists by Catherine the Great: freedom from military service. In 1892,

Alexander III curtailed land acquisition by non-Orthodox citizens in the west. To land-starved colonists who had established many new colonies and who doubtless had plans to start more, such a policy seemed to aim at their freedom of religion, which Catherine had also guaranteed.

Many families did send sons off to the army and navy. Even today pictures of young Germans in Russian uniforms are found in the homes of their American offspring. An anti-German wind was blowing across the steppes, however, and the colonists felt it. They had lost faith in the manifesto that brought their ancestors to Russia. Consequently, many sought new homes, some going to the United States and Canada and others journeying to South America. (Source:http://www.volgagermans.net/norka/emigration.html)

We find in a collection of documents from the Volgograd State Archive (GAVO) a set of passport applications for residents of Josefstal from 1876 to 1878. One of those is the passport application for Johann Georg Gerk and his sons, Johann Georg Gerk and his brother Georg Gerk.

At this point, we cannot see any confirmation that they actually left Russia during this time period…that they did in fact go at a later date will be discussed in this chapter later. Remember that our Johann Georg Gerk would have been 8-years old when his brother Johann Georg Gerk, age 23, applied for this passport.

Meanwhile, the year 1886 will be of great significance to our Gerk family line.

Johann Georg Gerk, father to both the "Georg Gerk's" will die on July 27, 1886. The status of head of the house will now pass on to the older Gerk brother.

Our Georg Gerk will find and marry a wife, Anna Margareta Rohwein, daughter of Heinrich Rohwein and Barbara Haberkorn. Anna Margareta was born 15 August 1868 in Josefstal, which made her one-year older than her husband.

They were married 4 November 1886 in the church in Josefstal, with Georg being 17 years old and wife Anna Margareta 18.

Almost nine months to the day, their first child, Barbara Gerk, was born on 6 July 1887. Sadly, Barbara will die on 23 April 1888, just shy of one year old. Their next child, Alois, was born 6 June 1889. Alois (commonly known as Louis in the West) will also die at a young age, at the age of 5 on March 6, 1895.

In keeping with the legal requirement, Georg will be drafted into the Russian military, in the year he turned 21 years of age. That would have made it approximately 1890.

Draft records for this time period for Josefstal are not available. We can only speculate that he answered the call and performed his military duty.

It was during this time period that we have, what is called, "a skeleton in the closet".

A baby born to Anna Margareta Gerk, labeled "illegitimate" and named "Tsirak" Gerk.

While illegitimate children were far from uncommon in Russia, there was just never any mention of this event.

More on this story can be found in the section "The Mystery of Michael Gerk".

Meanwhile, as the Gerk family grew in size and prospered, (eight more children were born up until 1911) rumors of war circulated.

These rumors and Russia's subsequent war with Japan, would force our Johann Georg Gerk to make an important decision.

Remember that in those days the Father of a household was an integral part of a family's survival.

To that end, our Johann Georg Gerk left Russia.

He made that decision, according to Historian James Long, because:

"The Russo-Japanese War suddenly and drastically interrupted the tranquil life of the colonists, who had never experienced the implications and ramifications of modern warfare, for being in the reserves during peacetime was no great burden. Although liable for training, but not more than twice and for periods not longer than six weeks, in fact because of reasons of economy, reservists usually were called up only once and for just two weeks. The 1904-5 mobilization weighed heavily on the colonists, causing many of them to fear and suspect future mobilizations, and may even help explain the recurring rumors of war which swept the colonies between 1906 and 1914.

Baptismal Record for Johann Georg Gerk, father of Paul Gerk. It states he was born in the village of Josefstal, Parish of Marienfeld, on 12 January 1869, and was baptized the same day. His parents were Johann Georg Gerk and Ekaterina Buss. Godparents were Johannes Schaeffer and Elisabetha Weichel. Source: GASO Fond 259

Johann Kaspar Gerk (498)
b. 1753
at Fulda, Hesse, Germany
m. circa 1776
m. circa 1790
+unknown
+Anna Marie Mützig
d. 14 Jan 1830
at Koehler, Saratov, RUS

→

Zacharius Gerk (512)
b. 1787
at Koehler, Saratov, RUS
m. circa 1809
at Koehler, Saratov, RUS
+Eva Elisabeta Schillig
at Saratov, RUS
d. 2 Feb 1843
at Koehler, Saratov, RUS

Johann Kaspar Gerk was the 1st child of Sebastian & Magdalena Gerk

Johann Georg Gerk (401)
b. 1826
at Koehler, Saratov, RUS
m. 3 Nov 1852
at Koehler, Saratov, RUS
+Katarina Buss
d. 27 Jul 1886
at Josefstal, Saratov, RUS

Johann Georg Gerk (847)
b. 8 Oct 1853
at Josefstal, Saratov, RUS
m. 14 Nov 1871
at Josefstal, Saratov, RUS
+Margareta Magdalena Haberkorn
d. Unknown
at ARGENTINA

Johann Georg Gerk (404)
b. 12 Jan 1869
at Josefstal, Saratov, RUS
m. 4 Nov 1886
at Josefstal, Saratov, RUS
+Anna Margareta Rohwein
d. 10 Feb 1925
at Josefstal, Stalingrad, USSR

59

Beginning in 1904, many Volga German reservists - men between the ages of twenty-five and forty-three, some of whom had been discharged as far back as 1886 - decided to emigrate illegally rather than being reactivated to fight in some distant war of no concern to them. These emigrants were not the single, twenty-one-year-old conscripts, but older men, now married, many with families, and some acting as the sole head of the household. Even a father could be mobilized, while his healthy nondrafted sons had no obligations. Thus the mobilization of reservists for the Russo-Japanese War involved thousands of colonists (about 20 to 25 percent of male villagers), while the annual conscription only affected about 500 young men with no family obligations. Consequently, most of those Volga Germans who fled Russia for military reasons were veterans who feared being recalled to active duty." -James W. Long: "From Privileged to Dispossessed - The Volga Germans 1860 - 1917" University of Nebraska Press

Elisabeth Dieser (Granny) Gerk stated in one of our interviews that although both Johann Georg Gerk's left for South America, our Georg Gerk would return.

passed down state that our Georg Gerk was able to retire at the age of 40, which would have been around the year 1909.

Granny Gerk (Elisabeth Dieser Gerk) stated that the Gerk family had the most up to date farm machinery…as well they had a home across from the Church in Josefstal, and another house out on their farm. The barns on the farm were "painted red".

As most of the Volga German villages prospered, regular land shortages became a problem. The Russian government gradually opened up new land for farming to the Volga Germans. Our Georg Gerk purchased some of this land…which was a few kilometers from the village of Josefstal, near the Russian village of Smorodinnoye.

One would think that the live of this Johann Georg Gerk would end in tranquility, allowing Georg to enjoy his children, grandchildren and the fruit of his labours.

This was not to be. War, Revolution, Civil War and a devastating famine would claim its toll.

Could it be? Hamburg, Germany Passenger list for 30 Aug 1905 lists a Georg Kerk of "Saratov" departing on the SS Cordoba, headed for Buenos Aires. It lists his age as 39, slightly older than our Georg Gerk, but not uncommon for a passenger list to have an incorrect age. As well, the Gerk name was often changed to Kerk to coincide to its' phonetic sound. Source: Hamburg Passenger Lists, 1850-1934 Volume: 373-7 I, VIII A 1 Band 169 Page: 1921 Microfilm Roll Number: K_1791

would return.

Family tradition states that our Georg Gerk returned to Russia under a general amnesty proclaimed by the Tsar, for all those who fled military duty, in honour of the birth of the heir to the Russian throne, the Tsarevich Alexei Nikolaevich.

Would the family have stayed in Russia? Would Georg Gerk move the entire family to Argentina, as did his older brother Georg?

These are questions without answers.

With the return of Georg Gerk to Russia, the family continued on to prosperity. Family stories

Two of his sons, Michael and Paul, will be forced to escape from Russia.

Johann Georg Gerk will die from stomach cancer on 10 February 1925 at the age of 56.

The search is still continuing on what happened to his older brother Johann Georg Gerk and where he and his family settled in Argentina.

And the question has to be asked…how much different our family would have been if our younger Johann Georg Gerk had made the decision to stay in Argentina and move his family there?

"This is my brother Georg, and this is my other brother Georg..."*

In many Volga German villages, especially the smaller ones, only a few names predominated. Common surnames were evidence of just how interrelated many Volga German households had become (although some villagers denied genealogical ties with individuals who bore the same family name). Beside common surnames, certain first names and middle names (or Doppelnamen, double-names) frequently were used. Traditionally, names like "Johannes Jakob" and "Anna Margareta" were contracted into more endearing terms like "Hanjakob" and "Amagret". Volga Germans tended to be very conservative in naming their children and thus it was not unusual to find several individuals in one village that bore the same first name, middle name, and surname.

In the early 1900's, the Protestant Pastor Eduard Seib served the Volga German villages of Messer (Ust Zolikha) and Warenburg (Privalnoye). Later he wrote about some of his experiences in the colonies, leaving behind a fascinating document that describes Volga German folkways. Pastor Seib recalled that the common use of certain Volga German names in the colonies gave rise to considerable confusion, especially on the part of ministers and schoolteachers. He described an interesting exchange between a village school teacher and two pupils - both of whom were named "Heinrich Franz Lipps." Since it was the first day of school, the teacher sought to find an easy way to tell the two pupils apart. And so the Schulmeister quizzed them for a little family history:

"Wie heisst dein Vater?" (What is your father's name?)
"Heinrich Franz"
"Und deiner?" ("And yours?" asked the teacher of the other pupil)
"Heinrich Franz"
"Wie heist deine Mutter?" (What is your mother's name?)
"Maria Katharina"
"Und deine?" (And yours?)
"Maria Katharina"
"Was fur eine geborene ist deine Mutter?" (What is your mother's maiden name?)
"'ne Radisen." (Radisen)
"Und deine?" (And yours?)
"'ne Radisen." (Radisen)
"Wie heist dein Grossvater?" (What is your grandfather's name?)
"Heinrich Franz."
"Und deiner?" (And yours?)
"Heinrich Franz."
"Wie heist deine Grossmutter?" (What is your grandmother's name?)
"Maria Katharina."
"Und deine?" (And yours?)
"Maria Katharina."
"Wie schreibt sich deine Grossmutter?" (What is your grandmother's last name")
"Geis."
"Und deine?" (And yours?)
"Zieg."

At last the flabbergasted schoolmaster had found a way to distinguish the two Volga German pupils who bore the same name of "Heinrich Franz Lipps." Thereafter, the one boy would be referred to as "Geisa-Lipps" and the other as "Ziega-Lipps"!

-Timothy J. & Rosalinda Kloberdanz:
"Thunder on the Steppe : Volga German Folklife in a Changing Russia" (1993)
(Used with permission)
*with apologies to the Newhart Show

A copy of the passport application for "America" of Johann Georg Gerk, wife Ekaterina and children dated January of 1877. The document includes a copy of a passport page. Source: GAVO Fond 270 Opis 1 2014, 2014b and 205. In the Cyrillic alphabet Gerk is spelled Герк

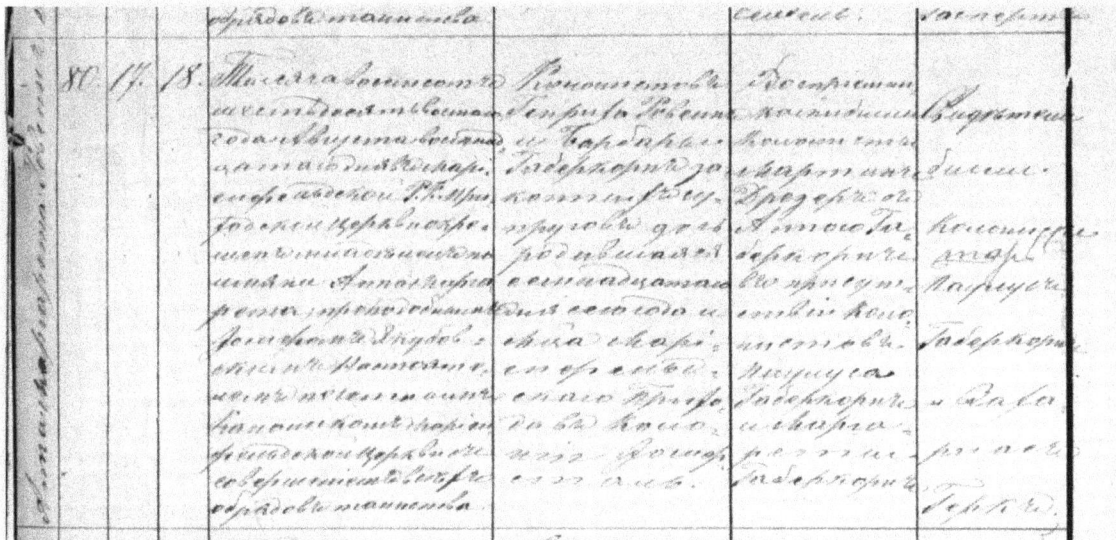

Baptismal Record of Anna Margareta Rohwein (pronounced Rovein). Born 17 August 1868 in Josefstal, and baptized on 18 August 1868. Daughter of Heinrich Rohwein and Barbara Haberkorn. God parents were Martin Dreckaser and Paulina Haberkorn. She will marry Georg Gerk in 1886.

Johann Georg Rohwein (615)
b. 1815
at Kamenka, Saratov, RUS
m. circa 1809
at Koehler, Saratov, RUS
+Franziska Roth
b. 1815
at Kamenka, Saratov, RUS
d. Unknown
at Josefstal, Saratov, RUS

Heinrich Rohwein (416)
b. 1846
at Kamenka, Saratov, RUS
m. circa 1867
at Josefstal, Saratov, RUS
+Barbara Haberkorn
b. unknown
at Unknown, RUS
d. circa 1923
at Josefstal, Stalingrad, USSR

Anna Margareta Rohwein (405)
b. 17 Aug 1868
at Josefstal, Saratov, RUS
m. 4 Nov 1886
at Josefstal, Saratov, RUS
+Johann Georg Gerk
b. 12 Jan 1869
at Josefstal, Saratov, RUS
d. 16 Sep 1957
at Krasnoturinsk, USSR

ЧАСТЬ ВТОРАЯ.—О ВѢНЧАЕМЫХЪ.

Преданіе вѣнчаніе	№	Числа вѣнчанія	Когда, гдѣ, кто и по коликократ-номъ оглашеніи вѣнчалъ бракъ?	Какихъ именно новобрачныхъ, какого состоянія, званія, воз-раста и прихода?	Кто по имени и прозванію ро-дители новобрачныхъ и кто поручители или свидѣтели?

Wedding Record of Joh. Georg Gerk, age 18, son of Georg Gerk and Ekaterina Buss, and A. Margareta Rohwein, age 19, daughter of Heinrich Rohwein and Barbara Haberkorn. Married on 4 Nov 1886 in Josefstal. In reality both Bride and Groom were a year younger than what is listed in their wedding record. Witnesses were Konrad Gette and Andreas Bauer.

РСФСР   КОПИЯ:
Область Немцев Поволжья
СКРИПАЛЕВСКИЙ СЕЛЬСКИЙ   УДОСТОВЕРЕНИЕ
        СОВЕТ   Иосефстальский с/совет Каменского к-на
КАМЕНСКОГО КАНТОНА   АССРНП удостоверяет, что смерть гр-на
II февраля 1925г.   Георг Гергова Герк I проживающ. в село
    № II   Иосефсталь происшедшая IО февраля 1925г.
село Скрипалево   зарегистрирован указан.с/советом II-го фев-
                             раля 1925г.
                                Удостоверение выдано на предмет предания те-
            по   земле
гербовая печать   Председатель :- подпись
                             секретарь:- подпись

Copy of the Soviet-era death record of Johann Georg Gerk who died 10 February 1925 in the village of Josefstal, Kamenka Kanton, Autonomous Republic of the Volga Germans, USSR. He was 56. Josefstal is also listed with its' Russian name, Skripalevo.

COLD CASE FILES:
The Mystery of
Michael Gerk

Dated 28 October 1893, the birth of Michael Gerk is a mystery. And not just because he was listed in his baptismal record as "illegitimate". His name is also different. Baptized on the 31 October 1893 with the name "Tsiriak" Gerk, listing his mother as A. Margareta Gerk, born Rohwein. His Godparents were Michael Rohwein and Kat. Barbara Haberkorn. No father's name is listed. *(GASO Fond 365 Opis1 Delo 797 List 413)*

But why the difference in names? Was Michael just a nickname? Both Elisabeth (Granny) Gerk and the youngest brother of Paul Gerk, Johannes, referred to him as Michael Gerk. Did they know?

Josefstal Military Draft records for 1914, show him still as "Tsiriak Gerk". *(GAVO Fond 270 Opis 1 del 212)* Interestingly, the 1914 record will also show him currently living in the Volga German village of Rosenberg. Why?

On 5 February 1912, "Tsiriak" will marry Margareta Stremel, the daughter of Johannes Stremel and Anna Maria Arnold.

"Tsiriak-Michael", his wife Margareta, and brother Paul, will all leave together in the fall of 1921 and try to escape Russia. Sadly, "Tsiriak-Michael" will die of typhoid, as did so many other Volga Germans, somewhere near Poland...while travelling in a railroad car. Widow Margareta will remarry after coming to Canada....to Anton Kloster. They will have one child, a son named John Kloster. John will ironically marry the daughter of Paul Gerk, Mary, on 20 November 1951.

"Tsiriak-Michael" Gerk was buried somewhere in an unmarked grave in Poland. This account remembers him.

Johann Georg
Gerk
Born:
12 Jan 1869
Died:
11 Feb 1925

Anna Margareta
Rohwein
Born:
17 Aug 1868
Died:
17 Sep 1957

Barbara Gerk
Born:
6 Jul 1887
Died:
23 Apr 1888

Tsiriak Gerk
Born:
28 Oct 1893
Died:
Dec 1921

Alois Gerk
Born:
6 Jun 1889
Died:
6 Mar 1895

Anna Gerk
Born:
29 Jan 1896
Died:
Feb 1983

Georg Gerk
Born:
21 Dec 1897
Died:
5 Mar 1943

Jakob Gerk
Born:
19 Feb 1900
Died:
3 Dec 1942

Paul Gerk
Born:
14 Jan 1902
Died:
3 Jun 1954

Katharina Gerk
Born:
18 May 1904
Died:
2 May 1985

Maria Gerk
Born:
27 Apr 1906
Died:
27 Apr 1999

Gottfried Gerk
Born:
3 May 1908
Died:
5 Nov 1980

Johannes
Gerk
Born:
22 Feb 1911
Died:
24 Apr 1996

**The children of Johann Georg Gerk
& Anna Margareta Rohwein**

DID YOU KNOW??

The "Return" of the Lost Photograph

This photograph of the Gerk family, taken in Josefstal in aprox 1917, was sent to Paul Gerk in the 1920's, by his sister Anna (Gerk) Kisser. Anna wrote on the back of the photo asking Paul to please make a copy and return it. Paul told his wife Elisabeth that he would do no such thing...Anna had all the family there while Paul had no one in Canada. After contact with the family was re-established in 1984, a copy of this photograph was sent to Johannes Gerk, Paul's youngest brother, in the USSR. Johannes wrote to us "...at last we have our photograph back which our brother Paul was to return so long ago..."

TOP PHOTO:
Standing left to right:
Kaspar Blattner, Gottfried Gerk, Johannes Gerk

Sitting left to right: Katharina (Gerk) Blattner, unknown child, Anna Margareta (Rohwein) Gerk, unknown child, Maria (Gerk) Leonardt, unknown child

BOTTOM PHOTO:
Standing left to right:
Unknown, Margareta (Stremel) Gerk

Sitting: left to right:
"Schwarz Liz", Piada Kisser, Kristina (Rausch) Gerk, Georg Gerk

TOP PHOTO: Standing far right:
Gottfried Gerk

Also in photograph: Andreas Holzman,
Konstantin Kisner, Peter Holmann

BOTTOM PHOTO: Standing left to right:
Gottfried Gerk, Barbara (Schmidt) Kisser,
Johannes Gerk

Sitting left to right: Elisabetha (Kisser) Gerk
Anna Margareta (Rohwein) Gerk

COLD CASE FILES:
How much land did
Johann Georg Gerk own?

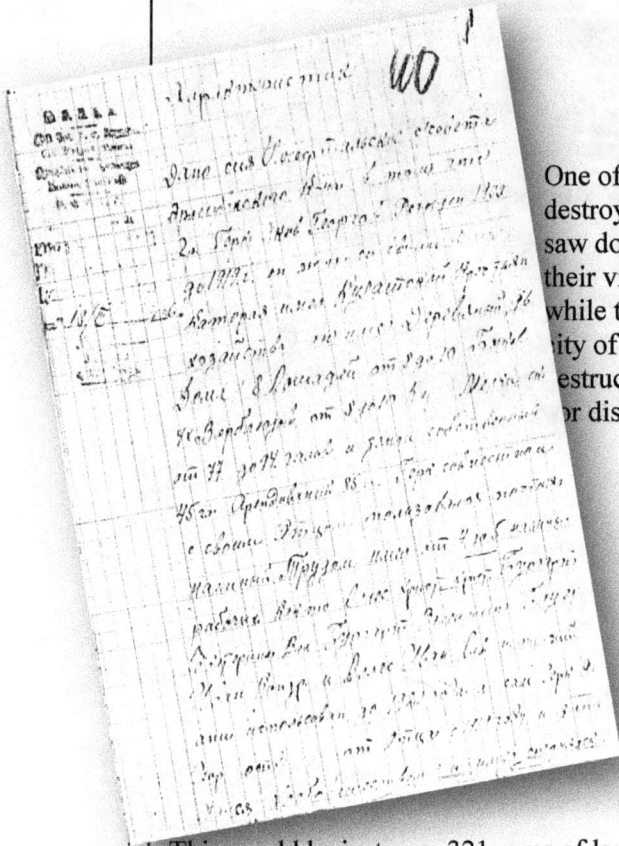

One of the first things the Bolsheviks did when they took power was destroy land records. Indeed, Paul Gerk told his wife Elisabeth that he saw documents with their family name on them being set on fire in their village of Josefstal, just after the Russian revolution. In 2009, while travelling in Russia, I was told by an archivist in the Russian city of Kamyshin that communists targeted land records for destruction, so there would be "no going back". No one could prove or disprove where their land was.

We have one clue to how much land the Johann Georg Gerk family had by this denunciation document, unearthed from secret Soviet archives. In it, it states the Gerk family owned:

...two wood houses, eight horses, from 8 to 10 bulls, 4 camels, 8 to 10 chickens, small livestock from 77 to 94, personal land of 45 hectares, rented land of 85 hectares.

This would be just over 321 acres of land. The family owned a house on the farm, and a house in the village.

So, is it true? We know from recollections of Elisabeth Gerk that the Gerk family indeed owned two homes, and had a large amount of livestock, including camels.

We can then assume that this document is a close reflection what the family actually owned and farmed in the Josefstal, Volgograd, Russia area.

(Source: GAVO Fond 2659 Op. 2 L.6) (Translation courtesy Rick Rye)

(This chapter was written mostly based on recollections of "Granny Gerk", also known as Elisabeth (Dieser) Gerk. Dates have been confirmed through the use of archival records. Paul is shown above at the age of 15.)

Paul Gerk was born in Josefstal, Province of Saratov, Russia, on January 14, 1902, to Johann Georg Gerk and his wife Anna Margareta Rohwein.

He was baptized in the village Church of Josefstal, parish of Marienfeld, on January 16, 1902. Godparents are listed as Paul Schaab and Elisabeth Domme.

Little is actually known about the life of Paul Gerk in Russia. We know he attended the village school in Josefstal, and later went to another village to further his education. His father, Johann Georg Gerk, believed in each son learning a craft or trade, so Paul was taught how to make shoes, a trade that would come in handy for survival while living in the Minsk, Russia area, waiting to escape to Germany through Poland.

We know that Paul could speak German and Russian fluently.

Paul spoke little about his experiences in Russia, which the reader is aware, were not pleasant. None of his children, Edward, Mary or John can ever remember him talking about life in Russia.

We know that on 15 September 1920, he will marry his child-hood sweetheart, Elisabeth Dieser. That wedding took place at a time of great turbulence in the lives of the Volga Germans. Both Paul and Elisabeth were just 18 years old at the time.

My father, John Gerk, once remarked to me: "Whenever friends of my parents who were from the old country, came by for a visit, we were shooed out the door. My Dad never said anything about Russia. It just was not talked about."

We do know that sometime after the Russian Revolution of 1917, the civil war brook out. Fighting was particularly heavy among the Volga German colonies, as was remembered by Paul's wife, Elisabeth Dieser. Paul was 15 years old during the Russian Revolution. We know that at least one brother, Jakob Gerk, made the decision to fight in the civil war that would occur just 2 years later in 1919.

Jacob's decision to battle the Soviets in that civil war would impact Paul directly.

The Soviets would come looking for Jacob. In hiding, Jacob was not immediately found. So the Soviet Commissars put in prison the next best thing they could find – Jacob's younger brother Paul.

So in June of 1921, Paul Gerk was arrested by the Bolsheviks for the simple reason that Paul's brother Jakob had fought with the White Cossacks against the Communists. Paul had indeed originally travelled with his brother to fight, but changed his mind and returned to Josefstal.

Paul was imprisoned in a jail in the nearby village of Erlenbach. His wife Elisabeth (Granny Gerk) visited him almost daily until July, when he was transferred along with other prisoners on foot north to the Volga German village of Balzer. The Balzer prison consisted of a root cellar and a barrel for a toilet. While incarcerated there, he discovered his brother Jacob had also been taken prisoner and was badly beaten and lay in the next room. There was no longer any reason

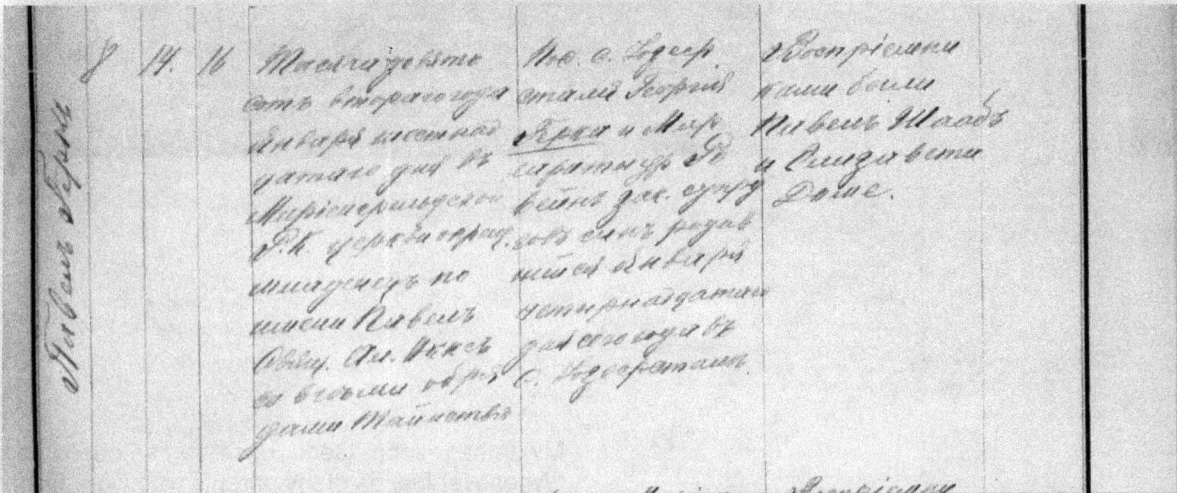

Baptismal record of "Pavel" Gerk, born 14 January 1902 and baptized on 16 January 1902 in the Catholic Church in Josefstal. Baptized by Father Alois Oks. Source: GASO Fond 365 Opis 1 Delo 1039 List 409

to actually hold Paul, but the local communist government was unrelentive.

As far as we know, fellow Josefstal villager and prisoner Josef Hoffman helped forge release papers, as some of the officials there could not properly read or write. Paul Gerk, Josef Hoffman, Alois Heinrich and Heinrich Dreckaser were released. Paul returned home to his wife Elisabeth, covered in lice and extremely ill.

All the men, upon their return, were treated to a large celebratory meal...the only exception being Alois Heinrich, as his wife was thinking clearly, and offered her husband a simple meal of eggs and milk. The rest of the men because seriously ill (probably because they had been close to starvation). Heinrich Dreckaser died. Josef Hoffman and Paul Gerk were both given the Last Rights as they were not expected to live.

Paul indeed did live.

After those incidents, Paul decided it was time to leave Russia

Russian 5 Rouble bank note Paul Gerk brought with him to Canada.

Readers will no doubt know about the Russian Revolution, and the imposition of Communism on Russia. Not well known is impact of communism on the Volga Germans, and the subsequent uprisings that occurred due to the intense Red Terror that accompanied communism where it went.

Remember these were peaceful farm people. But they had had enough. Members of the Gerk family took part in the uprisings, including the shooting of a Soviet Commissar in Josefstal. Although there is no written record of the uprising in Josefstal, the town was fired upon with cannon as punishment for their participation in the following events.

It was all these events that would convince Paul Gerk, his brother Michael and wife Margareta, and thousands of other Volga Germans to literally escape for their lives from Russia.

This account is taken from "*Verschollene Heimat an der Wolga*" *by* Edmund Imherr. (2000) Translation is courtesy of Joseph Gareis.

Dangerous it is the lion to wake
Ruinous are the tigers' teeth
But the most frightful fright of all
Is mankind in his delusion
Frederich Schiller - Songs of the Bell

The uprising in Köhler erupted on July 18, 1918. This was surely not a spontaneous event as has been suggested in several chronicles of the time, since uprisings began at exactly the same time in the colonies of Leichtling, Köhler, Hildman, and Semenowka.

Uprisings in the Volga region were not unheard of during the Russian civil war. For example, 13 people lost their lives across the Volga in Mariental in a revolt beginning March 13, 1921. However, none were comparable in scale or brutality to what happened in Köhler and Leichtling where on the first day alone 96 Bolsheviks and their sympathizers lost their lives. And that was only the beginning as many more deaths followed.

I hesitate to recall the uprising in my home village Köhler. Such a journey into the past is painful. On the other hand, it did happen and remains part of our History. These events can and must be viewed objectively.

I reviewed various accounts of the uprising over and over, and have done my best to reconcile reports from participants, eyewitnesses, culprits, and surviving victims. Unfortunately I have to conclude that the record is far from unanimous. According to one eye witness, Maria Klein, (nee Siebert) from Köhler, in a letter written the 13th of July, 1970 to Jacob Zorn:

(Heavy Volga dialect) on Monday night they started the killing, until Tuesday evening. I saw it with my own eyes. My father was hacked to death in the churchyard. When I got there, I saw Fr. H struck. With an iron bar, he was hit twice more. And many stood by his murder: Ulrich Peter and his sons, Hokor, Hanes, Plaze Krocher, Herich Jaschka. I took my father, held him, and the marrow and blood flowed onto my lap.

The name of victim referred to above is Martin Siebert, Köhler's mayor at the time of the uprising.

There exists a deeply moving account of the uprising that is both detailed and credible. It was written by Alexander Schmidtlein of Köhler, who at the time of the uprising was a teacher in nearby Hildmann. Schmidtlein wrote this account after leaving Russia, a step removed from the passions of the day. Although he lost an initial draft of it during the Second World War, he wrote it down again in 1964. To be sure, one may question some of his account. Witness that it repeatedly refers to the given name of the commissar of Köhler then as Andreas Berin while all other sources refer to him as Peter.

What caused the uprising? (By Alexander Schmidtlein):

With the fateful start of the First World War and the decisive defeat of the Russians in East Prussia (at Tannenberg), came scattered reports to households on the Volga that their sons had fallen. Complaints and mourning began. Village elders prophesized "The end of the world is at hand." Today in hindsight we know that they were right in a way. Although the world did not exactly come to an end, the world we knew was certainly torn apart.

For Russia, the war followed a disastrous course with Germany winning one battle after another. The search began for a scapegoat. Wherever one went, on trains or in crowded streets, the question could be heard: "Who is responsible for this disaster." The government circulated reports that it was the Germans living in Russia who were responsible. "We have too many Germans among us. They betray us! And the Tsarina is surely one of them." People told stories that the German-born Tsarina kept a radio under her bed so she could report everything to the Germans. "Rasputin must also be with the Germans."

Eventually the Tsar's uncle, Nikolai Nikolajewitsch, the governor of the Caucasus and commander of the army on the Turkish front ordered Germans away from the Western Front. They were instead formed into support units, assigned with keeping the supply lines in order or perhaps sent to build the small-gauge Turkish rail line between Saramysch and Erzerum (about 150 Kilometers) and Begburi.

With no weapons the Volga Germans colonists could do little to protect themselves. Many were killed in their tents at night at the hands of Kurds. How many Germans starved in Turkey when the supply lines failed? How many died of scurvy and typhus?

On top of the losses among our sons, husbands, and fathers in the War, more horrible news came as the year 1916 ended. The Russian regime announced plans to send all of the Volga Germans to Siberia, far from the arena of war. The malicious hatred of Germans was stirred-up from the top. One can imagine how this felt to us. I was a soldier myself and knew that our colonists remained fully loyal. The expulsion announcement caused massive unrest in the (Volga German) colonies.

On the second of March 1917 Tsar Nikolaus II abdicated as the February revolution was still in progress. The colonists breathed easier, although the reprieve would be short-lived.

At the end of October, the provisional government assembly was broken up by force as the Bolsheviks rose to power with Lenin in the lead. The Volga Germans had also drawn up voter lists and sent two delegates to the assembly. But the men turned around and were lucky to make it back alive. Workers and farmer soviets were instructed to bring about the "dictatorship of the proletariat."

Bolshevik agitators were sent from Petersburg to the war front where they urged soldiers: "Throw away your guns. Why shoot Germans? They are people just like use. Just make sure you make it home in time to share in the land being divided up among the people. There is no more military service. Those who believe in the cause will take up arms voluntarily to defend the Party. You will never again be forced to bear arms, nor forced to fight for something you do not believe in." During November and December of 1917, there were more deserters in the Russian army than soldiers left on the front. Lenin had after all vowed to sue for peace with Germany as soon as he returned to Russia.

Outside Petersburg and Moscow, soviets were established first in the big cities, next in the districts, then in the towns and villages. In the first two months of 1918 the soviet movement reached our villages. From Kamyshin came organizers, sent to form the so-called soviets. These men were mostly out-of-work Volga Germans. Most could spoke some Russian and maybe read and write a little, learned either in military service or during longer stays in the cities. They were often taken with socialist ideas and linked their fortunes to the Bolshevik standard. They though their time had come. At that time, no one would have believed that the Bolsheviks and Lenin were so dangerous, and would one day break every promise.

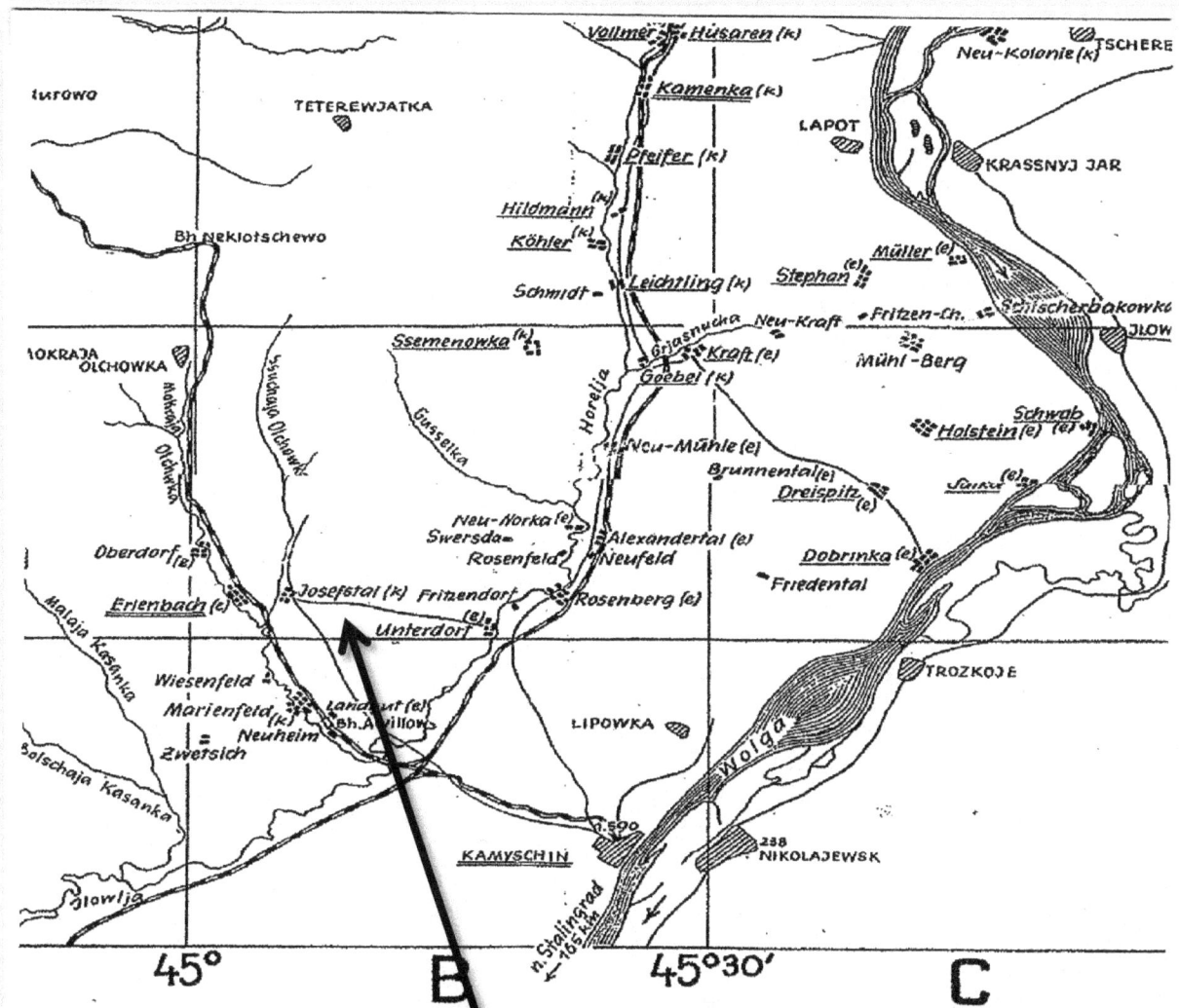

Area villages in which the 1918 uprising occurred, including Josefstal

We called these organizers idlers because they appear to have lost all appetite for honest work. Those with the gift of gab were best suited for this role.

Anarchy ruled in Russia at the time and the reins of power eluded Lenin's and Trotsky's grasp. They came up with the idea of freeing the prisoners and arming them, announcing this as part of a new order, "Wlastj na mestach" or martial law. Commissars were given absolute power over the life and death of the people in their district. If a military governor happened to have someone killed the affair would be forgotten.

During this period of anarchy, the economy broke down altogether. Transportation was no longer functioning. Sugar ran out and there was no more lamp oil to light homes. Prices spiraled upward with wheat prices increasing tenfold in only a few months.

The Bolsheviks took advantage of these circumstances, promising farmers sugar and oil if they would organize into soviets. But the soviets must represent the poor and this largely meant those who did not work. Respectable working farmers and craftsman were to be left out even though they were far from rich. Those who should get the power would of course be answerable to the Bolsheviks whether it was popular with the other villagers or not.

Anyone speaking out against the soviet agitators risked being branded to the district soviet as a counter-revolutionary and faced being hauled before the Revolutionary tribunal. We all knew very well what that meant. Village and city

75

leaders were pushed out of the way. Only when our farmers saw no way out did they form a soviet. But they left no role in this for the idlers. This quickly led to bad blood.

The poor wanted no part of the new inflated wheat prices. Instead they demanded the old rates. Bolshevik lectures concerning the duty of well-to-do farmers to subsidize the poor with lower wheat prices fell on deaf ears. The villagers stubbornly resisted! The community became divided between left and right. To the left, the revolutionaries and their ringleaders, to the right the wealthy "Burschujs." The gap between the classes widened daily.

Denied power in the village, the leftists met and decided to send a delegation under the leadership of Andreas Berin ("Ludwig") to the district soviet in Kamyshin to complain and demand that a "genuine" soviet be established in Köhler. Although this was done in secret it became common knowledge in the village.

Soon after that, around afternoon tea-time on a Sunday in May, when without warning came loud gunfire and two or three hand-grenade explosions. Red guards entered from two directions and occupied the village. It was a "Strafbataillons" (disciplinary force) under the command of war-commissar Orlow, or least that is what he called himself. The "Strafbataillons" units were formed to punish disobedient village soviets and bring them to their senses. If you were to take a closer look at these forces, however, you would see that it was made up of criminals released from prisons and stuck in the guard. The Russians said of them "Takaja schwalj!" (Such a rabble!)

As a result, the proletariat immediately took control of the soviet in Köhler. The 12 members of the dismissed soviet were all locked up. Villagers were called to an assembly at which the war-commissar read out the names of 33 men who must replace them in the new village soviet. These were of course drawn from the ranks of the "proletariat" who had demonstrated loyalty to the Bolshevik regime. Another seventeen of the most zealous troublemakers in the village were appointed red guards and given weapons. The red guards were responsible for keeping order, suppressing any resistance to the soviet, and, if necessary, shooting counter-revolutionaries. Wealthier villagers, as a group were, ordered to pay a penalty of 40,000 rubles and to come up with that amount within 2 hours.

The Bolsheviks from Kamyshin arrived with approximately 20 wagons. While commissar Orlow did his business at the schoolhouse, red guards drove to farms identified by the village proletariat and loaded up everything they could find: wheat, rye, flour, ham, bacon, fat, butter, eggs, and other stores. They barged into homes and granaries without leave, stealing peoples' supplies. In some homes they emptied out flour bins completely, leaving housewives with nothing to bake.

Their wagons filled to capacity with loot, the Bolsheviks gathered by the schoolhouse. Meanwhile, the 40,000 ruble fine was collected and delivered. The Bolsheviks pulled out in the evening, since it would be unsafe for them to remain overnight in the village.

In the 150 year history of our village, nothing like this had every happened before. The women, especially, were scared to death. All were embittered, particularly since it was some of their own neighbors who'd delivered their village to the robbers. The villagers vowed revenge, but for now their clenched fists were to remain hidden. The terror in the village had begun.

The new village administration consisted of 33-man soviet plus another 17 villages who had sold out. The new soviet mistreated the people, starting with the well-to-do farmers. Keep in mind that in our village there were no truly rich people, such as one might find in Saratov for example. One who worked could shape his situation but only to a degree.

The soviet issued slips of paper (ration coupons) telling us what and how much we could eat. If the soviet needed money, it would be collected by threat of force. Red guards patrolled the village with guns un-holstered by day, ready and aimed by night. They had to be very careful of the possibility of a revolt. They all knew very well that what they were doing ran contrary to the customs and norms of the colony, and that their cause was unjust. Among those with a conscience, pangs of guilt began to be felt.

Under the Bolshevik system, the church was to be separated from the state and from schools. Orders were issued forbidding religious instruction in the folk-schools and barring priests from the classroom. The teachers were divided on the issue of religious instruction. Some were opposed to having clergy in the classroom.

They argued that the Bolshevik order be carried out and had no difficulties with the official policy. Other teachers continued offering religious instruction while hiding any evidence of it from the official, public curriculum.

In the midst of the debate came a pastoral letter from the Bishop, Josef Aloisius Kessler of Saratov. This letter would become a decisive in explaining the events that followed. The Bishop wrote it after receiving alarming reports from the Catholic villages, pleading him for both advice and action. He warned in the letter that any people taking up the communist cause or even tolerating it risked excommunication. The letter was to be read from the pulpit by all the priests in the diocese.

Our pastor was the young Father Klemens Weissenburger from the village of Selz. At first he hesitated to read the bishop's letter, fearing that it would cause a riot. He did nevertheless read it at the Church on July 11, 1918. The result was as if a bomb were dropped in the village. It split even the Bolsheviks in the village. Leftists who were unwilling to deny their faith wanted nothing more to do with the communists. The more radical of the village soviet factions were unaffected by the announcement.

On the next Sunday, the 18th of July, at 8:30 AM, red guards occupied the entrance to the churchyard, denying people access to Mass that day. The pastor was to preach to an empty church. To be sure, a large crowd gathered at the doors of the church demanding entry. However, the red guards had strict instructions from their leader Andreas Berin to deny access to the church, even to shoot in the event it was necessary.

One of the red guards' own, "Springhannes" (likely John) Mildenberger refused to be denied access to the church. Mildenberger was a very poor man who had sided with the Bolsheviks for practical reasons, yet he remained true to his faith. With these courageous words: "You're not going to prevent me from going to Mass on account of the Bolshevik system," he approached the churchyard entry. Alerted to his approach, two red guards Peter Klein ("der Alte") and Peter Klug ("Balulja") barred him from passing with their rifles. Mildenberger grabbed Klein's gun, pushed it aside and moved to pass by. Klug quickly turned his gun around and shot Mildenberger, who within a few minutes lay dead. The people reacted with horror, and called "For God's sake, now they just shoot men dead!"

The men in the crowd took a threatening stance, as additional red guards hurried in and moved to disperse the crowd. "Go home or else you'll all be shot," yelled Berin. In the meantime Berin had sent a call for help to the war commissar at Leichtling, named Josef Schneider. Schneider was a native Leichtlinger and nephew of Father Johannes Schneider.

Reinforcements from Leichtling arrived to find a crowd of people, who had stayed on to see if anything more would happen. The "Almighty One in the Area," as Berin saw himself, yelled to any who came too close, "Just be glad that I wasn't there when it happened, or there'd be more than just one lying there now, instead there'd be a whole bunch! And you too!" As he circulated among the Köhler red guards, he asked them "why didn't you just go into the church and shoot the priest down from the alter. Then you'd have had quiet right away." "If (he continued to the crowd) you don't move out immediately and go home, I'll have you all shot." He himself was armed with two revolvers. Eventually the crowd gave way. People returned to their homes with bloodied hearts.

Peter Weissenburger and I left early that day for Hildmann. Weissenberger went to meet with Father Johannes Schonberger and to hold Sunday service and Vespers; I was to speak with the director concerning religious instruction in the schools. Father Schonberger had hidden himself, at the time, because the Bolshevik wanted to bring him in. They blamed him for hindering the formation of a soviet in the village. In addition to that, Schonberger read the pastoral letter as soon as he had received it.

As we were eating lunch at the Rectory, a messenger arrived with news of a call to military service from the district army command in Kamyshin, mobilizing those born between the years 1892 and 1896. Across the colonies, those affected by the mobilization assembled to protest to village soviets. "Why are we now being called into service" they asked? "Didn't Lenin himself say that from now on we would not be required to bear arms, against our wills? Only those who believed in the Bolshevik ideas would voluntarily pick up arms to defend that cause."

The order came from the top and they could do nothing, was the answer they got from the local soviets. That wasn't an acceptable answer to the protestors. "You guys are committed Bolsheviks, how come you don't go to the front (instead of us)? And further: "You just want to get rid of the best men so you can do what you please with our elders and women." In Leichtling, the response to the draft was equally defiant.

When war commissar Schneider returned to Leichtling from Köhler, the soviet reported to him on the threatening attitude of the reluctant draftees there. Schneider invited the assembled men to a discussion of the matter at the new schoolhouse. When they got there, though, he locked them up and declared them prisoners. His order was clear: "Anyone who tries to escape will be shot like a dog!" The schoolhouse was across from the district office and was closely watched by the Red Guards.

Not all of the soldiers accepted the district commissar's invitation. When they found out what had happened, they went from door to door informing villagers. Unrest grew. Throughout the streets and yards, people assembled and angrily discussed what was happening.

Schneider and his followers were at the district office, lying just beyond the edge of the village, right next to the river Lawl. They debated how many villagers they would have to shoot to restore order. Schneider wanted also to go after the draftees who had escaped. When he heard what had come to pass in the village, he immediately jumped up taking red guards with and raced through the village shouting: "Everyone from the streets! If you don't beat it right away, you'll all be shot into a heap." As usual, the commissar and his red guards offered nothing but threats for the villagers.

That night ended quietly in Köhler. The reds had the upper hand. The colonists had a dead man to bury.

Meanwhile in Hildmann, the mayor allowed the men in the village to assemble for meeting in the schoolhouse, where the young men affected by the mobilization order had already been gathering. The mayor was an honest, hard-working, and god-fearing man, although he was not at all rich. He was ordered by the war commissar to post three armed red guards at the schoolhouse. The draftees and the red guards began to quarrel and came to blows. The reds were beaten half to death and held under lock and key. When the war commissar heard of this, he fell on the village with a fury. Not knowing what to do, the people from Hildmann stood in front of the schoolhouse and waited not knowing what would happen next.

At that moment, a man from Köhler came into the picture and reported on what had just happened there. All were alarmed by the news. Had things gone so far that hard-working people could not even be sure of being able to practice their religion? Soldiers returning from the front often brought their guns home with them. Fearing that they would be used in an insurrection, the Bolsheviks confiscated weapons from various villages and took them to Kamenka. The Bolsheviks threatened to bring anyone owning guns or munitions to the Kriegsgericht (war court) where they would meet a pre-determined end. One of the boys in Hildmann who had been called to military service, suggested that they all ride to Pfeifer, and then men from both villages would proceed to Kamenka and take the arms and munitions that had recently been collected there.

This plan was accepted. Several wagons were prepared and the soldiers drove off. The older men accepted the task of surrounding the village and guarding it to ensure that no one escaped. The plans were withheld from Köhler or Leichtling, to reduce the chances that the plan would be betrayed to the enemy.

As we arrived in Pfeifer, we came across another gathering that had taken place over the question of the mobilization. The priest in Pfeifer then was Nikolaus Meier, who had been pastor in Köhler until 1913. The young soldiers in Pfeifer embraced the Hildmann plan enthusiastically. The gathering from both villages then proceeded to Kamenka. On the way, we cut the telegraph lines linking Kamenka and Saratov. Upon arriving in Kamenka, we occupied the post office, which included the telegraph station. A single clerk manned the soviet office there. He played dumb, claiming no knowledge of munitions stores. Some men from Kamenka came and they made some progress with the clerk, until he eventually pulled out the key to the basement. There we found only a part of the confiscated weapons. Where the others were hidden, we would never find out.

All the munitions that could be found were loaded onto wagons and driven back to Hildmann. Couriers were sent to Vollmer and Husaren inviting those villagers to join the uprising and proceed to Köhler and Leichtling. Word was to pass from village to village as far out as Balzer.

The size of the rebellion grew considerably as it proceeded, even though its leaders tried to move quietly. In Kamenka, we heard some more grim news: Two days earlier in Jakerinenburg, the Bolsheviks murdered Tsar Nikolaus II and his family. The war commissar there, named Jakubowski, ordered the shootings. It was done, he claimed, as the whites under Admiral Koltschak and the Czech legion under the command of Colonel Syrovy approached. Jakubowski feared the whites would free the Tsar and his family. This also meant that white armies had moved close to us, right up to the banks of the Volga. That explained the sudden need to mobilize. The Bolsheviks wanted to pit us against the whites! Southwest of us, General Deniken's troops crossed the Medwediza, a tributary of the Don and neared the rail line connecting Balaschow - Netkatschowo - Kamyshin. On top of that, the lines with the Cossacks remained only about 60 kilometers away. We decided that, early the next day, we should send a request for help to the Cossacks.

In Hildmann we were told that everything was still quiet. Two non-commissioned officers took command. Since we had too few guns for all the rebels, those equipped to shoot would be positioned in front. Approximately 30 to 35 men were armed with infantry rifles, the rest with pitchforks, axes, and clubs. In the dark, it was hard to estimate, but it appeared that there were about 200 of us, perhaps more.

On the way, as an advance guard approached Köhler, those armed with guns moved ahead as the others stayed in reserve, until the fight moved to close quarters. So as not to alert the Bolsheviks in Köhler, only whispers were allowed in the march and smoking was strictly forbidden. These precautions were important since the highway along which the column moved was not far from Köhler.

About two kilometers before Leichtling, the advance guard found 3 men outside the village. More men affected by the mobilization. They reported that everyone was still awake as war commissar Schneider continued to search throughout the village for draftees.

We planned to strike first at Schneider's district soviet in Leichtling and then march on Köhler. At 1:00 AM outside the village of Leichtling, all was quiet. A password -- "Key" -- was used to prevent us from shooting ourselves in the crowd. At a sign from the non-commissioned officers, we advanced along 3 streets running through the village towards the district office (Kreishaus). As the first of us arrived there, or so it was later told, the door soon opened and there was Schneider. He ran out down the steps, armed with a revolver in each hand, shouting in Russian, "Who's here? I'm the war commissar!"

Soon many shots rang out. The commissar slumped and fell sideways off the steps. A bullet had gone through his throat. He groaned loudly, bled awfully, and lay there in his last throws. He took one of our younger men with him in death, one armed with only pitchfork. The poor boy had failed to obey the order to stay back until later and paid for the mistake with his life.

A clerk in the district office, who had again locked the door, eventually opened it after we promised him that no hair on his head would be wrinkled. He informed us that other soviet members escaped out the back door, as they left denouncing as counter-revolutionaries all those in the district including the villages of Köhler, Leichtling, Hildmann, Gobel, and Semenowka who had participated, and vowing that they would be shot.

Schneider himself had been waiting for the Bolsheviks from Kamyshin. They were supposed to enforce the military call up and put down the rebellious solders with force. When he stepped out of the district office, and shouted in Russian "Who's' here? I'm the commissar!" he must have mistaken the rebels for the reinforcements from Kamyshin.

Soon we freed those who had been locked up in the Leichtling schoolhouse. The reds that were supposed to guard them had fled. Shortly after releasing the draftees, we heard voices from the other side of the river, from the direction of the brook at "Steintumpel." Our scouts reported immediately that it was men from Semenowka. They too wanted to see Commissar Schneider, with whom they had a score to settle and regretted very much that they had come too late.

There was hardly time for that alarm to be over when from the South, renewed shots and even hand grenade explosions were heard. This time we were all but certain that the Bolsheviks from Kamyshin had come and moved into position.

But again an all clear would be sounded. It was the men from Gobel, who also wanted to get to the district war commissar. So, except for those in Köhler, who were still imprisoned by the soviet and locked in the schoolhouse, all of the rebellious forces in the district had gathered in Leichtling.

To this day, there is one issue that remains unresolved: Although no conspiratorial discussions had taken place, all the soldiers in the named colonies appeared in Leichtling at almost the exactly same time, on the night of the 18th of July, to square accounts with the tyrant Schneider. It appears to have been a coincidence.

On the 19th of July, the battle escalated. The mobilized soldiers searched for all of the Bolsheviks in Leichtling and there were more than 50 of them and beat them dead. In one house 2 heavily armed red guards offered stubborn resistance. The second-in-command to the now-dead war commissar, Kaspar Mehler, along with one of his men, took up a position on a rooftop and shot at anyone who approached the house. These Bolsheviks wounded two of our men. When they ignored our threats that we would burn them out unless they surrendered, our soldiers stepped to the task. Later we found the blackened bodies of the two reds. Only their heads escaped burning as they had buried them in a mound of bran as protection against the flames.

The men on the river, who were to against an attack from the Bolsheviks in Köhler, were ordered to hold fire. We wanted the Bolsheviks to come to us so we could capture them. But when they did approach, one of our men fired anyway, evidently without authorization, and other shots followed. The plan was bungled. The reds drove their horses around and fled.

As we took up the pursuit with the horse-drawn wagons, we met a man from Köhler who told us the inhabitants had fled and now stayed in open fields behind the "Gumnes" and in the cemetery. What happened? The Bolsheviks in the village had spread word that "Our people from Kamyshin will be coming and they will shoot the whole village." Panic resulted. The red guards that we were pursuing had in the meantime returned to plunder the village's wealth. They then fled toward the forest. That the stolen goods of the town later would become fateful is another story.

As we approached Köhler, we saw a swarming mass of humanity overflowing the area from the cemetery up to the windmills. The villagers had their prized possessions with, stuffed in wagons and wheelbarrows. Women and children cried in despair, some older women kneeled as if in church and prayed fervently.

Our arrival calmed things down considerably. There was great joy. We were everywhere greeted enthusiastically and treated as rescuers. Several of us carried white flags and escorted some people back to their homes.

During the course of the day, outside the gardens, before the forest, one part of the "pitchfork-war" was staged in our own home. All of the Bolsheviks in Köhler were herded together, "judged," and beaten to death. Some truly terrible scenes were played out. As a slain Bolshevik lay in the middle of the street, a woman came from her house carrying a brick, shouting (Heavy dialect) "What . . . you have no butter? Wanted to steal the butter did you?" She then threw the brick into the dead man's head, shouting: "There, you've got your butter." This came from a woman who until then was known as an upright housewife. And that was certainly not the only such scene one would see that day.

Without making excuses, after dealing with the Bolsheviks, in just a short time the pious and orderly inhabitants of the village were turned into a mob. The soul of the people had been seized and wounded. Simple people had been stopped from going to church, even shot. Force breeds counter-force.

As of the 19th of July 1918, a total of 32 colonies had sent forces to Köhler to help its inhabitants in the battle with the Bolsheviks. Alas, for reasons unknown to this day the Cossacks never came. Perhaps an armored train moving along the Balaschow - Kamyshin line, cut the supply lines and prevented them from coming. The armored train bombarded two towns near Kamyshin -- "Spatzekutter" (Marienfeld) and "Schwobekutter" (Josefstal). The Kamyshin soviet pulled back on a Volga steamboat, and was covered by red guards.

The armored train bombarded two towns near Kamyshin -- "Spatzekutter" (Marienfeld) and "Schwobekutter" (Josefstal).

In total, there were then around 5,000 colonists in Köhler, surely more than there ever had been in the village's history. And these knew no mercy. In Kohler more than 50 red guards and sympathizers were killed, and in Leichtling no fewer were lost. Without judging and to repeat the fact once more: the force applied by the Bolsheviks produced a reaction in a village, which in its prior 150 years, had always been peaceful.

On the 20th of July greater uncertainty ruled. The members of the Bolshevik soviet were dead; a new soviet had not yet formed. No one knew for sure where to go from there, the less so since the villagers were divided among each other. It is very difficult for us now to understand, that at this critical moment most of the farmers returned to the fields to harvest their over-ripe crops.

The decisive turn came with the news that red guards were approaching from the forest. They rushed into the homes and took all the men with. As they poured into the village, the reds went directly after the men who had hurried from Leichtling in wagons to help the Köhlerites. They were immediately taken into custody, disarmed, and placed before the community assembly. This all took place

Russian Civil War poster 1919

before the new schoolhouse. The commissar -- it was again Orlow, the same one who had just plundered the village in May -- was beside himself and shouted at the crowd of people: "Which of you counter-revolutionaries killed our comrades? We'll find out soon enough." He had all the men of the village gathered together and divided into two groups. In one group, the wealthier farmers were placed. From the group of poorer farmers, Orlow picked out 11 men and had them surround the same number of prisoners. He gave each of the farmers a bayoneted rifle and ordered them: "When I call out 'attack,' each of you is to run through one of them (the prisoners)."

Among the captured soldiers (prisoners) was a childhood friend of mine, Michael Messler, who stood opposite one of his good friends Jakob Tomann. Michael called in despair, "cousin Jaschka, is there no deliverance? In God's name, help us!" As the commander gave the order, Jaschka stumbled and fell to the ground. Confusion followed. Michael tried to run away but was caught by one of the red guards and stabbed to death.

Another prisoner had more luck. Using the general commotion as cover, he ran in the opposite direction into the village. The red guards fired after him, but missed. He reached the back yard of the village then ran through the front yard to the streets, where he spotted a horse-drawn wagon. He jumped into the wagon, ripped the whip and reins from the hands of a boy who sat in the carriage and drove past the red guards.

None of the 11 obeyed the command to execute their neighbors. All were killed by the red guards.

Before moving on, Orlow had the village looted a second time. This time, however, not only did they take more provisions, but also dresses, valuables, pillows, bed clothing and anything else.

A family of teachers, named Schönfeld, happened to live in the village at the time. They had been evacuated to the village during the war. The wife had a golden, diamond ring on her finger that the Bolsheviks wanted. But when it did not come off smoothly, it was brutally ripped off, taking the skin from her finger.

After some time, another group of Bolsheviks rushed into Köhler. They told the people that they should now quietly return to their business. The war is now over and what was done is done. It has to stop sometime. So things stayed for about 10 days. But then the reds returned late in the evening looking for a targeted list of village inhabitants. With village soviet members acting as guides, they hauled people out of their beds and took them away. None of them were ever seen again. The terror grew: An eye for an eye.

The Bolsheviks investigated the uprising until they discovered that it all began in Hildmann. More suspected leaders (or instigators) were found, primarily, among draftees there. They searched for a certain Alexander Gallinger but couldn't find him. Also the priest from Pfeiffer, Father Nikolaus Meier, was under suspicion but they didn't risk taking him into custody, at least not yet.

However, in the fall of 1918, the Bolshevik move against the priests began in earnest, the immediate excuse being the pastoral letter from Bishop Dr. Aloisius Kessler. Fathers Meier and Schönberger were forced to flee. Luckily they made it to Germany. As for Father Klemens Weissenburger, he was forced to give up. After having read the pastoral letter from the pulpit on the 11th of July, Weissenburger gave up his position as Vicar in Köhler and returned south to his home village Selz.

The red guards also searched for me that night, though I'd already left. A red guard warned my Father, that I should not try to flee to Germany: "he won't make it, the borders are much too closely watched."

DID YOU KNOW??

*Декретъ о введенiи въ Россiй-
ской республикѣ западно-евро-
пейскаго календаря.*

Wrong Birth Dates?

The pre-Russian Revolution birth-dates of everyone in this history, including Paul and Elisabeth Gerk, are based on the Julian calendar.

Which mean they are wrong as we know them!

The explanation?

"Although there had been discussion and petitions in Russia to switch to the new calendar, the tsar never approved its adoption. After the Soviets successfully took over Russia in 1917, V.I. Lenin agreed that the Soviet Union should join the rest of the world in using the Gregorian calendar. In addition, to fix the date, the Soviets ordered that February 1, 1918 would actually become February 14, 1918. (This change of date still causes some confusion; for example, the Soviet takeover of Russia, known as the "October Revolution," took place in November in the new calendar.) So the Gregorian calendar was implemented in Russia on 14 February 1918 by dropping the Julian dates of 1–13 February 1918 pursuant to a Sovnarkom decree signed 24 January 1918 (Julian) by Lenin. The decree required that the Julian date was to be written in parentheses after the Gregorian date until 1 July 1918."
(Source: "Soviets Change the Calendar" @ about.com)

Given the horrible experiences of war and revolution, and the difficult task of changing dates on documents, Paul and Elisabeth Gerk kept the Julian calendar dates for their birthdates. In actuality, based on the Western Gregorian calendar, Paul's birthdate should now be January 27, 1902 and Elisabeth's birthdate should be September 1, 1902.

News clipping: *Partial Russian text of the decree adopting the Gregorian calendar in Russia as published in Pravda 25 January 1918 (Julian) or 7 February 1918 (Gregorian).*

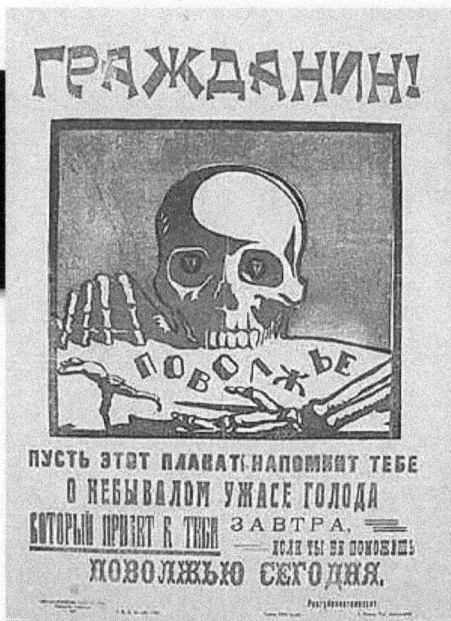

ГРАЖДАНИН!

ПОВОЛЖЬЕ

ПУСТЬ ЭТОТ ПЛАКАТ НАПОМНИТ ТЕБЕ
О НЕБЫВАЛОМ УЖАСЕ ГОЛОДА
КОТОРЫЙ ПРИЙДЕТ К ТЕБЕ ЗАВТРА,
ЕСЛИ ТЫ НЕ ПОМОЖЕШЬ
ПОВОЛЖЬЮ СЕГОДНЯ.

In March of 1918, a war-weary Russia signed a separate peace treaty with Germany. Thousands upon thousands of men returned to their homes only to find a different atmosphere - an atmosphere of fear and hate. Communism had secured itself as the system of government now ruling Russia. Many people, including the Volga Germans, did not lay themselves down to this new breach of their freedom without a fight.

And so Russia, fresh from its' own revolution, now experienced its own civil war.

"White Cossacks" fought for a restoration of the monarchy and the destruction of the new Soviet government headed by Lenin. Western allied nations, including the US and Britain, joined forces with the Cossacks, mounting "expeditionary" forces that basically invaded Russia. The reason for this "invasion" was the outrage over the fact that Lenin had pulled Russia out of the first World War.

White Cossacks made their way up the Volga, pushing the Red Army up as they went. May 1919 was a time of victory for the Cossacks, due in part to the assistance received by the allies. The Cossacks were surprised to learn how well the communist government had taken care of its opponents....buildings lay in ruins, churches had been burned to the ground or turned into barns...clergy had been shot.

June 1919 saw a major battle take place for the Volga city of Tsaritsyn (later to be called Stalingrad). White Cossacks managed to push

even further up the Volga, but were driven back to the city of Kamyshin. July 1919 saw major battles occur in the areas surrounding Josefstal and other Volga German villages.

Emma Schwabenland Haynes in her landmark book "History of the Volga Relief Society" (Portland, Oregon 1941) wrote about the fighting:

"...a great deal of fighting also took place between the Reds and so-called Whites. This latter army included many Cossack soldiers, who proceeded to steal everything that the Bolsheviks had failed to carry away. The Bergseite (hilly-side) towns especially lay in this zone of battle, and some of the German villages (ed. Note: including Josefstal) passed back and forth as many as seven different times until the communist won their final victories in the summer of 1919."

Elisabeth (Dieser) Gerk, aka Granny Gerk, recalled in her broken English, in a 1978 interview, what the fighting was like during this time:

"....I can still remember...like the devil coming. They came in the yard with their horses and threw hay and everything around...oh I hate to remember...."

She described what it was like to have the Cossacks in the village:

"When the Cossacks came around you didn't know the difference. Same clothes....same language. But the Cossacks came to the door, and knocked....saying...'Don't be afraid, we are the Cossacks, we are here and we want to help you fight the communists'. And when the communists came around, they always had a revolver in their hands, they didn't say 'don't be afraid'...they want something and if they wanted to eat and you haven't got anything, they sweared (sic). They make themselves at home." She added: "You can't believe even, what means the communist. I don't think the devil is worse than they are...God forgive me."

"Once a communist got shot. There was the front between our town and Marienfeld. They brought him in the house. The next day, they brought machine guns in and fired a salute. Our house was just shaking. They put him in a coffin and sent him home."

"There were lots of times we had to go and get bricks and pile them all the windows up. If you went to the window you were killed. The Cossacks fight - the communists lost, they had to go back, and then in a couple of days the Cossacks lost and the communists come back. They were always fighting."

Interestingly, while researching July 1919 and what it meant to the German villages along the Volga, I found confirmation from a variety of sources to what Granny Gerk was saying.

> "....I can still remember...like the devil coming.
>
> ...oh I hate to remember...."
>
> –Elisabeth (Dieser) Gerk on the events of 1918 and 1919

Indeed, one of the war "fronts' was right between Josefstal and Marienfeld. And I discovered that one of the simple statements she made to me, that she saw her first airplane during this time of fighting and turbulence, was fighting that was occurring between the Red Army and the 47th British Air Squadron.

July 1919 was a pivotal time for Wrangel's Cossacks, with the aid of the British, in trying to overthrow the Bolsheviks and reach their target of Moscow. Both the official air diary of the 47th Squadron and Soviet Red Army records state that late July 1919 is when much of the fighting occurred...and Red Army battle maps confirm the many battles taking place around the Volga German villages of Josefstal and Marienfeld....all near the Russian city of Kamyshin. Kamyshin itself was bombed on numerous occasions by the British D.H. 9 planes.

The Red Army victories of July 1919 would soon meld into the next terror to hit the Volga Germans - Famine!

Stated Elisabeth (Dieser) Gerk: "They were always fighting. That's what hit Russia so badly, because it was just in harvest time. You went out and started to harvest but the fight started so you had to go home. The grain that was cut went rotten because it rained and the grain that were not cut and still standing - the grain fell out and there was just the straw left. Then the next year - no rain - nothing to eat...there were no apples left, there were no potatoes left, no onions left, everything was black. That's when people starved in Russia."

Word of the drought did eventually leak out to the Western world. Soviet authorities would finally announce to the world, on July 23, 1921, that there was a major problem - and they needed help.

It should be noted that during the years 1914 to 1920, the population of the Volga German colonies went from 600,000 to 431, 000, with another 72,000 decrease in 1920-21. This decrease included those killed during the various battles in the colonies, executed, and those evacuated. (See Emma D. Schwabenland, History of the Volga Relief Society, 1941)

Groups in Germany, Argentina and the USA banded together to help stop the famine along the Volga. The American Relief Administration began distribution to various areas hard hit throughout Russia, gradually handing control of Volga area relied to the Volga Relief Society.

A circular distributed by the Volga Relief Society documented the amount of children being fed....which included 350 for our village of Josefstal alone!

Elisabeth (Dieser) Gerk recalled her younger sister Ludvina, curled up in a corner, chewing on her fingers, due to lack of food.

These events, and the ones documented earlier, would seal the decision of Paul Gerk to leave Russia, and ultimately, for the escape from Russia of Elisabeth Gerk as well.

JOHN W. MILLER, PRESIDENT   DAVID HILDERMAN, VICE-PRESIDENT   MRS. GEO. REPP, SECRETARY   GOTTFRIED GEIST, TREASURER

VOLGA RELIEF SOCIETY

PURPOSE: CONDUCT RELIEF WORK IN STRICKEN GERMAN COLONIES
LOCATED IN VOLGA RIVER DISTRICT, RUSSIA

623 LUMBERMENS BUILDING
PORTLAND, OREGON.

den 9. Februar 1922.

Neu Norka	. . . .	800
Rosenberg	. . . .	400
Unterdorf	. . . .	250
Josephthal	. . . .	350
Marienfeld	. . . .	500

Letter documenting that from 25 December 1921, there were 350 children in Josefstal being fed through special kitchens set up by the US-based Volga Relief Society. 500 children were being fed in nearby Marienfeld, both villages with Gerk's living in them.

Excerpt from War Diary of British 47th Air Squadron, documents bombing of Kamyshin and aerial reconnaissance of Volga German area surrounding Josefstal. Elisabeth (Dieser) Gerk recalled seeing her first airplanes in July 1919, during the allied intervention of Russia. The Airco DH.9 (from de Havilland 9) were used by the British during the intervention and was probably what she saw. Source: Air1/2375/226/11/2

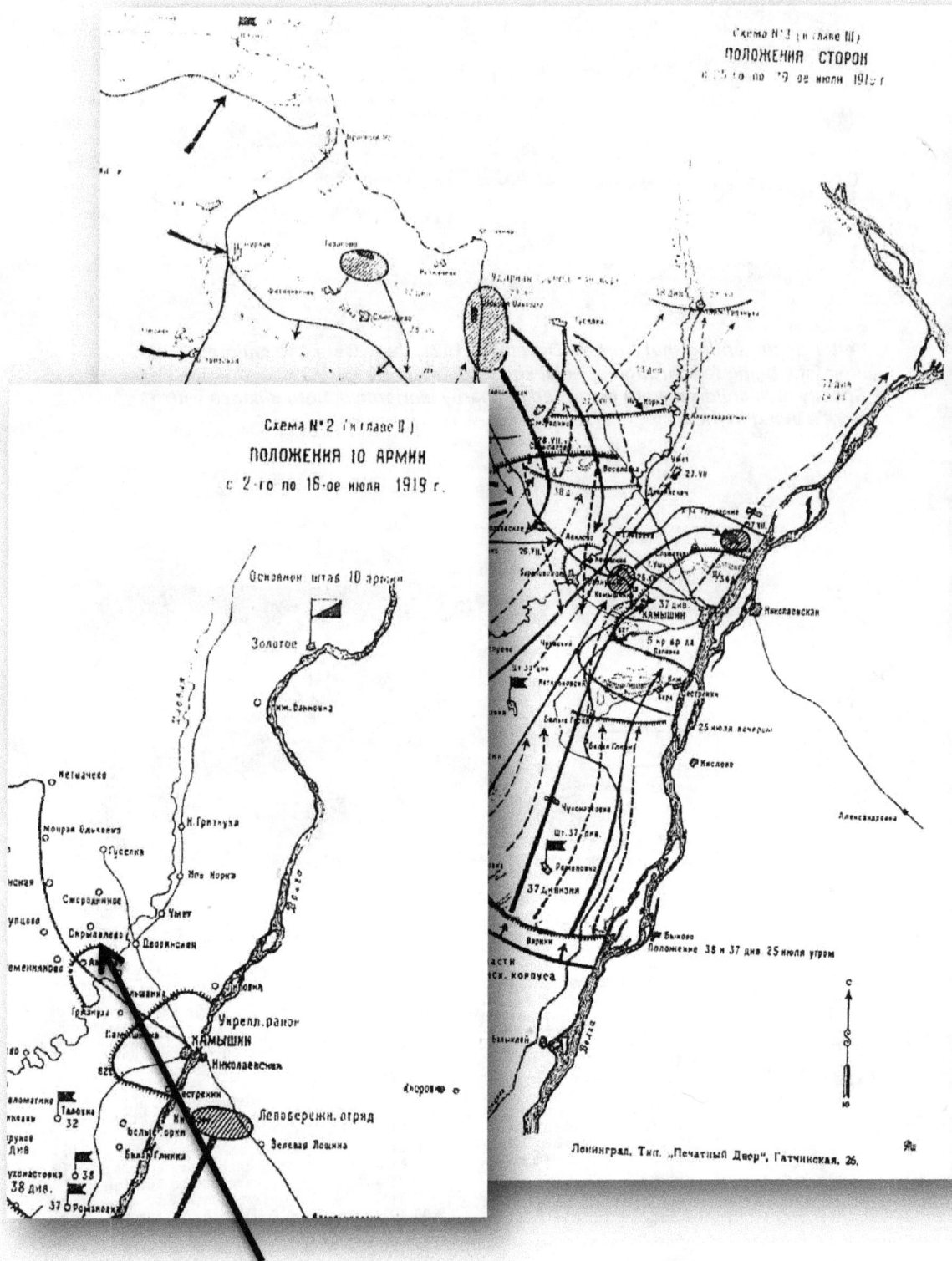

Soviet Red Army Battle maps of Volga German villages and the Russian city of Kamyshin, all during July 1919. Elisabeth (Dieser) Gerk described the events of July 1919 accurately, including insisting that a "front" was between her village of Josefstal and Marienfeld. Josefstal listed on the map by its Russian name of Skripalovo, or Скрипалево, Source: Kamyshinskaia operatsiia desiatoi Krasnoi Armii. liul' 1919 goda. S 3 skhemami na otdel'nykh listakh. Kliuev, L: 1928

After achieving his escape from Josefstal in 1921, Paul Gerk made his way to the Minsk area, joining with thousands of other Volga German refugees seeking to escape Russia. Travelling with others from Josefstal, including his brother Michael and wife Margareta Stremel Gerk, Paul Gerk did odd jobs including shoe repair while he waited for an opportunity to leave Russia. He managed to make his way to a refugee camp for Volga Germans located in Frankfurt on the Oder River in Germany. This article, translated from the original, was published in the German-language publication "Heimkehr", No. 2, 1923. (*The Volga Refugees from Minsk: A Visit in the Refugee camp Frankfurt/Oder*) It describes the exact conditions that Paul Gerk found himself at the time as he continued his flight to freedom, and includes information about the transport from Minsk that Paul was part of.

It is well known that a year ago, when the unmercifulness of hunger was felt more every day by the Volga settlers, a mad despair came over the unfortunate inhabitants of the German colonies, more and more Volga settlers left their homes and fled in every direction, trying to escape their ill fate. Some went westwards since they were hoping that their journey to reach Germany would not take them too long. It is still imprinted in everybody's memory the cruel expectations of most refugees were crushed: they were held back in the forests of Minsk for over half a year. The first refugees to arrive in Germany via White-Russia got here in 1922. So far, the largest transport of about 1000 people (222 men, 295 women and 436 children under the age of 16) reached the homecoming camp Frankfurt on the Oder on December 9, 1922, to

find a temporary residence in the barracks which used to house prisoners of war.

The impression the refugees give the visitor is at first unexpectedly good. The children are merrily playing ball on the grounds between the barracks, and the elders are not at all displaying a depressed state of mind, but are readily willing to answer any questions. When one considers the terrible conditions the refugees escaped, then it really doesn't come as a surprise that they are feeling pretty good in this desolate town of barracks. As our pictures are showing, there is a big diversity in their clothing. Besides the men's long sheep coats and the women's kerchiefs, you see very fashionably dressed folks. When we visited, we were greeted by Dr. Rothermel from the Society of the Volga Germans, a young, Volga-German doctor who devoted his energy to his unfortunate fellow countrymen. Then, Mr. Alexander Bier from Warenburg showed us around the barracks and related, from his own experiences and the lists he compiled what the refugees had gone through.

Beginning of last year, about 7000 Volga-Germans started out to Minsk, some with horse and wagon, some on foot or by train. In Saratov most of them had to go by train since the horses couldn't go on anymore. The way to White-Russia took several months, therefore it was March/April until the refugees arrived there. A lot of people were dying on the train already, and it got worse when everybody had to leave the train in Minsk. Women, men, children, the healthy and the sick were cramped in lonely houses and sheds without windows, tables, chairs and beds, and it wasn't long until the sick outnumbered the healthy. The typhoid fever was especially bad. One has to assume that more than half of the refugees died in Minsk.

We will only relate a few shocking individual stories. A man starts out with his wife and three children. On the way, first the wife dies, then two children, and shortly before the train leaves the third child dies too. From a family of twelve only one child could be saved. 56 people left a village, but only 11 arrived in Frankfurt. Other refugees were luckier. An ex prisoner of war by the name of Stressler from Warenburg, who for 3 ½ years worked on a farm in Münsterlande as a prisoner of war, managed, together with his wife and 2 children, to reach Frankfurt, where he now

looked after by the Caritas. All the refugees are still shaking, remembering what all they went through in the last years. Everything we were told here in Germany, from individual letters, news items, like the rampage of the Reds, the systematic robbery of the fruit, the horrible rebellions, the continuous dying in the Volga area, all this is the terrible truth, as we are now told by eyewitnesses. "It is difficult to be a

Aus Josestal Kath.

235. Gerk,	Paul		Georg	14. 1.02	Gottfr. Winter, Ft. Dalge Jowa.
236. "	Emilia, geb. Richter aus Schulz	Karl	2. 2.04	
237. Dieser,	Katharina		Heinrich	24. 10. 06	Jof. Mildenberger, Stiff, Colo., Box 304.
238. "	Heinrich		"	15. 3.09	
239. Berat,	Elif., geb. Lattner aus Göbel	Stephan	4. 12.90	Clemens Blattner, 1111 So. 4 St. Ford Dodge, Jowa.

The December 9, 1922 Minsk List was printed in the publication "Wolgadeutschen", January 1923. Paul Gerk is Number 235 on the list, hoping to travel to Gottfried Winter of Fort Dodge, Iowa. On this transport he was joined by over 900 other Volga Germans, including 4 others from Josefstal.

lives in the same barrack he was in as a prisoner in 1916. Another prisoner of war, Conrad Schauermann from Brunnental got back to Germany again as well.

The refugees' actual destination is America, where most of them have relatives who are longing to welcome their kin. Only the American money made it possible to feed the refugees in Poland and get them across the border into Germany. Already in Russia they had to sacrifice the money they had with them, just to get the exit permit, and they were robbed in other ways as well. They made a bare livelihood doing hardest work for small White-Russian farmers. Some were also working for the ARA (American Relief Administration), either in the kitchen or the transport system. It is estimated that altogether around 1700 – 1800 Volga-Germans came to Germany from Minsk, and that nearly as many stayed there. Besides ARA, the German Red Cross earned the love and thanks from the refugees, especially Dr. Carstens from the Red Cross, who brought the transport to Frankfurt, is looked upon and honored like a father to everybody.

Since there will be no entry permits for America issued before July 1st, the Volga-German refugees will stay in Frankfurt until further notice. Their living expenses here are paid for by their American friends. The future of the children, especially the numerous orphans, is mostly taken care of, some will go to Bethel by Bielefeld, some will go to Angerburg. The Catholic orphans are

Christian in such times" an earnest young man said apologetically, when he told us about the well-known Warenburger rebellion and about the atrocities, which were a revenge for even worse horror-deeds committed by the angered Volga farmers. Commissioners were clubbed to death, thrown into the icy water of the Volga or into a dung-hill. The number of people killed in the desperate rebellion in the Volga area, the center being the colony of Mariental, in the spring of 1921, is estimated to be 35,000. A single number illustrates the decrease of work animals: It is estimated that before the war there were 12,000 oxen, horses and camels in Warenburg; beginning 1922 all that could be found were 60 horses. The refugees don't know how many of them are left now.

It is more than understandable that the refugees yearn for a place where they can stay forever, that their biggest desire is peace and quiet and that they want to free themselves from the shadows of the past. They don't believe in the reconstruction of the colonies, because they suffered through such bad times, although they do concede that in general, at least since their escape, it is not gotten worse in Russia. What they are wishing for, old and young alike is to go to the United States of America and meet their friends and relatives. Several of the refugees have been there before. A family by the name of Kaiser from Hoffental left America 10 years ago and they are now going back as beggars. A few might possibly stay in Germany, like those ex-prisoners of war. Everybody, though, shows a

Wolgadeutsche Monatshefte

Monatsschrift für Kultur und Wirtschaft der Wolgadeutschen

Herausgegeben vom Verein der Wolgadeutschen E. V., Berlin NW. 52, Schloß Bellevue.
——— Erscheint am 1. jeden Monats. ———

Bezugspreis für das Vierteljahr:
Deutschland . . . . 550 Mark;
Vereinigte Staaten 50 Cents;
Kanada . . . . . . 50 Cents;
Argentinien . . . . 1½ Pesos

Einzelheft 200 Mark

Anzeigen: Die 4gespalt. Nonp.-Zeile 50 Mk.; Stellenangebote und -nachweise 50 Mk. Zahlungen sind zu richten: für Deutschland Postscheckkonto Berlin NW 7, Nr. 118997 und an die Kolonisenbank Berlin, Dorotheenstr. 24. Aus dem Ausland an den Verein der Wolgadeutschen E. V. NW 52, Schloß Bellevue.

| Nummer 5/6 | Berlin, März 1923 | II. Jahrgang |

31. Krämer, Friedrich,   von Weinberger, Friedrich.
32. Schönberger, Josef,   von Grünwald, Pankratius.
33. Eberle, Mathias in Argentinien.   von Gaßmann, Georg.
34. Gert, Georg,   von Gert, Paul.
35. Mitzig, Konrad,   von Mitzig, Peter.
36. Ehrlich, Jakob,   von Ehrlich, Lydia.
37. Werner, Josef   von Weht, Peter.
38. Stamm, Johannes,   von Hecht, Elisabeth geb. Stamm.
39. Hecht, Andreas angebl. Kopela Kant,   von Hecht, Elisabeth geb. Stamm.

Paul Gerk's uncle, Georg Gerk, is listed as being sought by Paul in the March 1923 edition of the Wolgadeutsche Monatshefte, published in Berlin. He is Number 34 on the list, which featured hundreds of such requests. It is not known if Georg Gerk, then living in Argentina, ever responded.

natural and sincere concern for Germany, its difficult situation is surprisingly readily understood, surprisingly especially when one considers the horrible loneliness and distance from all culture that the refugees had to endure the last few years. From own experiences and from the bottom of their hearts they perceive their fate to be one and the same with what happened to Germany. Their loyalty and understanding towards their mother country shall never be forgotten, and we hope for the day, when Germany can repay their loyalty through deeds.

Leaving Russia with no personal identity, Paul Gerk had to slowly try to re-construct his identity. Such a reconstruction was not impossible....authorities recognized the turbulence that refugees had gone through and made special provisions for identity papers and other documentation to be issued to the refugees. During this time, the Catholic Bishop of Tiraspol, covering Russia, was also in exile. He arranged for official baptismal documents to be made in Berlin for the future emigrants.

Initially, while on the 9 December 1922 Minsk transport to Germany, Paul would list Gottfried Winter of Fort Dodge Iowa as a contact in America whom he was trying to travel to.

Gottfried Winter was married to Elisabetha Gerk, the daughter of Johann Georg and Margareta (Bauer) Gerk, all from Josefstal. This Johann Georg Gerk and wife were the Godparents of Paul's youngest brother Johannes Gerk, born in 1911.

Paul probably did not realize it, but visa quotas for the United States meant his chances of getting a visa for the USA was small.

While housed in the refugee camp in Frankfurt/Oder, Paul also made an appeal in March of 1923, to the Volga German newspaper published in Berlin, the *"Wolgadeutsche Monatshefte"*. Looking for his uncle, the older brother of his father, Johann Georg Gerk who had settled in Argentina. Sadly, we do not know if the family in Argentina ever responded, or even if they saw Paul's appeal.

The next chapter in Paul Gerk's trek can be found in the following article - describing the next step of Paul's journey, selection as an immigrant farm worker to Canada and subsequent departure from Europe. This article, translated from the original, was published in the German-language periodical "*Clemens Blatt*", May 1924. It details the group that Paul Gerk was in and their departure in March of 1924. It was written by S. Feist of the "Kath. Fürsorge" (Catholic Social Welfare). He writes:

After the Canadian Catholic Church Members Society (Volksverein) had successfully arranged for the German refugees' emigration from the Volga and Black Sea Provinces to Canada and their settlement possibilities amongst the Canadian farmers, it was then their most important duty to assemble and conduct their transport, departure, and the travel route. Among the first duties of the authoritative St. Raphael Society in Hamburg regarding the assembling of the first refugee transport was to place it under our care, namely the Catholic Social Welfare. It accordingly then became our duty to prepare the emigrants for emigration. On March 19th I went to the refugee camp located in Frankfurt on the Oder to get and prepare a full and complete list of the emigrants. Immediately upon getting acquainted, those representing the Catholic Church Members Society in Canada, which had the prepared emigration requirements, declared that 76 persons were already listed for emigration; however, with the explicit wish that all concerned organizations might do their utmost to have the families of the emigrants soon follow them to Canada.

The transport's departure was firmly set for March 23rd. To lighten the parting of these emigrant heads of families, a wish was generally expressed that our Diocese Bishop, Cardinal Kessler, might conduct a solemn farewell Mass in the Frankfurt camp. Early in the morning of March 22nd Bishop Kessler and I traveled together to the camp, where we were cheerfully welcomed by the refugees.

In the considerably bleak and cold camp-church Bishop Kessler conducted high mass and at its end he gave a short speech. He stated that this approaching parting is a parting from wife and children, even though on unfamiliar soil. He further stated that he wanted the emigrants to always keep their holy faith and always keep in mind to be good Catholics in Canada just as they

had been in their homeland diocese. In all necessities he urged them to take refuge in prayer and never give up hope, and that after the bitter hour of parting there will be a happy reunion. He also stated that the St. Raphael Society and the Catholic Social Welfare in cooperation with the Canadian Catholic Church Members Society will exert every means possible to succeed in the shortest period of time to have their families soon rejoin them in Canada.

In the evening of March 23rd the emigrants, after a tearful and difficult departure, began their travel from the "Grube Fatherland" station, a branch depot of the Frankfurt-Cottbus line, in three already provided railway cars. Here, too, various speeches of comfort were spoken to the left-behind wives and children and the departing men.

At the railway station in Berlin via a telegraph notification the entire Board of Directors of our Catholic Social Welfare for Russia appeared. Here again the emigrating refugees received wishes for their infinite good, and were promised that everything will be set in motion so that their left-behind families can most quickly follow them.

On Sunday, March 23rd, we arrived in Hamburg and were welcomed by a representative of the St. Raphael's Society and an agent of the Emigration Office. Under the navigation agent's escort we came to the emigration hall. After the completion of the usual formalities, a breakfast was served for the refugees. Then after a medical examination they were brought into two pavilions. At the suggestion of the emigrants a vesper and rosary service was conducted. On Monday morning the Rev. Dr. Kralewsky of the St. Raphael Society conducted a high mass.

Then the emigrants stepped into the usual completion formalities for emigration. It must be emphasized that the medical examination is strictly undertaken. Up to the examination time the emigrants had been cheerful and their humour also had not failed them. After the last medical exam, then the medical examination results were announced resulting in a sad picture.

Of the 76 persons examined, 27 were denied emigration due to illness. It must also be mentioned that our (Catholic Social Welfare) emigration transport was praised by the Board of Directors and the Navigation Association as having made a good impression. It can therefore be determined that our emigrants also will make a good impression upon the American farmers.

On March 25th, the Annunciation Day, the General secretary of the St. Raphaelsvereins (St. Raphael Society), namely Rev. P. Timpe came and conducted a high mass in the chapel on the (emigration hall) site. P. Timpe at the end of the mass, which he kindly had set up for the refugees, gave a short speech to give courage to the departing emigrant group. He spoke of his hope that by their good and willing work in Canada the farmers there will be ready and willing to also help bring their families to them. On March 26th we escorted the 49 emigrants to the train station, from which they were to go Rotterdam. Rev. P. Timpe likewise was at the train station and once again delivered his promise and pledge before their eyes. Then the train started on its way and everyone shouted, "Auf Wiedersehen". (Till we meet again.)That same evening we traveled back with the emigrant-denied people going through Berlin to the Frankfurt camp. To give the American friends an opportunity to help them get to know the emigrants individually, we gave them photographs, which eventually could help establish acquaintanceships or kinships. In closing, I point out with firm satisfaction that the people we selected for the first transport have in all concerns made a very good impression. I also hope that the American farmers will also be satisfied with them. In conclusion, the following request is also made to the Canadischen Katholichen Volksverein (Canadian Catholic Church Members Society): that in due course they will want to do everything possible so that the left-behind family members can soon follow to join their loved ones.

† Joseph Aloysius Kessler,
Titular-Erzbischof v. Bosporus

Joseph Aloysius Kessler was the Bishop of the Russian Diocese of Tiraspol, in Saratov. He escaped from Russia and ministered among the Volga German refugees in Germany. He provided Paul Gerk with a signed baptism certificate.

From this point on, Paul Gerk traveled to Canada, accepting farm employment from the John Ehman family of Holdfast, Saskatchewan.

Paul will work one year, and during that time, they will offer him an arrangement to bring his wife, Elisabeth (Dieser) Gerk, to Canada, in exchange for an additional year of farm work.

Paul Gerk arrived in Saint John, New Brunswick on April 5, 1924.

He would have been met at the Port by Father Kierdorf, the Volksverein representative in Canada, and then travelled by train to Regina.

And so the Canadian chapter of the Gerk family began.

1924 signature of Paul Gerk on passenger list.

Name List of Refugees Travelling to Canada April 1924

Richelhof, Friedrich	Abt, Kilian	Weisbeck, Johannes	Mildenberger, Jakob	Stankowitz, Johannes
Diel, Adam	Burgardt, Peter	Gerk, Paul	Blattner, Jakob	Rau, Heinrich
Rutzman, Josef	Stalldecker, Albinius	Frank, Adolf	Weichel, Georg	Schermer, Adam
Storm, Alexander	Zelbel, Reinhold	Okulewitsch. Leo	Eckermann, Johannes	Dandörfer, Jakob
Abt, Florian	Neitzich, Peter	Gottseltig, Johannes	Weichel, Peter	Markel, Georg
Martel, Sebastian	Wagner, Clemens	Weingardt, Johannes	Weichel, Peter	Wucheuauer, Georg
Meringer, Michael	Herlein, Anton	Stremel, Georg	Seelmann, Heinrich	Werner, Georg
Eberhardt, Johannes	Terre, Johannes	Schönberger, Josef	Rolsing, Andreas	Specht, Georg
Schowalie, Johannes	Wander, Johann	Schönberger, Dionysius	Specht, Josef	Rohleder, Johann
Schowalie, Adolf	Weisbeck, Johannes	Schamber, Raymund	Dandörfer, Peter	Rieth, Georg

Personal Identity Papers used as a passport for Paul Gerk, born 14 Jan 1902, in "Josepfstal, Volga German Republic, Russia". It also states that "Gerk was in the refugee camp since 10 December 1922, and his behavior was excellent, and recommended him for travel to America.

TAUFZEUGNIS

Vor und Zuname : Name der Eltern : des Getauften :	Tag, Jahr und Ort : der Geburt :	Name des Taufspenders, Pfarrkirche, Diözese

Paul GERK   Sohn des *Georg* und dessen legitimen Ehefrau *Anna-Margarethe Rohwein*   Geboren am 14. Januar 1902 zu Josefsthal, Gebiet der Wolgadeutschen, Russland.   Die Taufe spendete der Pfarrer *Aloisius Ochs* in der röm.-katholischen Pfarrkirche zu Josefsthal, Diözese Tiraspol, Russland.

№ 575.

+ Joseph Kessler
Bischof von Tiraspol

Berlin, den 21. März 1924.
Michaelkirchstrasse 12

Nr.

Paul Gerk Baptism certificate issued by the then in-exile Bishop of the Diocese of Tiraspol, Joseph Kessler. It is dated 24 March 1924, in Berlin. It states that Paul was baptized in Josefstal by Father Aloisis Ochs, and that he was born January 14, 1902 to, Georg Gerk and legitimate wife Anna Margareta Rohwein.

Passenger List of Paul Gerk, March 28, 1924. S.S. Montrose Source: Library and Archives Canada. Form 30A, 1919-1924 (Ocean Arrivals). Ottawa, Ontario, Canada: Library and Archives Canada, n.d. RG 76. Department of Employment and Immigration Fonts. Microfilm Reels: T-14939 to T-15248. Photo: Public Archives Canada

CONTRACT.

THIS AGREEMENT made the   day of   A.D. 1924.

BETWEEN:-

Hereinafter called "the Immigrant,"
OF THE FIRST PART.

- and -

Hereinafter called "the Employer,"
OF THE SECOND PART,

- and -

Hereinafter called "the Local Committee,"
OF THE THIRD PART.

WITNESSETH: THAT in consideration of the covenants, agreements and undertakings on the part of the other or others of them hereinafter contained, the parties hereto covenant and agree each with the other or others of them, as follows:-

1. The Immigrant hereby agrees to enter into the service of the Employer and serve him faithfully and diligently as a farm laborer for the period commencing the   day of   192   and ending the   day of   192 .

2. The Employer hereby agrees to take the said Immigrant into his service as farm laborer for the said period at the yearly wages of $, payable monthly to the Local Committee as hereinafter provided, and further agrees to furnish the said Immigrant and his family with suitable living quarters and board on his farm during the said period.

3. The Immigrant hereby assigns, transfers and sets over to the Local Committee all wages due or to become due to him by the Employer, or any other Employer to whom the said Immigrant may be assigned to by the Local Committee as hereinafter provided. The receipt of the Local Committee to the said Employer for such wages shall be sufficient discharge to the Employer therefor.

4. The Local Committee shall allow the Immigrant a reasonable amount from time to time out of said wages for clothing and other necessaries for himself and family and shall apply the balance of such wages in payment of any costs or expenses incurred or guaranteed by the Employer or Local Committee for the transportation of the Immigrant and his family from   to   and any other amounts which may be due by the said Immigrant to the Employer or the Local Committee. What is a reasonable amount for clothing and other necessaries for the Immigrant and his family and the manner in which said wages shall be applied as aforesaid, shall be in the sole discretion of the Local Committee.

5. In order to prevent disputes or misunderstandings between the Immigrant and the Employer all matters of dissatisfaction on the part of the Immigrant caused by lack of sympathy of the Employer, maltreatment, abuse, unsuitable living quarters, or board, or unreasonable labor demands, and generally all matters of dissatisfaction on the part of the Immigrant or on the part of the Employer shall be adjusted between the Immigrant and the Employer by the Local Committee and the said Local Committee shall be and is hereby made, constituted and appointed sole umpire to decide such questions and matters. The decisions of the Local Committee which may be given from time to time as questions come up shall be binding and conclusive upon the Immigrant and the Employer.

6. In the event of any disagreement between the Immigrant and the Employer, or if for any other reasonable cause the Local Committee deem it advisable that the Immigrant shall be removed from the service of the Employer, it shall notify the Employer accordingly and thereupon the contract of service hereby entered into between the Employer and the Immigrant shall cease, but the Employer shall continue to be liable for all obligations incurred by him prior to such termination. In such an event the Local Committee shall have the right to allot the Immigrant to another Employer, and the Immigrant hereby agrees to enter the service of such other employer for the then remaining portion of the period referred to in paragraph 1 hereof, or such other period as may be agreed upon, upon the same terms and conditions as are herein contained.

IN WITNESS WHEREOF the said Parties have hereunto set their hands and affixed their seals on the day and year first above written.

SIGNED, SEALED AND DELIVERED)
in the presence of: }

Contract of the Canadischen Katholichen Volksverein (Canadian Catholic Church Members Society) or Volksverein as it was widely known. Paul Gerk signed one of these, in both English and German, promising to work as farm help for one year. In exchange for work and passage to Canada, the farmer also pledged to bring over any close relatives, such as a wife. Paul worked at least an additional year in order to cover the costs of travel for his wife, Elisabeth (Dieser) Gerk, from Russia. Source: Public Archives Canada

Paul Gerk – 1924 after arrival in Holdfast, Saskatchewan, Canada. He was sponsored by the Ehman family.

The Volksverein assisted Paul Gerk in immigrating to Canada in 1924. They assisted scores of families in their quest to come to Canada from Russia.

Statuten

— des —

Volksvereins

Deutsch-Canadischer Katholiken.

VD
CK

CONSTITUTIONS

— of the —

ASSOCIATION OF THE GERMAN-CANADIAN CATHOLICS.

Paul Gerk a Millionaire? Hardly! While in Germany, Paul Gerk collected the above bank notes, German Marks. Given the high inflation of the day, 20 Million Marks did not go very far….and it is worthless today. It remains part of the fascinating history of the time.

DID YOU KNOW??

Der Wolgadeutsche

Bezugspreis für das Vierteljahr: Deutschland 24 M. bei der Post (vom 1. Juli), direkt unter Kreuzband 30 M., Holland 1 Guld., Argentinien 2½ Pesos, Ver. Staaten von Nord-Amerika 1 Dollar, Kanada 3 Schilling (Ausland nur unt. Kreuzband)

Unabhängige Wochenschrift für die kulturelle und wirtschaftliche Förderung des Wolgadeutschtums

Erscheint jeden Sonnabend

Fernsprecher: Norden 11832 Schriftleitung: Berlin NW 6, Luisenstr. 31a Drahtanschr.: Wolgahilfswerk Berlin

Inserate: Die fünfgespaltene Zeile oder deren Raum 6.— M., Stellen-Angebote und -Gesuche 3.—M. Rabatt nach Tarif. Geldüberweisung: Postscheck-Konto Berlin NW 7, Nummer 36 661 und Bankkonto Raiffeisen-Bank, Berlin W 9

Nummer 4 | Berlin, 24. Juni 1922 | 1. Jahrgang

The Sad Case of the Gustav Gerk Family

The Gustav Gerk Family, of Koehler, according to Passenger lists, immigrated to the USA around 1905. Gustav, born 7 December 1871, arrived in New York on 27 April 1905 on the SS Patricia. His wife, Julianna (Feit) Gerk and children, Josef (born 3 Sep 1897), Klara (born 5 Apr 1899) and Elisabetha (born 10 May 1901) would arrive in 1906. The family settled in Denver Colorado, and are mentioned in the 1910 US Census.

At some point they must have returned to Russia. We lose track of the family until a mention of them is made in the June 24, 1922 German publication "*Der Wolgadeutche*", published in Berlin. It states that the family tried to escape Russia again, due to the famine...but tragedy struck. Documented in a letter written by Koehler school-teacher Peter Weinzettel, he states:

"Much worse, however, were those who in the autumn (of 1921) parted with all their property along with livestock and food for half its value to go to America by their friends and relatives...the Gustav Gerk family (7 persons) died, except one 8-year-old daughter and a daughter-in-law. This was the second time that this family attempted to seek a better life in America near friends and relatives. (Source: "Letter from the Volga: Koehler Balzer District Mid-May 1922)

Gustav was the son of Johann Adam Gerk and Magdalena Macht.

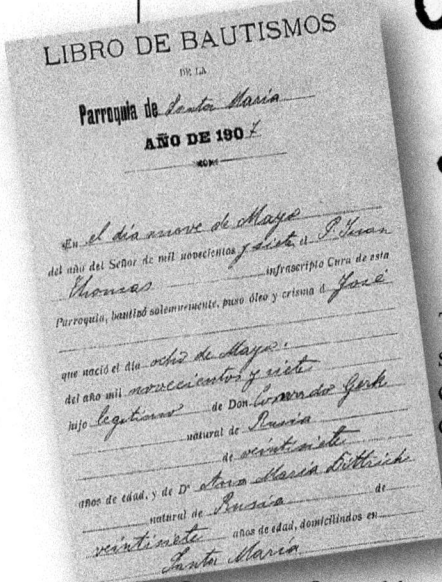

COLD CASE FILES:
The Mystery of Johann Georg Gerk

The uncle of Paul Gerk, Johan Georg Gerk, travelled to Argentina sometime in the early 1900's. As we have shown, Paul Gerk tried to contact this uncle, the older brother to his father. There is no documentation if the two families ever reconnected.

So what happened to Johann Georg Gerk, his wife Margareta Magdalena (Haberkorn) Gerk and their children?

After years of searching we know a few things about their trail:

The oldest daughter, Anna Maria Gerk (born 1874) married Adam Schaeffer in 1892. Then the family seems to have disappeared? South America perhaps?

One of Johan Georg's other children, Konrad Gerk, (born 1880) was married to Anna Maria Dietrich. A child of theirs, José (Josef) shows up in a Baptism record from Santa Maria, Buenos Aires, Argentina, dated 9 May 1907. The data trail continues and on 13 July 1954, José will marry Catalina Kippes in Santa Anita, Entre Ríos, Argentina. José died 17 December 1974 and is buried in Santa Anita.

Another of the children was Elisabetha Helena (Isabel) Gerk (b. 24 Aug 1885). She also travelled to Argentina, probably with her husband Johannes Kloster. He died in 10 March 1918 in Crespo, Entre Ríos, Argentina. She will remarry to Peter Alois Gerk, her second cousin, the son of Johannes Gerk and Margareta Pitz from Josefstal, on 12 August 1919. Members of this family will eventually move to the Province of Santa Fe in Argentina.

Daughter Franzsica stayed in Josefstal, Russia. As of 1925 she was still living in the village. Another daughter Barbara, born 1883, will marry Gottfried Stremel and have 7 children, before Gottfried dies in 1920. She will then marry Nikolaus Breit and die in 1967 in the USSR. The family now lives in Germany.

So what happened to Johann Georg and his wife? As of March 2018, we have tracked down living members of the family in Santa Anita, and in the Province of Santa Fe. The problem is that those family members have no information on what happned to the rest of the family. The old timers are gone, and with them, it would appear, is information that would help us solve this ongoing mystery!

TOP: Marriage record of Johan Georg Gerk & Ekaterina Buss (Grandparents of Paul Gerk),
dated 3 Nov 1852 in the parish church in Semenovka.
MIDDLE: Birth record of Ivan (Johann) Georg Gerk, uncle to Paul Gerk and oldest brother of Johann
Georg Gerk. Dated 8 Oct. 1853, born in Josefstal and baptized the same day.
It is a mystery to what happened to him and his family.
BOTTOM: Birth record of Konrad Gerk, born 8 Jul 1880 in Josefstal,
son of Johan Georg Gerk & Margareta Haberkorn (Paul's uncle and aunt)
Of the 10 children born to Johann Georg Gerk & Margareta Haberkorn, only 4 will survive to
adulthood.

Johann Kaspar Gerk (498)
b. 1753
at Fulda, Hesse, Germany
m. circa 1776
m. circa 1790
+unknown
+Anna Marie Mützig
d. 14 Jan 1830
at Koehler, Saratov, RUS

Zacharius Gerk (512)
b. 1787
at Koehler, Saratov, RUS
m. circa 1809
at Koehler, Saratov, RUS
+Eva Elisabeta Schillig
at Saratov, RUS
d. 2 Feb 1843
at Koehler, Saratov, RUS

Johann Kaspar Gerk was the 1st child of Sebastian & Magdalena Gerk

Johann Georg Gerk (401)
b. 1826
at Koehler, Saratov, RUS
m. 3 Nov 1852
at Koehler, Saratov, RUS
+Katarina Buss
d. 27 Jul 1886
at Josefstal, Saratov, RUS

Family moved to Josefstal in 1852

Johann Georg Gerk (847)
b. 8 Oct 1853
at Josefstal, Saratov, RUS
m. 14 Nov 1871
at Josefstal, Saratov, RUS
+Margareta Magdalena Haberkorn
d. Unknown
at ARGENTINA

Johann Georg Gerk is the uncle of Paul Gerk, brother to the "other" Johann Georg Gerk, the father of Paul Gerk.

Family moved to Argentina in 1904?

Anna Maria Gerk
b.1874

Franzisca Gerk
b.1876

Johan Peter Gerk
b.1878

Konrad Gerk
b.1880

Barbara Gerk
b.1883

Isabel Gerk
b.1885

Georg Gerk
b.1887

Elenora Gerk
b.1890

Georg Gerk
b.1892

Elisabeth Gerk
b.1895

The family of Elisabeth (Dieser) Gerk, "Granny Gerk", originally settled in Josefstal around 1868. Valentin Dieser, born 1828 just north of Josefstal, in the village of Semenoka, was married to Anna Margareta Bellendir.

The Dieser Family of Josefstal, like the Gerk family, was made up of various lines of Dieser's who first came to Russia in 1767.

The first Dieser to Russia was Johann Peter Dieser, born on 13 June 1744 in the German city of Seligenstadt, Hesse, Germany. He was married to Anna Marie Reis in Büdingen, Hesse, Germany, just shortly before leaving for Russia.

Due to the confusion of the recording of names, Johann Peter Dieser's name was recorded as Dreser, when in fact the correct German spelling would have been Disser.

Early settler lists show that Johann Peter and his wife settled in the Volga German village of Leichtling in 1767. After that, we can assume that his first wife, Anna Marie Reis will die. When exactly is not known. Records seem to show that he will remarry to Marie Reigert. Altogether, Johann Peter Dieser will have 11 known children.

Around 1793, it appears that some of the children will move to the neighboring Volga German village of Semenovka. Michael Dieser and family will settle there in 1793, with Samuel Dieser moving to Semenovka a few years later in 1817.

From son Michael, we have the family line leading to Valentin Dieser, and his granddaughter, Elisabeth Dieser.

For Elisabeth (Gerk) Dieser, her grandfather Valentin Dieser was not a first settler of Josefstal, Indeed, his line of Dieser's came to Josefstal in 1868. In fact, it would appear that a number of Dieser families would settle in Josefstal between the years of 1868 to 1872

Valentin Dieser was born in the Volga German village of Semenovka on January 2, 1828. He was married to Anna Maria Bellendir on January 22, 1852 in Semenovka. Elisabeth (Granny Gerk) was told that Valentin Dieser, when he moved to Josefstal, bought 4 plots of land across from the Church. These were intended for his family. However, the Dieser families remained close, and kept in regular contact with their relatives in Semenovka, even though some of the families had moved to Josefstal.

Not much is known after that. We know of 5 or 6 children born to the Valentin Dieser family. Research is still taking place to fill in missing pieces of the Dieser puzzle. But that's the subject of another book!

With the data we have from Russian archives, we can look at the family of Johannes Dieser and wife Marie Eva Heit, and examine the siblings of Elisabeth.

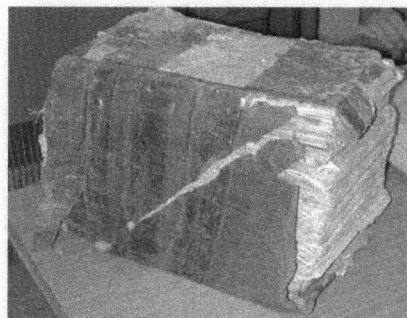

A census book from the Saratov Archives in Russia

*Baptism record for Valentin Dieser, born January 2, 1828, in Semenovka,
to parents Johannes Dieser and Theresia Getting (Gette). Valentin Dieser is the grandfather
of Elisabeth Dieser Gerk.*

*Marriage record for Valentin Dieser & Anna Maria Bellendir, dated January 22, 1852.
They are the grandparents of Elisabeth Dieser Gerk.*

Johannes Dieser (13)
b. 1794
at Semenovka, Saratov, RUS
m. circa 1817
at Semenovka, Saratov, RUS
+Teresia Gettlin (Gette)
d. unknown
at Semenovka, Saratov, RUS

Valentin Dieser (28)
b. 2 Jan 1828
at Semenovka, Saratov, RUS
m. 22 Jan 1852
at Semenovka, Saratov, RUS
+Anna Maria Bellendir
d. 12 Oct 1885
at Josefstal, Saratov, RUS

Family moved to Josefstal in 1868

Michael Dieser (7)
b. 1772
at Leichtling, Saratov, RUS
m. circa 1792
at Leichtling, Saratov, RUS
+Anna Maria Redling
d. unknown
at Semenovka, Saratov, RUS

Johannes Dieser (67)
b. 29 Jan 1874
at Josefstal, Saratov, RUS
m. circa 1893
at Semenovka, Saratov, RUS
+Marie Eva Heit
d. 13 Mar 1933
at Baku, USSR

Johan Peter Dieser (1)
b. 13 June 1744
at Seligenstadt, GER
m. unknown
m. unknown
at Büdingen, Hesse, GER
at Leichtling, Saratov, RUS
+Anna Maria Reis
+Maria Reigert
d. 1816
at Leichtling, Saratov, RUS

Elisabeth Dieser (74)
b. 19 Aug 1902
at Josefstal, Saratov, RUS
m. 15 Sept 1920
at Josefstal, Saratov, USSR
+Paul Gerk
d. 14 Aug 1991
at Kelowna, BC, CAN

Elisabeth Dieser Gerk and her connection to the
first Dieser settlers of Russia.

ЧАСТЬ ПЕРВАЯ О КРЕЩЕНЫХЪ.

Baptism record for Johannes Dieser (Elisabeth Dieser Gerk's father), born January 29, 1874, and baptized the next day.

Marriage record for Johannes Dieser & Marie Eva Heit, dated November 8, 1894
These are the parents of Elisabeth Dieser Gerk (Granny Gerk)

Johannes
Dieser
Born:
29 Jan 1874
Died:
13 Mar 1933

Marie Eva Heit
Born:
26 Oct 1873
Died:
2 Aug 1933

Georg
Dieser
Born:
1894
Died:
1900

Ekaterina
Dieser
Born:
3 Jul 1896
Died:
4 Aug 1988

Anna
Dieser
Born:
10 Jul 1900
Died:
Aug 1938

Elisabeth
Dieser
Born:
19 Aug 1902
Died:
14 Aug 1991

Maria Dieser
Born:
19 Dec 1904
Died:
23 Aug 1987

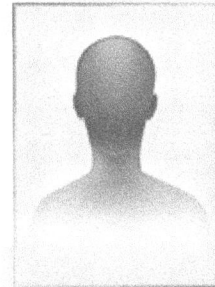

Adam Dieser
Born:
12 Jun 1907
Died:
20 Jan 1908

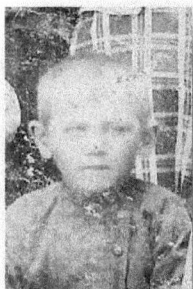

Peter Dieser
Born:
5 May 1910
Died:
Aug 1948

Ludvina
Dieser
Born:
14 Oct 1912
Died:
Nov 1934

Johannes
Dieser
Born:
26 Mar 1914
Died:
29 Dec 1970

The children of Johannes Dieser & Marie Eva Heit

DID YOU KNOW???

This family photo survived a World War, the Russian Revolution, the Russian Civil War, the Famine of the 1930's and Labour Camps!

The Johannes Dieser Family Photo from circa 1914
Back Row Left to Right: Marie Eva (Heit) Dieser, Johannes Dieser, Maria Dieser, Elisabetha Dieser (Granny Gerk), Anna Margareta (Gette) Heit
Front Row Left to Right: Peter Dieser, Ludvina Dieser

Elisabeth (Granny Gerk) remembered when this family photo was taken, as her father was "fighting in the war" (WW1). The photo was sent to her after re-establishing contact with her Dieser family in 1984!

DID YOU KNOW?

A Photograph, of a photograph, of a photograph

The only surviving photograph of Elisabeth Dieser Gerk's father, Johannes Dieser, taken while he was in the Russian army during World War 1.

Family members would painstakingly change the photograph, taking out any Tsarist symbols from his uniform. To have a photograph of a loved one with ANY former Russian regime insignia could get your entire family immediately sent to Siberia, or worse, shot, for being an Enemy of the People!
The photograph, of a photograph, of a photograph…was all designed to protect the owner.

Top Left Photograph: Johannes Dieser, younger brother to Elisabeth Dieser Gerk
Top Right Photographs: Katharina Dieser Heinrich, oldest sister to Elisabeth,
Maria Dieser Alles, next sibling to Elisabeth.

Both sisters were alive with Elisabeth found her family in 1984, allowing her to fill in the missing pieces of what happened to her family.

Bottom Photograph: Peter Dieser, brother to Elisabeth, and his wife, Anna Benz Dieser. Peter and his wife both died in 1948....family members said it was due to health complications from their years of starvation and their time in labour camps.

Elisabeth (Dieser) Gerk:

(This chapter was written based on recollections of "Granny Gerk", also known as Elisabeth (Dieser) Gerk. Dates have been confirmed through the use of archival records. The above photograph was taken in Kamyshin in 1925)

Elisabeth Dieser was born August 19, 1902, in Josefstal, Province of Saratov, Russia, to Johannes Dieser and wife Marie Eva Heit. Her Godparents were Georg Dieser and Elisabeth Klein.

Her mother, Marie Eva, was actually born in the nearby village of Semenovka, and had moved to Josefstal to seek employment as a maid for the Dieser family. The Dieser family was well-off and originally from Semenovka and Leichtling, both Volga German villages, but branches of the family moved to Josefstal around 1870.

Johannes Dieser was born in Josefstal, his father Valentin died when Johannes was very young. The story was told of Johannes, after being frustrated at not knowing his father, one day announced he was going to go to the cemetery and exhume his father's grave, so at least he could look upon him. The local parish priest is said to have talked him out of it.

Elisabeth was a shy girl, who could neither read nor write. Vision problems struck Elisabeth at a young age, and we know she underwent a number of surgeries to correct the medical problem, the result of which was she could not attend regular school. (She would one day learn how to sign her name, but that was all)

The story was told how one day Elisabeth's mother, Marie Eva, sent Elisabeth to the town store. She obediently went, but upon her arrival was struck by such fear that she could not explain to the storekeeper what she wanted. Her mother was about to scold her for this when the grandmother, the mother of her mother (Anna Margareta Gette Heit) reminded her that Elisabeth came by her shyness honestly, and that she remembered a little girl named Marie Eva who was just as shy when she was a child.

Elisabeth spent her childhood between the house in Josefstal, and the farm that was located some miles away from the village. As a farm girl she was not only expected to learn how to run a household, everything from cooking, cleaning and sewing, but she was also expected to often work in the fields.

Her first Holy Communion was at the traditional age, where Elizabeth dressed as other girls, in a beautiful white dress that could have almost passed for a wedding dress. The happy and solemn occasion was marred when someone behind her, holding a lighted candle, held it too close to Elizabeth's veil. The result which was as expected – her dress caught on fire. No damage was done, the fire was extinguished, and the ceremony resumed. But given Elizabeth's shyness, the embarrassment must have been excruciating.

Elisabeth was the fourth of nine children. She married Paul Gerk on September 15, 1920 in the church in Josefstal. The couple followed the Volga-German custom and moved into the Gerk household, with the rest of the Gerk family. A prospect and event Elizabeth grew to dislike immensely. She often told her children and grandchildren it was because of this that she would never move in with her children. Something she steadfastly refused to do. Elizabeth was in Josefstal throughout the Russian revolution, and remained in Josefstal during the Russian civil war.

Paul had escaped in hopes of finding a better home for his family. She moved back in with her parents, in much relief, but the memories were tarnished with the horror of the constant battles between Red and White troops battling it out for control of the Russian countryside.

After Paul secured his transport to Canada, and upon arrival, he immediately started work to bring his wife to Canada. His employer, John Ehman, said that it would not be a problem...all Paul had to do was to sign up for an extra year of farm work. Paul agreed.

Now came the task of paperwork. Elizabeth was helped in this regard by her father, Johannes Dieser. They would travel via horse and wagon to Saratov, some 200 miles north. There, they would take a small ferry to the city of Prokovsk (later named Engels). Elizabeth would obtain her passport and travel documents for the final leg of her journey.

While in Saratov, Father and daughter would attend Mass at the Catholic cathedral.

Her passport was stamped August 17, 1925.

On the way home, they would stop in the village of Semenovka. Here Elizabeth got to say farewell to many of her cousins, and as well see how the "triumph" of communism had turned many of her family members against their own family. She was able to see firsthand how a cousin who was a communist leader in Semenovka would not even allow his own mother to sleep in a regular bed.

Upon arrival in Josefstal, there was time to pack and say goodbyes.

The plan was for Elizabeth to travel to her husband in Canada, and then gradually arrange for transport for the rest of the Dieser family.

She left Josefstal on the train and traveled to Moscow. While in Moscow she obtained her visa for Latvia, since she would need to travel through that country in order to board a ship for Canada. She obtained her visa there on September 23, 1925.

After Moscow she traveled via train to Latvia, her traveling companions for this leg of the journey where many Mennonites also escaping Russia. At Riga she went through an inspection by officials with the Canadian government, on September 26, 1925. She then left for Canada, on September 30, 1925.

After a stop in England, where she would have boarded another ship, she left for this final part of her sea journey. She boarded the Canadian Pacific Railway Ship S.S. Minnedosa on October 8, 1925, and arrived at the port of Quebec on October 16, 1925.

Elisabeth then boarded a train and travelled to Holdfast, meeting her husband Paul Gerk there. It was a two day train journey.

They would live in the Holdfast area until 1929, when they would move to Rutland, now part of the city of Kelowna.

The rest is, as they say, history.

Rare and faded photograph taken in Josefstal of two of Elisabeth's sisters circa 1920: Left to Right: Georg Gette, Katharina (Dieser) Heinrich & child, Anna (Dieser) Gette

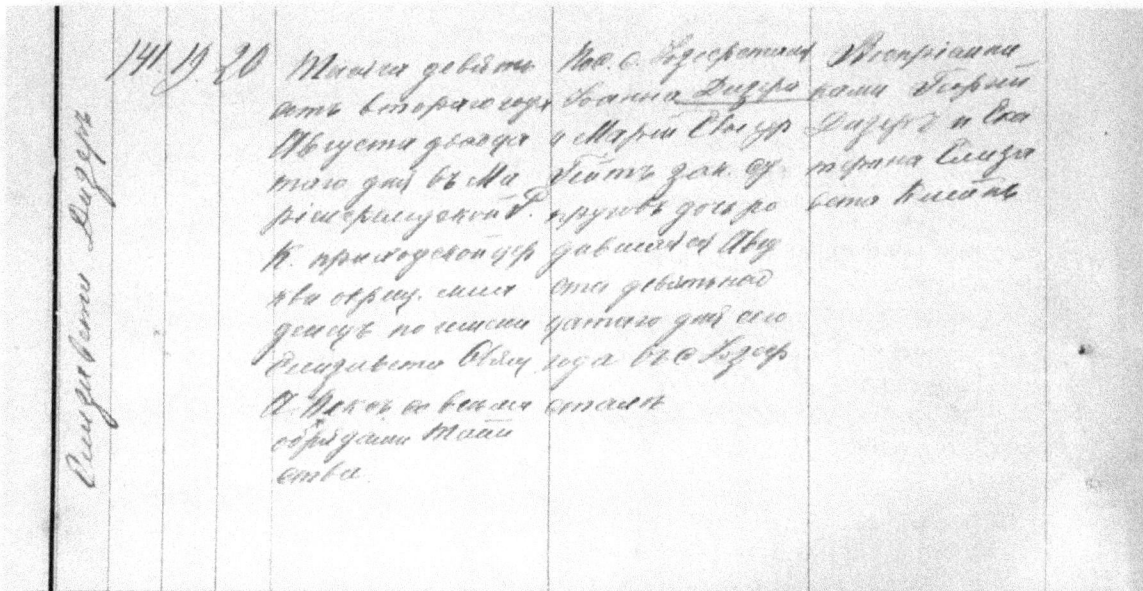

Baptismal record of Elisabeth Dieser born 19 August 1902 and baptized on 20 August 1902 in the church in Josefstal. Baptized by Father Alois Oks. Godparents were Georgi Dieser and Ekaterina Elisabetha Klein. Source: GASO Fond 365 Opis 1 Delo 1039 List 485

Elisabeth and her Father, Johannes Dieser, attended Mass at Saint Clemens Catholic Cathedral in Saratov, USSR, during August 1925. The Church will later be closed and converted into a theatre.

РОССИЙСКАЯ СОЦИАЛИСТИЧЕСКАЯ
ФЕДЕРАТИВНАЯ СОВЕТСКАЯ РЕСПУБЛИКА

REPUBLIQUE SOCIALISTE
FÉDÉRATIVE DES SOVIETS DE RUSSIE

ЗАГРАНИЧНЫЙ ПАСПОРТ

PASSEPORT POUR L'ETRANGER

Пред'явитель *иида* сего, граждан *ка* Российской Социалистической Федеративной Советской Республики *Герк Елизавета Иоганесовна*

L'aporteu *se* de la présente, citoyen *ne* de la République Socialiste Fédérative des Soviets de Russie *Gerk, Elisabeth, fille de Jean*

отправляется в *Канаду*

se rend en *Canada*

в удостоверение чего и для свободного проезда дан сей паспорт с приложением печати Народного Комиссариата по Внутренним Делам.

en foi de quoi et pour le libre passage le présent passeport est délivré avec apposition du sceau du Commissariat du Peuple aux Affaires Intérieures.

Настоящий паспорт действителен на *1 год*
по *17 Августа* 192 *6* г.,
выдан *17 Августа* 1925 г.
в гор. *Покровске АССРНП.*

Le présent passeport est valable pour *un an*
jusqu'au *17 août* 192 *6*.
et délivré *17 août* 192 *5*.
à *la ville de Pocrovsque, A.S.S. Rep. des Allemands s. l. Volga*

СВЕДЕНИЯ О ПРЕД'ЯВИТЕЛЕ:

SIGNALEMENT DU PORTEUR:

Время и место рождения *Иосефсталь Каменск к-на 19.8.1902 года*
Семейное положение *Замужняя*

Lieu et date de naissance *Josefstal, Canton Camenque, 19.8.1902.*
Etat de famille *mariée*

ПРИМЕТЫ:

SIGNES:

Рост	*средний*	Taille	*moyenne*
Глаза	*синие*	Yeux	*bleus*
Нос	*обыкновенный*	Nez	*droit*
Волосы	*блондинка*	Cheveux	*blonds*
Особые приметы	———	Signes particuliers	———

По Уполномочию Народного Комиссара по Внутренним Делам

Настоящий паспорт действителен для проезда Государственной границы до *17 Сентября* 1925 г. через Контрольно-Пограничный Пункт *Себеж*

Взыскано *33* руб. — коп.
Квитанция № *71136*

Soviet Passport of Elisabeth Dieser Gerk, dated 17 August 1925. Elisabeth had her passport photo taken in Kamyshin, then Elisabeth and her father, Johannes Dieser, traveled north to Saratov and Pokrovsk to obtain her passport.

SHEET NO. 23
THIRD CLASS

CANADIAN GOVERNMENT RETURN

S. S. "MINNEDOSA" **SAILING FROM** SOUTHAMPTON October 8th 19 25

			AGE				COUNTRY AND PLACE OF BIRTH	NATIONALITY COUNTRY OF WHICH A CITIZEN OR SUBJECT	RACE OR PEOPLE	IF IN CANADA BEFORE					WHAT LANGUAGE	BY WHOM WAS PASSAGE PAID
										BETWEEN WHAT PERIODS	AT WHAT ADDRESS					
LINE			M.	F.												
1	2	3	4	5	6		7	8	9	10	11	12	13	14	15	16
1	GERK , Elisabeth	Wife	25	M			Russia Josephstal	Russian	German	/ -		-	No	Yes	Yes	German	Husband

CANADIAN IMMIGRATION SERVICE

ARRIVING AT QUEBEC 16th October 19 25

SHEET NO. 23
THIRD CLASS

VOL 15 **PAGE** 23

	OCCUPATION		DESTINATION		HAVE YOU OR ANY OF YOUR FAMILY EVER BEEN			PASSPORT			ACTION TAKEN AND CIVIL EXAMINER
	WHAT TRADE OR OCCUPATION DID YOU FOLLOW IN YOUR OWN COUNTRY?	WHAT TRADE OR OCCUPATION DO YOU INTEND TO FOLLOW IN CANADA?	IF DESTINED TO RELATIVE, FRIEND OR EMPLOYER STATE WHICH AND GIVE NAME AND FULL ADDRESS. IF NOT JOINING ANY PERSON IN CANADA, GIVE THE ADDRESS TO WHICH YOU ARE GOING	GIVE NAME, RELATIONSHIP AND ADDRESS OF YOUR NEAREST RELATIVE IN THE COUNTRY FROM WHICH YOU CAME. IF A WIFE OR CHILDREN ARE TO FOLLOW YOU LATER TO CANADA. GIVE NAMES AND AGES	MENTALLY DEFECTIVE	PHYSICALLY DEFECTIVE	TUBERCULAR	NUMBER, PLACE AND DATE OF ISSUE	MONEY IN POSSESSION BELONGING TO PASSENGER	TRAVELLING INLAND ON	
LINE	18	19	20	21	22	23	24	25	26	27	28
1	Housewife	Housewife	Husband - Paul Gerk. Box 77, Holdfast, Sask.	Father - Hannes Thiese, Josephstal , Saratov.	No	No	No	45554 Pillau 17/8/25	$2.		LANDED Immigrant
2	Farming	Farming	Proceeding to Canada under the Auspices of the Mennonite Board Rosthern Sask.	Brother - Isaak Giebert - Ekaterinoslav				Certificate issued by the Central Admin of Dutch Dependants in Russia, $300			LANDED Immigrant LANDED

October 1925 S.S. Minedosa passenger list for Elisabeth Gerk.

*Source: Port of Arrival: Quebec Port of Departure: Southampton, England Roll: T-14720
Department of Employment and Immigration fonds. Library and Archives Canada Ottawa,
Ontario, Canada. Photo: Courtesy National Archives of Canada: PA195502*

Reunited – Paul Gerk with Wife Elisabeth Dieser Gerk – October 1925 with their sponsoring family the Ehman's of Holdfast, Saskatchewan.

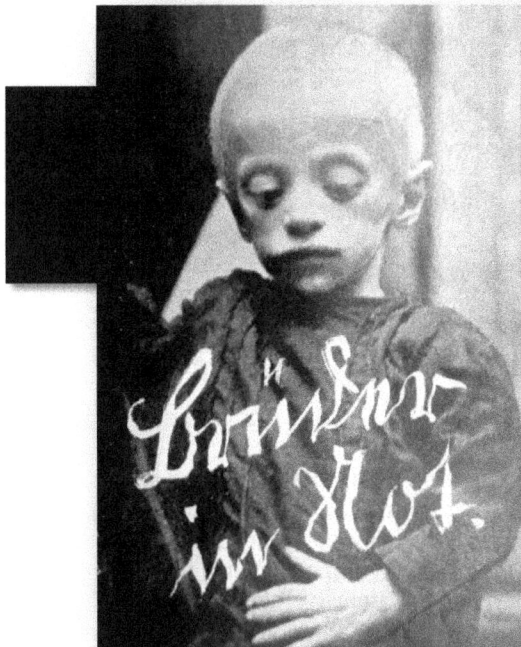

villages, local Commissars would have people shot for such activity. Then, in 1933, the tone of the letters became bold and desperate. Another famine had hit Russia. But this time, there would be no appeal by Soviet officials. The famine did not exist.

Johannes Gerk described what happened:

"Harvests weren't too bad in 1932 and they gave the collective farmers a little grain for their labours. Then in the winter it was taken away from them because they said they didn't have enough for planting in the spring. There was famine among the collective farmers and whole families died. They rationed food to 500 grams of bread per woman. In the spring they gave the men ten years prison for keeping grain during the spring planting. Most of them never returned." (Johannes Gerk 1989)

And so we look at the most treasured family heirloom we have: The last letters of our family, desperate for food, for contact with their family in Canada.

These last letters are all that survive of the heavy correspondence that took place with the family of Paul and Elisabeth.

They were written by Elisabeth Gerk's "Dieser" family.

It should be noted that all the while these letters arrived, Paul and Elisabeth would regularly send letters and money in response. Those letters and cash were never received by the family...they were stolen by Soviet postal workers.

That such mail to the Gerk family in Canada even made it to them was miraculous....mail sent in the

After their safe arrival in Canada, Paul and Elisabeth Gerk kept up a significant correspondence with their families back in Russia. Those letters were a life-line for the couple, who never intended their separation from their respective families to be permanent.

Plans were made and discussed. The possibility of sponsoring family members was paramount in their minds.

The parents of Elisabeth, Johannes and Marie Eva Dieser, were going to be the first sponsored out of Russia. The family in Russia hesitated. Son Peter Dieser was going to be drafted into the army...they did not want to leave without him.

As family hesitated....the "iron curtain" became just that. It not only closed, it slammed shut.

Mail continued between the families. Paul's brother, Jakob, would write letters with one side of the page left blank. This indicated that a "secret" message had been written...using various types of home-made invisible ink. Paul could read the propaganda in the regular letter, and held the letter up to a candle to get the real story of their life in Russia.

Soviet officials noted in archival documentation available to us now, that both Gerk and Dieser family members were receiving letters from Paul Gerk in "America". In some Volga German

Soviet Postal system was regularly censored and stolen... even mail going out.

For Paul and Elisabeth, the receipt of these letters were devastating.

Excerpt from former Soviet archives documenting the famine in Josefstal, specifically in February and March of 1933 – 20 people died. Source: GARF

Imagine, if you will, leaving your parents for a far-off country. Your only source of contact is the mail. And then you start to receive letters pleading for money because your loved ones will starve.

You receive a number of these letters...and then....silence.

Elisabeth Gerk, at the time of the writing of the letters, had two children and was expecting her third. She was so emotionally devastated, she thought she would lose her baby.

It is in that thought mode that we now turn to the letters that caused so much pain, anguish and mystery.

We started this book with the story of the reestablishment of contact with our German Russian family in the USSR. This chapter examines the last letters received before the "great silence" of 51 years.

The letters are pretty basic. The writers were concerned with conveying their faith, and then pleading for help.

The first were written either by or on behalf of Marie Eva (Heit) Dieser, the mother of Elisabeth Gerk.

In letter 2, half way through, another correspondent adds his name....that of Elisabeth's brother Peter. He too pleads for help to feed his family.

Then, on the last page of letter #2, page 2d, the letter is written by Elisabeth's brother-in-law, Alois Heinrich, married to her sister Katharina Dieser. Ironically, Alois Henirich was the same person who was arrested and put in prison with Elisbeth's husband Paul back in 1921!

The letters document the devastating famine taking place. The famine of the 1930's was a famine that was constantly denied by the government of the USSR. While families in the West received letter after letter begging for money because of looming starvation, Soviet Officials denied anything was wrong. After the collapse of the Soviet Union, and with the opening of the archives, slowly but surely, documents have been published that were never intended to see the light of day.

This is such a document.

Entitled: *"Secret summary of data collected by March 20th, 1933 prepared by the Secret Operations department of the territorial representative of OGPU [Joint Main Political Directorate] of the USSR for Lower Volga region [of the Russian Federation] regarding food shortages."* Original document: March 28th, 1933. Provided by the Central Archive of the Federal Security Service of the Russian Federation. *(Fond 2, Record Series 11, File 56, Pages 125 – 132, 136 – 137.)*

The document details some of the reports being compiled of the famine. For Josefstal, interestingly, named "Iosif-Stal" (as if the village was named after Josef Stalin- funny but not true) it (top of page 7) reports that during the months February and March 1933, there were 20 deaths from starvation registered in the village. Most of them were the villagers who "had returned to join the collective farm (again)". The bodies reportedly lay around without being buried for several days. (Former villagers tell me it was because no one had the strength to bury them).

Marie Eva (Heit) Dieser will die of starvation a few months later in August of 1933.

Interestingly, this is an "official" but still secret acknowledgement of the famine, and that Josefstal villagers, among others, were dying.

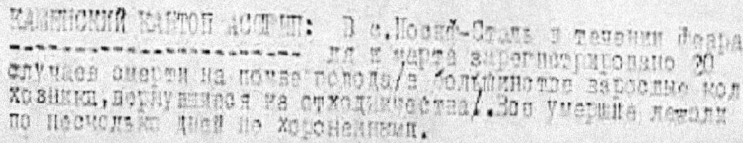

Letter #1 was written on January 5, 1933, by Marie Eva (Heit) Dieser, the Mother of Elisabeth (Dieser) Gerk.

Marie Eva will die from starvation on August 2, 1933.

The family in Russia never received the money nor the letters that Paul & Elisabeth had sent.

Photo: Marie Eva (Heit) Dieser

Flipside of Letter #1, dated January 5, 1933. Written in old German dialect, it reads:

May God grant you warmest greetings from your mother and mother-in-law to you children Paul and Elizabeth and your two children. I thank the dear Lord I am still halfway healthy and hope this letter finds you as healthy as when you left me. Further I want to tell you where the father has gone with the two children. They have gone further into the Kavkas (ed. note: Caucasus) and I am home alone. Dear children, conditions are difficult here with respect to food. Times are tough dear children. Yes dear children we are having a hard time getting food. Some people have had money sent to them. For one coin (taler) one pound of flour can be bought in Kamyshin. If you could come to my aid could you send me 5 (taler) which would give us five pounds of flour. Perhaps then I wouldn't starve to death, dear children. Again I ask if you can help me so that I don't have to starve. Now I will close this letter and greet you again and ask you to write quickly.

Letter #2a and 2b were written on January 12, 1933, and appears to be a family effort. Page 1 was written by Marie Eva (Heit) Dieser. Page 2 of the letter continues the dialogue, but then states it is written by the brother of Elisabeth (Dieser) Gerk, Peter Dieser. Letter 2c was also written by Peter Dieser. Letter 2d was written by Alois Heinrich, who was married to the oldest sister of Elisabeth (Dieser) Gerk, Katharina (Dieser) Heinrich.

Letter 2a, 2b and 2c written by Marie Eva (Heit) Dieser, mother to Elisabeth Gerk and Peter Dieser, brother to Elisabeth Gerk.
Written January 12, 1933

"God be with you. Hearty greetings from me your mother and mother-in-law Dizer to our dear children Paul and Elisabeth with your two children. We have the dear Lord to thank that we are still healthy and wish you the same health as ourselves, Amen. Further dear children I want to inform you how things are here. I am very poor because there is nothing more to eat here, dear children. If one does nothing, then there is nothing to eat. (No work, no food) Dear children, if you wish then you could come to my aid. Perhaps you want to know how. I can tell you with money (Taler) People have sent money to others and for the Taler one can buy flour in Kamyshin. Dear children, be so good and help me with money, so that I don't starve to death and if it is only 5 Taler then dear children I beg you again to be so good and come to my aid as soon as possible for there is nothing to eat here, except what I beg for here and there. Some days I get something to eat and some days I get nothing. So you can imagine how poor I am, dear children. If you can help me so that I don't starve to death. I want to tell you where the father is with the two children, they are in the Kavkas (Caucasus) and they can't help me because they get as much as they can get on by themselves."

So it is. We work for food but receive no pay, so again I must turn to you dear children. I ask you again, can you help me. Then I want to close my letter and greet you again and ask that you come to my greatest aid and write that God Bless you. A hearty greeting from me your brother-in-law Peter and sister Anna together with the children. We have the dear Lord to thank for our health and wish the same to you as myself. Amen. Further, dear brother-in-law Paul I beg you. Things are very poor here and if you could send me one Taler so that I can buy some flour in Kamyshin, because for a Taler one can get flour, I beg you to help us somewhat.

Above Photo: Peter Dieser & wife Anna (Benz) Dieser.

Letter 2d: written by Alois Heinrich, who was married to Elisabeth (Dieser) Gerk's oldest sister, Katharina.
Written January 12, 1933

"May God Bless you, a hearty greeting from your brother-in-law Alvis and sister-in-law Katharina together with our three children to our brother-in-law Paul and sister and your two children. We thank the dear Lord that we are still healthy and wish you the same health as we, Amen. You probably want to know how I'm getting along. Conditions here are pretty bad and if you can, dear brother-in-law, be so kind and help us a little, because things here are very bad. Perhaps you can send me something that I can get a little flour in Kamyshin I can write you a little..." (letter cuts off here)

Above Photo: Alois Henirich, wife Katharina (Dieser) Heinrich and unknown person.

DID YOU KNOW???

Big Brother **WAS** watching! Soviet authorities continuously monitored mail going both inside and outside of the country.

Local communist officials also produced and kept files on residents, able to provide documentation to any State official or agency that needed it. Many of those documents are housed in village files, once labelled "Secret". The Josefstal archive "Fond" was removed from this classification in the 1990's.

Two such files document the constant contact that Paul and Elisabeth Gerk had with members of their respective families. This first document is from "Characteristic" File of Elisabeth Gerk's brother, Johannes Dieser: "In the characteristics of draftee Ivan Ivanovich Dieser, issued by the Josefstal Village Council on 17 April 1937, No. 36, it is noted that the name of his brother-in-law, who resides in America, is Paul Georgievich Gerk" (GAVO Fond 2659, Op. 2, Delo. 14, L. 12 - 12 ob.)

Excerpt from the second document for Jacob Gerk shows that Jakob was also under observation for having contact with his brother Paul Gerk in Canada. In this case it was used against Jacob in a denunciation against him. (Source: GAVO Fond 2659 Op. 2, D 14 L 36)

PROLETARIER ALLER LÄNDER, VEREINIGT EUCH!   24. Jahrgang.

Nachrichten

Organ des Gebietskomitees der KPdSU(b) und des Obersten Sowjets
der ASSRdWD, des Stadtkomitees der KPdSU(B) und des Stadtsowjets
der Deputierten der Werktätigen von Engels

Nr. 204 | Sonnabend, den 30. August 1941 | Preis 15 Kop.

ERLASS

DES PRÄSIDIUMS DES OBERSTEN SOWJETS DER UNION DER SSR

Über die Übersiedlung der Deutschen, die in den Wolgarayons wohnen

Laut genauen Angaben, die die Militärbehörden erhalten haben, befinden sich unter der in den Wolgarayons wohnenden deutschen Bevölkerung Tausende und aber Tausende Diversanten und Spione, die nach dem aus Deutschland gegebenen Signal Explosionen in den von den Wolgadeutschen besiedelten Rayons hervorrufen sollen. Über das Vorhandensein einer solch großen Anzahl von Diversanten und Spionen unter den Wolgadeutschen hat keiner der Deutschen, die in den Wolgarayons wohnen, die Sowjetbehörden in Kenntnis gesetzt, folglich verheimlicht die deutsche Bevölkerung der Wolgarayons die Anwesenheit in ihrer Mitte der Feinde des Sowjetvolkes und der Sowjetmacht.

Falls aber auf Anweisung aus Deutschland die deutschen Diversanten und Spione in der Republik der Wolgadeutschen oder in den angrenzenden Rayons Diversionsakte ausführen werden und Blut vergossen wird, wird die Sowjetregierung laut den Gesetzen der Kriegszeit vor die Notwendigkeit gestellt, Strafmaßnahmen gegenüber der gesamten deutschen Wolgabevölkerung zu ergreifen.

Zwecks Vorbeugung dieser unerwünschten Erscheinungen und um kein ernstes Blutvergießen zuzulassen, hat das Präsidium des Obersten Sowjets der UdSSR es für notwendig gefunden, die gesamte deutsche in den Wolgarayons wohnende Bevölkerung in andere Rayons zu übersiedeln, wobei den Überzusiedelnden Land zuzuteilen und eine staatliche Hilfe für die Einrichtung in den neuen Rayons zu erweisen ist. Zwecks Ansiedlung sind die an Ackerland reichen Rayons des Nowosibirsker und Omsker Gebiets, des Altaigaus, Kasachstans und andere Nachbarortschaften bestimmt.

In Übereinstimmung mit diesem wurde dem Staatlichen Komitee für Landesverteidigung vorgeschlagen, die Übersiedlung der gesamten Wolgadeutschen unverzüglich auszuführen und die Überzusiedelnden Wolgadeutschen mit Land und Nutzländerein in den neuen Rayons sicherzustellen.

Vorsitzender des Präsidiums des Obersten
Sowjets der UdSSR M. KALININ.

Sekretär des Präsidiums des Obersten
Sowjets der UdSSR A. GORKIN.

Moskau, Kreml. 28. August 1941.

And so it began. As Germany invaded the USSR in 1941, Stalin and the government of the USSR ordered the deportation of an entire ethnic group, the Volga Germans.

The above notice, printed in the August 30, 1941 edition of the Soviet Volga German publication "Nachrichten", was the official announcement of the deportation.

Johannes Gerk, brother of Paul Gerk, described what happened:

"Then in 1941 the war began and by decree of August 28, 1941 from the Supreme Soviet of the USSR, thousands and hundreds of thousands were accused of sabotage and all Germans from all over the country were arrested and exiled to Siberia and Kazakhstan. They lost all their property and livestock. Only two or three remained at the collective farms, just a few. Everyone was evacuated to areas away from the front. This was at the end of August, beginning of September. Harvest of grain was going on in the fields, stacks of grain lay at the collection points. Almost all the implements, combines and tractors were taken for the war. Everything else was thrown to fate. People were taken on tractor carts pulled by horses to the railroad stations. My brother tried to take clothing and bedding and

other property without the bed. Even the chairs were left. At the railroad station we were loaded into box cars which had carried grain and livestock. Fifty people in one car, without any conveniences. They took us to Omsk. Ten days we were on the road. From Omsk they took us to collective farms where they gave us a place to stay in dug-outs without windows and doors. We had to work at the collective farms until January 1942."

From then on, the Volga Germans were "mobilized" into what was known as the "Trudarmii", or Worker's Army. This was just another term for slave labour in Russia's vast Gulag system.

The government issued decree was published in August of 1941, in various forms. Historian Otto Pohl writes:

On 28th August 1941, the Presidium of the Supreme Soviet issued Ukaz no. 21-160. This decree ordered the deportation of all the Volga Germans to Kazakhstan and Siberia. Unlike most deportation decrees this one was published soon after its approval. On 30 August 1941, the two largest newspapers in the Volga German ASSR, Nachrichten and Bolshevik, printed the deportation order in its entirety. Below I have reproduced a translated version of the decree as found in N.F. Bugai, ed., Iosif Stalin – Lavrentiiu Berii, "Ikh nado deportirovat'," Dokumenty, fakty, kommentarii (Moscow: Druzhba narodov, 1992), doc. 3, pp. 37-38.

"On Resettling the Germans, Living in the Region of the Volga"

28 August 1941

According to reliable reports received from military authorities among the German population living in the region of the Volga exist thousands and tens of thousands of diversionists and spies who are now awaiting a signal from Germany that they should conduct sabotage in the region settled by Volga Germans.

On the presence of this large number of diversionists and spies among the Germans, living in the region of the Volga, nobody informed the Soviet authorities, therefore the German population of the region of the Volga concealed amongst themselves enemies of the Soviet people and Soviet authorities.

In the case that diversionist acts are conducted, according to orders from Germany by German diversionists and spies in the Volga German Republic or its adjoining regions, bringing about bloodshed, the Soviet leadership would according to the laws of wartime be required to bring punitive measures against the entire German population of the Volga.

In order to avoid this undesirable occurrence and to prevent serious bloodshed the Presidium of the Supreme Soviet deemed it necessary to resettle the whole German population, living in the region of the Volga, to other regions, with the provision that the resettled will be allotted land and rendered state assistance for settling in their new regions.

Those to be resettled are to be assigned to areas of abundant arable land in the regions of Novosibirsk and Omsk oblasts, Altai Krai, Kazakhstan and other neighboring localities.

In connection with this the State Defense Committee is directed to quickly undertake the resettlement of all Volga Germans and allot those resettled – Volga Germans land in their new regions.

Chairman of the Presidium of the Supreme Soviet of the USSR
M. Kalinin

Secretary of the Presidium of the Supreme Soviet of the USSR
A. Gorkin

(Source: http://jpohl.blogspot.com/2006/08/ukaz-no-21-160.html)

Deportation Card File: All Volga German families had a card file filled out at the time of deportation to Siberia, dated August 31, 1941. This is the card for the Georg Gerk family, brother to Paul. It notes that Georg was "transferred" from another area, probably due to the fact he was living in southern Russia at the time where he could find work. The KGB caught up with him. It also lists his wife, Kristina, born 1897, and children living with her: Jackob born 1927, Ivan, born 1929 and Elisabeth, born 1937. Son Georg was not on the list.
Source: Procurator of Volgograd Oblast, Feb 2005 Number 14855

One day Lara went out and did not come back. She must have been arrested in the street, as so often happened in those days, and she died or vanished somewhere, forgotten as a nameless number on a list which was afterwards mislaid....

- "Doctor Zhivago" by Boris Pasternak

If only there were evil people somewhere insidiously committing evil deeds, and it were necessary only to separate them from the rest of us and destroy them. But the line dividing good and evil cuts through the heart of every human being. And who is willing to destroy a piece of his own heart?

-"The Gulag Archipelago" 1918-1956
(1973) by Aleksandr Solzhenitsyn

Jakob & Georg Gerk: Lost in the Gulag

When Johannes Gerk visited our family in the summer of 1989, he spent time, at my request, writing out a short history of our Gerk family. Even in 1989, the family was unsure what exactly happened to two of the Gerk brothers, Jakob and Georg.

Family members knew roughly what year they perished, and even had a rough idea what area they were sent to. But that was all. The concept of entire archives opening up was just not within the realm of possibility.

With the fall of communism, former Soviet archives opened to the world. Researchers could now investigate what was once forbidden. Families were now able to put pieces of the puzzle together, and discover details about long-lost loved ones.

Our first bit of detective work had me looking for Jakob Gerk. Jakob was the brother who kept in constant contact with his younger sibling Paul in Canada. I had connected with Jakob's daughter, Lydia, who had married Jakob Stremel from Josefstal. They had immigrated in the 1990's to Stuttgart, Germany.

In 2007, while on a visit in Germany to visit relatives, I had the privilege of visiting with Lydia and talking about her father, Jakob.

Shortly after that visit, I came across a published list of inmates to a specific labour camp. On that list, prisoner #872 was listed as Герн (Герк) Яков Георгиевич. This was Gern (Gerk) Jakob Georgevich, born 1900 in Josefstal. The list stated he entered the camp 28.09.42 and died 03.12.42. The camp listed was the УСОЛЬЛАГЕ or Usollage NKVD camp located in Perm Oblast. *(Source: GEDENKBUCH: Книга Памяти немцев-трудармейцев Усольлага НКВД/МВД*

СССР (1942-1947 гг.). Сост. Э.А. Гриб. Ред. В.Ф. Дизендорф. М.: Общественная академия наук российских немцев. - 2005.)

The next step was to contact the State Archive of Perm Oblast and ask for a copy of the complete file.

Archivists were very helpful and did indeed produce a copy of the file. Alas, there was no camp photo - all that could be produced was a lone fingerprint....all that is left of a man who was a hero to his family.

Lydia told me the background in Jakob's original incarceration. She would fill in for us the missing information on what happened to this brave man. He would go out of his way to look for ways to feed his children, even as communist officials would make it more and more difficult for people to survive. "Sow what you have hidden" was the command from these cruel taskmasters, to people who had nothing. Thousands would starve in the 1930's. Jakob would be arrested in 1938, charge with the crime of stealing grain to feed his children. He would be sentenced to 5 years in a labour camp, where he would die in 1942. A fellow prisoner would later contact the family to let them know how Jakob perished. But this would be years after the fact.

But even in 2007, Lydia had doubts about the rumours of her father's death....and hoped that someday, it would be learned that he had survived and not suffered the fate of so many millions.

Village files from Josefstal document the harassment of Soviet officials directed at Jakob.

His labour camp file shows that a sickly Jakob Gerk entered the camp at the end of September, 1942, and he would die shortly after, on December 3, 1942, in the nearby village of Danilov Lug. Jakob had entered a camp where the work was logging, barely able to walk, and given the conditions, men did not last long.

They were not meant to.

Jakob Gerk in 1917 and then with wife Elisabeth (Kisser) Gerk circa 1930.
Photo courtesy Lydia (Gerk) Stremel

Children & grandchildren of three Gerk brothers meet: Stuttgart 2007

Left to Right: Sevta Gerk, Konstantin Gerk, Lydia (Gerk) Stremel,
Edward Gerk.

Sveta and Konstantin are the grandchildren of Johannes Gerk, Lydia is
the daughter of Jakob Gerk and Edward is the grandson of Paul Gerk

Постановление №3 46

Форма № 4 (1-й экз.)

1935 г. Junii 2 дня город Oberdorf A.S.S.R.d.W.D.

Комиссия по наложению взысканий в административном порядке при Arbeiter u. Bauernmiliz d. Erlenbacher Kantons, рассмотрев материал на гр-н Gerk Jacob d. Georg

по нарушению обязательного постановления J.V.A.u.V.K.R. за № 13

от "21" September 1934 г., выразившемуся In dem, dass Gerk den Bremstoff sowie Lampenöl u. Bensin wehrend der Frühjahrssaat nicht weit vom Feuer stehen hat, was einer Feuergefahr droht.

ПОСТАНОВИЛА: гр-н Gerk Jacob d. Georg , проживающего в Unterdorf. Kanton Erlenbach улице A.S.S.R.d.W.D. в доме № кв. рабо- тающего в Tractorenbrigade №10 , в должности Tractorist , по социальному положению Mittelbauer подвергнуты: предупреждению, штрафу. на 25 рублей, принудработам на дней. K.V.A.d. Erlenbacher Kantons.

Постановление может быть обжаловано в президиум

Жалоба подается через орган, наложивший взыскание. Поданная жалоба в пятидневный срок, со дня выручения постановления, приостанавливает приведение постановления в исполнение.

Преседатель Члены Комиссии

Секретарь Hippes

Document, dated June 2, 1935, showing that Jakob Gerk was employed as a "Tractorist" in the village of Unterdorf, not far from Josefstal, as of 21 September 1934.
(Source: GAVO Fond 2659 24)

The Volga German Autonomous Soviet Socialist Republic (German: Autonome Sozialistische Sowjetrepublik der Wolgadeutschen; Russian: Автономная Советская Социалистическая Республика Немцев Поволжья, Avtonomnaya Sovetskaya Sotsialisticheskaya Respublika Nemtsev Povolzh'ya) was an autonomous republic established in Soviet Russia, with its capital at the Volga port of Engels (until 1931 known as Pokrovsk – across from Saratov).
This is the official Seal of the Republic. Many of the documents found here are "official" documents from this "Republic".
Source:
http://en.wikipedia.org/wiki/Volga_German_Autonomous_Soviet_Socialist_Republic

Translation: "Protocol of Inquiry"

September 16, 1936, Josefstal village soviet, Erlenbach kanton executive committee chairman, Josefstal village soviet Alles , conducted an inquiry into the matter of the loss of a military billet by presenter citizen Jakob Georgovich Gerk, born February 19, 1900, private, staff of unit No. 1, educational level 1, social status: middle, family situation: collective farm worker, 6 members of the family. Property situation: house, barn, stable. Place of work: Josefstal collective farm. Duties: tractor driver [illegible], laborer, village of Josefstal, Erlenbach kanton, Jakov Georg Gerk.
Not previously subject to fine for loss of billet, when and where issued: Dobrinka kanton, village of Kraft.
In 1919 he was declared fit for military duty and registered with the Josefstal village soviet.
Demonstrated: Citizen Jakov Georgov. Gerk, during the planting campaign of 1936 in the month of May, worked shift as a tractor driver and I lost my billet and documents.

Chairman of Soviet: Alles
Secretary: Rowein
Resolution Issued by the Josefstal village soviet, due to social ancestry, social situation, no fine will be levied.

 (Source: GAVO Fond 2659 2 14) (Translation courtesy Rick Rye)

DID YOU KNOW???

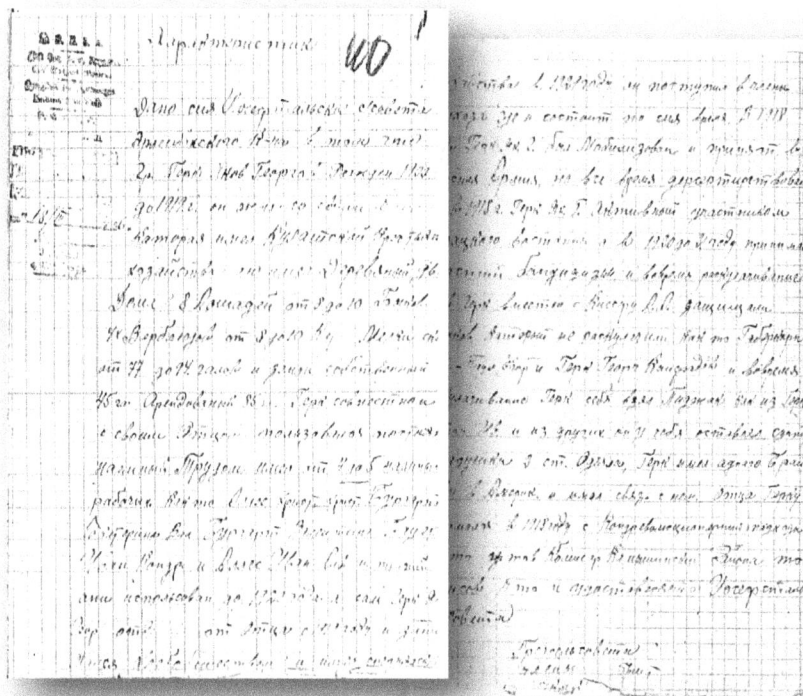

Were they out to get Jakob Gerk? This document, dated March 13, 1936 seems to confirm that view:

"Testimony given before the Josefstal village council, Ehrlenbach canton, that citizen Gerk, Jacob Georgov., born 1900 and until 1919 resided with his family who had a "kulak" peasant's farm with two wood houses, eight horses, from 8 to 10 bulls, 4 camels, 8 to 10 chickens, small livestock from 77 to 94, personal land of 45 hectares, rented land of 85 hectares.

Gerk and his father utilized constantly the labors of 4 or 5 hired hands, such as Christ. Christof. Burgart; Val. Burgart; Valentin Bauer; Ivan Konr. and Alles Ivan, and used them until 1920. Gerk Jacob Georg himself and his father from 1919 and his son-in-law farmed [unreadable], until 1929, and became members of the collective farm where they are up to this time. In 1918, Gerk Ja. G. was mobilized [conscripted, drafted] into the Red Army, but he deserted in 1918, and since 1918 Gerk Ja. G has actively participated in the kulak banditry, and since 1920 has been a bandit, and during the dekulakization, Gerk and A. D. Kisser have defended kulaks who were not dekulakized, such as Haberkorn, Peter- Paul Yegor, and Gerk, Georg Konradov. During the dekulakization Gerk himself stole a jacket from Anton Ivanov. Gerk. From others he stole 4 pillows, two blankets. Gerk had one brother Paul in America and has had contact with him. Since 1918, Gerk's father has been involved with counter-revolutionary campaigns. This is verified by the Comrade Commissar of the Kamyshin Region Council, and certified by the Josefstal village council."

Signed Representative of the President of the Council: Breit

(Source: GAVO Fond 2659 Op. 2 14 L40) (Translation courtesy Rick Rye)

Jakob Gerk's Labour Camp File: Worker's Army form No. 6 Ust-Usol Camp of the NKVD

Formulary to Personal File No. 6583

Surname (or nickname): Gerk
Name and patronymic: Jacob Georgovich
Year and place of birth: 1900, Josefstal, Erlenbach region, ASSRNP.
Nationality: German   Citizenship: USSR
Participated in which party activities and when: Member VKL (8), 1930-1934.
Served in the organs of the OGPU/NKVD: No. Served in the army (tsarist, white, foreign, red): 150th, from 1919-1921, private.
Place of residence before mobilization: [?] 5th [?] camp.
Profession and specialty: auto transport and tractor operator What work before mobilization: [Blank] Name of enterprise: Vitmastrans [?]tractor operator 1937 to 1938 Arrived in Usollag: 23/9/1942

Medium height, underweight, dark reddish hair, grey eyes, [?] normal, no special marks.

Documentation completed at Usollag on 23/9/1942
Signature of interrogatee: Gerk, Jacob Georgov. Gerk
completed by laborer of URCh.   Died 4//12/42
Thumbprint. Notes about relocations: Ust Yazva, 28/9/1942

(Source: Perm State Archive)

НКТП
Сталинградский
акторный завод
...учетный
СТОЛ

Спешно по призыву

КУДА _____

КОМУ _____

№ 10/40
г. Сталинград и-В.
Телефон № 10-62

Прошу дать исчерпывающую характеристику на допризывника 19___ года
рождения _____

происходящего из граждан _____
(селение, района область (край, город)

Характеристика должна быть обсуждена на общем собрании цеха, предприятия, учреждения, совхоза или колхоза и утверждена на заводе (фабрике), в учреждении, совхозе — треугольником и в сельской местности — президиумом сельсовета.

По утверждении, характеристику возвратить по адресу:

Военно-учетный стол
...ого Тракторного завода

Военный инспектор С
(Аканьев) Подпис

Сталинград, т.-л. изд-ва «Сталинградская правда» зак. № 5898 Уполкрайлит № В—5763, т. 5000.

Georg Gerk moved south to Stalingrad around 1932. Here is a inquiry document dated April 6, 1937 from the Military Accounting Office of the Stalingrad Tractor Factory to the chairman of the Josefstal village soviet and was sent May 16, 1937, NO. 1a/40, with a request to give a description of Georgii Georgievich Gerk, who until 1932 had resided in Josefstal and at the time he resided with his brother, Ivan Georgievich Gerk Source; GAVO Fond 2659 D. 20, L. 27).

Срочно по призыву

Председателю Иосиф. Стал........
сил совету

Присем перепровождаю Вам характеристика прошу в самом срочном порядке заполнит на допризивнику 191 года рождения гр-н. _____

и вернут по адрес. ССР Азирбаджана г. Кировабад Совхоз № 2 Кара-Еры Азсовхозтреста спец. часть прошу не задержат такаву ю).

НАЧАЛНИК СПЕЦ ЧАСТЬ
СОВХОЗА № 2 КАРА-ЕРЫ   /ЦЕРЕТИАН /

As of November 1936, Georg Gerk had moved to the Azerbaijan Soviet Socialist Republic, to the town of Kirovabad. In this document his name is spelled Kerk. Source; GAVO Fond 2659 D. 20, L. 52).

The labour camp at Chellyabinsk was called Chelyabmetallurgstroy of the NKVD of the USSR --
The Largest Forced Labor Camp for German-Russians.

Above Photo: Entry gate to the camp following the fencing in of its main zone Pershino, 1942.
Source: http://library.ndsu.edu/grhc/articles/magazines/german/kkvd.html

Bottom: Georg Gerk's labour camp file, documents his family and arrival in the camp on
March 17, 1942, and his death on March 3, 1943.

(Source: Chellyabinsk State Archive)

Additional documentation courtesy of the Chellaybinsk State Archive. No camp photograph exists, but a complete set of finger prints is all that remains of documenting the life of Georg Gerk. Also in the file was the death record, stating thet Georg Gerk died March 3, 1943. Included was an official document stating that Georg Gerk was "Rehabilitated" on October 18, 1991, meaning he was imprisoned unjustly and any charges against him were unfounded.

DID YOU KNOW???

ANATOMY OF A SMEAR

Under Soviet style socialism, citizens were encouraged to smear fellow citizens, often making false or exaggerated accusations. Such activities, while often unfounded, would hopefully prove the loyalty to the State of the person making the accusation.

Newspapers were no exception. Soviet newspapers such as "Nachrichten", the german-language newspaper of the Volga-Germans, were chalked full of petty and false accusations against, it would appear, anyone and everyone.

Here is an example of one such letter, published in 1930, written by someone with the initials JG. The letter goes after various individuals living in the village of Josefstal, including some members of the Gerk family. It reads:

The Josefstal Village Chairman Curbs the Grain Harvest

In Josefstal, Kanton Kamenka, all farm organizations did the harvest work under direction of the "Roter Stern" (Red Star) collective. Already on July 20, thanks to the increased work tempo, the collective had a Red Grain Train with 170 hundredweight of rye at the state granary. At the meeting taking place this day, the collectivists and single workers stated many others would follow that Red Grain Train. And truly, another 170 hundredweight of grain was brought to the granary on 27 July. Here the collectivists and single workers forcefully promised to bring all excess grain to the state in the shortest time.

All this speaks of a never previous enthusiasm among collectivists and non-collectivists. Duty of the officers of the collective and the village chairman especially is that they lead the work with similar spirit, put the enthusiasm of the masses on the right track, and place them into service of the thorough collectivization and terminal liquidation of kulakism. Unfortunately, this is not the case. The farmers are dissatisfied with this, and rightly so. Specifically, here the village chairman, the organ of the proletariat dictatorship in the village, is mentioned. He cannot justify his proposals in the full and correctly timed completion of the grain harvest, since he is misled by class enmity elements. This year, Jos. ds. Jos Rupp again begins to speculate grain and flour to Kamyshin, Katharina Breiet slaughtered her oxen and sold the meat to Kamyshin, Jak. Breidt did likewise, Ad. Dieser also participated in meat speculating, etc. Are these accomplices of the village chairman or agents of class enmity?

What concerns the officers of the collective is that chairman J. Gerk exchanged his hog for a better one in the collective, and the official accomplices Stremel, J.J. Gerk and J. Dieser secretly feast on cutlets from the kitchen of the collective and drink whiskey thereto. The collectivists and single workers see all of this. They realize quite well that such village chairman accomplices and collectivist-activists only serve the interests of the kulaks, that they might undermine the grain harvest and accomplishments of the thorough collectivization by their work. The collectivists and non-collectivists desire from the KVK that it hereby makes its own revisions and remove activists as assistant helpers to kulaks and puts them before a judge.- - J.G.

Source: Nachrichten (Pokrovsk): 11 August 1930, Nr. 176

Left Behind: "My Memories about our Gerk Family"
By Johannes Gerk

As has been noted, in 1984 contact was re-established with our Gerk family. One of the prolific writers to our family in the west was the youngest brother of Paul Gerk (Grandpa Gerk), Johannes Gerk. He came to be known as Uncle Vanya to us. He was able to visit our family in Canada in the summer of 1989 at the age of 78. While visiting, I asked him if he would write the following chapter for us, his family.
Remembering what he knew, and telling us what life was like for the family who stayed behind in Russia. The account is fascinating and sad for all of us in the family. What he never knew is that Soviet archives would open up and we would be able to document the disappearance and death of the 2 Gerk brothers, Jakob and Georg, and that so many of the family would make their way to Germany, leaving Russia once and for all. Johannes Gerk died April 24, 1996 in the city of Nizhnekamsk, USSR. This account documents what happened to the family and details the peril they all faced in Russia's labour camps.

Please note it was always the intention of Paul and Elisabeth Gerk to find a way to sponsor what family they could get out to the west, But the Iron Curtain was exactly that....a curtain of iron that would open for no one.

Our family was one of many children, farmers, who lived in the village of Josefstal, ASSRNP. Parents were father: Georg Georgievich Gerk, born in 1868 in the village of Josefstal. He died on February 10, 1925 in the village of Josefstal, from intestinal cancer. Mother: Anna Margaretha Heinrichovna Gerk was born in 1868? In the village of Josefstal. Her maiden name was Rohwein. She died on September 16, 1957 in the Urals, in the town of Krasnoturinsk after paralysis.

Our parents had 11 children, 7 sons and four daughters.

1.   Daughter Barbara, I don't know her birth date, died at a young age in Josefstal.
2.   Son Alois, I don't know his birth date, died at the age of 6 in Josefstal
3.   Son Michael, born about 1894 – 1895, was married to Margaretha Gerk, maiden name Stremel. He died in 1921 – 1922 in Poland on the way to Germany.
4.   Daughter Anna, born 1896 in the village of Josefstal, married Michael Kisser, and her second husband was Conrad Arnold. She died in 1983 – 1984 in the village of Chernikovka, Kazakstan of stomach cancer.
5.   Son Georg, born 1897, married Christina Gerk, maiden name Rausch, he died of starvation in 1942 in the Trudarmiya in the Chelyabinsk oblast.
6.   Son Jacob, born 1900 in Josefstal, married Barbara Gerk, maiden name Lambrecht. He died in prison in 1941 – 1943, unknown where.
7.   Son Paul, born in Josefstal in 1902, married Elisabeta Gerk, maiden name Dieser. He died in 1954 in Kelowna, Canada.
8.   Daughter Ekaterina, born in Josefstal in 1904, married Kaspar Bladner. She died from tuberculosis in 1985 in Angren, Uzbekistan.
9.   Daughter Maria, born 1906 in the village of Josefstal, married 1) Ivan Leonhard, 2) Kern Ivan, 3) Peter Walde; lives in the Omsk Oblast, village of Golubovka, USSR.
10.   Son Gottfried, born in Josefstal in 1908, died in 1980, Omsk Oblast, village of Novyi Khutor. Was married to Elizabetha Gerk, maiden name Kisser. Died from paralysis.
11.   Son Ivan, born 1911 in the village of Josefstal, married Barbara Gerk, maiden name Dieser, lives in Uzbek SSR, village of Angren. Before the revolution, the parents had their own farm 12 km from the village of Josefstal. They had a wooden house on the farm, and all

necessary farm buildings. They were farmers and raised livestock. There was a lot of working livestock on the farm: horses, bullocks, camels, cows, young calves, sheep. There were a lot of implements, plows, carts, sledges, harrows, mowers. Of course there was the plot of land. After the revolution, the land was taken away according to the rules of the Soviet Regional Committee of the USSR. After that they had to sell one of the two houses, so one was liquidated. After they moved to a home in the village of Josefstal. The house in the village was mostly of wood, but had all the necessary structures and workers, but then World War I came. All the horses were taken for the Army, almost all the livestock died of disease, and the farm became poor. There remained only 2 colts and 4 working bullocks on the farm, and two cows. In 1921, there was no harvest and people in the village died from starvation. Oldest brother Mikhail and his wife Margaretha in the summer of 1921 took one horse from father, took one cart and a saddle, and the brother and Margaretha left for Germany. Brother Jacob separated from our family. He received one horse. In 1922 brother Paul also went to Germany. At the beginning of 1922, sister Katya married, and in 1923 sister Maria married. Only four bullocks remained at our family. In 1924 brother Georg left the family, he received one working bull and a cow. Only four of us remained in the family with brother Gottfried and our parents. On February 10, 1925, father died, so it was just me, my brother Gottfried, and Mama alone at the farm. We had two bulls and one horse. In 1926 he married, so Gottfried stayed on the farm until 1929, the year I married. Only two horses remained, and we divided them between us, one horse each. At the end of 1929 – beginning of 1930, the collective farm was founded, and in 1930 we entered the collective. Brother Georg didn't enter the collective, but left for the neighboring village where he became the elder and built a house. Then our village authorities came and took his horse and cow and he had nothing. He and his son went to Stalingrad to work in a tractor factory. Then the rest of the family went to Stalingrad. From there he moved to the Kuban, and got set up at a collective farm. He lived there until he was exiled to Kazakhstan. Then in 1942 with his older son, he was taken into the worker's army and both of them didn't return.

Brother Jacob entered the collective farm and joined the communist party. In 1933 he was kicked out of the party and fined. He was sent to a tractor brigade as a student, and at the end of 1933 he was sent to the tractor course, where he worked as a tractor driver until 1937, when he was arrested and sent to prison. He never came back.

Brother Gottfried, after these events, was sent by the collective to study as a veterinary assistant, which he completed, and worked as a veterinarian at the veterinary station, first in the village of Josefstal, then in the village of Marienfeld, where he lived until the deportation. He then went to work after the deportation in the collective farms in the Omsk region until he retired.

A little information about those brothers and sisters who remained alive:

1.   Sister Anna had a son and a daughter
2.   Brother Georg had two sons and a daughter
3.   Brother Jacob had one son and a daughter
4.   Brother Paul had two sons and a daughter
5.   Sister Katy had two daughters
6.   Sister Maria had two sons and five daughters
7.   Brother Gottfried had four daughters
8.   From me, Ivan, there is one son, Volodya.

My recollections about the suffering of Soviet Germans during de-kulakization, collectivization, deportation to the Trudarmiya, and the komendantura, beginning in 1929

At the end of 1929 and beginning of the 30s, de-kulakization and collectivization began. Who were the "kulaks?" The workers in the villages, the farmers who worked day and night in the fields and who took care of their livestock so they could improve their village lives. Thanks to their tireless work they began to live well. But the other peasants who were not kulaks also had two horses and one cow on their farms were soon arrested and sent to jail. Their property was all confiscated, even the clothes they wore. All members of the family were sent to the northern Urals and the Komi ASSR in the north. Then in the forests the men were united with their families. They were given [sleeping] pallets, axes, saws, shovels. It was in the winter and the guards said that they could use these tools to make their own living quarters. The guards took over what had been built. They threw the pallets into the fire. Some began to live with their families, including children and the elderly.

Then they began to build barracks. Most of them died from starvation and the cold, especially children and the elderly. Then the criminal collectivization began. They forced all the farmers into collectives, seized all the livestock and the farm inventory. They gathered the livestock in groups during the winter, and because of the bad cold and the bad food, most of the livestock died during the winter. That next spring the collective farms didn't have enough livestock to plant the crops. Then the collective farmers took their own cows away and added them to the village collective in order to have enough for spring planting.

All the churches were closed and the clergy was sent to prison. Churches were used for warehouses, clubs, and dance halls.

Then in 1931-32, they began to replace some of the horses with tractors and the planting went better. Harvests weren't too bad in 1932 and they gave the collective farmers a little grain for their labours. Then in the winter it was taken away from them because they said they didn't have enough for planting in the spring. There was famine among the collective farmers and whole families died. They rationed food to 500 grams of bread per woman. In the spring they gave the men ten years prison for keeping grain during the spring planting. Most of them never returned. Then in 1937-38, repressions began again. People were arrested and sent to prison even though they were not guilty. Again, none of them returned. Then in 1941 the war began and by decree of August 28, 1941 from the Supreme Soviet of the USSR, thousands and hundreds of thousands were accused of sabotage and all Germans from all over the country were arrested and exiled to Siberia and Kazakhstan. They lost all their property and livestock. Only two or three remained at the collective farms, just a few. Everyone was evacuated to areas away from the front. This was at the end of August, beginning of September. Harvest of grain was going on in the fields, stacks of grain lay at the collection points.

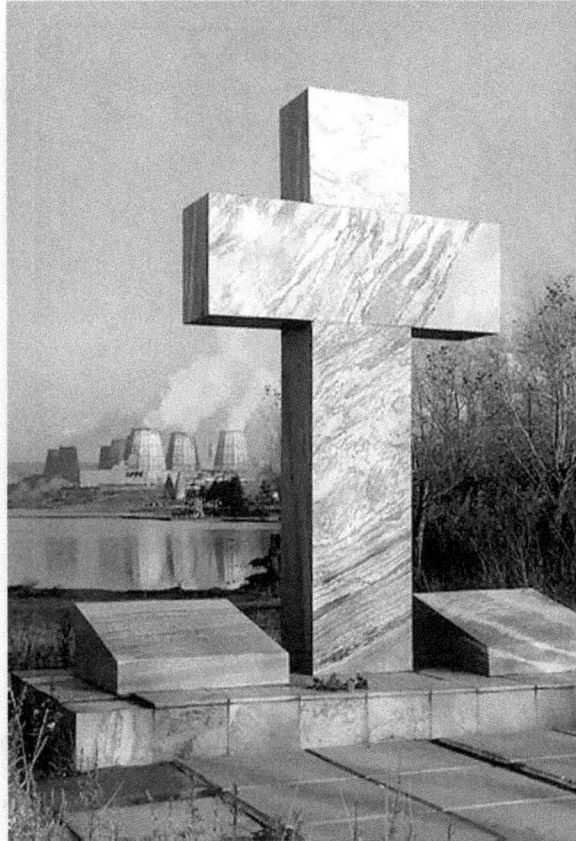

One of Russia's notorious labour camps in which thousands of Volga Germans lived, slaved away and died, was the Bogoslovlaga camp located in Sverdlovsk Oblast. Located near the city of Krasnoturinsk, the camp held over 20,000 people, mostly Volga Germans. Johannes Gerk, brother of Paul Gerk, and other members of the Gerk and Dieser families, were also incarcerated here. This is a Memorial set up near where the camp was housed. Source: rusdeutsch.ru

Almost all the implements, combines and tractors were taken for the war. Everything else was thrown to fate. People were taken on tractor carts pulled by horses to the railroad stations. My brother tried to take clothing and bedding and other property without the bed. Even the chairs were left. At the railroad station we were loaded into box cars which had carried grain and livestock. Fifty people in one car, without any conveniences. They took us to Omsk. Ten days we were on the road. From Omsk they took us to collective farms where they gave us a place to stay in dug-outs without windows and doors. We had to work at the collective farms until January 1942.

In January 1942 we men were mobilized by the Military Committee into the "Trudarmiya." Only families with children and the elderly remained. In such conditions many died from the cold and starvation, but in the summer they gathered the women and children older than 3 years. There was a woman who had to leave 5 – 6 children to the winds of fate. We men were taken to Omsk in horse drawn carts to the closest radio station. We were sent to a club where we waited for 13 days in railroad cars. Then we were transferred to wooden cars and transported to the northern Ural Mountains in the Trudarmiya to build the atomic factory.

On the way, which was 12 – 13 days, they kept us in barbed wire prison camps under military guard towers. They put us in two storey barracks, where we worked day and night almost naked and shoeless on the trees. In the camp were 13 barracks, but there was one bathhouse. People from only one barracks could go to the bath at a time and for sanitizing clothing. One evening we had to go to work. The bath house didn't operate during the day. All 13 barracks had to go and eat for 13 days without disinfection.

We were first fed 600 grams of bread, then the rations were reduced to 500 grams. We had to go to work at 6:00 am. There was also only one small kitchen in the camp. In the morning, we had to wait 3 hours to get soup from this kitchen. To get soup fed to all the Trudarmiya people, the first barracks had to get up at 3:00 am to go to the kitchen.

At 6:00 am we went through the gates under a strict count of everyone in the brigade. The counts had to be given to the office. We went to work under guard. It was 5 km to the site of construction. The rest of the people worked on dirt excavation, digging trenches 3 – 4 meters deep. It was winter work, and the temperature went to 40 below. The ground was frozen and the tools, like shovels, picks, mattocks, were iron and they broke.

The brigades were told how many cubic meters they had to excavate per day. If the brigade didn't excavate as much as they were told, the "desyatnik" [brigade leader] would not give them the note, and without the note from the desyatinik, the brigade would not be allowed back in the camp in the evening. Literally after a month

Taken in Krasnoturinsk, USSR. Standing Left to Right: Barbara (Dieser) Gerk, Johannes Gerk Sitting Left to Right: Anna Margareta (Rohwein) Gerk, Volodya (Waldemar) Gerk

people began dying along the road on the way home in the evening. We had to leave them lying along the road in the snow until a cart pulled by a horse could collect them.

The brigade wouldn't be allowed back in the camp until the watchman knew how many people were left. He would ask where the man was, and we would wait until they brought him. That is how people began to die. At the camps, all the leaders and head leaders were all Jews, and they lorded it over the Germans.

At the end of 1945, at the end of the war, the Trudarmiya was finished. But then came the "spetskomandatura," [Office of Special Populations] where we all had to be listed. They read to us and gave us a decree of permanent exile to sign where every month we had to report to the special office. We were forbidden to leave town without permission from the special office. Without permission, we could not even go to the railroad station, which was 3 kilometres from town, or to the next town, which was 15 km away. In 1965 the special office was eliminated, and we were given passports without the notation of "special population." But we were forbidden to go to our homeland. Then it was determined that we had no claims on our home at our homeland.

In 1971 I went to my homeland, to my village of Josefstal. There wasn't anything at all there. The village was completely liquidated. I found my father's large wooden house in another village named Novo-Nikolaevka, which earlier was Marienfeld. It was turned into a club, and was locked. Many villages in our republic have been completely liquidated today.

Those villages which still exist are in sorry condition. We Germans were removed from the special population, but that special population gave us obstacles and under the special population department there were Germans who were not allowed to get any work. For example, we worked temporarily for one steam electric station, and attached to our factory was a permanent steam electrostation. Because this big electrostation worked all the time, they closed our temporary station and tore it down. All the bosses and technical workers were all transferred to the big station, except for us Germans. They didn't give us any work. They wouldn't let us work at the electrostation, but moved us from the factory. Only now are German workers given responsible positions at various factories.

My memories about daily life.

I am Gerk, Ivan Georgievich, born February 22, 1911 in the village of Josefstal, ASSRNP, into a farming family. My parents were: father Gerk, Georg Georgievich, born 1868 in the village of Josefstal. He died on February 10, 1925 in Josefstal from intestinal cancer. Mama was Gerk, Anna Margaretha Heinrichovna, born 1868 in the village of Josefstal. Her maiden name was Rowein. She died on September 16, 1957 in the city of Krasnoturinsk, Sverdlovsk oblast after a stroke. The parents had 11 children, 7 sons and 4 daughters. I was the youngest of those brothers, having been born in Josefstal, ASSRNP on February 22, 1911.

I spent my childhood in Josefstal, I studied in the village 4-year school, which was also in Josefstal. After school I worked on my parents' farm. On October 24, 1929, I married Barbara Gerk, born 1909 in Josefstal. Her maiden name was Dieser. Until 1929 I farmed, then in 1930 I joined the collective farm, which sent me to courses at the tractor school. I completed courses at the tractor school in 1931-1932, and at the end of 1932 I went to the courses for the tractor brigade. At the end of 1933 I was drafted into the Red Army, where I was sent to school for junior commanders. I finished the courses with the rank of sergeant I served in the cavalry units

Johannes Gerk, youngest brother of Paul Gerk, circa 1971

until the beginning of 1938, when I was then chosen as the chairman of the collective farm where I worked until the end of 1939. Then I was chosen as the brigadier of a tractor brigade until the deportation in 1941. I was deported to the Omsk oblast in September 1941. At the beginning I worked as a combiner, then worked at a machine tractor station, as the brigadier in charge of tractor repair. On January 20, 1942, I was mobilized into the Trudarmiya, and went to work at the aluminum factory in the northern Urals. First I worked as a mechanic at the diesel electrostation, then I was transferred to the steam station as the master for repairs of the turbine department. From 1945 to 1953 I worked as the head of the turbine shop. In 1953 I was transferred to the aluminum factory where I worked as a master of repair work. I worked there until I retired in 1971.

In 1937 we had our daughter Valeria. She died at the age of 15 months in 1938. In 1939 son Volodya was born. Our second son, Eduard, was born in 1941, and he died in Siberia in 1942. When we were taken into the Trudarmiya, my family, mother, wife, and two aunts remained in the Omsk oblast at the collective farm. Later my brother Gottfried took my family to his place, because he lived in a different region 130 km. The move was made in February, on sleighs pulled by horses. On the way our second son Ewald contracted pneumonia and he died at the age of 16 months. In 1943 I was sent to the Omsk oblast section for the Trudarmiya, where I picked up my wife. My mother and son stayed with my brother. In 1946 I built a home in the city of Krasnoturinsk and brought my mother and son to the Urals. We lived there until August 1974, then we moved to Uzbekistan, to the city of Angren where we have lived until today. (Written Summer, 1989)
(Text Translated by Rick Rye)

143

Soviet-era Birth certificate for Ivan (Johannes) Gerk confirms his birth on February 22, 1911 in Josefstal. It was probably made using the Baptism record as a reference.

Soviet-era death certificate for Ivan (Johannes) Gerk confirms his death on April 25, 1996 in the city of Nizhnekamsk, USSR.

8 pages in his own hand-writing, transcribed in July of 1989, Johannes Gerk (Uncle Vanya) told me he would not sign the finished work. "I still have to go back to Russia…"

The House than John Built. This is the house that Johannes Gerk built once released from the Bogoslovlaga labour camp in Krasnoturinsk, in the Sverdlovsk (Yekaterinburg) Oblast of Russia. Standing Left to Right: Sveta (Gerk) Volkomurov, Alexander Gerk, Waldemar Volkomurov Photo courtesy Waldemar Volkomurov

Johannes Gerk, youngest brother of Paul Gerk, visited Canada in August of 1989. He is here standing at the grave of his brother Paul Gerk in Saint Theresa's Catholic cemetery, Kelowna, BC

DID YOU KNOW???

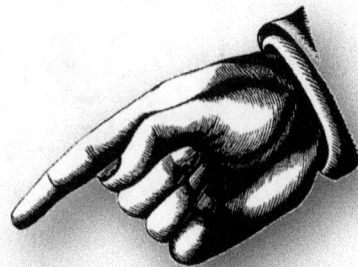

The Labour Camp that housed Johannes Gerk also had over twenty-thousand German-Russian inmates, all performing slave labour for the government of the USSR.

This one camp saw over 18 male members of the Gerk family live and work there. They included:

Gerk, August Ivanovich Born 1923 Kamenskii
Gerk, Adam Johannevich, born 1913 Iosefstal
Gerk, Georg Mateasovich, born 1912 Iosefstal
Gerk, Johannes Georgovich, born 1911 Iosefstal
Gerk, Johannes Jakoblevich, born 1911 Marienfeld
Gerk, Johannes Johannesovich, born 1903 Keller
Gerk, Johannes Mateasovich, born 1900 Iosefstal
Gerk, Johannes Iosefovich, born 1908 Marienfeld
Gerk, Iosef Mateasovich, born 1910 Iosefstal
Gerk, Iosef Robertovich, born 1923 Iosefstal
Gerk, Iosef Jakobevich, born 1909 Marienfeld
Gerk, Iosef Iosefovich, born 1921 Kamenskii
Gerk, Klementii Iosefovich, born 1908 Pfeifer
Gerk, Kospar Michaelovich, born 1904 Marienfeld
Gerk, Nikodemus Petrovich, born 1913 Iosefstal
Gerk, Robert Davidovich, born 1909 Iosefstal
Gerk, Franz Ivanovich, born 1912 Pfeifer
Gerk, Emanuel Iosipovich, born 1923 Pfeifer

Source: Kirillov V.M. , Kuz'mina P.M. (ed.)
GEDENKBUCH: «Kniga pamiati nemtsev-trudarmeitsev Bogoslovlaga. 1941-1946»

M.Distergeft. A step to the right, a step to the left ... (prisoners under escort). 1943. Camp in Karpinske. Ural Mountains. A paper, a pencil. Michael Vasilevich Distergeft (battalion (№687), with 1942 Museum «Creativity and a Gulag life» at International "Memorial"

Life in the USSR:
Top Photo: Gottfried Gerk and daughters circa 1962
Bottom Photo circa 1962: Standing Left to Right: Katarina (Gerk) Blattner, Kaspar Blattner,
Barbara (Dieser) Gerk, Johannes Gerk, Maria (Gerk) Valde, Peter Valde.
The Gerk's were all siblings of Paul Gerk

Little did they know….Anna Margareta (Rohwein) Gerk, mother of Paul Gerk, outlived Paul by 3 years. She died in Krasnoturinsk, USSR on September 16, 1957, without ever knowing if her son Paul was still alive. Paul died in 1954, not knowing whatever happened to his Mother. Top Photo: circa 1951 Bottom Photo: Funeral from September 1957
Source: Johannes Gerk

Top Photo: Standing Left to Right: Johannes Gerk, unknown daughter of Gottfried, Gottfried Gerk
Sitting: Left to Right: Elisabeth (Kisser) Gerk, Barbara (Dieser) Gerk, Anna (Gerk) Arnold
Circa 1962

Bottom Photo: Kaspar Blattner and wife Katharina (Gerk) Blattner, son Georg Blattner

The Gerk's were all siblings of Paul Gerk

Johannes Gerk kept in close contact with all the Gerk family. He is shown in the above photo with Lydia (Gerk) Stremel, the daughter of his brother Jakob Gerk, and her husband Jakob Stremel. The other photos are all taken around 1971 and are taken with his wife, Barbara (Dieser) Gerk.

Johannes Gerk visited Canada in 1989.

Grave of Maria (Gerk) Valde who died April 27, 1989 in Russkaya Poliana, Omsk Oblast, USSR.

Bottom Photo: Johannes Gerk stands at the burial of his sister Katharina (Gerk) Blattner, who died May 1, 1985 in Angren, Tashkent Oblast, USSR.
The Gerk's were all siblings of Paul Gerk

Photos of Kaspar Blattner and wife Katharina (Gerk) Blattner, with Johannes Gerk and wife Barbara (Dieser) Gerk
The Gerk's were all siblings of Paul Gerk

The Life of Paul & Elisabeth Gerk in Photographs

In Canada, Paul & Elisabeth lived without the threat of a knock on the door. They lived in a variety of homes, as Paul gradually bought and sold property to provide for his family. After 2 children were born to them in Holdfast, Saskatchewan (Edward & Mary) they came to the Rutland area of Kelowna around 1929, thanks to a tip by their close friends Georg & Katarina Stremel. Living on Black Mountain, their son Johnny was born in 1933.

The family lived in their little shack on Black Mountain until the early 1940's, where they moved around the Okanagan, with Paul building a small family home in Osoyoos. Both Paul & Elisabeth worked in the Osoyoos Hotel, with Paul managing it and Elisabeth working as a maid.

Eventually they moved back to the Kelowna area, up until the time of Paul's death on June 3, 1954.

Church was an important part of their family life. Both were extremely aware of the value of faith, and how that comforted and guided them from Russia...and the eventual tragedy of losing contact with their loved ones back in the Soviet Union.

Paul became a prominent member of the Catholic Knights of Columbus, obtaining their highest order as a 4th Degree Knight in June of 1953.

Through it all, the family never lost hope that sometime, somewhere, they would re-establish contact with family.

Sadly, Paul's ongoing health issues dealing with a serious ulcer, necessitated surgery in May of 1954. An abscessed tooth not reported to the physician gave Paul a serious infection, in which he succumbed to complications on June 3, 1954, at the age of 52.

The family was devastated.

This account in photographs and old documents, remembers our brave parents, grand-parents & great-grandparents, Paul & Elisabeth (Dieser) Gerk, and their children, Ed, Mary & Johnny.

Lonely cross stands in the abandoned cemetery in the village of Josefstal, Russia, where Paul & Elisabeth were born and raised.

Transition from Holdfast, Saskatchewan to Rutland, British Columbia. The children of Paul & Elisabeth Gerk: Edward, Mary & Johnny

Life on the farm on Black Mountain, Rutland.
First Communion of Ed & Mary. The 1930's

Life on the farm on Black Mountain, Rutland. The Bunkhouse. Son Johnny & friend. The 1930's

Bunk House on Black Mountain, Rutland.
The 1930's

Life on the farm on Black Mountain, Rutland.
The 1930's

DOMINION OF CANADA

NUMBER
15370

SERIES H

THE NATURALIZATION ACT

CERTIFICATE OF ACQUISITION OF BRITISH NATIONALITY BY A MARRIED WOMAN
WHOSE HUSBAND IS NATURALIZED UNDER THE SAID ACT.

I, the undersigned Secretary of State of Canada, do certify and declare that ELIZABETH GERK whose particulars are endorsed hereon, has acquired British nationality under the provisions of Section 13 subsection 3 of the said Act. In testimony whereof I have hereunto subscribed my name and affixed the Seal of the Department of the Secretary of State of Canada this SIXTEENTH day of DECEMBER 1936

THIS CERTIFICATE SHALL BE EFFECTIVE ON AND
FROM THE SIXTEENTH DECEMBER 36

E. H. Coleman

Particulars

ELIZABETH GERK

RUTLAND, BRITISH COLUMBIA, CANADA

HOUSEWIFE

JOSEPHSTHAL, RUSSIA
19TH AUGUST 1902

RUSSIAN

NONE

...S DECLARATION RUSSIAN

PAUL GERK

HIS OCCUPATION LABOURER

HIS NATIONALITY BRITISH

AGE 34 YEARS. HEIGHT 5 FEET 4 INCHES.

COLOUR WHITE COMPLEXION DARK

COLOUR OF EYES BLUE

Particulars

FULL NAME PAUL GERK

ADDRESS RUTLAND, BRITISH COL...

TRADE OR OCCUPATION LABOURER

PLACE AND DATE OF BIRTH (WHEN KNOWN) JOSEPHSTHAL 14TH JANUARY 1902

SUBJECT OF CITIZEN RUSSIA

MARRIED SINGLE WIDOWER (WIDOW) MARRIED

NAME OF WIFE (NOT HEREBY NAT...)

PARENTS SUBJECTS OF RUSSIA

AGE 34 YEARS HEIGHT 5 FEET 8

COLOUR WHITE COMPLEXION DARK...

COLOUR OF EYES GREY COLOUR OF HAIR BLACK

VISIBLE DISTINGUISHING MARKS MOLE ON CHIN AND OVER LEFT EYE

COUNTERSIGNED

DOMINION OF CANADA

NUMBER
143125

SERIES A

THE NATURALIZATION ACT

Certificate of Naturalization

I, the undersigned Secretary of State of Canada, do hereby certify and declare that PAUL GERK whose particulars are endorsed hereon, is hereby naturalized as a British subject that he is entitled to all political and other rights, powers and privileges, and subject to all obligations duties and liabilities to which a natural born British subject is entitled or subject and that he has to all intents and purposes the status of a natural born British subject. In testimony whereof I have hereunto subscribed my name and affixed the Seal of the Department of the Secretary of State of Canada this ELEVENTH day of JUNE 1936

THIS CERTIFICATE SHALL BE EFFECTIVE ON AND
FROM ELEVENTH DAY OF JUNE 36

E. H. Coleman

Paul & Elisabeth took their citizenship very seriously, both becoming Canadian citizens in the 1930's.

*Life on the farm on
Black Mountain,
Rutland. The 1930's*

*The house in
Penticton
Ed, Johnny & Mary*

Johnny Gerk at Black Mountain.

Life on the farm on Black Mountain, Rutland. Mary, Paul, Elisabeth and Johnny. The 1930's

Life in Osoyoos

Working at the Osoyoos Hotel

DOMINION OF CANADA
NATIONAL REGISTRATION REGULATIONS, 1940
REGISTRATION·CERTIFICATE

This certificate must always be carried upon the person of the registrant.

Electoral District No. 243 Yale (Name)
Polling Division No. 58 Osoyoos (Name if any)

THIS IS TO CERTIFY THAT

Paul Gerk

residing at Osoyoos

was duly registered under the above-mentioned Regulations this 19 day of Aug 1940.

D. E. Bimgee
Deputy Register.

Signature of Registrant
Paul Gerk

DOMINION OF CANADA
NATIONAL REGISTRATION REGULATIONS, 1940
REGISTRATION CERTIFICATE

This certificate must always be carried upon the person of the registrant.

Electoral District No. 243 Yale (Name)
Polling Division No. 58 Osoyoos (Name if any)

THIS IS TO CERTIFY THAT

Elizabeth Gerk

residing at Osoyoos B.C.

was duly registered under the above-mentioned Regulations this 19 day of Aug 1940.

D. E. Bimgee
Deputy Registrar.

Signature of Registrant
Elizabeth Gerk

KNIGHTS OF COLUMBUS

KofC

_____ Council No. ___
of _____ British Columbia

This is to Certify that

George Paul Gerk

received the honors of the Third Degree of the Knights of Columbus on _____ July _____ 19__

Francis P. Matthews
Supreme Knight

Joseph F. Lamb
Supreme Secretary

_____
Grand Knight

_____
Financial Secretary

COUNCIL SEAL

162

Above: Paul & Elisabeth and friends

Above: Paul & Elisabeth's son, Johnny Gerk

Above: Paul Gerk took this photo of the old Kelowna Post Office.
Left: Paul & Elisabeth with their close friends, the Georg & Katharine Stremel family of Kelowna. Stremel's were friends from Josefstal, Russia.

June 1953 was when Paul Gerk became a 4th Degree Knights of Columbus. He is seen here with wife Elisabeth and their friends the Dreiling family.

Blessing of new Saint Theresa Church: Paul Gerk can be seen leaving at the far left of the photo.

Paul Gerk purchased the cross that sits atop Saint Theresa's Church in Rutland. The gift was recorded as anonymous as per Paul's wishes.

Left: Paul & Elisabeth with granddaughter, Sharon Gerk

June 1953 was when Paul Gerk became a
4th Degree Knights of Columbus.

Obituary for Paul Gerk:
The Prospector
June 11, 1954 No. 30
Long-time friend Georg Stremel stands as an
honour guard at the grave of Paul Gerk

Large Numbers at P. Gerk Funeral

RUTLAND—On Saturday, June 5, Requiem High Mass was sung at St. Theresa's Church, Rutland for the repose of the soul of Paul Gerk; Rev. Father Frank Flynn being the celebrant, with B. Bachman as choirmaster.

Joe Dreiling and George Stremel, 4th degree Knights of Columbus, as was the departed brother Knight, and long time friends, formed a guard of honor. The pallbearers were George Bohn, Martin Dillman, Denis Schonberger, John Weisbeck, Paul Bach and Alex Sieben.

PRESIDENT OF KNIGHTS

Paul Gerk was born in Russia 52 years ago and came to Canada 30 years ago, and to the Rutland district, 5 years later. At the time of his passing he was head of the Knights of Columbus in the parish, having always been active in the affairs of that organization and in those of the parish in general.

A very large number assisted at the Requiem Mass, demonstrating the high esteem in which Paul was held by his fellow Knights and by the people of the parish.

He leaves to mourn his passing, his widow, two sons, Edward and John of Copper Mountain, one married daughter, Mrs. John Kloster and three grandchildren.   R.I.P.

Gerk family photo taken in 1946. Everyone in the family apparently hated this photograph!
Standing: Left to Right: Ed Gerk, Mary Gerk, John Gerk
Sitting Left to Right: Elisabeth (Dieser) Gerk, Paul Gerk

Elisabeth (Dieser) "Granny" Gerk
Photo: 1979

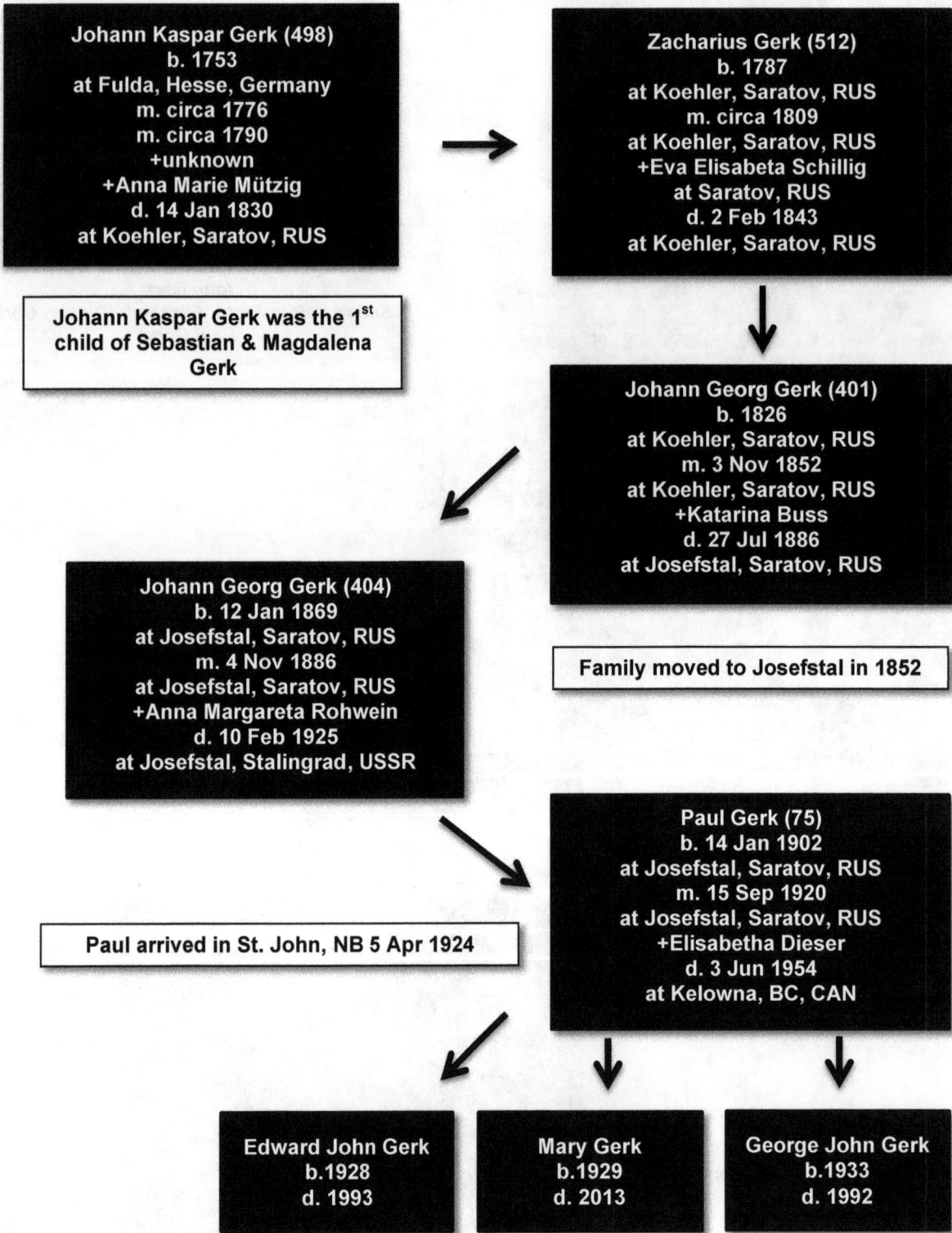

Johann Kaspar Gerk (498)
b. 1753
at Fulda, Hesse, Germany
m. circa 1776
m. circa 1790
+unknown
+Anna Marie Mützig
d. 14 Jan 1830
at Koehler, Saratov, RUS

Zacharius Gerk (512)
b. 1787
at Koehler, Saratov, RUS
m. circa 1809
at Koehler, Saratov, RUS
+Eva Elisabeta Schillig
at Saratov, RUS
d. 2 Feb 1843
at Koehler, Saratov, RUS

Johann Kaspar Gerk was the 1st child of Sebastian & Magdalena Gerk

Johann Georg Gerk (401)
b. 1826
at Koehler, Saratov, RUS
m. 3 Nov 1852
at Koehler, Saratov, RUS
+Katarina Buss
d. 27 Jul 1886
at Josefstal, Saratov, RUS

Johann Georg Gerk (404)
b. 12 Jan 1869
at Josefstal, Saratov, RUS
m. 4 Nov 1886
at Josefstal, Saratov, RUS
+Anna Margareta Rohwein
d. 10 Feb 1925
at Josefstal, Stalingrad, USSR

Family moved to Josefstal in 1852

Paul Gerk (75)
b. 14 Jan 1902
at Josefstal, Saratov, RUS
m. 15 Sep 1920
at Josefstal, Saratov, RUS
+Elisabetha Dieser
d. 3 Jun 1954
at Kelowna, BC, CAN

Paul arrived in St. John, NB 5 Apr 1924

Edward John Gerk
b.1928
d. 1993

Mary Gerk
b.1929
d. 2013

George John Gerk
b.1933
d. 1992

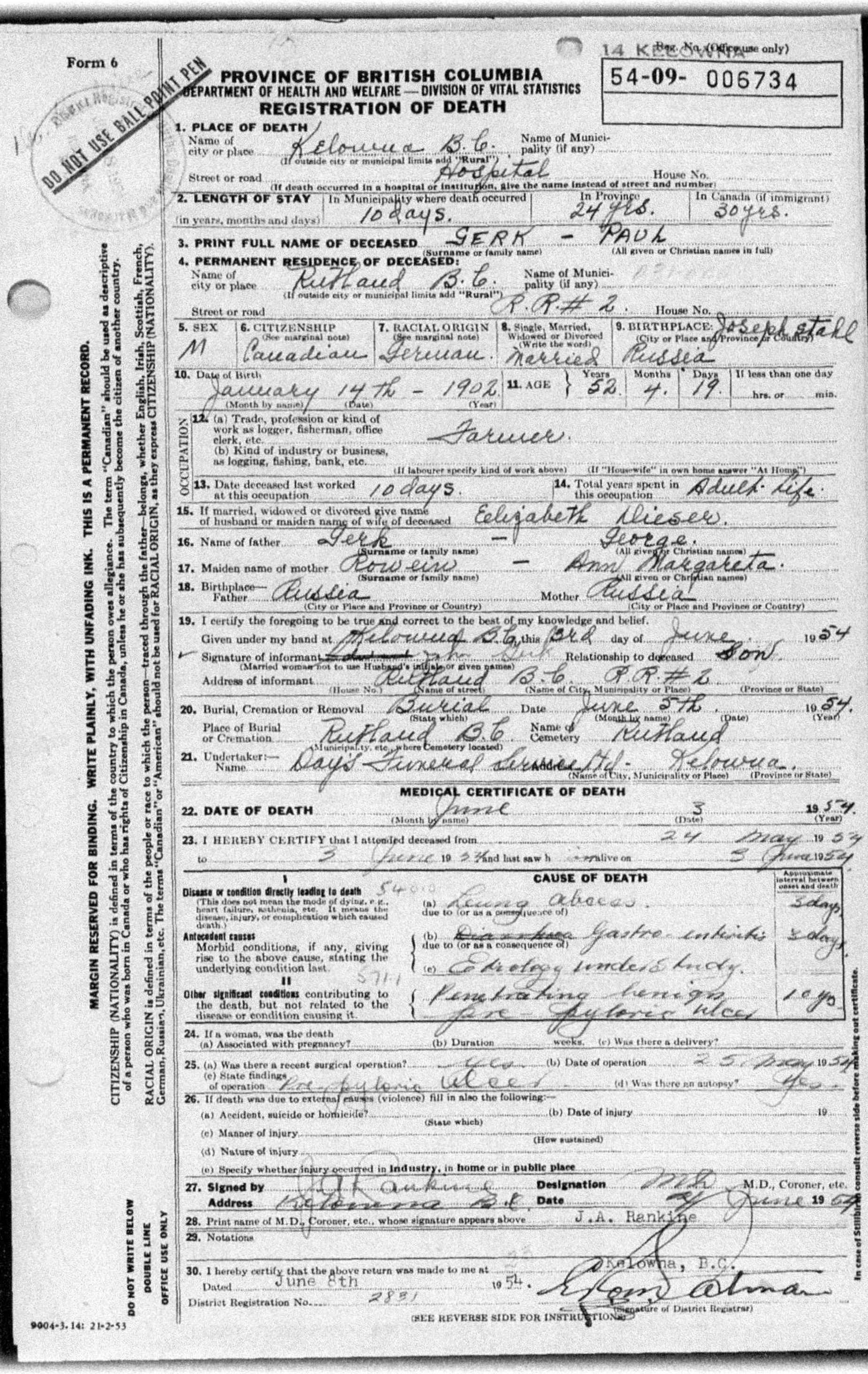

Death Record for Paul Gerk, 1954

Province of British Columbia
Ministry of Health
DIVISION OF VITAL STATISTICS

REGISTRATION OF
DEATH

Registration No.
(Department Use Only)
014303

SHADED AREAS — FOR OFFICE USE ONLY

THIS IS A PERMANENT LEGAL RECORD - TYPE OR PRINT PLAINLY - COMPLETE ALL ITEMS
DO NOT USE RED OR GREEN INK
(See reverse for legal requirements under the Vital Statistics Act)
IMPORTANT: Any change or correction made in the completion of this form must be initialled by the person certifying the original information

NAME OF DECEASED
1. SURNAME (Print or Type)
Gerk
ALL GIVEN NAMES (Print or Type)
Elizabeth
2. SEX M ☐ F ☑ UK ☐
DATE OF DEATH MM 08 DD 14 YY 91

PLACE OF DEATH
3. NAME OF HOSPITAL OR INSTITUTION (Otherwise give exact location where death occurred)
Kelowna General Hospital
L-302
CITY, TOWN OR OTHER PLACE (by name)
Kelowna
POSTAL CODE 3501Q V1Y 1T2
INSIDE MUNICIPAL LIMITS? STATE: ☑ YES ☐ NO

RESIDENCY INFORMATION AND USUAL ADDRESS
B.C. RESIDENT ☑   NON-RESIDENT ☐   IF BRITISH COLUMBIA RESIDENT, B.C. CARE CARD NO.
4. COMPLETE STREET ADDRESS if rural give exact location (Rtd Post Office or Rural Room address)
3 Links Manor 1449 Kelglen Cres. 3501Q
CITY, TOWN OR OTHER PLACE (by name) Kelowna
POSTAL CODE V1Y 8P4
INSIDE MUNICIPAL LIMITS? STATE: ☑ YES ☐ NO
PROVINCE (or country) B.C.

MARITAL STATUS
5. STATE 3
☐ SINGLE ☐ MARRIED ☑ WIDOWED ☐ DIVORCED
6. IF MARRIED, WIDOWED OR DIVORCED GIVE FULL NAME OF HUSBAND OR FULL MAIDEN NAME
Paul Gerk

OCCUPATION
7. KIND OF WORK DONE DURING MOST OF WORKING LIFE
Housewife
8. KIND OF BUSINESS OR INDUSTRY IN WHICH WORKED
At Home

BIRTHDATE
9. MONTH (by name), DAY, YEAR OF BIRTH
Aug. 19, 1902
10. AGE (YEARS) 88
IF UNDER 1 YEAR MONTHS 5 DAYS / IF UNDER 1 DAY HOURS MINUTES

BIRTHPLACE
11. CITY, TOWN OR OTHER PLACE
Russia
PROVINCE (or country) OF BIRTH 643
12. NATIVE INDIAN? ☐ YES ☐ NO

FATHER
13. SURNAME AND GIVEN NAMES OF FATHER (Print or Type)
Dieser: John
14. BIRTHPLACE – CITY OR PLACE, PROVINCE OR COUNTRY
Russia 643

MOTHER
15. MAIDEN SURNAME AND GIVEN NAMES OF MOTHER (Print or Type)
Unknown
16. BIRTHPLACE – CITY OR PLACE, PROVINCE OR COUNTRY
Russia 643

INFORMANT
SIGNATURE X Mary Kloster
DATE SIGNED Aug. 15/91
RELATIONSHIP TO DECEASED Daughter
ADDRESS OF INFORMANT 320 Patterson Rd. Kelowna, B.C.
POSTAL CODE V1X 2L2

TO BE COMPLETED BY FUNERAL DIRECTOR ONLY

DISPOSITION
17. TYPE OF DISPOSITION ☑ BURIAL ☐ CREMATION ☐ OTHER (SPECIFY)
18. BURIAL PERMIT No. AG 4810
19. DATE OF BURIAL / DISPOSITION MM 08 DD 17 YY 91
NAME AND ADDRESS OF CEMETERY, CREMATORIUM OR PLACE OF DISPOSITION
St. Theresa's Cemetery Kelowna, B.C.

FUNERAL DIRECTOR
NAME OF FUNERAL DIRECTOR OR PERSON IN CHARGE OF REMAINS (Print or Type)
The Garden Chapel
CLIENT NO. 892
ADDRESS 1134 Bernard Ave. Kelowna, B.C.

DO NOT WRITE BELOW THIS LINE – OFFICE USE ONLY

NOTATIONS

CERTIFICATION OF DISTRICT REGISTRAR
I CERTIFY THAT THIS RETURN WAS ACCEPTED BY ME ON THIS DATE AT:
Kelowna
BRITISH COLUMBIA
DATE Month 08 Day 15 Year 91
SIGNATURE OF DISTRICT REGISTRAR
REGISTRATION DISTRICT No. (24)

HLTH 406 REV 00/02

ATTENDING PHYSICIAN
MEDICAL CERTIFICATE OF DEATH

REGISTRATION No. (Department Use Only)
014303

of Death promptly to avoid delaying funeral arrangements. If the attending able to complete the Medical Certificate within 48 hours of death, the shall notify a coroner.

ALL GIVEN NAMES
ELIZABETH
AGE (YEARS) 88 yrs
SEX M ☐ F ☑ UK ☐
M.S.P. NUMBER

Kelowna Gen. Hospital

DE HYDRATION, HYR PROTEIN 2 WEEKS
5 YRS

MONTH AUG DAY 14 YEAR 91
DATE SIGNED MONTH AUG DAY 15 YEAR 91

Death Record for Elisabeth (Dieser) Gerk, 1991

170

The End?

The things that began to happen...were so great and beautiful that I cannot write them. And for us this is the end of all the stories, and we can most truly say that they all lived happily ever after. But for them it was only the beginning of the real story. All their life in this world and all their adventures in Narnia had only been the cover and the title page: now at last they were beginning Chapter One of the Great Story, which no one on earth has read: which goes on forever: in which every chapter is better than the one before.   -C.S. Lewis –The Chronicles of Narnia: The Last Battle

The history of the "Alberta Gerks" began with Peter and Suzanna Gerk. While Peter was born and raised in Russia, Suzanna was born in Argentina. Her father, Joseph Schenfeld, had a wandering spirit and had moved from Russia to Argentina with his wife, Anne Marguerite Burkhart, and their first two children. Anne Marguerite missed her family back in Russia, so they moved back to Russia.

In 1909, Joseph Schenfeld traveled to the United States. Joseph farmed in the US Mid-West for a number of years, saving his money, which he then converted to Russian currency. Joseph had hoped to return to Russia, but Russian currency became worthless during the first World War and he lost everything. He had to start saving again.

While Joseph was in the United States, the Russian Revolution took place and the Bolsheviks brought about national Communism. Peter and Suzanna married in 1920 and lived in a German village in Russia, where they had been allowed to keep their German customs and religion prior to the Revolution. As non-Russian minorities, Peter and Suzanna were forced by the Bolsheviks to work on the railroad for daily pay of one loaf of bread for their entire family. The Bolsheviks also set their main house on fire, so the family was forced to live in their summer cookhouse. During this time, Suzanna gave birth to four children. The first died as an infant.

Joseph had tried unsuccessfully to gain US citizenship, so he went to Canada in the winter of 1926 after hearing this country was still accepting new immigrants. Although Anne Marguerite still did not want to leave her family and home in Russia, she joined him in Canada in August 1927.

In August 1928, Peter and Suzanna left for Canada with their three small children. Peter spent all the money he had to bribe the local authorities to allow his family to leave Russia. Suzanna was also 7 months pregnant at the time. Pregnant women were not allowed on the boat to Canada, but Suzanna was a round woman and she lied to the doctors. The whole family only had one suitcase, with just their clothes and some food in it.

The family arrived in Quebec on September 1, 1928 on the *Empress of Scotland*. They waited overnight in Montreal before beginning a long train ride to Southern Alberta. There were no seats on the train for part of the journey, so the family had to stand. Their food also ran out, so Peter went off when the train stopped to work for bread and cheese, or to pick berries along the train tracks.

The family joined Suzanna's parents in Compeer, Alberta, which was located directly on the Alberta-Saskatchewan border. Peter worked helping in the fall harvest. Suzanna dug vegetables from neighbors who offered them to the family to help them. She gave birth to her fifth child, the first born in Canada, in early October 1928.

Farming had been easy in southern Alberta when Joseph arrived there due to the fertile soil, but the year after Peter and Suzanna arrived, the area had 7 years of drought. Peter and Suzanna struggled to feed their family while farming on a crop-share basis because they did not own any land.

In the fall of 1934, Peter, Suzanna and their children moved to the Peace Country near Brownvale, Alberta. The government offered them an incentive to move north, giving them a couple train box cards to move their household effects and stock. They lived in an empty, weed infested log shack on an abandoned farm, and Suzanna worked hard to make it into a home. The next spring, Peter began farming on leased land.

Together, Peter and Suzanna had a total of fifteen children. Suzanna was backbone of the family. She was often working in the fields while pregnant, and returned to work shortly after giving birth. She sewed clothes for her family and loved to cook. She was well known for her homemade bread. Moving to the Peace Country forced Suzanna to learn to speak English as she was very social by nature. She was also a very strong Catholic.

Peter was an easygoing man. He made homemade wine, tanned his own leather, and made harnesses and shoes for his horses. As his children got older, he often sent them to work outside of the home and used the money they earned to buy necessities for the family. Over the years, Peter managed to purchase about 6 quarters of land. Peter and Suzanna farmed for many years until they eventually retired to Fairview, Alberta, and both passed away there.

1958 Photograph of Peter Gerk, Susanna (Schoenfeld) Gerk, and Elisabeth (Dieser) Gerk. The families knew each other from Russia. Photo taken in front of Saint Theresa's Church in Rutland, BC.

Peter & Susanna Gerk & Family, circa 1970.
Source: Charmaine Gerk Moeller

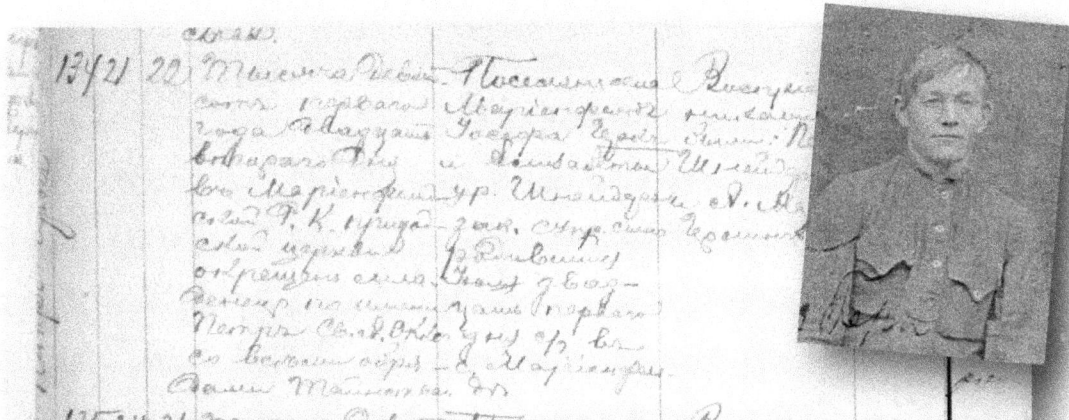

Baptism record for Peter Gerk dated 21 July 1901 in the village of Marienfeld. Peter was baptized the next day. The parents were Josef Gerk and Elisabetha Schneider
Source: GASO

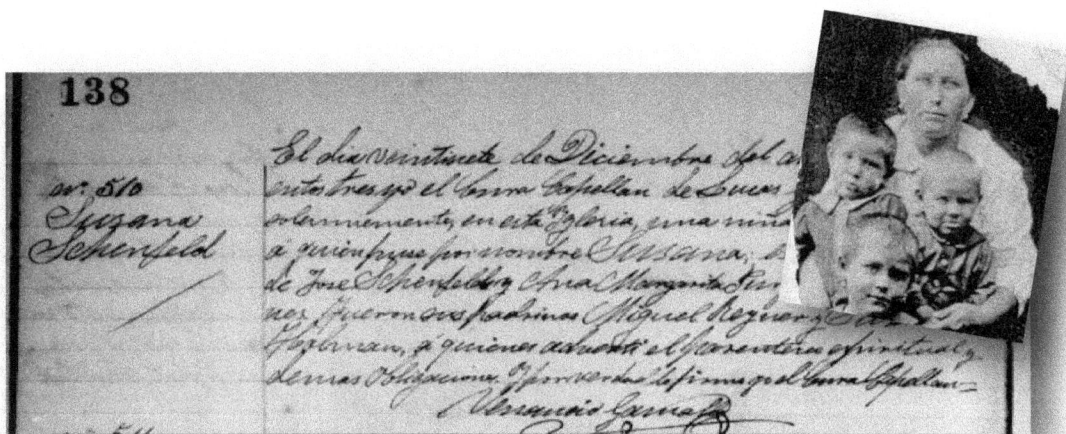

Baptism record for Susana Schenfeld, dated 26 December 1903 in the church at San Lucas Evangelista, Lucas González, Nogoyá, Entre Ríos, Argentina
Susana was baptized the next day. The parents were Josef Schenfeld and Anna Margareta Burkhardt
Source: familysearch.org

Photograph of Johannes Gerk, and his wife, Elisabeth Rachschreiba, circa
1929 in Marienfeld.
Johannes was a brother to Peter and was born in 1908 in Marienfeld
Source: Charmaine (Gerk) Moeller

Photograph of Kaspar Gerk, and his wife, Margaret Schoenfeld in Siberia
Kaspar was a brother to Peter and was born in 1903 in Marienfeld
Source: Charmaine (Gerk) Moeller

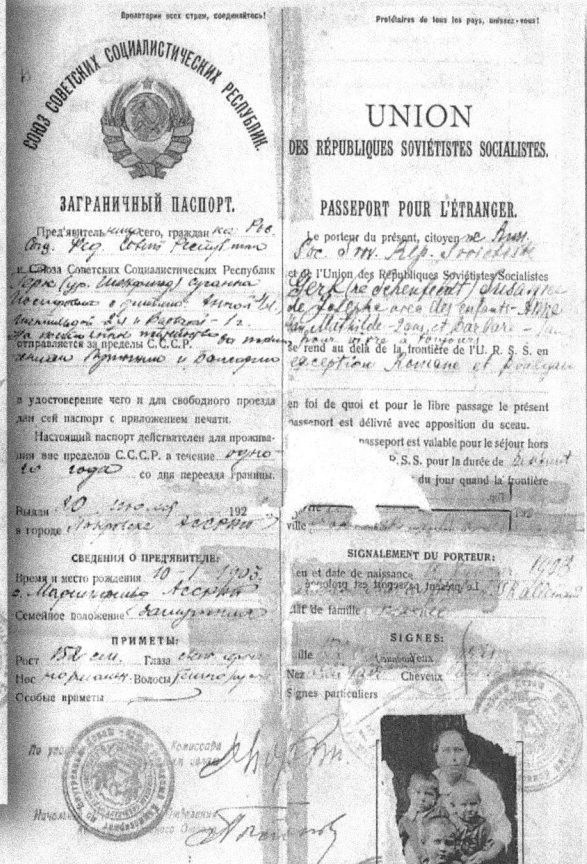

1928 Soviet Passports of Peter & Susanna Gerk
Source: Charmaine (Gerk) Moeller

Final Resting place of Peter & Susanna Gerk,
Friedenstahl cemetery near Fairview, Alberta.
Source: Charmaine (Gerk) Moeller

Johann Adam Gerk (501)
b. 1768
at Koehler, Saratov, Russia
m. 1788
+Barbara Schenk
d. 1816
at Koehler, Saratov, RUS

Johann Georg Gerk (570)
b. 1792
at Koehler, Saratov, Russia
m. 24 Jan 1810
+ Elisabetha Ruhl
d. 1831
at Koehler, Saratov, RUS

Johann Adam Gerk was the 6th child
of Sebastian & Magdalena Gerk

Johann Heinrich Gerk (572)
b. 26 Oct 1815
at Koehler, Saratov, Russia
m. 1838
+ Anna Maria Schectel
d. 18 May 1864
at Marienfeld, Saratov, RUS

Zacharius Gerk (816)
b. 1842
at Koehler, Saratov, Russia
m. 18 Nov 1862
m. 14 Nov 1867
+ Margareta Kloster
+Katarina Hergenrater
d. 5 Feb 1908
at Marienfeld, Saratov, RUS

Family moved to Marienfeld in 1852

Peter Gerk (907)
b. 15 Aug 1901
at Marienfeld, Saratov, Russia
m. 12 Feb 1920
+ Susanna Schoenfeld
d. 26 Mar 1975
at Fairview, Alberta, CAN

Arrv in
Quebec from
Southampton
1 Sept 1928
aboard SS
Empress of
Scotland

Josef Gerk (834)
b. 6 Sep 1871
at Marienfeld, Saratov, Russia
m. 11 Oct 1893
+ Elisabetha Schneider
d. 1915
at Marienfeld, Saratov, RUS

Josef Gerk
b.1921

Annie Gerk
b.1923

Matilda Gerk
b.1924

Barbara Gerk
b.1927

Peter Gerk
b.1928

Susanne Gerk
b.1929

Joseph Gerk
b.1931

John Gerk
b.1933

Amelia Gerk
b.1934

Wendlin Gerk
b.1935

Aloysius Gerk
b.1936

Marie Gerk
b.1938

Francis Gerk
b.1939

George Gerk
b.1940

Dennis Gerk
b.1945

This article was written by Geoff Gerk and is used with permission of the author. Taken from the book: "Whistlewind Recollections of Northeastern Colorado. (Copyright 1978)

You've Come A Long Way

Everybody throughout their lives listens to different stories and histories of their family. As a youngster, my grandfather, Jake Gerk, told me many stories of his life. Now as I have grown to appreciate the love of my grandfather, I have also grown to appreciate his stories. Here is the story of his life.

In the small town of Marienfeld, Russia, John Gerk and his wife gave birth to a son, Michael, on September 2, 1856. Mike grew up in this small farming community. In his early twenties, Mike met Katherine Kloster who became his wife. They farmed in this small German settlement for about five years. During these years they had two of their children, Barbara and Rose. After Rose was born, Mike decided to get out of Russia and go to South America. He found some land in the province of Entre Rios, Argentina, where he bought a section of land and started to farm again. He acquired this when a rancher was selling out. About 40 families bought this ranch and divided it. The owner gave these families the deal, "one for all and all for one." This proposition meant that if one farmer defaulted and failed to make his payments, the rancher could get all of the other family farms back. Mike nearly had his farm paid for when some other farmer defaulted. Mike had been farming since 1892 in Argentina.

"While he was there, he and my mother had six more children, Catherine, John, Elizabeth (Lizzy), Mary, Jake, that's me, and Mike. After the rancher took our land away he asked us to stay on and farm. We did until 1908, "stated Jake.

During that spring, Jake's father and some men were reading a farming magazine, and in the back with the ads, there was an article stating there was land to be homesteaded in Canada. Without even seeing the land, Mike and two other families sold all their possessions and headed for Canada.

"Not knowing what we were getting into, we left Argentina on May 10, 1908. We had two options on how to get there (Canada). We could go by ship to some part of the southern United States and then travel by rail to Canada, or we could travel to England, and from there go across the Atlantic Ocean again, and through the St. Lawrence Seaway. We went by way of England because it was cheaper. We made three stops in South America on our way to England. We left Buenos Aries and stopped at Montevideo, Uruguay and Rio de Janeiro, which was the original capitol of Brazil," said Jake.

On the steamship, they then headed out across the Atlantic for a long trip to Lisbon, Portugal. After a short stopover there, they went to Vigo, Spain, and finally, after twenty-one days at sea, they landed at their destination of Southampton, England. They then traveled by railroad across Britain to London and on to Liverpool. In Liverpool they boarded another steamship for the final leg of their journey from England to Canada.

Jake told me, "Shortly after leaving England, we were about to eat. We were below deck when the whole ship started to shake. It vibrated so bad that our supper spilled everywhere. We all ran to the top of the deck. We asked the deckhand what had happened. He told us a barge cut in front of our steamship. To keep the two ships from colliding, the captain shifted the ship into reverse while we were going about 15 knots to avoid the crash. Had the captain not done this, we surely would have wrecked." That was one of the few adventures the Gerk family had on their month long trip across the Atlantic. They sailed without a stop straight through the St. Lawrence Seaway to Quebec, Canada. The family then boarded a train to Montreal and then on to Winnipeg.

"Between Montreal and Winnipeg we had to get off onto a side rail to let another train pass. They had only one way traffic, so when another train came along, one of them had to pull off on the side or extra rails. The west bound trains had the right-of-way. While waiting for the train to pass, the passengers got out of the train," Jake recalled. "The strawberries on the ground were so thick that when we re-boarded the train, our shoes were stained red."

decided to end their journey in Hayes, Kansas, where they heard other Germans from Russia were living. Here they stayed during the months of July and August. Jakes' father, Mike, worked there on a farm as a hired hand.

In September of 1908, the Gerk family moved to Colorado. They moved to Windsor, where the area farmers were harvesting their crop of sugar beets. The family helped with the beets all autumn. The Gerk family would have taken up permanent residence in Windsor, but they had no Catholic Church, and Mike wanted his family to grow up where there was a church.

Mike and his family moved to Sterling in January

July 1908 is when the Michael Gerk family left Canada for the United States, according to Cross Border records.

Source: Citation: National Archives and Records Administration (NARA), Washington, D.C.; Manifests of Passengers Arriving at St. Albans, VT, District through Canadian Pacific and Atlantic Ports, 1895-1954; Record Group: 85, Records of the Immigration and Naturalization Service; Microfilm Serial: M1464: Microfilm Roll: 77: Line: 7

When the train resumed, it continued on to the province of Saskatchewan. Inside the province they went to their destination of Battleford. It was around this area they intended to purchase and homestead the land to start a new life.

There were no houses, so the three families had to spend their nights in tents. It was now the end of June, but the temperature was still very cold. Mike Gerk and the two other men left to see the future farmland. From the livery barn they rented a horse and buggy. They went with the realtor to see the land. The area was heavily wooded, and in many of the shaded areas there were snow drifts six to eight feet deep. After seeing the snow, the three men came to the unanimous conclusion that they had had enough of Canada.

The following day the Gerk family bade farewell to Canada as they loaded on a train for Kansas, USA. Their destination was not certain, so they

of 1909. He had raised enough money during that period of time to purchase a house. Some land, twenty miles north of Sterling, became available, so Mike, at the age of 54, bought a dry land farm in January of 1910. The family moved to the farm between Christmas and New Years to their newly acquired farm four miles north of the North Sterling Reservoir.

The land seemed to produce good crops of wheat and even a little dry land corn. Mike wanted to enlarge his farm after working it for eight years. He borrowed enough money to obtain the quarter section of land adjacent to his own farm in 1918. This was when some of the leaner years came along. Very little moisture fell on the Gerk farm between 1918 and 1923, and being dry land farming, the Gerks couldn't quite make it with the additional payments on the new land.

They sold out their farm and left their homestead and moved to the Iliff community. They farmed

Addendum to the February 15, 1857 tax census for Marienfeld adds the name of "illegitimate" Michael Gerk as the son of Johannes Gerk, and states Michael was 1 ½ at the time of the census. GAVO Fond 299, Opis 1, Delo 375

for one year on a rented farm four miles north of Iliff. The following year they moved their operation two miles south and farmed the Richardson place.

Early in January of 1825, Mike held a farm sale. At this time he sold all of his machinery. It was during 1925 that Jake and his younger brother, Mike Jr., purchased a threshing machine. This was Jake's first job away from the farm. They continued the business and were able to rent their own house.

Now with the appearance of Margaret Sommers, Jake heard wedding bells. On February 1, 1926, Mike Jr. moved out to Jake's house when the marriage took place. Margaret and Jake have had twelve children over 51 years of happy marriage.

Their early years of marriage were not easy. Mike retired at the age of 69. He and his wife moved into the house with the newlyweds. In 1928 Jake's mother, Katherine, died. Jake's father continued to live with them until his death 17 years later in September of 1943.

Jake and his brother Mike continued to operate their threshing machine as partners until 1836. On October first of that year, Jake bought a car repair shop on the south end of Iliff. For five years he repaired cars for the community, but farming was still in his blood. In 1942 Jake purchased a farm just west of Iliff. This farm had no improvements on it. The only structure standing on it was a chicken barn. The land was not in good condition to be farmed. On one end, there was a duck pond where water would drain and stand. Jake had dirt brought in and filled in the pond. During the spring, Jake had the entire farm leveled and heavily fertilized so the ground would contain enough nutrients in it to produce a good crop. To help build up the soil, Jake and his boys planted sweet clover, and when it had grown to maturity they plowed it under to strengthen the land. In the months and years that followed, Jake and his family constructed many buildings on their farm. Nine of their children were old enough to help with the building of the house, barn, garage, chicken coop, granary, and other small storage buildings.

"This place looked like hell when I bought it.

People said I was a damn fool for buying a place like this," Jake said, as he sat in his wooden chair. In this chair, at the age of 78, Jake can look out the window and see one of the best farms in the community. One of his sons, Herman, now does the majority of the farming, but Jake keeps very active. He and his wife Margaret live in the same house they build in the 1940's. In this house their twelve children, Joe (my father, Lawrence, Rose Mary, Margaret, Stanley, Dorothy, Regina, Agnes, Rita, Herman, Loretta, and Bill, have all grown up and left. They have 34 grandchildren and two great-grandchildren.

Only five years ago Jake could hardly get around with the aid of crutches. Since then he has had both of his arthritic hips operated on and replace. Now you may see him walking around his farm (without crutches) with a look of satisfaction on his face. As you look over his life you must say, "You've come a long way Jake Gerk-a long way."

Some addendums: Since writing this in 1978, research found Michael Gerk to be adopted by his father John (Johannes) Gerk in Russia.

This story is pretty much taking direct quotes from my grandfather, a man of few words, as he told the story in his heavily accented voice that I audio taped and then typed for a school project.

There are many other details that I've learned or knew but didn't include in the school project.
* I now have the crucifix that Michael carried in his hands during the entire trip from Argentina to Colorado.

* Mike left Russia because the Russian army wanted him to join their forces. He claimed to be German and not required to join their army. He got out, but others were forced to serve. Other Germans from Marienfeld settled in Iliff years later and had horror stories about the Russian army.

*When arriving in Hayes, Kansas, Michael found that his two brothers, whom he had left in Russia, were now in America. He thought they were working in steel mills in Pittsburgh, but found them in Hayes. They came to Colorado with Mike, and Peter settled 50 miles from Mike in Julesburg, Colorado. Joseph returned to Russia and was seldom heard from, with no communication after the early 1920's. He died in 1935, but this was not known until 2004.

* My grandfather remembered leaving his two oldest sisters in Argentina, as they were already

married and had families of their own by 1908. The last photos they had were of Rose and her husband Kaspar Stremel and their four children, and Barbara and her husband Lawrence Acevado and their five children. As my grandfather put it, they, "lost contact with them."

*Michael's daughter Mary lived in California. All of the other five children lived in Logan County, Colorado, and are buried in Sterling in the Catholic section of Riverside Cemetery. (Catherine Lell died November 1, 1918 in Sterling, Colorado. Her husband Peter Lell died July 25, 1933, also in Sterling).

* Mike spoke German, Russian, and Spanish, but said he was too old to learn another language so he spoke little English. German was spoken at home with him until he died. My father was fluent in German, having learned it prior to English. Iliff had many German and German from Russia families who spoke German, so Michael was able to communicate with his neighbors.

* Jake's farm is now operated primarily by grandsons Allen and Randy, and owned by his son, Herman.

My grandmother was also born in Argentina, and came to Colorado after arriving in Galveston, Texas, and then traveling by train to Colorado. Her parents, too, were Germans from Russia. Jake died October 11, 1986. Margaret died July 11, 1996. Their son Joe died May 12, 2003, and daughter Rose Mary died March 29, 2012.

> **Michael, Peter & Joseph Gerk of Colorado were second cousins of Jakob Gerk of South Dakota, and also second cousins of Peter Gerk of Santa Anita, Argentina.**

The Gerk Family: Taken Christmas 1909 or 1910
Front Row: Joseph Gerk, Katharina (Kloster) Gerk, Michael Sr. Gerk , Peter Gerk
Middle Row: Mike Jr. Gerk, Jake Gerk
Back Row: Elizabeth Gerk, John Gerk, Mary Gerk Source: Julie Gerk Campbell

Final resting place of Rosa "Kerk" Stremel, a daughter of Michael and Katarina Kloster Gerk. Rosa stayed in Argentina, marrying Kaspar Stremel in Crespo, Argentina in 1905. The photo is from the Crespo cemetery.

Photo courtesy Sergio Keiner

Final resting place of Gerk family patriarch Michael and his wife Katharina (Kloster) Gerk. Also Final resting place of Peter and Catherine (Dittler) Gerk. Riverside Cemetery, Sterling, Colorado. Photos courtesy Geoff Gerk

COLD CASE FILES:
The Mystery of the
Missing Gerk brother

Michael Gerk had two brothers, Peter and Joseph, who also settled in the United States. Around 1909, Joseph Gerk returned to his wife and family in Marienfeld. Nothing was heard from him after 1919. After numerous attempts at discovering what happened to him, the Gerk family in Colorado was finally reunited with members of Joseph's family in 2005. Joseph Hollman, Joseph Gerk's grandson, (son of Joseph's daughter, Rosa) tracked down members of the Gerk family from his new home in Germany.

Joseph Gerk (pictured above) died January 25, 1935 in Marienfeld. His wife, Katarina (Naab) Gerk, died in 1958.

Joseph Hollmann wrote:

"My mother is Rosalie Gerk, the daughter of Josef Gerk, also my grandfather. He had two brothers, Michaael and Peter, who with their families immigrated to Argentina 100 years ago. Before this, they lived in the village of Marienfeld, in the Saratov region on the Volga in Russia.

When my grandfather, Josef, went to Argentina he came to see his brother. I believe it was Michael. There was a wedding. His daughter got married. The wedding guests called Michael and told him that there were guests from Russia and among them his brother Josef. Michael was supposed to guess who among them was his brother. In front of Michael stood four men. (When Michael left Russia, his brother Josef, was still small, the youngest child in the family.) Then Michael said, "This young black man!" And they hugged each other. When Michael left for Argentina my grandfather was still small. His mother is deceased and later also his father and he was with his sisters until he was grown up.

After two years of being in Argentina (and the US), my grandfather came back to Marienfeld, and he wanted to go back to Argentina. But his wife didn't want to live away from her parents and siblings.

This entire history, I heard from my mother. She told me that often and then I made notes and paid attention.

In the year of 1941, all of my relatives were deported to Siberia and Kazakhstan. In January 1942, everybody sixteen years old and older, had to work in the Ural Mountains. Many died but the children of my grandfather made it despite hardship and hunger!

Now they are all deceased and their graves are scattered in Siberia, Kazakhstan and on the Volga. Between 1993-2002, most all of the Gerks left for Germany.

Together we are a large family: Hollmann, Naab, Meisler, Reich, Prediger. Our closeness helped us to survive."

As the family fills in the blanks over the history of the family and the tragedies they suffered, there is the satisfaction that the circle is now complete.

COLD CASE FILES:
The Mystery of the Colorado Michael Gerk

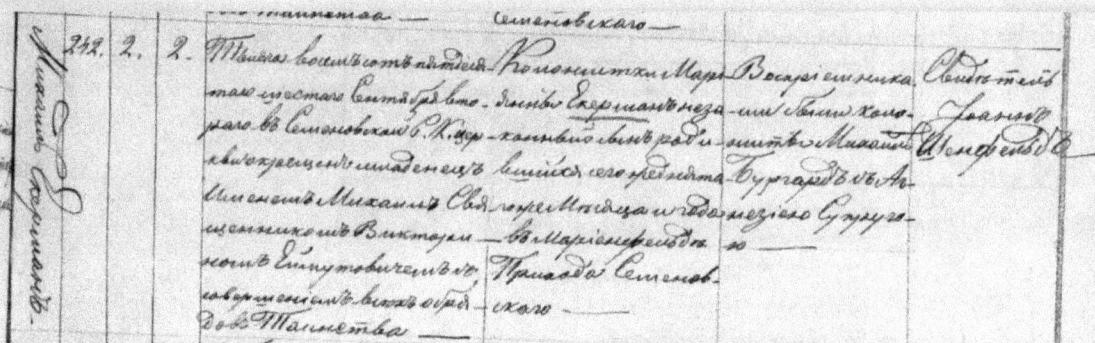

Sometimes, genealogy can uncover whispered secrets long since forgotten. That was the case with Michael Gerk, born September 2, 1856 in Marienfeld, Saratov Province, Russia. While researching the Gerk family, I was able to acquire the 1858 census for Marienfeld. Church records seemed silent about Michael's birth, which I just chalked up to a mistake by the archives. But the census should have shown his birth. I knew that, according to Church records, Michael's parents, Johannes Gerk and Maria Anna Eckerman, were married in Marienfeld on February 10, 1857.

But the original 1858 census that I obtained showed no children for both Johannes and Maria Anna.

Puzzled, I turned to the Gerk's of Colorado. They confirmed for me the rumours in the family about the situation…that Michael was indeed adopted. Individuals in the family had heard the story for years, but thought nothing of it…nor did they desire to spread was potentially just simple gossip.

But the situation still is a mystery. Who was Michael's real father? Was it Johannes Gerk? I later managed to obtain another copy of the original Russian census. There on the last page, was an addendum, listing Michael Gerk. It states that Michael was the "illegitimate child of Johannes Gerk's wife".

Given the strict religious conditions of the day, Michael's father was courageous for taking in and adopting a child that may or may not have been his.

But as to his origins…who knows? Finally, to add to the mystery, in 2017, I was able to obtain the baptism record for Michael Eckermann, born to Maria Eckerman on September 2, 1856. Michael's godfather was Michael Burgahrdt. Maria and Johannes would marry just a few months after Michael's birth.

We do know this. Michael lived in a loving home, raised a large family, courageously moved his family from Russia and proudly carried the name Gerk until his dying day.

Johann Adam Gerk (501)
b. 1768
at Koehler, Saratov, Russia
m. 1788
+Barbara Schenk
d. 1816
at Koehler, Saratov, RUS

Johann Adam Gerk was the 6th child
of Sebastian & Magdalena Gerk

Peter Gerk (573)
b. 1796
at Koehler, Saratov, Russia
m. 1817
+Anna Elisabeth Leonardt
d. 28 May 1854
at Marienfeld, Saratov, RUS

Family moved to Marienfeld in 1852

Johannes Gerk (734)
b. 25 Nov 1836
at Koehler, Saratov, Russia
m 10 Feb 1857
m. 7 Feb 1883
+Maria Anna Eckermann
+Margareta Schneider
d. 21 Nov 1902
at Marienfeld, Saratov, RUS

Michael Gerk (1204)
b. 2 Sep 1856
at Marienfeld, Saratov, Russia
m circa 1876
m. 7 Jun 1882
+Anna Marie Dittler
+Katarina Kloster
d. 4 Sep 1943
at Iliff, Colorado, USA

Family moved to Marienfeld in 1852

Left Hamburg 11 Nov 1886 for Argentina

Josef Gerk (741)
b. 27 Jul 1878
at Marienfeld, Saratov, Russia
m 29 Oct 1902
+Katarina Naab
d. 25 Jan 1935
at Marienfeld, USSR

Peter John Gerk (740)
b. 30 Jan 1876
at Marienfeld, Saratov, Russia
m 7 Nov 1900
+Katarina Dittler
d. 29 Oct 1957
at Julesburg, Colorado, USA

Arrv in Baltimore from Bremen
15 Apr 1908 Returned to Russia
circa 1910

Arrv in New York from Bremen 26 Nov 1910

Baptism record for Johannes Gerk dated 25 November 1836 in the village of Koehler. Johannes was baptized 6 Jan 1837. The parents were Peter Gerk and Anna Elisabeth Leonardt. Johannes is the father of Michael, Peter and Joseph Gerk.
Source: GASO

Marriage record for Johannes Gerk and Mariana Eckerman, dated 10 Feb 1857 in the village of Marienfeld.
They were the parents of Michael, Peter and Joseph Gerk.
Source: GASO

Death Record of Mariana Gerk, born Eckermann, the mother of Michael & Peter Gerk, dated 15 May 1882 in Marienfeld. It lists her husband as Johannes Gerk and children: Michael, Peter, Josef, Katarina and Margareta.
Source: GASO

Marriage record for widower Michael Gerk age 25 and widow Katharina Ziegler, nee Kloster age 24, dated 7 June 1882 in the village of Marienfeld.
Source: GASO

Baptism record for Josef Gerk dated 27 July 1878 in the village of Marienfeld. Josef was baptized the same day. The parents were Johannes Gerk and Marie Anna Eckermann
Source: GASO

Baptism record for Peter Gerk dated 30 Jan 1876 in the village of Marienfeld. Peter was baptized the next day. The parents were Johannes Gerk and Marie Anna Eckermann. Godparents were Phillip Roskof and Ekaterina Hergenrater.
Source: GASO

The Gerk Family of Iowa
By Lucille Hemann Mueller

(This article is an excerpt from the book: "The Families of Michael Halbach and John Brumm" by Lucille Hemann Mueller. Copyright: Palatine, Ill. : L.H. Mueller, 1990, Used with permission of author. The above photo is the grave of Heinrich and Lucrezia Gerk courtesy Sandra Huemann-Kelly)

The Gerk family came from Uffhausen by Grossenlüder in the German state of Hesse. At the time our ancestor Henry Gerk left there, Hesse would have been in the north central part of Germany. But after World War II and the division of that country, it formed the northeastern border of Western Germany. (Editors note: The borders have returned to their pre-WWII status with the reunification of Germany) Exactly what prompted Gerk to leave is not known since there appears to be no records and none of the living descendants can recall ever having been told a story about the emigration. One could venture a guess that the motivation was economic. What is known is that at the age of 26 he sailed from Bremen on the ship "Rosa" in April of 1844 with 300 gulden (a fairly sizeable amount of money) and arrived in New York on June 13th of that year. On the passenger list he is #88.

At this point the story gets very interesting because passenger #89 is Lucretia Seiring. The only information given on her is her age, 28 years old. (that being the case, it means she was born in 1816. But years later her gravestone gave her birth years as 1819) Unfortunately, no place of origin is shown for her, nor is there any mention of her being in the company of a relative, for instance a married sister who would not have the Seiring name. So how she happened to be the next passenger on the list after Gerk remains a mystery. The next record found on these two individuals is a marriage certificate issued only 3 weeks later in Schlessinger, Wisconsin, They were married at St. Peter and Paul Catholic Church on July 3, 1844. One descendant claims to have been told that Lucretia said she and Henry met on the boat which is possible since a search of Church records from the Uffhausen area does not show the Seiring name. By the same token, extensive research in communities in Germany (both East and West) that have or have had families by that name has not yielded a clue as to the origins of our Seiring.

There is also something of a question with regard to the number of children they had. Again, one descendant recalls hearing that there 13, but actual records of births and/or deaths can only be found on 9. Often times in the 19th century a child's name was not included in the family list until he was at least a year old. That would help explain the discrepancy in numbers. Nevertheless, at least one child is included who died the day of her birth. Be that as it may, the Gerk's show up in the census in Wisconsin for 3 decades. Sometime in the 1870's or 80's they joined several of their married children in Stacyville (Iowa) where they lived to celebrate their Golden Wedding in 1894.

ADDITIONAL INFORMATION:
Henricus Gerk, Sr. (son of Joannis Gerk and Maria Elisabetha Schlitzer) was born July 27, 1818 in Uffhausen, Kreis Fulda, Germany, and died February 13, 1904 in Stacyville, Iowa. He married Lucrezia Seiring on June 30, 1844. Lucrezia Seiring was born about January of 1819 in Kassel, Hesse Province, Germany, and died July 22, 1894 in Stacyville, Iowa.

DID YOU KNOW???

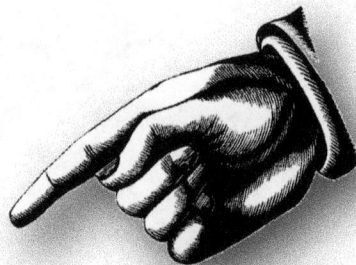

Henricus Gerk, Sr. (son of Joannis Gerk and Maria Elisabetha Schlitzer) was born July 27, 1818 in Uffhausen, Kreis Fulda, Germany. He immigrated June 13, 1844, to New York City, NY. The Fulda area is the same area that Sebastian Gerk, the first Gerk to Russia, was originally from.

Henry & Lucretia Gerk (undated photo)
Photo courtesy Bonnie (Halfmann Schiemann) Burnson

Henricus Gerk, Sr. was baptized
July 27, 1818, in St. George Church in
Grossenlüder, Diocese Fulda, Germany.
(Photo October 1994
by Edward Roy Gerk)

Application of Intent for U.S.
Citizenship of Henricus (Henry)
Gerk, Sr. April 5, 1847 Wisconsin

Catholic Cemetery, Stacyville, Mitchell County, Iowa. Graves of Heinrich and Lucrezia Gerk and other members of the Gerk family. Source: Sandra Huemann-Kelly

The hunt for information on the Gerk's of South Dakota was illusive. At times I wasn't even sure if it could be pursued, due to the little information available.

But persistence paid off, despite the fact that at the time of writing this book (2012) there no longer are any Gerk's who reside in this American state. In the 1980's I corresponded with Donald Gerk living in Minnesota, who was directly descended from the Gerk's of this area, through his father, Peter Gerk. Knowing little about the history of his family, he stated that he was always led to believe that the first Gerk to settle here was from Frankfurt, Germany.

New research has shown that this is not the case. Census records show that the first Gerk to South Dakota was Jakob Gerk, born in August of 1850 in Koehler, Saratov Province. His family will later move to the Province of Stavropol, Russia. According to the history of Marienfeld, in 1865, 17 people resettled in the village of Semenovka, and 29 people resettled in the village of Rozhdestvenskoye in the Kuban District [Caucasus].

Naturalization papers for Jakob confirm his birth in Russia, as do census records for the year 1900, 1920 and 1930.

What also can be ascertained from these archival documents show that Jakob was married twice, the second time to Ottilia Koehler, born in 1863, probably in the village of Semenovka, Saratov Province, Russia.
She was the daughter of Andreas Kehler and Anna Koch. The Jakob Gerk family moved from Russia via Hamburg on December 10, 1884, sailing on the SS Petropolis. Two of their children were born in Argentina, in the town of Tres Arryos, Province of Buenos Aires, Argentina. The family returned to Europe, probably in transit on their way to North America sometime in 1891 or 1892, where one child, William Philip, was born in 1892. They then traveled to the United States, arriving in the port of New York on September 3, 1892 aboard the SS Gallia. They then settled first near Marion Junction, South Dakota, and then in 1894 to Yankton, South Dakota.

Jakob and Ottilia were married in Russia Nov. 3, 1882. Jakob died Dec 2, 1935 in Yankton. Ottilia died 22 January, 1918 also in Yankton. Both are buried in Sacred Heart Catholic cemetery in Yankton. Their children were:

1. Jakob born Nov. 12, 1880 in Russia, died Nov 27, 1941 in San Diego CA.

2. Anna, born 1883 in Russia.
Married to John McInerrey on October 9, 1899.

3. Peter born Sept 16, 1888 in Tres Arroyos, Province of Buenos Aires, Argentina, died Nov 16 1960 in Minneapolis MN. Married to Agnes Knutson. These are Donald James Gerk and Robert Eugene Gerk's parents.

4. Valentine (Charles) born March 5, 1890 Tres Arroyos, Province of Buenos Aires, Argentina. Married to Anna K. Peshek on Sept. 4, 1911. He died in Jan 1967 in Deer Lodge, Montana.

5. William Philip born Aug 1892 in England. He died Jan 18, 1941 in South Sioux City, Nebraska.

6. Christina born Jan 1895 in Yankton, South Dakota. She had a son, Anton Gerk, born April 8, 1915. She married George Davies on April 9, 1951.

7. Maria born Mar 9, 1897 in Yankton, South Dakota.

8. Clara born Jan 1899 in Yankton, South Dakota. Married to Fred Moderegger on Nov 2, 1913.

9. John Arthur born Jul 9 1900 in Yankton, South Dakota. He died in May 1979 in Garland, Arkansas.

10. Joseph born Jun 24, 1905 in Yankton, South Dakota, died Jun 14, 1982 in Denver, CO.

The family farmed for many years in the Yankton area, and then the children seem to have moved to numerous areas in the United States.

Cemetery photo courtesy Don Freidel, Sacred Heart cemetery, Yankton, South Dakota

> **Michael, Peter & Joseph Gerk of Colorado were second cousins of Jakob Gerk of South Dakota.**

> **Johann Adam Gerk (501)**
> **b. 1768**
> **at Koehler, Saratov, Russia**
> **m. 1788**
> **+Barbara Schenk**
> **d. 1816**
> **at Koehler, Saratov, RUS**

> **Heinrich Gerk (574)**
> **b. 1799**
> **at Koehler, Saratov, Russia**
> **m. 1819**
> **+Kristina Ziegler**
> **d. 10 Sept 1848**
> **at Koehler, Saratov, RUS**

> **Johann Adam Gerk was the 6th child of Sebastian & Magdalena Gerk**

> **Family moved to Marienfeld in 1852**

> **Valentin Gerk (591)**
> **b. 1821**
> **at Koehler, Saratov, Russia**
> **m. 1841**
> **m. 26 Nov 1846**
> **+Katarina Mildenberger**
> **+Marie Eva Graf**
> **d. circa 1885**
> **at Rozhdestvenskoye, RUS**

> **Jakob Gerk (1959)**
> **b. 12 Aug 1850**
> **at Koehler, Saratov, Russia**
> **m. 6 Aug 1873**
> **m. 3 Nov 1882**
> **+Annastasia Roth**
> **+Ottilia Koehler**
> **d. 2 Dec 1935**
> **at Yankton, SD, USA**

> **Family moved to Rozhdestvenskoye, Stavropol Province, Russia, circa 1869**

Family #54 is the Valentin Gerk family from Koehler. The family consists of 12 people that include: Valentin Gerk, age 36, Valentin Gerk's wife Maria Eva Graf, age 29, 1st daughter Elisabeta age 4, 2nd daughter Katarina, age 2, 1st son Peter age 9, 2nd son Jakob age 6 ½, 3rd son Johannes age 8 days, Valentin's brother Johannes age 31, Johannes' wife Katarina age 27, 1st daughter Elisabeta age 8, 2nd daughter Katarina age 5 and Valentin's 2nd brother Johannes age 17. Valentin's son Jacob, age 6 ½ at the time of this census, will settle in South Dakota. Source: 1857 Koehler census GAVO Fond 299, Opis 1, Delo 375

Further proof that Jacob Gerk's parents were Valentin Gerk and Marie Eva Graf is found in the civil registration for birth of Jakob's son Charles Valentin Gerk, born March 5, 1890 in Tres Arroyos, Argentina. The grandparents, that are the parents of father Jakob Gerk, are listed on the document as Valentin Gerk and Eva Kraf. Source: Lorna (Gerk) Elberson

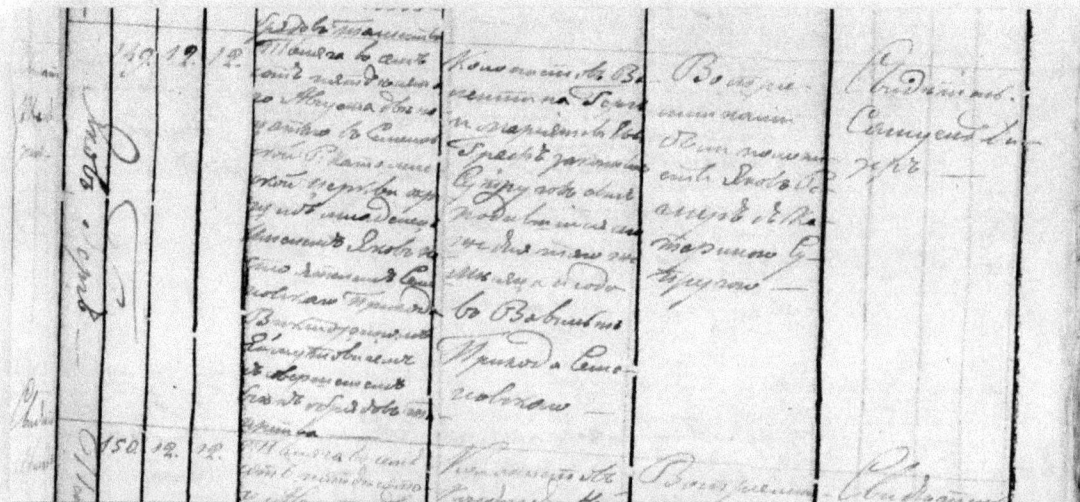

Birth/Baptism record for Jacob Gerk. Born 12 August 1850 in the Volga German village of Koehler, Baptized the same day in the Parish Church in Semenovka, just a few Kilometers away. Parents are Valentin Gerk and Eva Graf.

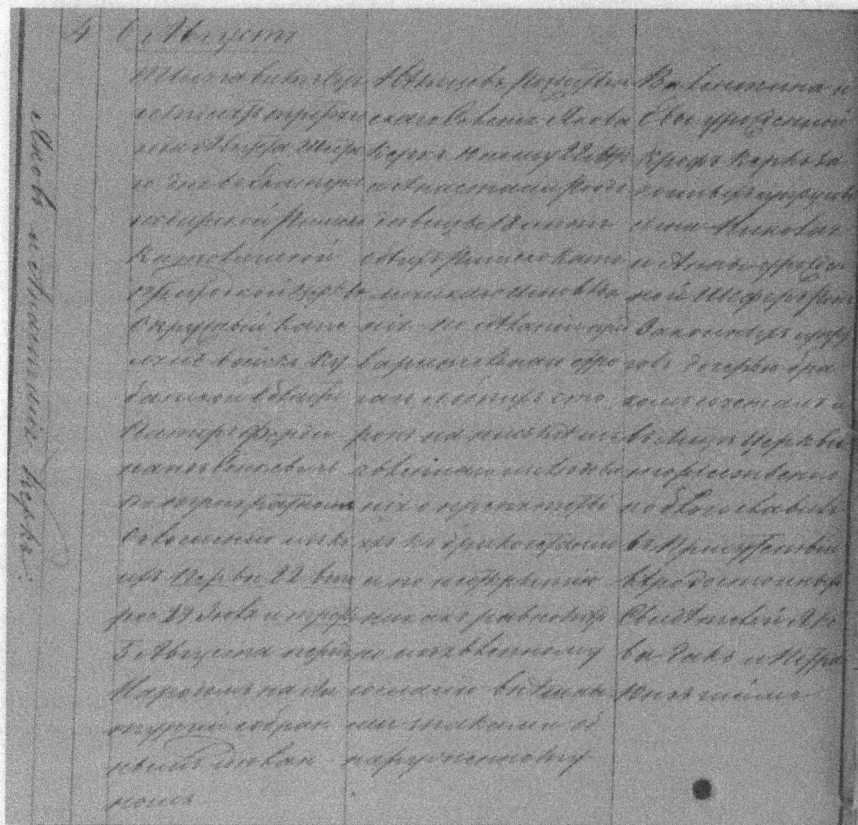

Marriage record for Jakob Kerk, age 22, and Annastasia Roth, age 18. Married in the Catholic Church in Ekaterinodar, Stavropol region, Russia, on 6 August 1873. Parents are Valetin Kerk and Eva Graf, and Nicolaus Roth and Anna Schaefer. This is Jakob's first wife. She would die shortly after, possibly after their first child was born, Jakob Jr. Note that the Gerk name was spelled phonetically, as "Kerk". Source: GASO

Top: Marriage record for widower Jakob Kerk, age 32 and Ottile Koehler, age 20. Married in the Catholic Church in Semenovka, Stavropol region, Russia, on 3 Novemeber 1882. Parents are Valetin Kerk and Eva Graf, and Andreas Koehler and Anna Koch.

Bottom: Jacob Gerk Jr.'s application for a certificate of American Citizenship, dated 1918. It wrongly states that he was born in Yankton, South Dakota.

Naturalization Record for Jacob Gerk dated March 6, 1899, confirming his birth in Russia.

1915 South Dakota State census also confirms Russia as the birthplace for Jakob & Ottilia Gerk.
Source: familysearch.org

DEATH OF MRS. JACOB GERK

Mrs. Jacob Gerk, after an illness of three years, died at 9:40 a. m. yesterday at the pioneer family home in east Yankton. The funeral has been arranged for 10 a. m. tomorrow, Thursday, from Sacred Heart church, Rev Lawrence Link officiating

Otillie Keller was born in Caucasus province, Russia, and was married in her native land in 1882 to Jacob Gerk. In 1884 they emigrated to South America, and in 1892, with their family, they came to South Dakota, settling first at Marion Junction, for two years, and then moving to Yankton to reside permanently. The deceased was quite well known and was highly regarded by a number of close friends.

The children are Jacob of San Diego, Cal.; Mrs. Anna McInerny, of Boston, Mass.; Peter, of Minneapolis, now home; Charles, of Miles City, also here; William, of old Company "M," Jersey City, or perhaps just sailed for France; Mrs. Christina Davis, of Yankton; Mrs. Marie Koontz, of Sioux City; Mrs. Fred Medewgger, also of Sioux City; John, of the sameplace, and Joe, of Yankton. The deceased

JACOB GERK DIES; FUNERAL THURSDAY

Jacob Gerk, 86, long time resident of Yankton, died at 5 o'clock Monday afternoon at the state hospital where he had been cared for recently. He resided for many years south of the lower highway on Fourth street, at the east outskirts of Yankton.

Funeral services will be held Thursday morning at 9:30 o'clock from Sacred Heart church. Until the hour for the funeral the body will be at the Kabeiseman and Donohoe Funeral Home on east Sixth street.

Mr. Gerk was preceded in death by his wife. Surviving are four daughters and six sons, most of whom reside at a distance. They are: Mrs. Anna Mack and Jacob Gerk, living in California; Mrs. George Davis, Yankton; Mrs. M. Kuntz, Stevens, S. D.; Mrs. Frank Dyer, Whiting, Ia.; Peter, Minneapolis; Charles, Deer Lodge, Mont.; William, South Sioux City, Neb.; Joseph, Auburn, Neb.; and John, of Blue Island, Ill.

Obituary for Otillie Gerk, January 24, 1918 Yankton Press & Dakotan

Obituary for Jacob Gerk, December 4, 1935 Yankton Press & Dakotan

Death record for Jacob Gerk states he was born in Germany.....which caused confusion among family members who then thought Jacob was born in Germany...not Russia.

Top: Left to Right: Christina Gerk, younger Gerk children, Marie Gerk.
Middle: Charles Gerk, Anna (Gerk) McInerney, john McInerney; Bottom:
Jakob Gerk and son Peter Gerk at Gerk family grave in Yankton Sacred
Heart Catholic Cemetery; Jakob Gerk, Yankton, South Dakota. Photos
courtesy Lorna Elberson

The Leopold Gerk Family of Wisconsin

Leopold Wilhelm Gerk and Julia Nauman came to America from Velbert, Germany (near Düsseldorf, Germany) in 1913 with their 7 children: Gottfried, Walter, Elfrieda, Emily, Emma, Leo, and Ernst. Left Antwerp, Belgium, on April 26, and sailed on the ship The Kroonland. Arrived at Ellis Island on May 7, 1913. Originally went to North Dakota. After a year, Leopold was injured in a fall from a hayloft, and moved to Sheboygan, WI, a large German community they had learned about. The entire Gerk family and descendants (except for 5) all still live in the Sheboygan Area.

Leopold was born December 30, 1871 in Steele, Germany (now Essen). Leopold Wilhelm Gerk´s father was Leopoldus Gerk, born 1844-Nov.-17 in Großenlüder/Germany. His wife: Gertrud Krämer, born 1852-Nov.-04 in Kruft/Germany.

Grossenlüder is in the Fulda area, ironically, the same area that the Gerk family of Iowa originated from. Of course, this is also the same area where Sebastian Gerk, the first Gerk to Russia, also originated.

(Thanks to Erica Gerk and Eva Gerk Zwickel for this background information)

WE DELIVER! . . . PHONE 2097

GERK BROS. CO.

IN THE
A. & P. STORE
1232 MICHIGAN AVENUE

Leopold Gerk Sr. Passes Away Here After An Illness

Leopold Gerk, Sr., aged 60, died this morning at 6:55 o'clock at his home, 1609 S. Fourteenth street.

Mr. Gerk was born in Germany December 30, 1871 and was married there to Julia Nauman on Nov. 22, 1896. The family came to this country in 1913, directly to this city. Mr. Gerk was employed at the Kohler company as a pattern maker for the past seventeen years. He was a member of the G. U. G. Germania society No 13.

Besides his wife, he is survived by three daughers, Mrs. Arthur Shuh and Mrs. John Wirtz of this city and Mrs. Harold Ertel of Kohler; four sons, Gottfried, Walter and Leo Jr., of this city and Ernst at home. There are also thirteen grandchildren and a brother in Germany.

Funeral services will be held Friday afternoon at 3 o'clock at the Gerk residence, 1609 S. Fourteenth street. The Rev. Martin Hueter of St Andrew's Lutheran church will officiate and burial will be made in Wildwood cemetery.

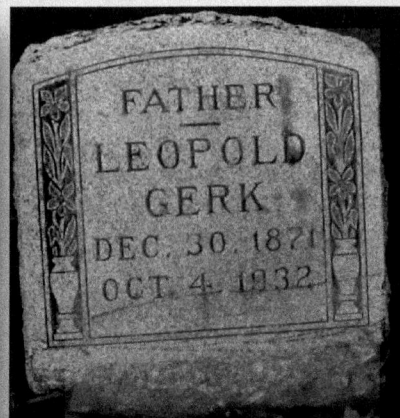

FATHER — LEOPOLD GERK
DEC. 30, 1871
OCT. 4, 1932

MOTHER — JULIA GERK
AUG 21, 1877
SEPT. 11, 1960

MRS. JULIA KALK

Mrs. Julia Kalk, 83, of 1537 S. 14th St., died Sunday morning at Sheboygan Memorial Hospital.

Mrs. Kalk, widow of Albert, was born in Germany Aug. 21, 1877, a daughter of the late Wilhelm and Julia Nauman.

She was educated in Germany and married there to Leopold Gerk in November, 1896.

The family came to America in the spring of 1913, settling first at Cancel, N.D., then moving to Sheboygan in the fall of that year.

Mr. Gerk died in October, 1932, and in 1938 she was married to Mr. Kalk of Sheboygan. He died in 1953.

She was a member of the South Side Golden Age Club.

Surviving are four sons, Gottfried, Walter, Leo and Ernst Gerk, all of Sheboygan; two daughters, Mrs. John (Emma) Wirtz, Sheboygan, and Mrs. Carl (Emily) Becker, Sacramento, Calif.; three stepsons, Isadore, Elmer and Anthony Kalk, all of Sheboygan; two stepdaughters, Mrs. Catherine Arnoldi, Sheboygan, and Mrs. Earl Krueger, East Troy, Wis.; a brother, John Nauman, Milwaukee; two sisters, Mrs. Emma Gruen and Mrs. Bertha Walthers, both in Germany; and 16 grandchildren and 39 great-grandchildren.

A daughter preceded her in death.

Services will be at 2 p.m. Wednesday at the Ramm Funeral Home with the Rev. August Grollmus, pastor of St. John's United Church of Christ, officiating. Burial will be in Wildwood Cemetery.

Friends may call at Ramm's from 4 p.m. Tuesday.

Previous page: Passenger List for the Leopold Gerk family. Source Citation: Year: 1913; Microfilm Serial: T715; Microfilm Roll: T715_2071; Line: 29; Page Number: 116. Passenger Lists of Vessels Arriving at New York, New York, 1820-1897; (National Archives Microfilm Publication M237, 675 rolls); Records of the U.S. Customs Service, Record Group 36; National Archives, Washington, D.C.

Above: Advertisement for the Gerk Brothers in the 1930's. Obituary for Leopold Gerk, October 4, 1932 Source: The Sheboygan Press. Obituary for Julia (Gerk) Kalk, widow of Leopold Gerk, September 12, 1960, The Sheboygan Press; Grave of Leopold & Julia Gerk, Wildwood cemetery.

According to research done by Helmut Gerk, Joseph A. Gerk of St. Louis, Missouri, was born on September 26, 1874, to John Francis Gerk and Barbara Hesch.

John Francis Gerk was born in Uffhausen, Hesse, Germany, in 1824. Uffhausen being a village in the Fulda area, where so many Gerk's originated from.

He emigrated and arrived in New York on May 17, 1847 aboard the SS Theodor Korner. Interestingly, he travelled with Martin Gerk, age 30, from the village of Müs, very close to Uffhausen. Martin will also settle in the St. Louis area.

John Francis Gerk married Barbara Hesch on October 6, 1849, in St. Louis, Missouri. They had 7 known children. He will die January 3, 1886.

Joseph was the youngest child. He would marry twice and have two known children, Joseph A. Gerk Junior, on November 6, 1902. Son Joseph will die on March 7, 1931. A daughter, Margaret, was born January 1, 1911. Joseph Senior will die April 7, 1957 in St. Louis.

Joseph Gerk was a well-known Police Officer in the St. Louis area, with him being Police Chief from 1925 to 1934.

Not much else is known about this family, as descendants seem to be largely unknown.

Death records for Joseph A. Gerk and his second wife, Corinne Gerk.
Source: Missouri State Archives

Graves of Joseph A. Gerk, wife Corinne Gerk and their son Joseph A. Gerk Jr.

Burial: Oak Grove Cemetery, St. Louis, Missouri

Source: Find A Grave

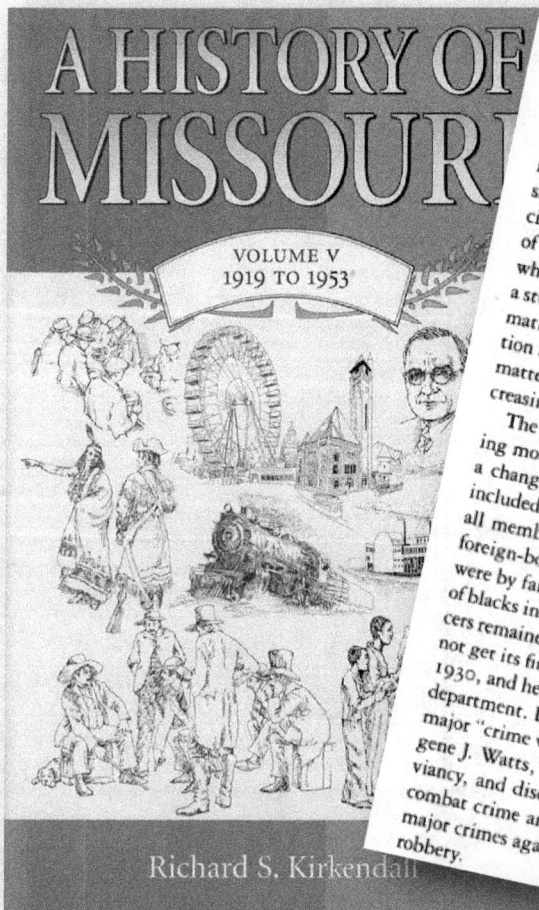

Missouri did have some tough and highly regarded policemen. Joseph Gerk, a veteran of the force, became chief in St. Louis in 1925 and served for over nine years. In that office, he was an implacable foe of gangs and police corruption, and his views on issues of law and order, frequently quoted in a press that had long admired him, included criticism of parole boards as ineffective and unnecessary and insistence that criminals should serve every day of their sentences. His fame extended beyond the city, and his peers elected him president of the International Association of Chiefs of Police for 1930–1931. "Gerk had the good fortune to be a student of the St. Louis police department at a particular point in the organization's history," whatever was rewarded at a particular point in the organization's history," matic and heroic when that mattered and gained recognition and promotion into the appropriate ranks. He became a technical expert when that mattered most, and was rewarded still further by an organization increasingly in need of his expertise."

The police force in which Gerk served was a very active one. Containing more officers than ever before, it was undergoing reform following a change from a Democratic to a Republican police board. Reforms included a rise in the level of education required of recruits. Nearly all members were white males, few were immigrants, but many had foreign-born parents, and Irish-Americans and German-Americans were by far the best-represented ethnic groups. Although appointment of blacks increased after Hyde's election, the number of black police officers remained small, only 1.4 percent of the force by 1930. The force did not get its first black sergeant until 1923, its first black lieutenant until 1930, and he, Ira Cooper, had been the first college graduate to join the department. Dominated by a conviction that the city was in the grip of a major "crime wave," the department engaged in what its historian, Eugene J. Watts, has called an "almost fanatical police war on crime, deviancy, and disorder." It relied heavily on wholesale apprehensions to combat crime and increased the arrest rate dramatically, especially for major crimes against people and property, such as murder, assault, and robbery.

Joseph Gerk was a "highly regarded policeman" who fought both "gangs and police corruption". See: A History of Missouri (V5), Volume V, 1919 to 1953, by Richard S. Kirkendall (University of Missouri Press)

253/47

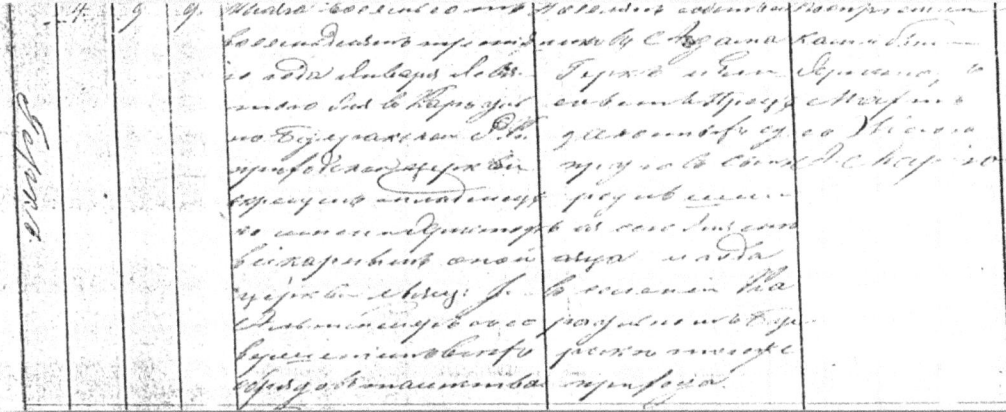

Baptism record of Christof Gerk, born 9 Jan 1883 in the village of Koehler, to Adam Gerk and Elisabetha Bretz. Baptized also on 9 Jan 1883. Source: GAVO

Top Photo: Christof Gerk circa 1943
Back Left to Right: Elisabeth (Kirchgessner) Gerk (wife of Christoph Gerk), Ferdinand Gerk, Wilhelm Gerk holding Alois & Wilhelm Gerk, Viktoria (Dietrich) Gerk with Erna Gerk, Maria Gerk
Front Left to Right: Johannes Gerk, Nikolaus Gerk

Johann Kaspar Gerk (498)
b. 1753
at Fulda, Hesse, Germany
m. circa 1776
m. circa 1790
+unknown
+Anna Marie Mützig
d. 14 Jan 1830
at Koehler, Saratov, RUS

Johann Heinrich Gerk (530)
b. 1802
at Koehler, Saratov, RUS
m. circa 1820
m. 21 Jul 1853
at Koehler, Saratov, RUS
+Maria Margareta Ziegler
+Margareta Schrack
d. 6 Jan 1877
at Koehler, Saratov, RUS

Johann Kaspar Gerk was the 1st child
of Sebastian & Magdalena Gerk

Johann Adam Gerk (643)
b. 1 Jan 1830
at Koehler, Saratov, RUS
m. 27 Jan 1848
m. 28 Jun 1882
at Koehler, Saratov, RUS
+Magdalena Macht
+Konstanzia Dieser
d. circa 1890
at Koehler, Saratov, RUS

Johann Adam Gerk (646)
b. 16 Feb 1853
at Koehler, Saratov, RUS
m. 6 Feb 1873
at Koehler, Saratov, RUS
+Elisabetha Bretz
d. Unknown
at Koehler, Saratov, RUS

Christof Gerk (1058)
b. 9 Jan 1883
at Koehler, Saratov, RUS
m. 8 Nov 1901
at Koehler, Saratov, RUS
+Elisabetha Kirchgessner
d. 1948
at Kassel, GER

Family moved to
Minsk in 1932
Family moved to
Germany in 1943

Maria Gerk
b.?

Barbara Gerk
b.?

Katarina Gerk
b.?

Adam Gerk
b.1904

Johannes Gerk
b.1912

Wilhelm Gerk
b.1915

208

The Gerk Family of Brazil
By Alexandre Gonçalves Gerk

Once upon a time there was a Gerk family living in Slivje, a small Slovenian village. Jožef Gerk (original Slovenian name), son of Antonio Gerk and Ines Rotow, had nine kids with his wife Katarina Abram: José, João, Chico, Maria, Tereza, Antônio, José (Pepe), André and Gaspar (all names here are in Portuguese).

At that time, Slovene wasn't a free country, but it was part of Austro-Hungarian Empire. They were a poor family, living in a very difficult time, and America was a very promising land.

In 1888 slavery was abolished in Brazil, and Brazil was encouraging people in Europe to immigrate.

Jožef Gerk, along with his wife Katarina Abram and their sons, (all but José, the eldest one), set sail from the port of Genova, Italy, aboard of the steam ship Orion. After a trip of one month, they arrived in Rio de Janeiro, Brazil, in December 24th of 1888. It is supposed that José didn't come on the same ship, but came later, alone.

They had come to work in the coffee plantations of Cantagalo. But after about one year, Jožef went back to Europe along with his eldest son José - and his kids -, and Maria - who married a Slovenian that came on the same ship Orion -, leaving his wife and all other children in Brazil. Jožef settled in Trieste, Italy, and their sons José and Maria (and her husband) went to Bosnia.

In approximately 1891, the whole family that was in Brazil, but Chico, went back to Europe. Once they arrived in Europe, they regretted what they did because there was no place for them. The money they could make working was barely enough to eat. They wanted to come back, but now they would have to pay the trip ticket

because they were not going as emigrants anymore….and they could not afford this.

João Gerk (Janez, in Slovene) went to work in the construction of a railway to make some money to help the family and to try to get back to Brazil, where he knew the conditions of living where better. He started working as a laborer, but the money he was making wasn't enough. He got a promotion latter, but also got sick, starved, and almost died. It was a very difficult time. When he arrived in Belarus, he already spoke 7 languages, and he could understand the Belarussian. He met a group of Belarussians that were going to Brazil, but they couldn't speak Portuguese. João offered himself to come with them to Brazil as a translator, in exchange he wouldn't have to pay the trip ticket. Finally João returned to Brazil.

Once again in Brazil, João Gerk worked in the coffee plantations, and the money he made with one year of work was enough to bring part of the family again – Tereza, Pepe, Antônio, and his mother Katarina. Jožef Gerk - his father -, and his brothers José, André, Maria and Gaspar, all died in Europe. After World War II, João Gerk helped José's son Roberto to go to Brazil with 3 of their 4 children (the forth seems to have settled in Australia).

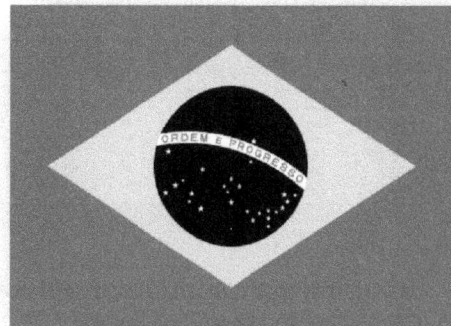

Brazil State Flag

209

Circa 1907: Left to Right: Mary Margaret, Christina and Rosaria, Maria (Purger) Gerk, Jannes Gerk, Jannes Jr Gerk Antonio Gerk.

As noted in this chapter, some of these Gerk's moved to Italy from Slovenia. They then immigrated to the United States, with many settling in the Ohio area. Here is the example of Joseph Gerk, born in Slivia, Italy, and arrived in the Port of New York on 27 Nov 1920 aboard the SS Argentina. But are they connected to the Gerk family that settled in Brazil? Source: Source Citation: Year: 1920; Microfilm Serial: T715; Microfilm Roll: T715_2881; Line: 21; Page Number: 239.

Ancestor

Dear Ancestor
Your tombstone stands among the rest; neglected and alone,
The name and date are chiseled out on polished marbled stone.
It reaches out to all who care, it is too late to mourn.
You did not know that I exist. You died and I was born.
Our blood contracts and beats a pulse entirely not our own.
Dear ancestor, the place you filled one hundred years ago
Spreads out among the ones you left,
who would have loved you so.
I wonder if you lived and loved. I wonder if you knew
That someday I would find this spot, and come to visit you.

Author: Unknown

The Martin Gerk Family of Santa María, Buenos Aires, Argentina

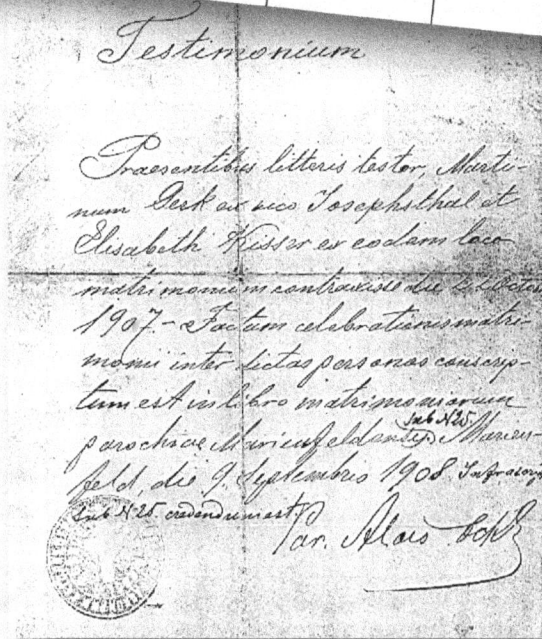

Photos Clockwise: 1908 Russian Passport of Martina and Elisabetha (Kisser) Gerk, Baptism record of Martin Gerk, born 10 Aug 1888 and baptized 11 Aug 1888 in Josefstal. (Source: GASO Fond 365, Op. 1, Del 696 List 317. Marriage record for Martin Gerk & Elisabetha Kisser, Tombstone of Martin and Elisabeth Gerk. Source: Maria Alicia Gerk

Johann Kaspar Gerk (498)
b. 1753
at Fulda, Hesse, Germany
m. circa 1776
m. circa 1790
+unknown
+Anna Marie Mützig
d. 14 Jan 1830
at Koehler, Saratov, RUS

Kristian Gerk (532)
b. 9 Aug 1807
at Koehler, Saratov, RUS
m. 2 Nov 1827
m. 28 Oct 1840
at Koehler, RUS
+Anna Maria Weisheim
+Maria Elisabetha Bisheimer
d. 23 Dec 1877
at Josefstal, Saratov, RUS

Johann Kaspar Gerk was the 1st child
of Sebastian & Magdalena Gerk

Family moved to Josefstal in 1852

Johann Georg Gerk (890)
b. 13 Jun 1856
at Josefstal, Saratov, RUS
m. 7 Jun 1877
m. 7 Nov 1883
at Josefstal, Saratov, RUS
+Anna Marie Senger
+Margareta Elisabetha Bauer
d. 1933
at Josefstal, Saratov, RUS

Nikolaus Gerk (555)
b. 21 Nov 1831
at Koehler, Saratov, RUS
m. 24 Nov 1853
at Josefstal, Saratov, RUS
+Katarina Margareta Ziegler
d. Unknown
at Josefstal, Saratov, RUS

Family moved to Josefstal in 1852

Martin Gerk (893)
b. 10 Aug 1888
at Josefstal, Saratov, RUS
m. 22 Oct 1907
at Josefstal, Saratov, RUS
+Elisabetha Kisser
d. 8 Oct 1953
at Pueblo Santa María, ARG

Elisa Gerk
b.1910

Margareta Gerk
b.1912

Andreas Gerk
b.1914

Jorge Gerk
b.1916

Sailed to Rio de Janeiro, Brazil
aboard SS Wurzburg 10 Oct 1908

Barbara Gerk
b.1921

Martin Gerk
b.1925

Anastasia Gerk
b.1918

José Gerk
b.1920

Juan Gerk
b.1926

Maria Gerk
b.1928

Baptismal record for Peter Gerk, born 2 Jul 1858 in the village of Koehler, and baptized on 3 Jul 1858. Parents were Kristof Gerk and Maria Margareta Kirchgessner. Source: GAVO

Photograph circa 1914, is of Peter Gerk, Elisabeth Sanger and 4 of their children.

Source: Juan Alberto Saccomani

Johann Kaspar Gerk (498)
b. 1753
at Fulda, Hesse, Germany
m. circa 1776
m. circa 1790
+unknown
+Anna Marie Mützig
d. 14 Jan 1830
at Koehler, Saratov, RUS

Johann Heinrich Gerk (530)
b. 1802
at Koehler, Saratov, RUS
m. circa 1820
m. 21 Jul 1853
at Koehler, Saratov, RUS
+Maria Margareta Ziegler
+Margareta Schrack
d. 6 Jan 1877
at Koehler, Saratov, RUS

Johann Kaspar Gerk was the 1st child
of Sebastian & Magdalena Gerk

Kristof Gerk (534)
b. 1823
at Koehler, Saratov, RUS
m. 11 Nov 1841
at Koehler, Saratov, RUS
+Maria Margareta Kirchgessner
d. 21 Dec 1874
at Koehler, Saratov, RUS

Peter Gerk (1875)
b. 2 Jul 1858
at Koehler, Saratov, RUS
m. 12 Oct 1876
at Koehler, Saratov, RUS
+Elisabeth Sanger
d. 25 Mar 1939
at Crespo, ARG

Family moved to Argentina in 1886

Nikolaus Gerk
b.1878

Margareta Gerk
b.1879

Jakob Gerk
b.1881

Elisabetha Gerk
b.1883

Valentine Gerk
b.1887

Isabel Gerk
b.1888

Juan Gerk
b.1890

Nikolaus Gerk
b.1892

Pedro Gerk
b.1893

Maria Gerk
b.1896

Theresia Gerk
b.1898

Jesus! Maria!

„Selig sind d
sterben, spricht
sie von ihren L.
löhnen nach."

Zum frommen Andenken im Gebete
an den selig im Herrn entschlafenen

Jakob Gerk

Er war geboren am 15. November 1881 in
der Kolonie Kohler (Rußland) als Sohn der
Eheleute Peter Gerk und Elisabeth Sänger,
mit denen er 1896 nach Argentinien kam.

Er starb, gut vorbereitet, am 25. August
1941 und hinterläßt seine tiefbetrübte Ehefrau
Elisabeth Sommer, mit welcher er seit 1903
in glücklicher Ehe lebte; außerdem 2 Söhne.

Gebet

O Herr, allmächtiger Gott, wir bitten Dich
um des kostbaren Blutes Jesu willen, Du
wollest die Seele Deines Dieners **Paul**
in die ewigen Freuden aufnehmen, der Du
lebst und regierst in Ewigkeit. Amen.

Herr, gib ihm die ewige Ruhe, und das
ewige Licht leuchte ihm. Laß ihn ruhen in
Frieden. Amen.
(300 Tage Ablaß)
„Alles für Dich, heiligstes Herz Jesu."
(300 Tage Ablaß)

Mein Jesus, Barmherzigkeit!
(300 Tage Ablaß.)

Süßes Herz Mariä, sei meine Rettung!
(300 Tage Ablaß.)

Jesus, Maria, Joseph! Euch schenke ich mein
Herz und meine Seele!
(7 Jahre Ablaß.)

Jesus, Maria, Joseph! Steht mir bei im
letzten Todeskampfe!
(7 Jahre Ablaß.)

Jesus, Maria, Joseph! Möge meine Seele
mit Euch im Frieden scheiden!
(7 Jahre Ablaß.)

Vater unser... Gegrüßet seist du... Ehre sei...

Mit firchlicher Gutheißung.

Baptismal record for Jakob Gerk, born 21 October 1881 Old Style, in the village of Koehler, and baptized the same day. Parents were Peter Gerk and Elisabeth Sanger. Jakob was the only child born in Russia before the family moved to Argentina. Jakob's death announcement states he was born in November of 1881, an attempt to match Old Style date with New Style. Source: GAVO

Baptismal record for Peter Gerk, dated 17 Dec 1893, born in the village of Crespo. Notice how the last name has been changed to "Kerck".

Son of Pedro Kerck and Isabella Kerck.

Source: familysearch.org

217

Top Photo: This 1915 photo, is the marriage of Peter Gerk and Margarita Kloster.

Bottom: Peter Gerk and children circa 1942

Source: Juan Alberto Saccomani; familysearch.org/

Marriage record for Peter Alois Gerk and
Isabel Elena Gerk, dated 12 Aug 1919 in
Crespo, Entre Ríos, Argentina. Isabel is the
cousin of Paul Gerk. Peter Alois Gerk was
also the 2nd cousin of Paul Gerk. The
whereabouts of this family remain a mystery.
Source: familysearch.org

Birth record for Rafael Gerk, born
16 Nov 1920 in Crespo. Whatever
happened to him?
Source: familysearch.org

Marriage record for Santiago
Kerg and wife Rose Schonfeld,
(pictured here) dated 12 April
1932 in Bovril. Santiago lists
his parents as Pedro Kerg and
Catalalina Prit, which are Peter
Gerk and Catarina Breit. On
this document there is no
known residence for
Santiago's parents. Santiago
died 10 Mar 1982 in Sunchales,
Santa Fe, Argentina.
Source: Gustavo Kerk

Johann Kaspar Gerk (498)
b. 1753
at Fulda, Hesse, Germany
m. circa 1776
m. circa 1790
+unknown
+Anna Marie Mützig
d. 14 Jan 1830
at Koehler, Saratov, RUS

Zacharius Gerk (512)
b. 1787
at Koehler, Saratov, RUS
m. circa 1809
at Koehler, Saratov, RUS
+Eva Elisabeta Schilling
b. 1790
at Saratov, RUS
d. 2 Feb 1843
at Koehler, Saratov, RUS

Johann Kaspar Gerk was the 1st child
of Sebastian & Magdalena Gerk

Gottlieb Gerk (515)
b. 1822
at Koehler, Saratov, RUS
m. 25 Nov 1846
at Koehler, Saratov, RUS
+Julia Gittlein
d. 1 Jul 1894
at Josefstal, Saratov, RUS

Johannes Gerk (752)
b. 25 Jan 1849
at Koehler, Saratov, RUS
m. 9 Nov 1865
at Josefstal, Saratov, RUS
+Margareta Pitz
d. 28 Aug 1877
at Josefstal, Saratov, RUS

Family moved to Josefstal in 1852

Peter Alois Gerk (754)
b. 28 Jan 1871
at Josefstal, Saratov, RUS
m. 16 Nov 1897
m. 12 Aug 1919
at Josefstal, Saratov, RUS
at Crespo, Entre Ríos, ARG
+Anna Katarina Breit
+Elisabetha Helena Gerk
d. unknown
at Argentina

Magdalena Gerk
b.1906

Georg Gerk
b.1908

Sailed from
Bremen,
Germany to
Rio de
Janeiro, Brazil
aboard SS
Coblenz
23 Jan 1909

Santiago Kerg
b.1911

Juan Gerk
b.1915

Juan Gerk
b.1917

Kaspar Gerk
b.1917

Rafael Gerk
b.1920

Miguel Gerk
b.1925

The Johann Adam Gerk Family of San Miguel Arcángel, Buenos Aires, Argentina

Johann Adam Gerk of San Miguel Arcángel, Argentina was the 1st cousin of Joseph Gerk, also of San Miguel Arcángel.

Baptism record of Johann Adam Gerk, born 27 March 1877 in Marienfeld and baptized the same day. Son of Zacharius Gerk and Katarina Hergenraeder. Godparents were Adam Lambrecht and Anna Marie Konrad. Source: GASO Fond 365

Top Photo: Johann Adam Gerk and Anna Marie Gette.
Bottom Photo: Grave of Johann Adam Gerk and Anna Marie Gette-Gerk in Bahía Blanca, Buenos Aires, Argentina.
Source: Apolo Ramírez Redel

Johann Adam Gerk (501)
b. 1768
at Koehler, Saratov, Russia
m. 1788
+Barbara Schenk
d. 1816
at Koehler, Saratov, RUS

Johann Georg Gerk (570)
b. 1792
at Koehler, Saratov, Russia
m. 24 Jan 1810
+ Elisabetha Ruhl
d. 1831
at Koehler, Saratov, RUS

Johann Adam Gerk was the 6th child
of Sebastian & Magdalena Gerk

Zacharius Gerk (816)
b. 1842
at Koehler, Saratov, Russia
m. 18 Nov 1862
m. 14 Nov 1867
+ Margareta Kloster
+Katarina Hergenrater
d. 5 Feb 1908
at Marienfeld, Saratov, RUS

Johann Heinrich Gerk (572)
b. 26 Oct 1815
at Koehler, Saratov, Russia
m. 1838
+ Anna Maria Schectel
d. 18 May 1864
at Marienfeld, Saratov, RUS

Johann Adam Gerk (821)
b. 27 Mar 1877
at Marienfeld, Saratov, Russia
m. 28 Nov 1900
+ Anna Marie Gette
d. 10 Jul 1949
at Bahía Blanca, Buenos Aires, ARG

Family moved to Marienfeld in 1852

Margareta Gerk
b.1901

Adam Gerk
b.1903

Alexander Gerk
b.1905

Pedro Gerk
b.1908

Anna Gerk
b.1912

Manuel Gerk
b.1915

Rosa Gerk
b.1916

Juan Gerk
b.1918

Nicolás Gerk
b.1921

Clemente Gerk
b.1923

Bárbara Gerk
b.1924

Cataline Gerk
b.1926

Maria Gerk
b.???

Family moved to
Argentina circa 1905

222

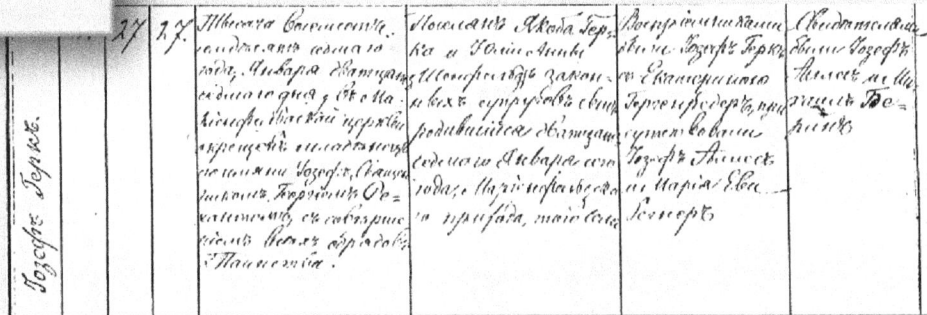

Baptism record of Josef Gerk, born 27 Jan 1877 in Marienfeld and baptized the same day. son of Jakob Gerk and Juliana Schoenfeld. Godparents were Josef Gerk and Ekaterina Hergenraeder. Source: GASO Fond 365

Family arrived from Hamburg to Buenos Aires, ARG on 1 May 1905 on SS Cap Blanco

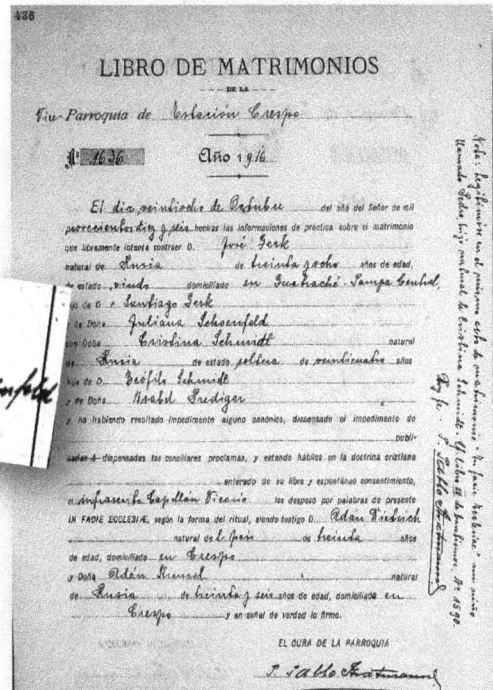

From the Hamburg Passenger Lists: The Joseph Gerk family left Hamburg on 21 Apr 1905 for Buenos Aires, Argentina. Joseph travelled with his wife Katharina and son Joseph. Katharina will pass away before 1918.
Source: Staatsarchive Hamburg; Volume: 373-7 I, VIII A 1 Band 165; Seite: 868; Mikrofilm Number: K_1788.

Marriage record for Joseph Gerk and Kristina Schmidt, dated 28 Oct 1918 in Crespo, Argentina.
Source: familysearch.org

Johann Adam Gerk (501)
b. 1768
at Koehler, Saratov, Russia
m. 1788
+Barbara Schenk
d. 1816
at Koehler, Saratov, RUS

Johann Georg Gerk (570)
b. 1792
at Koehler, Saratov, Russia
m. 24 Jan 1810
+ Elisabetha Ruhl
d. 1831
at Koehler, Saratov, RUS

Johann Adam Gerk was the 6th child
of Sebastian & Magdalena Gerk

Johann Heinrich Gerk (572)
b. 26 Oct 1815
at Koehler, Saratov, Russia
m. 1838
+ Anna Maria Schectel
d. 18 May 1864
at Marienfeld, Saratov, RUS

Jakob Gerk (713)
b. 24 Mar 1838
at Rothammel, Saratov, Russia
m. 17 Nov 1859
+ Juliana Schoenfeld
d. 2 Jul 1897
at Marienfeld, Saratov, RUS

Family moved to Marienfeld in 1852

Joseph Gerk (721)
b. 27 Jan 1877
at Marienfeld, Saratov, Russia
m. 29 Sep 1897
m. 28 Oct 1918
+ Katarina Stang
+Kristina Schmidt
d. 1958
at Bahía Blanca, Buenos Aires, ARG

Family arrived in Buenos Aires, ARG
on 1 May 1905 on SS Cap Blanco

Katarina Gerk
b.1898

Josef Gerk
b.1903

Luisa Gerk
b.1906

Juan Gerk
b.1909

Felipe Gerk
b.1918

Nicodema Gerk
b.1922

Ana Gerk
b.1926

Adan Gerk
b.?

Georg Gerk
b.?

Apolonia Gerk
b.?

Juan Pedro Gerk
b.?

TOP: Death records for Dorothea (Evangelista) Gerk – Sept 11, 1938
& Georg Gerk, June 3, 1944, in Santa Anita.
BELOW: Marriage record for Georg Gerk, age 20, & Dorothea Hartwig, age 18. Married in the Catholic Church
in Josefstal on 17 Nov 1887. Parents are Ivan Gerk and Barbara Dittler,
and Konrad Hartwig and Barbara Dittlow.
Source: Carina Kerke; GASO Fond 365 Op. 1 Delo 682 List No. 86

Birth & Baptism records for Georg Gerk, born 12 Dec 1888 in Josefstal, and Peter Gerk, born 5 Jan 1894
also in Josefstal. Both were children of Georg and Dorothea (Hartwig) Gerk,
and both will settle in Santa Anita, Argentina.
Source: GASO Fond 365 Op. 1 Delo 696 List No. 326 and Delo 825, List No. 298

Johann Kaspar Gerk (498)
b. 1753
at Fulda, Hesse, Germany
m. circa 1776
m. circa 1790
+unknown
+Anna Marie Mützig
d. 14 Jan 1830
at Koehler, Saratov, RUS

Kristian Gerk (532)
b. 9 Aug 1807
at Koehler, Saratov, RUS
m. 2 Nov 1827
m. 28 Oct 1840
at Koehler, RUS
+Anna Maria Weisheim
+Maria Elisabetha Bisheimer
d. 23 Dec 1877
at Josefstal, Saratov, RUS

Johann Kaspar Gerk was the 1st child
of Sebastian & Magdalena Gerk

Family moved to Josefstal in 1852

Johannes Gerk (743)
b. 4 Mar 1845
at Koehler, Saratov, Russia
m. 9 Nov 1865
+ Barbara Dittler
d. Unknown
at Unknown

Georg Gerk (745)
b. 7 Jun 1867
at Josefstal, Saratov, Russia
m. 17 Nov 1887
+ Dorothea Hartwig
d. 3 Jun 1944
at Santa Anita, Entre Ríos, ARG

Family travelled to
Rio de Janeiro, Brazil, on SS Würzburg
10 Oct 1908 from Bremen, GER, then to
Argentina

Georg Gerk
b.1888

Ana Katarina Gerk
b.1891

Peter Gerk
b.1894

David Gerk
b.1896

Elisabeth Gerk
b.1897

Barbara Gerk
b.1899

Johann Gerk
b.1903

Anna Gerk
b.1907

Adan Gerk
b.1909

Adan Gerk
b.1911

Georg Gerk of Santa Anita was the 2nd cousin 1st time removed of Peter Alois Gerk of Crespo, Argentina

The Peter Gerk Family of Santa Anita, Entre Ríos, Argentina

Birth record of Peter Gerk, born 17 April 1857 in Marienfeld, Russia, and baptized 20 April 1857. Parents are Johannes Gerk and Ekaterina Schaeffer.
Source: GASO Fond 365 Op. 1 Delo 61 List No. 65

Marriage record for widower Pedro Gerk and Leonora Gareis. Married on 18 August 1887 in Valle María, Entre Ríos, Argentina
Source: familysearch.org

Death record for Peter Gerk, confirming birth in Marienfeld. Peter died 11 September 1923 in Santa Anita.
Source: Carina Kerke

Johann Adam Gerk (501)
b. 1768
at Koehler, Saratov, Russia
m. 1788
+Barbara Schenk
d. 1816
at Koehler, Saratov, RUS

Heinrich Gerk (574)
b. 1799
at Koehler, Saratov, Russia
m. 1819
+Kristina Ziegler
d. 10 Sept 1848
at Koehler, Saratov, RUS

Johann Adam Gerk was the 6th child
of Sebastian & Magdalena Gerk

Johannes Gerk (1703)
b. 1826
at Koehler, Saratov, Russia
m. 1 Nov 1848
+Katarina Schaeffer
d.27 May 1886
at Marienfeld, Saratov, RUS

Peter Gerk (2436)
b. 17 Apr 1857
at Marienfeld, Saratov, Russia
m. 26 May 1877
m. 18 Aug 1887
+27 May 1886
+Elisabetha Dietler
+Leonora Gareis
d. 11 Sep 1923
at Santa Anita, Entre Ríos, ARG

Family moved to Marienfeld in 1852

Elisabetha Gerk b.1880	Anna Marie Gerk b.1882	Johannes Gerk b.1885	Catalina Gerk b.1888
Adán Gerk b.1890	Anamaria Gerk b.1892	Margareta Gerk b.1893	Anna Maria Gerk b.1895
Catalaina Gerk b.1896	Juan Gerk b.1898	Anna Gerk b.1900	Ana Margareta Gerk b.1901
Helena Gerk b.1902	Barbara Gerk b.1904	Nicolas Gerk b.1905	Rosa Gerk b.1907
Barbara Gerk b.1909	Elisa Gerk b.1911		

Family moved to
Argentina circa 1887

Members of the Peter Gerk family of Santa Anita, Argentina.
Top Photo: Adan Gerk & Family
Middle Photos Left to Right: Barbara & Elisa Gerk;
Juan and Catalina Gerk; Nikolaus
and Catalina Gerk;
Bottom Photo: Leonora (Gareis) Gerk (wife of Peter
Gerk) and Family.
Source: Cristian Gerk

Members of the Peter Gerk family of Santa Anita, Argentina.
Top Photo: Ana Gerk and family
Bottom Photo: Rosa Gerk Kranevitter and husband,
Margareta Gerk Glasman, José Glasman.
Source: Cristian Gerk

COLD CASE FILES:
The Mystery of August Gerk

August Gerk was born in Josefstal on 11 Jan 1894 to Peter Gerk and wife Kristina Klein. His mother passed away shortly after, and Peter remarried to Anna Marie Breit.

Sometime around 1904, Peter sought a better life for his family in Argentina. In 1905, the family that remained in Josefstal, sought permission to leave Russia, and applied for a Russian passport. Seen on the following page, the passport application was for Anna Marie Gerk, age 23, and son August, age 11; son Georg age 2 and daughter Anna age 4 months. They were to join Peter in "America".

We can trace the family to the area of Coronel Suárez, in Buenos Aires Province of Argentina, by the fact that they show up in Church records there. The 1906 confirmation lists for the parish of Nuestra Señora del Carmen, shown above, show August being confirmed, as well as brother Georg, and sister Anna. Peter Gerk's sister, Teresia Gerk, who was married to Josef Schaeffer, is also listed as being confirmed at the same time.

But then, the family vanishes.

Tradition and the descendants of this family tell us that Anna Marie (Breit) Gerk will return to Russia with Georg and Anna. Peter will stay in Argentina, if only for a time, with his son August. Eventually, Peter will return, but August made the decision to stay and to enter Religious life.

The Peter Gerk family became caught up in the sad events in Russia. …eventually moving from Josefstal to the Caucasus area in order to survive…and of course suffering the deportation to Siberia in 1941.

But what happened to August Gerk? Did he remain in the Priesthood? What was his ultimate fate? It remains one of those mysteries that we may never uncover.

August Gerk Birth record Source: GASO Fond 365; Confirmation record Source: familysearch.org

Passport application for Anna Marie Gerk and children.
Photo: The Gerk Family circa 1952 in the USSR
Artur Gerk, Lisa (Simon) Gerk, Adam Gerk, Paul Grizfeld.Alexander Gerk, Lydia
Gerk, Frida Gerk, Maria (Maier) Grizfeld, Berta (Grizfeld) Gerk, Georg Gerk, Amme
(Breit) Gerk, Georg Gerk, Maria (Dreser) Gerk.

Peter Gerk, the father of August, was Confirmed in the Parish Church in Pueblo
San José in 1905. San Jose is located near Coronel Suárez. Source: familysearch.org

Peter Gerk's sister, Teresia (Gerk) Schaeffer, was also Confirmed in 1906 in Coronel Suárez. As
far as we know, her family stayed in the area. Also Confirmed with August and family were his
brother Georg and sister Anna.

Source: familysearch.org

Johann Kaspar Gerk (498)
b. 1753
at Fulda, Hesse, Germany
m. circa 1776
m. circa 1790
+unknown
+Anna Marie Mützig
d. 14 Jan 1830
at Koehler, Saratov, RUS

Kristian Gerk (532)
b. 9 Aug 1807
at Koehler, Saratov, RUS
m. 2 Nov 1827
m. 28 Oct 1840
at Koehler, Saratov, RUS
+Anna Maria Weisheim
+Maria Elisabetha Bisheimer
d. 23 Dec 1877
at Josefstal, Saratov, RUS

Johann Kaspar Gerk was the 1st child
of Sebastian & Magdalena Gerk

Peter Gerk (705)
b. 20 Jan 1836
at Koehler, Saratov, RUS
m. 10 Nov 1859
at Josefstal, Saratov, RUS
+Anna Marie Wagner
d. Unknown
at Josefstal, Saratov, RUS

Family moved to Josefstal in 1852

Peter Gerk (711)
b. 4 Oct 1873
at Josefstal, Saratov, RUS
m. 19 Nov 1891
m. 17 Sep 1901
at Josefstal, Saratov, RUS
+Kristina Klein
+Anna Marie Breit
d. 1932
at Caucasus, USSR

Family moved to Argentina in 1904-05, then
returned to Russia. August Gerk stayed in
Argentina.

August Gerk
b.1894

Magdalena Gerk
b.1902

Georg Gerk
b.1903

Anna Gerk
b.1905

Katarina Gerk
b.1907

Anton Gerk
b.1908

Johannes Gerk
b.1910

Maria Gerk
b.1911

Nikodema Gerk
b.1913

A Prayer for our Family

Father,

Help us to recognize and create love in our families

Teach us gentleness.
Families need tender moments.

Teach us to be merry.
Families need laughter.

Teach us forgiveness.
Families can hurt each other.

Teach us honesty.
Family members do not need to hide from each other.

Teach us to be faithful.
Family members cannot give up on each other.

Teach us to believe in each other.
If we are to support each other, we can do anything

Teach us to be open to your will.
Families need your love to find their way.

Amen

(Source: Fully Alive)

The Descendants of Sebastian & Magdalena Gerk

It Never Ends....

This is a record of the descendants of Sebastian and Magdalena Gerk. To claim that this is the "complete" record, would be presumptuous, to say the least. It is a record, a database, that took 30 years to compile. Hundreds of letters, emails and old documents were the source for what lies in the subsequent pages.

Any errors are mine and mine alone. Since I am only human, I expect that I sometimes read things wrong, got mixed up, or generally misunderstood the collection of English, German, Russian and Spanish documentation that was before me.

So...simply put...please do not be annoyed if I got you wrong. I didn't mean to. You ARE an important part of this family. I can correct any errors found here... but I need to hear from you! And, if you want me to keep you updated on changes to this "Descendent Roster", drop me a line as well.

You can write me:

Edward Gerk
621 Grandview Road
Kelowna, BC
Canada V1V 2C8

Or even email me: tedgerk@yahoo.com

And I promise, in subsequent printings, to correct the misinformation I have. This descendant record can also be made available as an update, where you can simply place a copy into your original book. I will be making those available via email to those who have purchased a copy of this book.

Also, new research data, information and corrections not finding its way into this book will be made available at: http://faithofourfathers2012.blogspot.ca/

Thanks for your understanding and for sharing your family information!

Descendants of Sebastian & Magdalena Gerk

I. Johann Sebastian[1] Gerk (496) was born on 30 Apr 1725 at Müs, Fulda, Hesse, GER. He married Magdalena Helwig (497) on 12 Nov 1752 at Blankenau, Fulda, Hesse, GER. He immigrated on 20 May 1766. He died in 1797 at Koehler, Saratov, RUS.

    A. Johann Kaspar[2] Gerk (498) was born in 1753 at Fulda, Hesse, GER. He married Unknown (--?--) (522) circa 1776 at Koehler, Saratov, RUS. He married Anna Maria Mützig (525) circa 1790 at Koehler, Saratov, RUS. He died on 14 Jan 1830 at Koehler, Saratov, RUS.

        1. Maria Anna Barbara[3] Gerk (523) was born in 1777 at Koehler, Saratov, RUS.

        2. Margareta[3] Gerk (524) was born in 1781 at Koehler, Saratov, RUS.

        3. Zacharius[3] Gerk (512) was born in 1787 at Koehler, Saratov, RUS. He married Eva Elisabeta Schilling (513) circa 1809 at Koehler, Saratov, RUS. He died on 2 Feb 1843 at Koehler, Saratov, RUS.

            a) Katarina[4] Gerk (3690) was born on 13 Aug 1809 at Koehler, Saratov, RUS.

            b) Katarina[4] Gerk (2738) was born on 17 Jul 1810 at Koehler, Saratov, RUS. She married Peter Helmer (2737), son of Johannes Helmer (3665) and Maria Margareta Ulrich (3666), on 24 Jan 1828 at Koehler, Saratov, RUS. She died in 1849 at Koehler, Saratov, RUS.

                (1) Johannes[5] Helmer (3668) was born in 1830 at Koehler, Saratov, RUS.

                (2) Maria Anna[5] Helmer (3667) was born in 1834 at Koehler, Saratov, RUS.

                (3) Elisabeta[5] Helmer (3692) was born in 1842 at Koehler, Saratov, RUS.

                (4) Kristof[5] Helmer (2736) was born in 1849 at Koehler, Saratov, RUS. He married Anna Maria Gerk (581), daughter of Zacharius Gerk (575) and Katarina Schoenberger (577), on 30 Aug 1869 at Josefstal, Saratov, RUS.

                    (a) Ann Maria[6] Helmer (2753) was born on 12 Sep 1870 at Josefstal, Saratov, RUS.

                    (b) Johann Peter[6] Helmer (2754) was born on 24 Jun 1872 at Josefstal, Saratov, RUS.

                    (c) Nikolai Kristof[6] Helmer (2755) was born on 7 Sep 1874 at Josefstal, Saratov, RUS.

            c) Elisabeta[4] Gerk (3680) was born on 9 Feb 1815 at Koehler, Saratov, RUS.

            d) Zacharius Peter[4] Gerk (514) was born in 1820 at Koehler, Saratov, RUS. He married Katarina Schmidt (662) on 24 Jan 1839 at Koehler, Saratov, RUS. He died on 2 Sep 1852 at Josefstal, Saratov, RUS.

                (1) Christopher[5] Gerk (3047) was born on 31 May 1840 at Koehler, Saratov, RUS. He died on 16 Feb 1843 at Koehler, Saratov, RUS, at age 2.

                (2) Josef[5] Gerk (520) was born on 9 Jan 1843 at Koehler, Saratov, RUS. He married Elisabeta Schank (2760) on 16 Jan 1867 at Josefstal, Saratov, RUS. He married Teresia Buss (7346), daughter of Paul Buss (2451) and Marianna Magdalena Schiefelbein (2452), on 5 Nov 1897 at Josefstal, Saratov, RUS. He died on 11 Mar 1914 at Josefstal, Saratov, RUS, at age 71.

                    (a) Valentin[6] Gerk (1253) was born in 1868 at Josefstal, Saratov, RUS. He married Ekaterina Barbara Urich (1254), daughter of Johannes Urich (1266) and Magdalena Gerling (1267), on 9 Nov 1887 at Josefstal, Saratov, RUS.

                        i) Magdalena Margareta[7] Gerk (1255) was born on 3 Dec 1888 at Josefstal, Saratov, RUS. She married Peter Alois Kisser (2254), son of Wilhelm Kisser (2255) and Anna Marie Haspert (2256), on 7 Oct 1908 at Josefstal, Saratov, RUS.

                            (a) Georg[8] Kisser (2344) was born on 1 Aug 1909 at Josefstal, Saratov, RUS.

                            (b) Anna[8] Kisser (3581) was born in Jan 1910 at Josefstal, Saratov, RUS. She died on 18 Mar 1910 at Josefstal, Saratov, RUS.

                            (c) Johann[8] Kisser (2345) was born on 7 Jan 1911 at Josefstal, Saratov, RUS.

                        ii) Anna[7] Gerk (1256) was born on 20 May 1891 at Josefstal, Saratov, RUS. She married Johann Winter (2257), son of Georg Winter (2258) and Barbara Gette (2259), on 4 Nov 1909 at Josefstal, Saratov, RUS.

                            (a) Katarina[8] Winter (2292) was born on 8 Jul 1911 at Josefstal, Saratov, RUS.

                            (b) Johannes[8] Winter (4727) was born in 1913 at Josefstal, Saratov, RUS.

(c) Anna[8] Winter (4382) was born on 22 Jan 1916 at Josefstal, Saratov, RUS.

iii) Johannes[7] Gerk (1257) was born on 27 Sep 1894 at Josefstal, Saratov, RUS. He died on 19 May 1895 at Marienfeld, Saratov, RUS.

iv) Anna[7] Gerk (1258) was born on 24 Mar 1896 at Josefstal, Saratov, RUS. She married Josef Heinrich (3701), son of Johann Peter Heinrich (1107) and Katarina Gerk (723), on 22 May 1916 at Josefstal, Saratov, RUS.

    (a) Josef[8] Heinrich (8227) was born on 6 Feb 1918 at Josefstal, Saratov, RUS.

v) Katarina[7] Gerk (1259) was born on 1 Apr 1898 at Josefstal, Saratov, RUS.

vi) Andreas[7] Gerk (1268) was born on 1 Apr 1898 at Josefstal, Saratov, RUS.

vii) Johannes[7] Gerk (1260) was born on 15 Feb 1901 at Josefstal, Saratov, RUS.

viii) Marie Ann[7] Gerk (1265) was born on 16 Dec 1902 at Josefstal, Saratov, RUS. She died on 17 Mar 1910 at Josefstal, Saratov, RUS, at age 7.

ix) Barbara[7] Gerk (1261) was born on 6 Feb 1905 at Josefstal, Saratov, RUS. She died on 23 Jan 1908 at Josefstal, Saratov, RUS, at age 2.

x) Josef[7] Gerk (1262) was born on 7 Jan 1907 at Josefstal, Saratov, RUS.

xi) Margarita[7] Gerk (1263) was born on 2 May 1908 at Josefstal, Saratov, RUS.

xii) Susanna[7] Gerk (1264) was born on 30 May 1910 at Josefstal, Saratov, RUS. She died on 22 Dec 1911 at Josefstal, Saratov, RUS, at age 1.

(b) Johannes[6] Gerk (2309) was born on 15 Apr 1870 at Josefstal, Saratov, RUS. He married Anna Elisabeth Hollmann (Schaab) (1032), daughter of Michael Hollmann (2310) and Anna Maria Schaab (2311), on 16 Oct 1890 at Josefstal, Saratov, RUS.

i) Anna Maria[7] Gerk (2312) was born on 25 Aug 1891 at Josefstal, Saratov, RUS. She died on 13 Jun 1896 at Josefstal, Saratov, RUS, at age 4.

ii) Barbara[7] Gerk (2313) was born on 12 Dec 1893 at Josefstal, Saratov, RUS. She died on 1 Jun 1896 at Josefstal, Saratov, RUS, at age 2.

iii) Nikolaus[7] Gerk (3543) was born on 8 Nov 1897 at Josefstal, Saratov, RUS. He married Anna Breit (3700), daughter of Jakob Breit (5296) and Marie Anna Flohr (7507), on 26 Jan 1916 at Josefstal, Saratov, RUS. He died in 1925 at Josefstal, Saratov, RUS.

    (a) Josef[8] Gerk (7493) was born on 8 Aug 1919 at Josefstal, Saratov, RUS.

iv) Paul[7] Gerk (2314) was born on 6 Dec 1899 at Josefstal, Saratov, RUS. He died on 12 Oct 1900 at Josefstal, Saratov, RUS.

v) Katarina[7] Gerk (2315) was born on 8 Aug 1901 at Josefstal, Saratov, RUS.

vi) Barbara[7] Gerk (2316) was born on 13 May 1904 at Josefstal, Saratov, RUS.

vii) Johann[7] Gerk (2317) was born on 20 Mar 1906 at Josefstal, Saratov, RUS.

viii) Maria[7] Gerk (1033) was born on 5 Sep 1908 at Josefstal, Saratov, RUS.

ix) Jakob[7] Gerk (1034) was born on 1 Aug 1910 at Josefstal, Saratov, RUS. He married Anna Margareta Heinrich (7950) in 1929 at Josefstal, Saratov, USSR. He died in 1938 at USSR.

x) Rosa[7] Gerk (1035) was born on 14 Dec 1913 at Josefstal, Saratov, RUS.

(c) Margareta[6] Gerk (2763) was born on 2 Jun 1872 at Josefstal, Saratov, RUS. She died on 13 Jun 1876 at Josefstal, Saratov, RUS, at age 4.

(3) Peter[5] Gerk (3048) was born on 6 Oct 1845 at Koehler, Saratov, RUS.

(4) Elisabeta Katarina[5] Gerk (3105) was born on 25 Nov 1848 at Koehler, Saratov, RUS. She died on 17 Nov 1851 at Koehler, Saratov, RUS, at age 2.

e) Gottlieb[4] Gerk (515) was born in 1822 at Koehler, Saratov, RUS. He married Juliana Gitlein (2720), daughter of Wilhelm Gitlein (3114) and Konstanzia Kolb (3115), on 25 Nov 1846 at Koehler, Saratov, RUS. He married Katarina Heinrich (2729), daughter of Feit Heinrich (4383) and Elisabeta Wallentor (4386), on 5 Feb 1868 at Josefstal, Saratov, RUS. He died on 1 Jul 1894 at Josefstal, Saratov, RUS.

(1) Johannes Georg^5 Gerk (4049) was born on 26 Jan 1847 at Koehler, Saratov, RUS. He died on 1 Aug 1848 at Koehler, Saratov, RUS, at age 1.

(2) Johannes^5 Gerk (752) was born on 25 Jan 1849 at Koehler, Saratov, RUS. He married Margareta Pitz (753), daughter of Johannes Pitz (2761) and Appolonia Burgardt (2762), on 9 Nov 1865 at Josefstal, Saratov, RUS.

(a) Anna Marie^6 Gerk (2195) was born in 1866 at Josefstal, Saratov, RUS. She married Josef Trinaka (2196), son of Georg Trinaka (2197) and Katarina Altmeier (2198), on 15 Nov 1883 at Josefstal, Saratov, RUS.

(b) Barbara^6 Gerk (751) was born on 27 Feb 1867 at Josefstal, Saratov, RUS. She died on 12 Mar 1867 at Josefstal, Saratov, RUS.

(c) Peter Alois^6 Gerk (754) was born on 28 Jan 1871 at Josefstal, Saratov, RUS. He married Anna Katarina Breit (918), daughter of Josef Breit (2176) and Magdalena Helmert (2177), on 16 Nov 1897 at Josefstal, Saratov, RUS. He emigrated on 23 Jan 1909. He married Elisabeta Elena Gerk (1289), daughter of Johann Georg Gerk (847) and Margareta Magdalena Haberkorn (846), on 12 Aug 1919 at Crespo, Entre Ríos, ARG.

    i) Magdalena^7 Gerk (927) was born on 2 Jul 1906 at Josefstal, Saratov, RUS. She married Johannes Bahl (928), son of Juan Bahl (2860) and Luisa Schulz (2861), on 9 Sep 1924 at Crespo, Entre Ríos, ARG.

    ii) Georg^7 Gerk (930) was born on 13 Aug 1908 at Josefstal, Saratov, RUS. He married Elena Kloster (6022), daughter of Johannes Kloster (919) and Elisabeta Elena Gerk (1289), on 2 Apr 1929 at Seguí, Entre Ríos, ARG.

        (a) Maria Amelia^8 Gerk (7979) was born in 1944 at ARG. She married Ovidio Bivas (7980) on 21 Jun 1962 at Gessler, Santa Fe, ARG.

    iii) Santiago^7 Kerg (3749) was born on 17 Jan 1911 at Nogoyá, Entre Ríos, ARG. He married Rosa Schonfeld (3454), daughter of Ignacio Schonfeld (3455) and Teresa Gette (3456), on 12 Apr 1932 at Bovril, Entre Ríos, ARG. He died on 10 Mar 1982 at Sunchales, Santa Fe, ARG, at age 71.

        (a) Juana^8 Kerg (5503) was born at ARG. She married Siluerio Daga (5504).

        (b) Ángela^8 Kerk (5505) was born at ARG. She died in 1961 at Santa Fe, ARG.

        (c) María Nieves^8 Kerk (5506) was born at ARG.

        (d) Eugenio^8 Kerg (5507) was born at ARG.

        (e) Gerardo^8 Kerk (5508) was born at ARG.

        (f) Irma^8 Kerg (5509) was born at ARG. She married Juan Nuri (5510) at ARG.

        (g) Rosa^8 Kerk (5511) was born at ARG. She married Benjamín Altamirano (5512).

        (h) Oscar^8 Kerk (5513) married Belkis Larrea (5514) at ARG. He was born in 1943 at ARG. He died in 2007 at ARG.

            i) Monica^9 Kerk (5517) was born at ARG. She married Germán Sobrero (5518) at ARG.

            ii) Gustavo^9 Kerk (5515) married Laura Pelegrino (5516). He was born on 28 Jun 1977 at ARG.

                (a) Julian^{10} Kerk (7492) was born on 27 Mar 2006 at Sunchales, Santa Fe, ARG.

    iv) Juan^7 Gerk (2373) was born on 6 Jun 1915 at Crespo, Entre Ríos, ARG. He died on 13 Jun 1915 at Crespo, Entre Ríos, ARG.

    v) Juan^7 Gerk (2121) was born on 10 Oct 1917 at Crespo, Entre Ríos, ARG. He died on 10 Oct 1917 at Crespo, Entre Ríos, ARG.

    vi) Kaspar^7 Gerk (2012) was born on 10 Oct 1917 at Crespo, Entre Ríos, ARG. He died on 10 Oct 1917 at Crespo, Entre Ríos, ARG.

    vii) Rafael^7 Gerk (2122) was born on 16 Nov 1920 at Crespo, Entre Ríos, ARG.

    viii) Miguel^7 Gerk (2930) was born on 12 Aug 1925 at Crespo, Entre Ríos, ARG. He married Ancila Teresa Giovedoni (2931), daughter of Valentin Giovedoni (3209) and Angela Pretto (3210), on 14 Mar 1956 at Lehman, Santa Fe, ARG.

        (a) Juan Remigio^8 Gerk (3100) was born on 24 Feb 1956 at Lehman, Santa Fe, ARG.

(d) Wilhelm^6 Gerk (755) was born on 12 Apr 1873 at Josefstal, Saratov, RUS. He died on 14 Dec 1873 at Josefstal, Saratov, RUS.

(e) Johannes Friedrich[6] Gerk (756) was born on 1 Oct 1877 at Josefstal, Saratov, RUS. He died on 13 Dec 1878 at Josefstal, Saratov, RUS, at age 1.

(f) Johannes[6] Gerk (2237) was born in 1879 at Josefstal, Saratov, RUS. He married Margareta Mollentor (2238), daughter of Josef Mollentor (2239) and Magdalena Prediger (2240), on 24 Nov 1905 at Josefstal, Saratov, RUS. He emigrated on 10 Oct 1908 from Bremen, GER.

(3) Johann[5] Gerk (3054) was born on 19 Mar 1851 at Koehler, Saratov, RUS. He died on 26 Feb 1853 at Josefstal, Saratov, RUS, at age 1.

f) Johann Georg[4] Gerk (401) was born in 1826 at Koehler, Saratov, RUS. He married Ekaterina Buss (415), daughter of Johannes Buss (3529) and Ekaterina Seibert (3530), on 3 Nov 1852 at Josefstal, Saratov, RUS. He died on 27 Jul 1886 at Josefstal, Saratov, RUS.

(1) Johann Georg[5] Gerk (847) died at ARG. He was born on 8 Oct 1853 at Josefstal, Saratov, RUS. He married Margareta Magdalena Haberkorn (846), daughter of Gottlieb Haberkorn (2739) and Anna Margareta Leonardt (2740), on 14 Nov 1871 at Josefstal, Saratov, RUS.

(a) Anna Maria[6] Gerk (845) was born on 17 Feb 1874 at Josefstal, Saratov, RUS. She married Johan Adam Schaefer (5682), son of Friedrich Schaefer (856) and Eva Lambrecht (857), on 9 Nov 1892 at Josefstal, Saratov, RUS.

(b) Franzisca[6] Gerk (1284) was born on 7 Aug 1876 at Josefstal, Saratov, RUS.

(c) Johann Peter[6] Gerk (848) was born on 22 Aug 1878 at Josefstal, Saratov, RUS. He died on 4 May 1888 at Josefstal, Saratov, RUS, at age 9.

(d) Konrad[6] Gerk (850) was born on 8 Jul 1880 at Josefstal, Saratov, RUS. He married Anna Maria Dietrich (2178), daughter of Johannes Dietrich (2179) and Sophia Gareis (2180), on 20 Oct 1898 at Josefstal, Saratov, RUS.

i) Johann[7] Gerk (2346) was born in 1899 at Josefstal, Saratov, RUS. He died on 7 Apr 1899 at Josefstal, Saratov, RUS.

ii) Barbara[7] Gerk (7885) was born in 1901.

iii) José[7] Gerk (5519) was born on 8 May 1907 at Pueblo Santa María, Buenos Aires, ARG. He married Catalina Kippes (5520), daughter of Georg Kippes (5526) and Marianna Desch (5527), on 13 Jul 1954 at Santa Anita, Entre Ríos, ARG. He died on 17 Dec 1974 at Villaguay, Entre Ríos, ARG, at age 67.

(a) Juan José[8] Gerk (5528) was born on 24 Jun 1956 at Santa Anita, Entre Ríos, ARG.

(b) Pedro Conrado[8] Gerk (5529) was born on 27 Jun 1957 at Santa Anita, Entre Ríos, ARG. He died in 2010 at Santa Anita, Entre Ríos, ARG.

(c) Mario Osvaldo[8] Gerk (5530) married Irma Lucia Rhor (6500) at Entre Ríos, ARG. He was born on 19 Nov 1958 at Santa Anita, Entre Ríos, ARG.

i) Martin Alejandro[9] Gerk (6501) was born on 13 Apr 1999 at Santa Anita, Entre Ríos, ARG.

ii) Micaela Antorella[9] Gerk (6502) was born on 21 May 2002 at Santa Anita, Entre Ríos, ARG.

iii) Emiliano[9] Gerk (6503) was born on 11 Apr 2004 at Santa Anita, Entre Ríos, ARG.

(e) Barbara[6] Gerk (849) was born on 10 Jan 1883 at Josefstal, Saratov, RUS. She married Gottfried Stremel (1932), son of Johann Andreas Stremel (2181) and Magdalena Arnold (2182), on 26 Oct 1899 at Josefstal, Saratov, RUS. She married Nikolaus Breit (1751), son of Johannes Breit (1752) and Elenora???? (--?--) (5310), circa 1920 at Josefstal, Saratov, USSR. She died on 23 Oct 1967 at USSR at age 84.

i) Katarina[7] Stremel (1933) was born on 14 Sep 1900 at Josefstal, Saratov, RUS.

ii) Margarita[7] Stremel (1934) was born on 9 Sep 1902 at Josefstal, Saratov, RUS.

iii) Johannes[7] Stremel (1935) was born on 1 Oct 1904 at Josefstal, Saratov, RUS. He died on 3 Dec 1908 at Josefstal, Saratov, RUS, at age 4.

iv) Georg[7] Stremel (1936) was born on 8 Mar 1909 at Josefstal, Saratov, RUS.

v) Ferdinand[7] Stremel (1937) was born on 6 Mar 1911 at Josefstal, Saratov, RUS.

vi) Michael[7] Stremel (3699) was born on 26 Apr 1913 at Josefstal, Saratov, RUS.

vii) Rudolph[7] Stremel (3750) was born on 25 May 1915 at Josefstal, Saratov, RUS.

viii) Anna[7] Breit (1753) married Paul Schaab (1754), son of Johannes Schaab (1755) and Katarina Benz (1756). She was born on 10 Aug 1922 at Josefstal, Saratov, USSR.

    (a) Erika[8] Schaab (1757) was born in 1947 at USSR.

    (b) Anna[8] Schaab (1758) was born in 1950 at USSR.

    (c) Paul[8] Schaab (1760) was born in 1954 at USSR.

    (d) Katarina[8] Schaab (1759) was born in 1957 at USSR.

    (e) Viktor[8] Schaab (1761) was born in 1958 at USSR. He died in 1987 at USSR.

(f) Elisabeta Elena[6] Gerk (1289) was born on 24 Aug 1885 at Josefstal, Saratov, RUS. She married Johannes Kloster (919), son of Alois Kloster (2856) and Anna Maria Froschauer (2857), on 21 Apr 1903 at Puán, Buenos Aires, ARG. She married Peter Alois Gerk (754), son of Johannes Gerk (752) and Margareta Pitz (753), on 12 Aug 1919 at Crespo, Entre Ríos, ARG. She died in 1959 at Sunchales, Santa Fe, ARG.

    i) Catalina[7] Kloster (2858) was born on 12 Jul 1905 at Puán, Buenos Aires, ARG. She married Leon Bahl (2859), son of Juan Bahl (2860) and Luisa Schulz (2861), on 9 Sep 1924 at Crespo, Entre Ríos, ARG.

    ii) Johannes[7] Kloster (7520) was born on 13 Feb 1907 at San José, Entre Ríos, ARG. He married Rosa Exner (7521) on 19 Feb 1935 at Entre Ríos, ARG.

    iii) Elena[7] Kloster (6022) was born on 16 Jan 1909 at Crespo, Entre Ríos, ARG. She married Georg Gerk (930), son of Peter Alois Gerk (754) and Anna Katarina Breit (918), on 2 Apr 1929 at Seguí, Entre Ríos, ARG.

        (a) Maria Amelia[8] Gerk (7979) (see above)

    iv) Andreas[7] Kloster (7804) was born on 28 May 1910 at Santa Anita, Entre Ríos, ARG. He married Susana Kessler (7805), daughter of Juan Kessler (8082) and Anna Margareta Trinak (8083), on 13 Feb 1935 at Crespo, Entre Ríos, ARG.

    v) Aloisius[7] Kloster (7806) was born on 20 Jan 1912 at Santa Anita, Entre Ríos, ARG.

    vi) Ignacio[7] Kloster (7807) was born on 16 Dec 1914 at Santa Anita, Entre Ríos, ARG.

    vii) Rafael[7] Gerk (2122) (see above)

    viii) Miguel[7] Gerk (2930) (see above)

        (a) Juan Remigio[8] Gerk (3100) (see above)

(g) Georg[6] Gerk (851) was born on 8 Jul 1887 at Josefstal, Saratov, RUS. He died on 18 Jul 1888 at Josefstal, Saratov, RUS, at age 1.

(h) Elenora[6] Gerk (852) was born on 9 Feb 1890 at Josefstal, Saratov, RUS. She died on 12 Feb 1894 at Josefstal, Saratov, RUS, at age 4.

(i) Georg[6] Gerk (853) was born on 3 Jun 1892 at Josefstal, Saratov, RUS. He died on 7 Feb 1894 at Josefstal, Saratov, RUS, at age 1.

(j) Elisabeta[6] Gerk (854) was born on 12 Mar 1895 at Josefstal, Saratov, RUS. She died on 30 Aug 1896 at Josefstal, Saratov, RUS, at age 1.

(2) Kaspar[5] Gerk (1189) was born on 22 Nov 1855 at Josefstal, Saratov, RUS. He died on 20 Feb 1857 at Josefstal, Saratov, RUS, at age 1.

(3) Anna Marie[5] Gerk (1190) was born on 19 Feb 1858 at Josefstal, Saratov, RUS.

(4) Kaspar[5] Gerk (508) was born on 7 Jun 1859 at Josefstal, Saratov, RUS. He died on 14 May 1861 at Josefstal, Saratov, RUS, at age 1.

(5) Anna-Margareta Katarina[5] Gerk (509) was born on 26 Jul 1862 at Josefstal, Saratov, RUS. She died on 5 Feb 1870 at Josefstal, Saratov, RUS, at age 7.

(6) Eva Katarina[5] Gerk (510) was born on 11 Jul 1864 at Josefstal, Saratov, RUS. She died on 26 Feb 1867 at Josefstal, Saratov, RUS, at age 2.

(7) Anna Maria Magdalena[5] Gerk (511) was born on 25 Dec 1866 at Josefstal, Saratov, RUS. She died on 29 Jan 1870 at Josefstal, Saratov, RUS, at age 3.

(8) Johann Georg[5] Gerk (404) was born on 12 Jan 1869 at Josefstal, Saratov, RUS. He married Anna Margareta Rohwein (405), daughter of Heinrich Rohwein (416) and Barbara Haberkorn (417), on 4 Nov 1886 at Josefstal, Saratov, RUS. He died on 10 Feb 1925 at Josefstal, Stalingrad Oblast, USSR, at age 56.

   (a) Barbara[6] Gerk (603) was born on 6 Jul 1887 at Josefstal, Saratov, RUS. She died on 23 Apr 1888 at Josefstal, Saratov, RUS.

   (b) Alois[6] Gerk (406) was born on 6 Jun 1889 at Josefstal, Saratov, RUS. He died on 6 Mar 1895 at Josefstal, Saratov, RUS, at age 5.

   (c) Tsirian Michael[6] Gerk (407) was born illegitimate on 28 Oct 1893 at Josefstal, Saratov, RUS. He married Margareta Stremel (418), daughter of Johannes Stremel (943) and Anna Marie Arnold (944), on 5 Feb 1912 at Josefstal, Saratov, RUS. He died circa Dec 1921 at Minsk, RUS.

   (d) Anna[6] Gerk (408) was born on 29 Jan 1896 at Josefstal, Saratov, RUS. She married Michael Kisser (422), son of Johan Adam Kisser (1986) and Elisabeta Simon (1987), on 23 Oct 1912 at Josefstal, Saratov, RUS. She married Konrad Arnold (438) in 1934 at Josefstal, Stalingrad Oblast, USSR. She died in Feb 1983 at Angren, Tashkent Oblast, USSR, at age 87.

   i) Beata[7] Kisser (459) was born on 28 Oct 1913 at Josefstal, Saratov, RUS. She died circa 1973 at USSR.

   ii) Isabella[7] Kisser (460) was born on 5 Apr 1915 at Josefstal, Saratov, RUS. She died in 1933 at ?

   iii) Paul[7] Kisser (461) was born on 10 Mar 1917 at Josefstal, Saratov, RUS. He died in 1942.

   iv) Josef[7] Arnold (462) was born in 1935 at Josefstal, Stalingrad Oblast, USSR.

   v) Anna[7] Arnold (463) was born in 1937 at Josefstal, Stalingrad Oblast, USSR.

   (e) Georg[6] Gerk (409) was born on 21 Dec 1897 at Josefstal, Saratov, RUS. He married Kristina Rausch (420), daughter of Franz Rausch (3815) and Barbara Leonhardt (6861), on 6 Jan 1916 at Josefstal, Saratov, RUS. He died on 5 Mar 1943 at Chelyabmetallurgstroy Labour Camp, Chelyabinsk Oblast, USSR, at age 45.

   i) Georg[7] Gerk (464) was born on 6 Jan 1917 at Josefstal, Saratov, RUS. He died in 1942 at USSR.

   ii) Jakob[7] Gerk (465) was born on 21 Apr 1927 at Josefstal, Stalingrad Oblast, USSR. He married Alina Meier (6261) circa 1949 at USSR. He died on 18 Apr 1985 at Kaliningrad, RUS, at age 57.

      (a) Valentin[8] Gerk (6262) was born on 3 Jan 1950 at Shimanaeha, Kazakstan, USSR. He married Vera Starceva (6862) on 20 Apr 1971 at Frunze, USSR.

         i) Vechaslav[9] Gerk (6863) was born on 6 Feb 1972 at Frunze, USSR.

         ii) Sergey[9] Gerk (6864) was born on 15 Oct 1973 at Frunze, USSR. He married Helen Ovcharenko (6865) on 5 Jun 1993 at Mariupol, Ukraine, USSR.

            (a) Paul[10] Gerk (6866) was born on 12 Jul 1994 at Noyabrsk, RUS.

            (b) Iliya[10] Gerk (6867) was born on 1 Nov 1998 at Noyabrsk, RUS.

            (c) Ester[10] Gerk (6868) was born on 18 Jun 2000 at Noyabrsk, RUS.

            (d) Liza[10] Gerk (6869) was born on 17 Feb 2010 at Noyabrsk, RUS.

      (b) Olga[8] Gerk (6263) married (--?--) Hanneberg (6276) at USSR. She was born on 7 Oct 1954 at USSR.

      (c) Jakob[8] Gerk (6264) was born on 5 May 1956 at USSR.

   iii) Elisabeta[7] Gerk (466) was born on 20 Jan 1937 at Josefstal, Stalingrad Oblast, USSR. She married Igor Filmonov (6272) on 9 Aug 1958 at USSR.

      (a) Natalia[8] Filmonov (6273) was born on 11 Jul 1958 at USSR.

      (b) Sergei[8] Filmonov (6274) was born on 19 Mar 1960 at USSR.

      (c) Juri[8] Filmonov (6275) was born on 19 Apr 1964 at USSR.

   iv) Eduard[7] Gerk (1028) was born at Josefstal, Saratov, RUS.

   v) Johannes[7] Gerk (601) was born on 10 Oct 1929 at Josefstal, Stalingrad Oblast, USSR. He married Katharina Rausch (6265) in 1950 at USSR.

(a) Anna[8] Gerk (6266) married (--?--) Martemjanov (6269) at USSR. She was born on 5 Mar 1951 at USSR.

(b) Valentin[8] Gerk (6267) was born in 1952 at USSR. He died in 1970 at USSR.

(c) Olga[8] Gerk (6268) was born on 5 May 1955 at USSR.

(d) Lydia[8] Gerk (6270) was born on 19 Jan 1958 at USSR.

(e) Nikolai[8] Gerk (6271) was born on 4 Nov 1960 at USSR.

(f) Jakob[6] Gerk (410) was born on 19 Feb 1900 at Josefstal, Saratov, RUS. He married Barbara Lambrecht (446), daughter of Georg Lambrecht (4621) and Barbara Bellendir (4622), circa 1919 at Josefstal, Saratov, USSR. He died on 3 Dec 1942 at Usollag Labour Camp, Danilov Lug, Perm Oblast, USSR, at age 42.

i) Leo[7] Gerk (467) married Teresia Dreser (1772) at USSR. He was born in 1919 at Josefstal, Saratov, USSR. He died in 1942 at USSR.

ii) Lydia[7] Gerk (468) was born on 13 Oct 1924 at Josefstal, Saratov, USSR. She married Jakob Stremel (602), son of Jakob Stremel (679) and Katarina Kess (949), on 27 Jun 1948 at Krasnoturinsk, Sverdlovsk Oblast, USSR.

(a) Viktor[8] Stremel (681) was born on 10 May 1949 at Krasnoturinsk, Sverdlovsk Oblast, USSR. He married Katarina Schaab (686) in 1970 at Kotovo, Volgograd Oblast, USSR. He married Nadeschda (--?--) (688) in 1981 at Kotovo, Volgograd Oblast, USSR.

i) Dima[9] Stremel (687) was born at Kotovo, Volgograd Oblast, USSR.

ii) Julia[9] Stremel (689) was born on 24 May 1982 at Kotovo, Volgograd Oblast, USSR.

(b) Anna[8] Stremel (682) was born on 12 Feb 1951 at Krasnoturinsk, Sverdlovsk Oblast, USSR.

i) Elena[9] (--?--) (690) was born at Kotovo, Volgograd Oblast, USSR.

(c) Waldemar[8] Stremel (683) married Katarina Schaab (691) at Kotovo, Volgograd Oblast, USSR. He was born on 5 May 1953 at Krasnoturinsk, Sverdlovsk Oblast, USSR.

i) Vitali[9] Stremel (692) was born on 3 Aug 1977 at Kotovo, Volgograd Oblast, USSR.

ii) Ina[9] Stremel (693) was born on 14 Oct 1984 at Kotovo, Volgograd Oblast, USSR.

(d) Irma[8] Stremel (684) married Alexander Jantscharkin (694). She was born on 10 Jul 1955 at Schelano, Omsk Oblast, USSR.

i) Natalia[9] Jantscharkin (695) was born on 6 Oct 1976 at USSR.

ii) Sergei[9] Jantscharkin (696) was born on 4 May 1979 at USSR.

(e) Valentina[8] Stremel (685) married Alexander Graf (697). She was born on 10 Jan 1958 at Smorodino, Kotovo Region, Volgograd Oblast, USSR.

i) Svetlena[9] Graf (698) was born on 24 May 1977 at Krasnoturinsk, Sverdlovsk Oblast, USSR.

ii) Anna[9] Graf (699) was born on 8 Oct 1979 at Krasnoturinsk, Sverdlovsk Oblast, USSR.

iii) Adam[7] Gerk (469) married Elisabeth Bensak (951). He was born on 18 Aug 1926 at Josefstal, Stalingrad Oblast, USSR.

(a) Anna[8] Gerk (1096) married (--?--) Leonardt (1767). She was born in 1956 at USSR.

(b) Galina[8] Gerk (1097) was born in 1959 at USSR.

(c) Lydia[8] Gerk (1098) married (--?--) Aristova (1768). She was born in 1962 at USSR.

(d) Aleksander[8] Gerk (1099) was born in 1964 at USSR.

(e) Valentina[8] Gerk (1100) married (--?--) Saks (1765). She was born in 1967 at USSR.

(f) Nadia[8] Gerk (1101) married (--?--) Saks (1766). She was born in 1972 at USSR.

iv) Anna[7] Gerk (470) married Viktor Weimer (680). She was born on 4 Apr 1930 at Josefstal, Stalingrad Oblast, USSR. She died on 20 Nov 1992 at Germany at age 62.

(a) Vadimir[8] Weimer (1769) was born at USSR.

(b) Valentina[8] Weimer (1770) was born at USSR.

(c) Viktor[8] Weimer (1771) was born at USSR.

(g) Paul[6] Gerk (75) was born on 14 Jan 1902 at Josefstal, Saratov, RUS. He married Elisabeta Dieser (74), daughter of Johannes Dieser (67) and Marie Eva Heit (68), on 15 Sep 1920 at Josefstal, Saratov, RUS. He died on 3 Jun 1954 at Kelowna, B.C., CAN, at age 52.

i) Edward John[7] Gerk (402) was born on 26 Jan 1928 at Holdfast, Sask, CAN. He married Ann Lingor (442) in 1946 at Kelowna, Kelowna, B.C., CAN. He married Sharron Howe (445), daughter of Samuel Thomas Howe (3224) and Elizabeth Ann Brown (3225), on 6 Dec 1975 at Summerland, B.C., CAN. He died on 31 May 1993 at Hedley, BC, CAN, at age 65.

(a) Sharon[8] Gerk (443) was born on 27 Jun 1947 at Kelowna, Kelowna, B.C., CAN. She married Gordon Solloway (701) in 1967 at Kelowna, BC, CAN.

i) Sherrie[9] Solloway (702) was born at Kelowna, BC, CAN.

ii) Gordon[9] Solloway (703) was born at Kelowna, BC, CAN.

(b) Ronald[8] Gerk (444) was born on 4 Dec 1952 at Kelowna, B.C., CAN. He married Debra Turner (1290), daughter of Robert James Turner (1293) and Mildred Johnston (1294), on 17 May 1980 at CAN.

i) Dustin James[9] Gerk (1291) was born on 16 Jul 1981 at Penticton, BC, CAN. He married Jayme Esler (7873) on 13 Sep 2014 at Penticton, BC, CAN.

(a) Foster Lloyd Ronald[10] Gerk (8077) was born on 25 Aug 2016 at Penticton, BC, CAN.

ii) Amber Nicole[9] Gerk (1292) was born on 29 Dec 1983 at Penticton, BC, CAN. She married Frank Chirico (6559) in Jul 2012 at Penticton, BC, CAN.

(c) Carol[8] Gerk (521) was born on 20 May 1949 at Kelowna, BC, CAN. She died on 21 May 1949 at Kelowna, BC, CAN.

ii) Mary[7] Gerk (403) was born on 6 Sep 1929 at Holdfast, Sask, CAN. She married John Kloster (425), son of Anton Kloster (450) and Margareta Stremel (418), on 20 Nov 1951 at Kelowna, B.C., CAN. She died on 12 Jan 2013 at Kelowna, BC, CAN, at age 83.

(a) Diane Mary[8] Kloster (447) was born on 20 Sep 1952 at Kelowna, B.C., CAN. She married Terry De Meo (656) on 14 Oct 1972 at Kelowna, B.C., CAN. She married James Michael Budd (660), son of William Leo Budd (661), on 11 Jun 1983 at Calgary, Alberta, CAN.

i) Steven John[9] De Meo (657) was born on 18 Jun 1974 at Winnipeg, Manitoba, CAN.

ii) Derek Paul[9] De Meo (658) was born on 30 Jun 1976 at Kelowna, B.C., CAN.

iii) Christopher Leo[9] Budd (659) was born on 26 Apr 1984 at Calgary, Alberta, CAN. He married Andrea Lynne Crump (6420), daughter of Lance Crump (6422) and Debra Crump (6421), on 20 Aug 2011 at Niagara-on-the-Lake, ON, CAN.

(b) James Paul[9] Kloster (448) was born on 3 Mar 1955 at Kelowna, B.C., CAN. He married Susan Gordon (664) on 26 Jan 1974 at Kelowna, BC, CAN. He married Gwen McPherson (668) on 28 Jun 1980 at Kelowna, BC, CAN.

i) Jason James[9] Kloster (665) was born on 27 Apr 1974 at Kelowna, BC, CAN. He married Tana Ross (666) on 1 Aug 1998 at Kelowna, BC, CAN.

(a) Haley[10] Kloster (667) was born on 18 Jul 1999 at Kelowna, BC, CAN.

ii) Darren James[9] Kloster (669) was born on 7 Aug 1981 at Kelowna, BC, CAN.

(c) Kathleen Elisabeth[8] Kloster (449) was born on 15 Dec 1960 at Kelowna, B.C., CAN. She married Brian Hilstob (455) on 1 Sep 1979 at Kelowna, BC, CAN.

i) Nicole Lyn[9] Hilstob (670) was born on 7 May 1983 at Kelowna, BC, CAN.

ii) Kayla Elizabeth[9] Hilstob (671) was born on 2 Dec 1987 at Kelowna, BC, CAN.

iii) John George[7] Gerk (256) was born on 1 Sep 1933 at Kelowna, B.C., CAN. He married Margaret Ann Skelton (388), daughter of Thomas William Skelton (611) and Elizabeth Isabelle Martell (614), on 10 Oct 1953 at Princeton, B.C., CAN. He died on 27 Nov 1992 at Kelowna, B.C., CAN, at age 59.

(a) John William⁸ Gerk (397) was born on 29 Oct 1954 at Kelowna, B.C., CAN. He married Joyce Beverly Kunz (427), daughter of Clarence Kunz (1093) and Charlotte Helen Bley (1094), on 8 Jun 1974 at Kelowna, B.C., CAN.

> **i)** Kimberley Ann⁹ Gerk (428) was born on 19 Dec 1977 at Kelowna, B.C., CAN. She married Chris McKinnon (4632) on 15 Jul 2006 at Kelowna, BC, CAN.
>
>> **(a)** Hudsyn Charlotte¹⁰ McKinnon (6247) was born on 8 Oct 2011 at Revelstoke, BC, CAN.
>>
>> **(b)** Emmersyn Jaymes¹⁰ McKinnon (6687) was born on 17 Nov 2013 at Kelowna, BC, CAN.
>
> **ii)** Jordan John⁹ Gerk (429) was born on 6 Jul 1979 at Kelowna, B.C., CAN. He married Jennifer Hope Castonguay (3143), daughter of Richard Castonguay (3144), on 25 Oct 2003 at Jefferson Idabel, Oklahoma, USA.
>
>> **(a)** Logan William¹⁰ Gerk (6561) was born on 15 Dec 2012 at Plano, TX, USA.

(b) William Paul⁸ Gerk (398) was born on 31 Jan 1956 at Princeton, B.C., CAN. He married Deborah Roth (419), daughter of Gary Roth (1763) and Viola Roth (1764), on 5 Apr 1975 at Kelowna, B.C., CAN. He married Cathy Makra (672), daughter of Louis Makra (1749) and Helen Sipas (1750), on 25 May 1996 at Kamloops, BC, CAN.

> **i)** Joshua William⁹ Gerk (430) was born on 30 May 1980 at Kamloops, B.C., CAN.
>
> **ii)** Matthew Paul⁹ Gerk (431) was born on 8 Apr 1983 at Vancouver, B.C., CAN. He married Lindsay Nicole Mallory (5614) on 11 Jul 2008 at Kelowna, BC, CAN.
>
>> **(a)** Emmit¹⁰ Gerk (5645) was born on 1 Jan 2009 at Kelowna, BC, CAN.
>>
>> **(b)** Dean Matthew John¹⁰ Gerk (6560) was born on 2 Sep 2012 at Kelowna, BC, CAN.

(c) Thomas James⁸ Gerk (399) was born on 29 Dec 1957 at Kelowna, B.C., CAN. He married Jamie Gawne (432) on 23 Apr 1977 at Calgary, Alberta, CAN. He married Patricia Murray (1016) on 12 Aug 2000 at Kelowna, B.C., CAN.

> **i)** Kristin Marjory Ann⁹ Gerk (433) was born on 1 Feb 1978 at Red Deer, Alberta, CAN. She married Peter Auclair (604) on 9 Aug 1997 at Calgary, Alberta, CAN.
>
>> **(a)** Kayla Christine¹⁰ Auclair (2969) was born on 17 Apr 2003 at Calgary, Alberta, CAN.
>>
>> **(b)** Kyle Michael¹⁰ Auclair (4608) was born on 27 Feb 2006 at Calgary, Alta, CAN.
>
> **ii)** Scott Thomas⁹ Gerk (434) was born on 6 Jan 1979 at Red Deer, Alberta, CAN. He married Nicole Lynn Grant (6507) on 4 Aug 2012 at Summerland, BC, CAN.
>
>> **(a)** Wesley Scott Grant¹⁰ Gerk (5312) was born on 3 Jul 2003 at Penticton, BC, CAN.
>>
>> **(b)** Mya Lynn¹⁰ Gerk (6518) was born on 23 Oct 2007 at Penticton, BC, CAN.
>
> **iii)** Jennifer Jamie⁹ Gerk (435) was born on 29 Mar 1984 at Kelowna, BC, CAN. She married Greg Owen Jackson (5311) on 3 Jun 2006 at Penticton, BC, CAN.
>
>> **(a)** Madison Paige¹⁰ Jackson (5894) was born on 20 Jan 2010 at Penticton, BC, CAN.
>
> **iv)** Thomas James Jordon⁹ Gerk (436) was born on 2 Aug 1981 at Kelowna, B.C., CAN.
>
> **v)** Alex Michael⁹ Gerk (437) was born on 30 Dec 1988 at Kelowna, BC, CAN. He married Candace Ann Gillard (6517) on 3 Sep 2011 at Penticton, BC, CAN.
>
>> **(a)** Abigail Rae¹⁰ Gerk (6558) was born on 11 Aug 2012 at Penticton, BC, CAN.
>>
>> **(b)** Emilia Rose¹⁰ Gerk (7445) was born on 3 Jul 2016 at Penticton, BC, CAN.
>
> **vi)** Jennifer Lee⁹ Abney (6250) was born on 23 Sep 1983 at CAN.
>
> **vii)** Nicole Marie Edith⁹ Abney (6249) was born on 15 Apr 1984 at Mission, BC, CAN. She married Frank James Christian Gosselin (6253) on 6 Dec 2012 at Cancun, Mexico.
>
>> **(a)** Taylor Anne Marie¹⁰ Gosselin (6254) was born on 27 May 2003 at Kelowna, BC, CAN.
>>
>> **(b)** Dominic Christian¹⁰ Gosselin (6255) was born on 3 Sep 2008 at Kelowna, BC, CAN.
>>
>> **(c)** Lincoln James¹⁰ Gosselin (6256) was born on 18 Aug 2011 at Kelowna, BC, CAN.

viii) Amanda Mae[9] Abney (6251) was born on 18 Sep 1986 at Kelowna, BC, CAN. She married Devon Michael Robertson (6252) on 26 Nov 2011 at West Kelowna, BC, CAN.

(a) Gracie May[10] Robertson (6257) was born on 11 Oct 2009 at Kelowna, BC, CAN.

(d) Edward Roy (Ted)[8] Gerk (396) was born on 27 Jun 1960 at Kelowna, B.C., CAN. He married Marina Loewen (389), daughter of Hans Loewen (597) and Elsa Wiebe (598), on 1 Aug 1981 at Kelowna, B.C., CAN.

i) Elissa Marie[9] Gerk (395) was born on 7 Apr 1983 at Kelowna, B.C., CAN.

(a) Sierra Cameron[10] Gerk (7872) was born on 14 May 2018 at Kelowna, BC, CAN.

ii) Rebecca Lynn[9] Gerk (394) was born on 19 Oct 1984 at Kelowna, B.C., CAN. She married Brandon William David Lowe (5896), son of Kelly Lowe (6258) and Donna Cook (6259), on 22 Aug 2010 at Kamloops, BC, CAN.

(a) Carter Levi[10] Lowe (6384) was born on 17 Apr 2012 at Kelowna, BC, CAN.

(b) Everly Elizabeth Margaret[10] Lowe (6811) was born on 30 Oct 2014 at Grande Prairie, AB, CAN.

iii) Natalia Ann[9] Gerk (393) was born on 26 Jan 1987 at Vancouver, B.C., CAN. She married Devon Kiyoshi Mori (7488), son of Brian Keishi Mori (7489) and Debra Jill Tittsworth (7490), on 10 Jul 2016 at Kelowna, BC, CAN.

(a) Tatyana Ashley[10] Wiechnik (5851) was born on 30 Jul 2009 at Calgary, AB, CAN.

iv) Andrew Paul[9] Gerk (392) was born on 18 Jul 1988 at Kelowna, B.C., CAN.

v) David Michael[9] Gerk (391) was born on 19 Jan 1990 at Kelowna, B.C., CAN. He married Sharan Sandhar (5895) on 20 Feb 2010 at Kelowna, BC, CAN.

(a) Ashton Pavel[10] Gerk (6004) was born on 19 May 2010 at Kelowna, BC, CAN.

(b) Mason Jude[10] Gerk (7491) was born on 23 Sep 2016 at Calgary, AB, CAN.

vi) Stephanie Grace[9] Gerk (390) was born on 17 Sep 1991 at Kelowna, B.C., CAN.

vii) Kristina Esther[9] Gerk (504) was born on 4 Jul 1993 at Kelowna, BC, CAN.

viii) Kimberly Joy[9] Gerk (505) was born on 5 Jan 1995 at Kelowna, B.C., CAN.

ix) Steven Jesse John[9] Gerk (506) was born on 28 Jul 1997 at Kelowna, BC, CAN.

x) Josiah Edward[9] Gerk (507) was born on 17 Feb 1999 at Kelowna, BC, CAN.

xi) Ashley Elsa Margaret[9] Gerk (1092) was born on 17 May 2001 at Kelowna, B.C., CAN.

(e) Deborah Ann[8] Gerk (400) was born on 16 Jul 1967 at Kelowna, B.C., CAN.

(h) Katharina[6] Gerk (411) was born on 18 May 1904 at Josefstal, Saratov, RUS. She married Kaspar Blattner (423), son of Johan Georg Blattner (4315) and Konstansia Kaes (4316), in Jan 1922 at Josefstal, Saratov, RUS. She died on 1 May 1985 at Angren, Tashkent Oblast, USSR, at age 80.

i) Georg[7] Blattner (471) was born in 1926 at Josefstal, Stalingrad Oblast, USSR. He died in 1970 at Angren, Tashkent Oblast, USSR.

ii) Anna[7] Blattner (472) married (--?--) Petrova (4620) at USSR. She was born on 22 Nov 1922 at Josefstal, Saratov, USSR. She died on 27 Aug 2007 at Buzuluk, Orenburg, Russia, at age 84.

iii) Elizabeta[7] Blattner (473) was born in 1924 at Josefstal, Saratov, USSR. She died in 1994 at Angren, Uzbekistan.

(i) Maria[6] Gerk (412) was born on 27 Apr 1906 at Josefstal, Saratov, RUS. She married Johannes Leonardt (424), son of Josef Leonardt (4895) and Anna Margareta Zink (4896), in Jan 1923 at Josefstal, Saratov, RUS. She married Johannes Kern (439), son of Johannes Kern (5569) and Elisabetha Gerling (5570), in 1933? at Josefstal, Stalingrad Oblast, USSR. She married Peter Valde (440) in 1943? at USSR. She died on 27 Apr 1999 at Russkaya Polyana, Omsk Oblast, RUS, at age 93.

i) Anna[7] Leonardt (474) was born circa 1924 at Josefstal, Saratov, USSR.

ii) Palina[7] Leonardt (475) was born circa 1925 at Josefstal, Saratov, USSR.

iii) Peter[7] Kern (476) was born circa 1934 at Josefstal, Stalingrad Oblast, USSR.

iv) Piada[7] Kern (477) was born circa 1936 at Josefstal, Stalingrad Oblast, USSR.

v) Maria[7] Kern (478) was born circa 1938 at Josefstal, Stalingrad Oblast, USSR.

vi) Andrea[7] Kern (479) was born circa 1941 at Josefstal, Stalingrad Oblast, USSR.

vii) Nadya[7] Kern (480) was born circa 1940 at Josefstal, Stalingrad Oblast, USSR.

(j) Gottfried[6] Gerk (413) was born on 3 May 1908 at Josefstal, Saratov, RUS. He married Elisabetha Kisser (421), daughter of Josef Kisser (2246) and Barbara Schmidt (2247), in 1925 at Josefstal, Stalingrad Oblast, USSR. He died on 5 Nov 1980 at Lusino, Omsk Oblast, USSR, at age 72.

i) Elisabeta[7] Gerk (481) was born on 20 Feb 1926 at Josefstal, Stalingrad Oblast, USSR. She married Arkadii Gerasimov (6277) in 1950 at USSR. She married Michael Root (6319) in 1951 at USSR.

(a) Michael[8] Root (6320) was born on 28 Jan 1952 at USSR.

(b) Raisa[8] Root (6321) was born on 20 Apr 1953 at USSR.

(c) Ludmilla[8] Root (6322) was born on 9 Nov 1955 at USSR.

(d) Sergei[8] Root (6323) was born on 10 Jan 1957 at USSR.

(e) Waldemar[8] Gerk (6318) was born in 1951 at USSR.

ii) Lydia[7] Gerk (482) was born on 18 Apr 1937 at Josefstal, Stalingrad Oblast, USSR. She married Alexei Ivanov (6278) circa 1959 at USSR.

(a) Sergei[8] Ivanov (6279) was born on 7 Jul 1960 at USSR. He died in 1974 at USSR.

(b) Ludmilla[8] Ivanov (6280) married (--?--) Litvinov (6281) at USSR. She was born on 24 Sep 1961 at Omsk, USSR.

i) Alexander[9] Litvinov (6314) was born in 1978 at USSR. He died in 1995 at RUS.

ii) Daniel[9] Litvinov (6315) was born on 14 Jan 1996 at RUS.

iii) Paul[9] Litvinov (6316) was born on 21 Jan 1998 at RUS.

iii) Maria[7] Gerk (483) married Nikolai Jarikov (6282) at USSR. She was born on 1 Apr 1945 at USSR. She died in 1993 at Azinsk, RUS.

iv) Barbara Valentina[7] Gerk (700) married Nikolai Nikitina (6317). She was born on 15 Sep 1933 at Josefstal, Stalingrad Oblast, USSR. She died in 2009 at Tyumen, RUS.

(k) Johannes[6] Gerk (414) was born on 22 Feb 1911 at Josefstal, Saratov, RUS. He married Barbara Dieser (110), daughter of Adam Paul Dieser (105) and Anna Margareta Schaab (106), on 24 Oct 1929 at Josefstal, Stalingrad Oblast, USSR. He died on 24 Apr 1996 at Nizhnekamsk, Kazan Oblast, USSR, at age 85.

i) Valeria[7] Gerk (484) was born on 1 May 1937 at Josefstal, Stalingrad Oblast, USSR. She died in 1938 at Josefstal, Stalingrad Oblast, USSR.

ii) Waldemar[7] Gerk (485) married Lila Aul (487), daughter of Konrad Aul (678). He was born on 1 Feb 1939 at Josefstal, Stalingrad Oblast, USSR. He died on 6 May 2002 at Stuttgart, Germany, at age 63.

(a) Svetlena[8] Gerk (489) was born on 17 May 1962 at Krasnoturinsk, Sverdlovsk Oblast, USSR. She married Vladimir Volkomurov (673) in 1988.

i) Alexander[9] Volkomurov (674) was born on 6 Mar 1989 at Tumen, USSR.

(b) Konstantin[8] Gerk (488) married Ludmilla Jost (675), daughter of Rudolph Jost (677). He was born on 6 May 1964 at Krasnoturinsk, Sverdlovsk Oblast, USSR.

i) Johannes[9] Gerk (676) was born on 9 Jul 1990 at Nizhnekamsk, Kazan Oblast, USSR.

iii) Eduard[7] Gerk (486) was born in 1941 at Josefstal, Stalingrad Oblast, USSR. He died in Feb 1942 at Omsk Oblast, USSR.

(9) Jakob[5] Gerk (4281) was born in 1855 at Josefstal, Saratov, RUS. He died on 25 Jan 1858 at Josefstal, Saratov, RUS.

g) Maria Anna^4 Gerk (516) was born on 24 Oct 1828 at Koehler, Saratov, RUS. She married Adam Schaefer (4048) on 14 Feb 1850 at Kamenka, Saratov, RUS.

h) Elisabeta^4 Gerk (517) was born on 23 Oct 1830 at Koehler, Saratov, RUS. She married Andreas Kelbermerter (3575), son of Valentin Kelbermerter (3576) and Anna Marie Flohr (3577), on 3 Nov 1852 at Josefstal, Saratov, RUS. She died on 10 Sep 1859 at Josefstal, Saratov, RUS, at age 28.

(1) Nikolaus^5 Kelbermerter (3578) was born in 1857 at Marienfeld, Saratov, RUS.

i) Katarina^4 Gerk (518) was born on 21 Mar 1834 at Koehler, Saratov, RUS. She married Kaspar Domme (3523), son of Kaspar Domme (3524) and Gertrude (--?--) (3579), on 3 Nov 1852 at Josefstal, Saratov, RUS. She died on 10 Dec 1897 at Josefstal, Saratov, RUS, at age 63.

(1) Wilhelm^5 Domme (3525) was born in 1855 at Josefstal, Saratov, RUS. He married Anna M Hubert (6100) in 1876 at Josefstal, Saratov, RUS.

(a) Georg^6 Domme (6814) was born in 1869 at Josefstal, Saratov, RUS. He married Elisabetha Arnold (8113), daughter of Johan Adam Arnold (4445) and Anna Margareta Urich (--?--) (6816), on 15 Nov 1895 at Josefstal, Saratov, RUS.

(b) Johannes^6 Domme (5500) was born in 1877 at Josefstal, Saratov, RUS.

(c) Anna Maria^6 Domme (6840) was born in 1879 at Josefstal, Saratov, RUS. She married Johannes Arnold (6822), son of Johan Adam Arnold (4445) and Anna Margareta Urich (--?--) (6816), on 14 Feb 1899 at Josefstal, Saratov, RUS.

i) Johannes^7 Arnold (6857) was born in 1903 at Josefstal, Saratov, RUS. He died on 15 Jun 1913 at Josefstal, Saratov, RUS.

ii) Margareta^7 Arnold (6858) was born in 1906 at Josefstal, RUS. She died on 14 Sep 1913 at Josefstal, Saratov, RUS.

iii) Rose^7 Arnold (6859) was born in 1909 at Josefstal, Saratov, RUS. She died on 11 Sep 1913 at Josefstal, Saratov, RUS.

iv) Katharina^7 Arnold (6854) was born on 27 Nov 1911 at Josefstal, Saratov, RUS. She died on 23 Jun 1913 at Josefstal, Saratov, RUS, at age 1.

v) Angela^7 Arnold (6855) was born on 3 Mar 1913 at Josefstal, Saratov, RUS.

vi) Peter^7 Arnold (6856) was born on 22 Apr 1914 at Josefstal, Saratov, RUS.

vii) Georg^7 Arnold (6860) was born on 10 Jan 1916 at Josefstal, Saratov, RUS.

(d) Kristof^6 Domme (4292) was born on 9 Jan 1885 at Josefstal, Saratov, RUS. He married Anna Benz (6103) in 1909.

i) Jose^7 Domme (6104) was born on 20 Oct 1909 at Pubelo San José, Coronel Suárez, Buenos Aires, ARG.

ii) Beate^7 Domme (6144) was born on 9 Jul 1911 at Josefstal, Saratov, RUS. She died on 25 Dec 1911 at Josefstal, Saratov, RUS.

iii) Monika^7 Domme (6145) was born on 1 Jan 1913 at Josefstal, Saratov, RUS.

iv) Georg^7 Domme (6146) was born on 12 Jun 1915 at Josefstal, Saratov, RUS.

(e) Pedro^6 Domme (6102) was born in 1891 at Josefstal, Saratov, RUS.

(f) Susanna^6 Domme (6101) was born in 1901 at Josefstal, Saratov, RUS.

(2) Kaspar^5 Domme (4523) was born on 20 Apr 1861 at Josefstal, Saratov, RUS. He married Elisabetha Strack (5922) in 1882 at Josefstal, Saratov, RUS. He emigrated on 9 Nov 1908 from Bremen, GER. He died on 2 Oct 1930 at Pueblo San Jose, Coronel Suarez, Buenos Aires, ARG, at age 69.

(a) Matias^6 Domme (2123) was born on 22 Dec 1890 at Josefstal, Saratov, RUS. He married Katarina Schaefer (813), daughter of Stephan Schaefer (784) and Katarina Gerk (762), on 19 Nov 1920 at San José, Coronel Suárez, Buenos Aires, ARG.

(b) Elisabetha^6 Domme (5924) was born in 1900 at Josefstal, Saratov, RUS.

(c) Anna^6 Domme (5925) married Pedro Pascal (6107) at Pubelo San José, Coronel Suárez, Buenos Aires, ARG. She was born in 1906 at Josefstal, Saratov, RUS.

(3) Mattias^5 Domme (4574) was born on 27 Sep 1864 at Josefstal, Saratov, RUS. He married Anna Maria Blattner (4575) in 1884 at Josefstal, Saratov, RUS.

   (a) Georg^6 Domme (4577) was born on 7 Oct 1884 at Josefstal, Saratov, RUS. He married Elisabeta Erdle (4578) on 20 Jan 1910 at Josefstal, Saratov, RUS.

   i) Anna^7 Domme (4589) was born in 1911 at Josefstal, Saratov, RUS. She died on 5 Oct 1913 at Josefstal, Saratov, RUS.

   ii) Georg^7 Domme (4588) was born on 7 Jan 1913 at Josefstal, Saratov, RUS. He died on 9 Jan 1913 at Josefstal, Saratov, RUS.

   iii) Elena^7 Domme (5809) was born on 23 May 1915 at Josefstal, Saratov, RUS.

   (b) Mattias^6 Domme (4576) was born on 12 Jun 1886 at Josefstal, Saratov, RUS. He married Margareta Heinrich (4586) on 13 Sep 1911 at Josefstal, Saratov, RUS.

   i) Katarina^7 Domme (4587) was born in 1912 at Josefstal, Saratov, RUS. She died on 12 Oct 1912 at Josefstal, Saratov, RUS.

   ii) Andrew^7 Domme (4623) was born on 5 Oct 1913 at Josefstal, Saratov, RUS.

   (c) Kaspar^6 Domme (4579) was born on 11 Mar 1887 at Josefstal, Saratov, RUS. He married Julia Simon (4590) on 10 Oct 1913 at Josefstal, Saratov, RUS.

   i) Johannes^7 Domme (4624) was born on 20 Feb 1915 at Josefstal, Saratov, RUS.

   (d) Katarina^6 Domme (4625) was born in 1889 at Josefstal, Saratov, RUS. She married Georg Heinrich (4391), son of Johann Peter Heinrich (1107) and Katarina Gerk (723), on 3 Nov 1907 at Josefstal, Saratov, RUS.

   i) Maria^7 Heinrich (4626) was born on 10 Nov 1909 at Josefstal, Saratov, RUS.

   ii) Friedrich^7 Heinrich (4627) was born on 9 May 1911 at Josefstal, Saratov, RUS.

   (e) Igantius^6 Domme (4580) was born in 1892 at Josefstal, Saratov, RUS.

   (f) Anna^6 Domme (4373) was born on 1 Nov 1892 at Josefstal, Saratov, RUS. She married Friedrich Weigel (4359), son of Kaspar Weigel (2203) and Margareta Mitsig (2204), on 3 Nov 1910 at Josefstal, Saratov, RUS. She immigrated on 6 May 1914 to Baltimore, Maryland, USA. She died on 30 Oct 1918 at Topeka, Kansas, USA, at age 25.

   i) Elenora^7 Weigel (4374) was born on 26 Oct 1911 at Josefstal, Saratov, RUS.

   (g) Johannes^6 Domme (4583) was born on 15 Oct 1894 at Josefstal, Saratov, RUS.

   (h) Josef^6 Domme (4581) was born in 1896 at Josefstal, Saratov, RUS. He died on 12 Mar 1907 at Josefstal, Saratov, RUS.

   (i) Jakob^6 Domme (4584) was born on 4 Jun 1898 at Josefstal, Saratov, RUS.

   (j) Elisabetha^6 Domme (4585) was born in 1901 at Josefstal, Saratov, RUS.

   (k) Valentin^6 Domme (4582) was born in 1906 at Josefstal, Saratov, RUS. He died on 12 Mar 1907 at Josefstal, Saratov, RUS.

(4) Barbara^5 Domme (3526) was born on 25 Jun 1868 at Josefstal, Saratov, RUS.

(5) Margareta^5 Domme (3527) was born on 2 Mar 1871 at Josefstal, Saratov, RUS.

(6) Margareta^5 Domme (3528) was born on 20 Nov 1873 at Josefstal, Saratov, RUS. She married Josef Breit (7494), son of Josef Breit (2176) and Magdalena Helmert (2177), circa 1893 at Josefstal, Saratov, RUS.

   (a) Elisabetha^6 Breit (7496) was born in 1901 at Josefstal, Saratov, RUS.

   (b) Josef^6 Breit (7497) was born in 1903 at Josefstal, Saratov, RUS.

   (c) Phillip^6 Breit (7498) was born in 1905 at Josefstal, Saratov, RUS.

   (d) Pauline^6 Breit (7495) was born on 28 May 1907 at Josefstal, Saratov, RUS.

4. Elisabeta^3 Gerk (3693) was born in 1781 at Koehler, Saratov, RUS. She married Johan Georg Döring (3694), son of Johan Döring (3696) and Margarata Heil (3697), in 1798.

a) Barbara[4] Döring (3695) was born in 1798 at Koehler, Saratov, RUS.

5. Maria Barbara[3] Gerk (527) was born in 1791 at Koehler, Saratov, RUS. She died on 11 Jan 1805 at Koehler, Saratov, RUS.

6. Magdalena[3] Gerk (528) was born in 1793 at Koehler, Saratov, RUS. She died on 4 Jan 1805 at Koehler, Saratov, RUS.

7. Katarina[3] Gerk (529) was born in 1795 at Koehler, Saratov, RUS. She married Jakob Leonhardt (4046) on 22 Jan 1812 at Koehler, Saratov, RUS.

8. Johann Heinrich[3] Gerk (4102) was born in 1796 at Koehler, Saratov, RUS. He died in 1800 at Koehler, Saratov, RUS.

9. Michael[3] Gerk (526) was born in 1798 at Koehler, Saratov, RUS.

10. Johann Heinrich[3] Gerk (530) was born in 1802 at Koehler, Saratov, RUS. He married Maria Margareta Ziegler (533) circa 1820 at Koehler, Saratov, RUS. He married Margareta Schrack (4053) on 21 Jul 1853 at Koehler, Saratov, RUS. He died on 6 Jan 1877 at Koehler, Saratov, RUS.

    a) Maria Margareta[4] Gerk (540) was born in 1821 at Koehler, Saratov, RUS. She married Peter Weinzettel (4077) on 11 Nov 1841 at Koehler, Saratov, RUS. She married Philipp Dietrich (4078) on 23 Nov 1848 at Koehler, Saratov, RUS.

    b) Kristof[4] Gerk (534) was born in 1823 at Koehler, Saratov, RUS. He married Maria Margareta Kirchgessner (535) on 11 Nov 1841 at Koehler, Saratov, RUS. He died on 21 Dec 1874 at Koehler, Saratov, RUS.

        (1) Gottlieb[5] Gerk (3041) was born on 11 Nov 1843 at Koehler, Saratov, RUS.

        (2) Johannes Adam[5] Gerk (536) was born on 3 Sep 1845 at Koehler, Saratov, RUS.

        (3) Johannes[5] Gerk (3042) was born on 5 Oct 1846 at Koehler, Saratov, RUS. He married Susanna Gareis (3958), daughter of Josef Gareis (4554) and Kunigunda Klein (4555), on 22 Jan 1863 at Koehler, Saratov, RUS. He died on 19 Feb 1876 at Koehler, Saratov, RUS, at age 29.

            (a) Adam[6] Gerk (4058) was born on 13 Mar 1864 at Koehler, Saratov, RUS. He married Elisabetha Klug (4059) on 15 Nov 1883 at Koehler, Saratov, RUS. He died on 28 Sep 1888 at Koehler, Saratov, RUS, at age 24.

                i) Johan[7] Gerk (4062) was born in 1884 at Koehler, Saratov, RUS. He died on 5 Aug 1887 at Koehler, Saratov, RUS.

                ii) Katarina[7] Gerk (4061) was born on 3 Oct 1887 at Koehler, Saratov, RUS. She died on 22 Sep 1889 at Koehler, Saratov, RUS, at age 1.

            (b) Gottfried[6] Gerk (4065) was born in 1868 at Koehler, Saratov, RUS. He married Anna Maria Haspert (4066) on 13 Nov 1890 at Koehler, Saratov, RUS. He died in 1892 at Koehler, Saratov, RUS.

                i) Barbara[7] Gerk (4068) was born on 14 Oct 1891 at Koehler, Saratov, RUS.

            (c) Peter[6] Gerk (4057) was born on 5 Jul 1871 at Koehler, Saratov, RUS. He died on 14 Mar 1876 at Koehler, Saratov, RUS, at age 4.

            (d) Nikolaus[6] Gerk (3959) was born on 26 Aug 1873 at Koehler, Saratov, RUS.

        (4) Katarina[5] Gerk (537) was born on 3 Apr 1849 at Koehler, Saratov, RUS. She married Gottfried Remisch (4074) on 28 Nov 1867 at Koehler, Saratov, RUS.

            (a) Barbara[6] Remisch (7753) was born on 12 Dec 1873 at Koehler, Saratov, RUS.

            (b) Peter[6] Remisch (7754) was born on 26 Dec 1881 at Koehler, Saratov, RUS.

            (c) Peter[6] Remisch (7755) was born on 18 Mar 1885 at Koehler, Saratov, RUS.

        (5) Magdalena[5] Gerk (3043) was born on 5 Sep 1851 at Koehler, Saratov, RUS. She died on 14 Sep 1852 at Koehler, Saratov, RUS, at age 1.

        (6) Philipp[5] Gerk (538) was born on 21 Jul 1853 at Koehler, Saratov, RUS. He died on 21 Nov 1859 at Koehler, Saratov, RUS, at age 6.

        (7) Heinrich[5] Gerk (3044) was born on 28 Jan 1856 at Koehler, Saratov, RUS. He died on 24 Oct 1856 at Koehler, Saratov, RUS.

        (8) Peter[5] Gerk (1875) was born on 2 Jul 1858 at Koehler, Saratov, RUS. He married Elisabeta Sanger (1876) on 12 Oct 1876 at Koehler, Saratov, RUS. He died on 25 Mar 1939 at Crespo, Entre Ríos, ARG, at age 80.

(a) Nikolaus^6 Gerk (4070) was born on 23 Apr 1878 at Koehler, Saratov, RUS.

(b) Margareta^6 Gerk (4071) was born on 1 Jul 1879 at Koehler, Saratov, RUS. She died on 3 Jun 1885 at Koehler, Saratov, RUS, at age 5.

(c) Jakob^6 Gerk (1877) was born on 15 Nov 1881 at Koehler, Saratov, RUS. He married Elisabeta Sommer (1878), daughter of Adam Sommer (2167) and Katarina Schoenfeld (2168), on 15 Sep 1903 at Crespo, Entre Ríos, ARG. He died on 25 Aug 1941 at Crespo, Entre Ríos, ARG, at age 59.

   i) Barbara^7 Gerk (2358) was born on 13 Jan 1904 at San José, Entre Ríos, ARG. She died on 23 Apr 1905 at Crespo, Entre Ríos, ARG, at age 1.

   ii) Catalina^7 Gerk (1915) was born on 17 Aug 1905 at San Arnold, Crespo, Entre Ríos, ARG. She married Jorge Jacob (1916), son of Kaspar Jacob (2370) and Catalina Schmidt (2371), on 7 Oct 1924 at Crespo, Entre Ríos, ARG. She died on 4 Nov 1972 at Crespo, Entre Ríos, ARG, at age 67.

   iii) Mónica Barbara^7 Gerk (1917) was born on 11 Jul 1907 at Crespo, Entre Ríos, ARG. She married Pedro Goette (1918), son of Peter Goette (5374) and Katarina Wilberger (5375), on 24 Apr 1927 at Crespo, Entre Ríos, ARG. She died on 23 Mar 1928 at Crespo, Entre Ríos, ARG, at age 20.

   iv) Nicolas^7 Gerk (2359) was born on 27 May 1909 at Crespo, Entre Ríos, ARG. He married Barbara Haberkorn (2360) on 26 Aug 1930 at Crespo, Entre Ríos, ARG.

      (a) Teófilo Alfredo^8 Gerk (2979) was born on 22 Oct 1933 at Crespo, Entre Ríos, ARG.

      (b) Amanda^8 Gerk (2980) was born on 22 Mar 1936 at Crespo, Entre Ríos, ARG.

   v) Magdalena^7 Gerk (2363) was born on 8 Jul 1911 at Crespo, Entre Ríos, ARG. She married Adam Baumann (2364) on 5 Apr 1932 at Crespo, Entre Ríos, ARG.

      (a) Jorge^8 Baumann (2835) was born on 27 Jan 1933 at Crespo, Entre Ríos, ARG.

      (b) Teresa^8 Baumann (2836) was born on 26 Apr 1934 at Crespo, Entre Ríos, ARG. She married Martin Del Valle (2837) in 1957 at Crespo, Entre Ríos, ARG.

      (c) Ernesto^8 Baumann (2838) was born on 2 Aug 1935 at Crespo, Entre Ríos, ARG.

      (d) Elisa Agustina^8 Baumann (2829) was born on 14 Apr 1937 at Crespo, Entre Ríos, ARG. She married Nicasio Orozco (2830), son of Higinio Orozco (2839) and Paula Rojo (2840), on 27 Jun 1964 at Crespo, Entre Ríos, ARG.

         i) Mercedes del Carmen^9 Orozco (2832) married Juan Francisco Kownacki (2841) at ARG. She was born on 8 Nov 1965 at Jose C. Paz, Buenos Aires, ARG.

            (a) Cesar Adrian^{10} Kownacki (2842) was born on 8 Sep 1989 at San Isidro, Buenos Aires, ARG.

            (b) German Dario^{10} Kownacki (2843) was born on 1 Jan 1994 at San Isidro, Buenos Aires, ARG.

            (c) Leonardo Manuel^{10} Kownacki (2844) was born on 1 Jan 1994 at San Isidro, Buenos Aires, ARG.

         ii) Laura Estela^9 Orozco (2833) was born on 9 Jun 1967 at Jose C. Paz, Buenos Aires, ARG.

         iii) Mauricio Hernán^9 Orozco (2834) married Monica Noemi Crespi (2845) at ARG. He was born on 16 Mar 1970 at Jose C. Paz, Buenos Aires, ARG.

            (a) Jackeline Vanina^{10} Orozco (2846) was born on 20 Jan 1998 at Moreno, Buenos Aires, ARG.

            (b) Brian Ezequiel^{10} Orozco (2847) was born on 20 Feb 1998 at Moreno, Buenos Aires, ARG.

         iv) Amalia^9 Orozco (2831) was born on 22 Jul 1982 at San Miguel, Buenos Aires, ARG.

      (e) Andres^8 Baumann (2848) married Emilia Abarza (2849). He was born on 15 May 1939 at Crespo, Entre Ríos, ARG.

      (f) Anita^8 Baumann (2850) was born on 7 Jun 1941 at Crespo, Entre Ríos, ARG. She married Anibal Carrazco (2851) in 1976 at ARG.

      (g) Aurelio^8 Baumann (2852) was born on 20 Mar 1944 at Crespo, Entre Ríos, ARG.

      (h) Amanda^8 Baumann (2853) was born on 5 May 1946 at Crespo, Entre Ríos, ARG. She married Alberto Dana (2854) in 1967 at ARG.

(i) Maria Elvira[8] Baumann (2855) was born on 7 Jun 1950 at Valle Maria, Entre Ríos, ARG.

vi) Pedro[7] Gerk (2361) was born on 14 Apr 1914 at Crespo, Entre Ríos, ARG. He married Delfina Frank (2362) on 21 Jul 1949 at Crespo, Entre Ríos, ARG.

vii) Maria[7] Gerk (2367) was born on 10 Jul 1916 at Crespo, Entre Ríos, ARG. She married Francisco Pedro Rau (3024), son of Francisco Rau (3025) and Rosa Unrein (3026), on 28 Jan 1936 at Hernandez, Entre Ríos, ARG.

viii) Elisa[7] Gerk (2365) was born on 6 Sep 1918 at Crespo, Entre Ríos, ARG. She married Pedro Prediger (2366) on 26 Oct 1946 at Crespo, Entre Ríos, ARG. She died on 4 Jul 1972 at Olivos, Buenos Aires, ARG, at age 53.

ix) Cristina[7] Gerk (2368) was born on 16 Sep 1920 at Crespo, Entre Ríos, ARG. She married Pedro Alois Hollman (2369) on 9 Oct 1943 at Crespo, Entre Ríos, ARG.

x) Isabel[7] Gerk (2925) was born on 15 Mar 1923 at Crespo, Entre Ríos, ARG.

xi) Bárbara Fidela[7] Gerk (2926) was born on 25 Jan 1925 at Crespo, Entre Ríos, ARG. She married Agustin Schonfeld (2927) on 28 Jan 1949 at Maria Luisa, Entre Ríos, ARG.

xii) Josefa[7] Gerk (2928) was born on 28 Mar 1927 at Crespo, Entre Ríos, ARG.

xiii) Inés[7] Gerk (2981) was born on 17 Jun 1930 at Crespo, Entre Ríos, ARG.

(d) Elisabetha[6] Gerk (4073) was born on 30 Dec 1883 at Koehler, Saratov, RUS.

(e) Valentine[6] Gerk (2164) was born on 3 Mar 1887 at Valle Maria, Entre Ríos, ARG.

(f) Isabel[6] Gerk (2163) was born on 17 Aug 1888 at Valle Maria, Entre Ríos, ARG.

(g) Juan[6] Gerk (2165) was born on 3 May 1890 at Valle Maria, Entre Ríos, ARG.

(h) Nicolas[6] Gerk (1879) was born on 18 Jan 1892 at Crespo, Entre Ríos, ARG. He married Catalina Baron (1880), daughter of Juan P. Baron (1881) and Barbara Bahl (1882), on 2 Sep 1913 at Crespo, Entre Ríos, ARG. He married Ana Haberkorn (2804) circa 1930 at Crespo, Entre Ríos, ARG. He died on 10 Sep 1969 at Crespo, Entre Ríos, ARG, at age 77.

i) Barbara[7] Gerk (2173) was born on 11 Jan 1915 at Crespo, Entre Ríos, ARG.

ii) Isidoro[7] Gerk (2174) was born on 5 Apr 1917 at Crespo, Entre Ríos, ARG.

iii) Teresa[7] Gerk (1919) was born on 16 Mar 1919 at Crespo, Entre Ríos, ARG. She died on 29 May 1919 at Crespo, Entre Ríos, ARG.

iv) Salvador[7] Gerk (2175) was born on 12 Jul 1920 at Crespo, Entre Ríos, ARG. He married Erlinda Blanca Carlutti (2386) on 16 Feb 1956 at Córdoba, Córdoba, ARG.

v) Santiago[7] Gerk (2806) was born on 13 Jun 1923 at Crespo, Entre Ríos, ARG. He died on 3 Feb 1933 at Crespo, Entre Ríos, ARG, at age 9.

vi) Maria Elvira[7] Gerk (2929) was born on 8 Jul 1925 at Crespo, Entre Ríos, ARG.

vii) Anita Erminda[7] Gerk (2970) was born on 7 Jun 1927 at Crespo, Entre Ríos, ARG.

viii) Susana[7] Gerk (2805) was born on 21 Apr 1931 at Crespo, Entre Ríos, ARG. She died on 26 Jan 1933 at Crespo, Entre Ríos, ARG, at age 1.

ix) Maria Elena[7] Gerk (2971) was born on 3 May 1932 at Crespo, Entre Ríos, ARG.

x) Anastasia[7] Gerk (2972) was born on 19 Apr 1934 at Crespo, Entre Ríos, ARG.

xi) Jorge Ernesto[7] Gerk (2973) was born on 2 Nov 1935 at Crespo, Entre Ríos, ARG. He married Norma Walter (2974) on 11 Nov 1980 at Crespo, Entre Ríos, ARG.

xii) Santiago Louis[7] Gerk (2807) married Susana Bernz (2808) at Crespo, Entre Ríos, ARG. He was born on 7 Sep 1937 at Crespo, Entre Ríos, ARG. He died on 4 Apr 1977 at Crespo, Entre Ríos, ARG, at age 39.

xiii) Pedro Agustín[7] Gerk (2975) was born on 27 Dec 1937 at Crespo, Entre Ríos, ARG.

xiv) Cecilia[7] Gerk (2976) was born on 3 May 1939 at Crespo, Entre Ríos, ARG.

xv) Antonio[7] Gerk (1889) was born in 1940 at ARG.

xvi) Victor Hugo[7] Gerk (2977) was born on 28 Apr 1941 at Crespo, Entre Ríos, ARG. He married Esther Bruch (2978) in Nov 1976 at Crespo, Entre Ríos, ARG. He died on 13 Aug 2004 at Crespo, Entre Ríos, ARG, at age 63.

xvii) Natalio[7] Gerk (2999) was born on 22 Nov 1942 at Crespo, Entre Ríos, ARG.

xviii) Pablo Nicolás[7] Gerk (3000) was born on 16 Nov 1944 at Crespo, Entre Ríos, ARG. He married Ester del Valle (3074) in Oct 1969 at Crespo, Entre Ríos, ARG. He died on 6 Sep 1999 at Crespo, Entre Ríos, ARG, at age 54.

    (a) Mariá[8] Gerk (3098) was born on 28 Oct 1969 at Crespo, Entre Ríos, ARG.

    (b) Pablo Ernesto[8] Gerk (3075) was born on 14 May 1978 at Crespo, Entre Ríos, ARG.

    (c) Claudia[8] Gerk (3099) was born on 1 Mar 1972 at Crespo, Entre Ríos, ARG.

xix) Irma Catalina[7] Gerk (3001) was born on 16 Nov 1946 at Crespo, Entre Ríos, ARG. She married Emilio Borré (3003) on 25 Sep 1971 at Crespo, Entre Ríos, ARG.

xx) Carlos[7] Gerk (3002) was born on 16 May 1948 at Crespo, Entre Ríos, ARG.

(i) Pedro[6] Gerk (1885) was born on 17 Dec 1893 at Crespo, Entre Ríos, ARG. He married Margarita Kloster (1886), daughter of Antonia Kloster (1887) and Isabel Edelmann (1888), on 26 Oct 1915 at Crespo, Entre Ríos, ARG. He died in 1957 at Hernandez, Entre Ríos, ARG.

i) Juan[7] Gerk (1898) was born at ARG. He died in 1980 at ARG.

ii) Maria[7] Gerk (2171) was born on 12 May 1916 at Crespo, Entre Ríos, ARG. She died on 12 May 1916 at Crespo, Entre Ríos, ARG.

iii) Isabel[7] Gerk (2172) was born on 21 Jan 1918 at Crespo, Entre Ríos, ARG. She died in 2002 at Hernandez, Entre Ríos, ARG.

    (a) David[8] Gerk (3012) was born on 6 Dec 1939 at Hernandez, Entre Ríos, ARG.

iv) Teresa[7] Gerk (1891) was born on 21 Dec 1919 at Crespo, Entre Ríos, ARG. She married Teodoro Gottig (1901), son of Jorge Gottig (3022) and Margarita Köning (3023), circa 1947 at Hernandez, Entre Ríos, ARG. She died on 14 Jan 2001 at Crespo, Entre Ríos, ARG, at age 81.

v) Florentina[7] Gerk (1920) was born on 18 Sep 1921 at Crespo, Entre Ríos, ARG. She died on 30 Jan 1922 at Crespo, Entre Ríos, ARG.

vi) José[7] Gerk (2924) was born on 22 Nov 1922 at Crespo, Entre Ríos, ARG. He died in 1992 at Paso del Rey, Buenos Aires, ARG.

vii) Adam[7] Gerk (2372) was born on 28 Jul 1924 at Crespo, Entre Ríos, ARG. He died on 4 Aug 1924 at Crespo, Entre Ríos, ARG.

viii) Amalia[7] Gerk (1890) was born on 20 Sep 1925 at Hernandez, Entre Ríos, ARG. She married Francisco Ramírez (2984) on 2 Feb 1943 at Hernandez, Entre Ríos, ARG.

    (a) Hilda[8] Ramírez (2985) married Jorge Aga (2992). She was born on 12 Jan 1944 at ARG.

    (b) Leonor[8] Ramírez (2986) married Abelino González (2993). He was born on 1 Apr 1945 at ARG.

    (c) Olga Esther[8] Ramírez (2987) married José Díaz (2994). She was born on 12 Apr 1946 at ARG.

    (d) Francisco[8] Ramírez (2988) married Maria Rosa Noguero (2995). He was born on 27 Jul 1947 at ARG.

    (e) Susana Beatriz[8] Ramírez (2989) married Oscar Acosta (2996). She was born on 30 Apr 1952 at ARG.

    (f) Mirta Esther[8] Ramírez (2990) married Alberto Cardoso (2997). She was born on 12 Nov 1953 at ARG.

    (g) Marta Esther[8] Ramírez (2991) married Domingo Gómez (2998). She was born on 16 Dec 1958 at ARG.

ix) Regina[7] Gerk (1894) married (--?--) Salvatierra (1903). She was born on 7 Sep 1927 at Hernandez, Entre Ríos, ARG.

(a) Susana Trinidad^8 Salvatierra (3076) married Savior Ledesma (3077). She was born on 12 Aug 1954 at Buenos Aires, ARG.

  i) Susana Noemi^9 Ledesma (3078) was born on 15 Jun 1975 at ARG.

  ii) Jesica Laura^9 Ledesma (3079) was born on 30 May 1984 at San Clemente, ARG.

x) José^7 Gerk (1892) was born in 1930 at Hernandez, Entre Ríos, ARG. He died in May 1999 at Paso del Rey, Buenos Aires, ARG.

xi) Elisa^7 Gerk (1893) married (--?--) Peles (1902) at Hernandez, Entre Ríos, ARG. She was born in 1931 at Hernandez, Entre Ríos, ARG.

xii) Antonio^7 Gerk (1895) married Elena Mohr (1904) at San Antonio, Entre Ríos, ARG. He was born on 15 Feb 1932 at Hernandez, Entre Ríos, ARG.

  (a) Ricardo^8 Gerk (1905) married Liliana Finella (1908). He was born on 10 Jun 1958 at San Martín, Buenos Aires, ARG.

  (b) Liliana Mónica^8 Gerk (1906) was born on 24 Dec 1961 at San Martín, Buenos Aires, ARG. She married José Carlos Riffel (1909) circa 1983.

  i) Pablo Andrés^9 Riffel (2863) was born on 2 Dec 1983 at ARG.

  ii) Matías José^9 Riffel (2862) was born on 26 Jul 1985 at Crespo, Entre Ríos, ARG.

  iii) Leandro Daniel^9 Riffel (2864) was born on 2 May 1987 at ARG.

  (c) Maria Elena^8 Gerk (1907) was born on 2 Mar 1971 at Capital Federal, Buenos Aires, ARG.

xiii) Paulina^7 Gerk (1897) was born on 28 Feb 1935 at Hernandez, Entre Ríos, ARG. She married Pedro Javier Saccomani (1900) on 14 Jul 1956 at Buenos Aires, Buenos Aires, ARG. She died on 18 Mar 1996 at Villa Deveto, Buenos Aires, ARG, at age 61.

  (a) Juan Alberto^8 Saccomani (1910) was born on 31 Dec 1956 at Buenos Aires, ARG. He married Lucy Gianninoto (1911) in 1985 at Buenos Aires, Buenos Aires, ARG.

  i) Juan Manuel^9 Saccomani (1912) was born in 1986 at Buenos Aires, Buenos Aires, ARG.

  ii) Juan Facundo^9 Saccomani (1913) was born in 1988 at Buenos Aires, Buenos Aires, ARG.

  iii) Maria Malvina^9 Saccomani (1914) was born in 1991 at Buenos Aires, Buenos Aires, ARG.

xiv) Jorge^7 Gerk (1899) was born in 1939 at Hernandez, Entre Ríos, ARG.

xv) Gaspar^7 Gerk (1896) was born on 14 Mar 1940 at Hernandez, Entre Ríos, ARG.

(j) Maria^6 Gerk (1883) was born on 14 Nov 1896 at Crespo, Entre Ríos, ARG. She married Kaspar Goettig (1884), son of Johann Peter Goettig (2169) and Isabel Heinrich (2170), on 22 Sep 1914 at Crespo, Entre Ríos, ARG. She died on 13 Sep 1962 at Crespo, Entre Ríos, ARG, at age 65.

(k) Theresia^6 Gerk (2166) was born on 24 Jul 1898 at Crespo, Entre Ríos, ARG. She died on 20 May 1915 at Crespo, Entre Ríos, ARG, at age 16.

(9) Sophia^5 Gerk (3046) was born on 19 Jul 1861 at Koehler, Saratov, RUS.

(10) Philipp^5 Gerk (4056) was born in 1865 at Koehler, Saratov, RUS. He died on 10 Oct 1868 at Koehler, Saratov, RUS.

c) Josef^4 Gerk (4051) was born on 12 Mar 1827 at Koehler, Saratov, RUS. He died on 11 Dec 1827 at Koehler, Saratov, RUS.

d) Elisabetha^4 Gerk (4075) was born on 21 Nov 1828 at Koehler, Saratov, RUS. She died on 12 Mar 1829 at Koehler, Saratov, RUS.

e) Johann Adam^4 Gerk (643) was born on 1 Jan 1830 at Koehler, Saratov, RUS. He married Magdalena Macht (644), daughter of Johann Adam Macht (3101) and Magdalena Heist (3102), on 27 Jan 1848 at Koehler, Saratov, RUS. He married Konstanzia Dieser (4141), daughter of Valentin Dieser (12) and Katarina Breuning (4503), on 28 Jun 1882 at Koehler, Saratov, RUS. He died circa 1890 at Koehler, Saratov, RUS.

(1) Katarina^5 Gerk (3106) was born on 19 Oct 1848 at Koehler, Saratov, RUS. She married Gottlieb Freiberger (4145), son of Peter Freiberger (7211) and Margareta (--?--) (7212), on 19 Nov 1868 at Koehler, Saratov, RUS. She died on 24 Feb 1882 at Koehler, Saratov, RUS, at age 33.

(a) Peter[6] Freiberger (7738) was born on 17 Jul 1873 at Koehler, Saratov, RUS.

(b) Phillip[6] Freiberger (7739) was born on 9 Sep 1880 at Koehler, Saratov, RUS.

(2) Kristof Josef[5] Gerk (3059) was born on 25 May 1850 at Koehler, Saratov, RUS. He married Katarina Bellendir (4152) on 19 Nov 1868 at Koehler, Saratov, RUS.

(a) Peter[6] Gerk (4160) was born on 5 Oct 1869 at Koehler, Saratov, RUS. He died on 8 Apr 1870 at Koehler, Saratov, RUS.

(b) Valentin[6] Gerk (4167) was born on 25 Aug 1872 at Koehler, Saratov, RUS. He married Katarina Haas (7803) on 13 Nov 1894 at Rozhdestvenskoye, Stavropol, RUS.

(c) Gottlieb[6] Gerk (4161) was born on 24 Mar 1875 at Koehler, Saratov, RUS. He married Elisabetha (--?--) (4236) in 1902 at Koehler, Saratov, RUS.

i) Adam[7] Gerk (4237) was born in 1905 at Koehler, Saratov, RUS.

ii) Johannes[7] Gerk (4238) was born in 1916 at Koehler, Saratov, RUS.

(d) Katarina[6] Gerk (4163) was born on 5 Dec 1879 at Koehler, Saratov, RUS.

(e) Margareta[6] Gerk (4166) was born on 13 Dec 1881 at Koehler, Saratov, RUS.

(f) Katarina[6] Gerk (4164) was born on 25 Oct 1884 at Koehler, Saratov, RUS.

(g) Margareta[6] Gerk (4165) was born in 1886 at Koehler, Saratov, RUS. She died on 22 Jul 1886 at Koehler, Saratov, RUS.

(h) Elisabetha[6] Gerk (4162) was born on 26 Jul 1887 at Koehler, Saratov, RUS. She died on 3 May 1888 at Koehler, Saratov, RUS.

(3) Johann Adam[5] Gerk (646) died at Koehler, Saratov, RUS. He was born on 16 Feb 1853 at Koehler, Saratov, RUS. He married Elisabeta Bretz (1055), daughter of Johannes Adam Bretz (1056) and Elisabetha Barbara Zigler (1057), on 6 Feb 1873 at Koehler, Saratov, RUS.

(a) Elisabetha[6] Gerk (4168) was born on 23 Aug 1873 at Koehler, Saratov, RUS. She died on 10 Jun 1874 at Koehler, Saratov, RUS.

(b) Johannes[6] Gerk (3057) was born on 18 Apr 1875 at Koehler, Saratov, RUS. He died on 5 Nov 1875 at Koehler, Saratov, RUS.

(c) Barbara[6] Gerk (3058) was born on 17 Oct 1880 at Koehler, Saratov, RUS. She died on 29 Oct 1890 at Koehler, Saratov, RUS, at age 10.

(d) Christoph[6] Gerk (1058) was born on 9 Jan 1883 at Koehler, Saratov, RUS. He married Elisabeth Kirchgessner (1059), daughter of David Kirchgessner (1060) and Elisabeta Hasenauer (1061), on 8 Nov 1901 at Koehler, Saratov, RUS. He died in 1948 at Kassel, Germany.

i) Maria[7] Gerk (1679) was born at Koehler, Saratov, RUS. She married (--?--) Schmidt (1680).

ii) Katarina[7] Gerk (1681) was born at Koehler, Saratov, RUS. She married (--?--) Macht (1682).

iii) Barbara[7] Gerk (1683) was born at Koehler, Saratov, RUS. She married (--?--) Schmidt (1684).

iv) Adam[7] Gerk (1062) was born on 16 May 1904 at Koehler, Saratov, RUS. He married Barbara Ruhl (1068) in 1924 at Koehler, Saratov, USSR. He married Klara Burkard (1065), daughter of Konrad Burkardt (1066) and Elisabeta Tetzel (1067), on 15 Jul 1938 at Minsk, USSR.

(a) Maria[8] Gerk (1069) was born on 23 Dec 1924 at Koehler, Saratov, USSR.

(b) Alexander[8] Gerk (1070) was born on 22 Mar 1932 at Minsk, USSR.

(c) Viktoria[8] Gerk (1071) was born on 27 Jul 1935 at Minsk, USSR.

v) Johannes[7] Gerk (1063) was born on 8 Oct 1912 at Koehler, Saratov, RUS. He married Pauline Binneder (1072), daughter of Fritz Binneder (1073) and Katarina Schreffer (1074), on 1 Jan 1933 at Minsk, USSR. He died in 1971 at Reichenbach, Germany.

vi) Wilhelm[7] Gerk (1064) was born on 14 Mar 1915 at Koehler, Saratov, RUS. He married Viktoria Ditrich (1078), daughter of Johannes Ditrich (1084) and Anna Maria Ulrich (1085), on 27 Apr 1935 at Minsk, USSR. He died on 15 Apr 1967 at Kassel, Germany, at age 52.

(a) Monika[8] Gerk (1610) was born at Germany. She married Eugen-Hans Keil (1611) on 20 Dec 1966 at Kassel, Germany.

(b) Erna[8] Gerk (1613) was born at Germany. She married Hans-Jürgen Becker (1614) on 4 Mar 1966 at Kassel, Germany.

(c) Johannes[8] Gerk (1079) was born on 16 Mar 1936 at Minsk, USSR. He married Irma Bruhn (1605) on 13 Mar 1959 at Kassel, Germany.

(d) Nikolaus[8] Gerk (1080) was born on 19 Nov 1938 at Minsk, USSR. He married Elfriede Burgardt (1606), daughter of Konrad Burgardt (2669) and Anna Katharina Schmidt (2670), on 30 Jul 1959 at Kassel, Germany.

> **i)** Harald Ferdinand[9] Gerk (2671) was born on 5 Feb 1960 at Kassel, Germany. He married Petra Luise Pfannkuche (2688), daughter of Heinrich Wilhelm Pfannkuche (2689) and Edith Anni Schmidt (2690), circa 1982 at GER.
>
> > **(a)** Alexander[10] Gerk (2674) was born on 9 Apr 1983.
> >
> > **(b)** Katharina[10] Gerk (2672) was born on 6 Jun 1985.
> >
> > **(c)** Anna Lena[10] Gerk (2673) was born on 25 Jul 1987.

(e) Ferdinand[8] Gerk (1081) married Helga Koenig (1607). He was born on 5 Apr 1940 at Minsk, USSR.

(f) Maria[8] Gerk (1082) was born on 4 Sep 1941 at Minsk, USSR. She married Gisbert Kaube (1608) on 17 May 1963 at Kassel, Germany.

(g) Wilhelm[8] Gerk (1083) was born on 5 May 1943 at Litzmannstadt, Poland. He married Lieselotte Eisenträger (1609), daughter of Johann Georg Eisenträger (2681) and Hilda Frieda Herz (2682), on 15 Jul 1964 at Kassel, Germany. He married Brigit Elke Müller (2687) on 3 Nov 1990 at Erfurt, Germany.

(h) Alois[8] Gerk (1612) was born on 11 Sep 1944 at Kassel, Germany. He died on 20 Jan 2001 at Kassel, Germany, at age 56.

(i) Lilli[8] Gerk (1615) was born on 13 Dec 1951 at Kassel, Germany. She married Klaus Seguin (2683), son of Fritz Otto Seguin (2684) and Hildegard Stachowiak (2685), on 15 Mar 1972 at Kassel, Germany.

> **i)** Michael[9] Seguin (2686) was born on 14 Nov 1975 at Kassel, Germany. He died on 20 Jun 1999 at Kassel, Germany, at age 23.

(e) Johann[6] Gerk (4169) was born on 2 Aug 1884 at Koehler, Saratov, RUS.

(f) Adam[6] Gerk (4170) was born on 11 Mar 1887 at Koehler, Saratov, RUS. He died on 29 Jan 1891 at Koehler, Saratov, RUS, at age 3.

(4) Anna Maria[5] Gerk (648) was born on 31 Dec 1854 at Koehler, Saratov, RUS. She married Kristof Macht (4147) on 6 May 1874 at Koehler, Saratov, RUS.

(a) Elizabetha[6] Macht (7745) was born on 2 Feb 1875 at Koehler, Saratov, RUS.

(b) Adam[6] Macht (7743) was born on 13 May 1880 at Koehler, Saratov, RUS.

(c) Peter[6] Macht (7750) was born on 22 Feb 1882 at Koehler, Saratov, RUS.

(d) Barbara[6] Macht (7744) was born on 22 Aug 1883 at Koehler, Saratov, RUS.

(e) Maria[6] Macht (7749) was born on 27 May 1891 at Koehler, Saratov, RUS.

(5) Magdalena[5] Gerk (649) was born on 22 Nov 1856 at Koehler, Saratov, RUS. She died on 18 Jul 1862 at Koehler, Saratov, RUS, at age 5.

(6) Elisabetha Isabel[5] Gerk (2802) was born on 20 Dec 1858 at Koehler, Saratov, RUS. She married Jakob Gareis (2803) on 12 Jul 1877 at Koehler, Saratov, RUS. She died on 25 Jul 1951 at Crespo, Entre Ríos, ARG, at age 92.

(a) Elisabetha[6] Gareis (7741) was born on 6 Mar 1885 at Koehler, Saratov, RUS.

(b) Juan[6] Gareis (2809) was born in 1888 at ARG. He married Apolonia Ruhl (2810) on 20 Oct 1908 at Crespo, Entre Ríos, ARG. He died on 10 Feb 1909 at Crespo, Entre Ríos, ARG.

(c) Isabel[6] Gareis (2811) died at ARG. She was born in 1890 at ARG. She married Wilhelm Schlottboom (2812) on 20 Oct 1908 at Crespo, Entre Ríos, ARG.

(d) Santiago[6] Gareis (2813) died at ARG. He was born on 25 Dec 1892 at Crespo, Entre Ríos, ARG. He married Rosa Walther (2814) on 11 Feb 1913 at Crespo, Entre Ríos, ARG.

(e) Adán[6] Gareis (2815) died at ARG. He was born on 26 Nov 1894 at Crespo, Entre Ríos, ARG. He married Catalina Ruhl (2816), daughter of Johannes Ruhl (2819) and Isabel Ruhl (2820), on 28 Oct 1915 at Crespo, Entre Ríos, ARG.

(f) Johannes[6] Gareis (2817) died at ARG. He was born on 7 Nov 1896 at Crespo, Entre Ríos, ARG. He married Isabel Ruhl (2818), daughter of Johannes Ruhl (2821) and Isabel Schaab (2822), on 8 Oct 1918 at Crespo, Entre Ríos, ARG.

(g) Georg[6] Gareis (2823) was born in 1898 at ARG. He married Catalina Hollmann (2824), daughter of Michael Hollmann (2825) and Catalina Kissner (2826), on 17 Oct 1921 at Crespo, Entre Ríos, ARG.

(h) Pedro[6] Gareis (2827) was born in 1901 at ARG. He married Magdalena Hollmann (2828) on 3 Oct 1922 at Crespo, Entre Ríos, ARG.

(7) Susanna[5] Gerk (4148) was born on 18 Feb 1864 at Koehler, Saratov, RUS. She married Friedrich Ditrich (4149) on 22 Jun 1888 at Koehler, Saratov, RUS.

(a) Adam[6] Dietrich (7736) was born on 8 Oct 1892 at Koehler, Saratov, RUS.

(8) Peter[5] Gerk (4143) was born on 23 Apr 1866 at Koehler, Saratov, RUS. He died on 7 Aug 1866 at Koehler, Saratov, RUS.

(9) Elisabetha[5] Gerk (4150) was born on 18 Sep 1867 at Koehler, Saratov, RUS. She married Jakob Frick (4151) on 22 Jun 1888 at Koehler, Saratov, RUS.

(a) Anna[6] Frick (7740) was born on 13 Apr 1890 at Koehler, Saratov, RUS.

(10) Martin[5] Gerk (4144) was born on 29 Jul 1869 at Koehler, Saratov, RUS.

(11) Margareta[5] Gerk (4158) was born in 1870 at Koehler, Saratov, RUS. She married Kristof Koehler (4159) on 4 Mar 1891 at Koehler, Saratov, RUS. She died on 16 Dec 1891 at Koehler, Saratov, RUS.

(12) Gustav[5] Gerk (4153) was born on 7 Dec 1871 at Koehler, Saratov, RUS. He married Julianna Feit (4154) on 25 Nov 1896 at Koehler, Saratov, RUS. He immigrated on 27 Apr 1905 to New York, NY, USA. He died circa 1921 at Minsk, USSR.

(a) Josef[6] Gerk (4155) was born on 3 Sep 1897 at Koehler, Saratov, RUS.

(b) Klara[6] Gerk (4156) was born on 5 Apr 1899 at Koehler, Saratov, RUS.

(c) Elisabetha[6] Gerk (4157) was born on 10 May 1901 at Koehler, Saratov, RUS.

(d) Paul[6] Gerk (4230) was born in 1908 at Denver, CO, USA.

(e) Johann[6] Gerk (4231) was born in 1910 at Denver, CO, USA.

(13) Gottfried[5] Gerk (4146) was born on 4 Feb 1875 at Koehler, Saratov, RUS. He died on 7 Mar 1875 at Koehler, Saratov, RUS.

f) Konrad[4] Gerk (4076) was born on 29 Feb 1832 at Koehler, Saratov, RUS. He died on 13 Nov 1833 at Koehler, Saratov, RUS, at age 1.

g) Magdalena[4] Gerk (541) was born on 22 Feb 1834 at Koehler, Saratov, RUS. She married Johann Geist (4052) on 11 Nov 1852 at Koehler, Saratov, RUS.

(1) Heinrich[5] Geist (4270) was born on 2 Jul 1855 at Koehler, Saratov, RUS. He died in 1876 at Koehler, Saratov, RUS.

(2) Magdalena[5] Geist (4274) was born in 1863 at Koehler, Saratov, RUS. She married Johannes Schwemmler (4276), son of Michael Schwemmler (4277), on 12 Jun 1878 at Diamante, Entre Ríos, ARG.

(3) Valentin[5] Geist (4271) was born on 24 Mar 1869 at Koehler, Saratov, RUS. He married Anna Maria Dietz (4275) on 19 May 1884 at Valle Maria, Entre Rios, ARG.

(4) Baltasar[5] Geist (4272) was born on 21 Feb 1871 at Koehler, Saratov, RUS.

(5) Johanes[5] Geist (4273) was born on 1 Jul 1873 at Koehler, Saratov, RUS. He married Barbara Schonfeld (4278), daughter of Michael Schonfeld (4279) and Katarina Burgardt (4280), in 1891 at Diamante, Entre Ríos, ARG.

h) Heinrich[4] Gerk (539) was born on 12 Oct 1838 at Koehler, Saratov, RUS. He married Elisabeth Dietrich (3084) on 21 Jan 1858 at Koehler, Saratov, RUS. He married Elisabetha Senger (4079) on 4 Nov 1882 at Koehler, Saratov, RUS. He died on 6 Sep 1889 at Koehler, Saratov, RUS, at age 50.

    (1) Katarina[5] Gerk (4086) was born on 30 Oct 1858 at Koehler, Saratov, RUS. She married Philipp Klug (4087) on 14 Nov 1877 at Koehler, Saratov, RUS.

    (2) Josef[5] Gerk (3085) was born on 13 Jan 1860 at Koehler, Saratov, RUS. He married Agnesia Heim (3086), daughter of Anton Heim (3088) and Maria Anna Weigel (3089), on 7 Feb 1895 at Koehler, Saratov, RUS.

    (3) Elisabetha[5] Gerk (4088) was born on 21 May 1862 at Koehler, Saratov, RUS. She married Peter Macht (4089) on 17 Jan 1884 at Koehler, Saratov, RUS.

        (a) Georg[6] Macht (7746) was born on 15 Oct 1884 at Koehler, Saratov, RUS.

        (b) Gottlieb[6] Macht (7747) was born on 8 Mar 1890 at Koehler, Saratov, RUS.

    (4) Margareta[5] Gerk (4082) was born on 11 Mar 1864 at Koehler, Saratov, RUS. She died on 11 Dec 1864 at Koehler, Saratov, RUS.

    (5) Adam[5] Gerk (4083) was born in 1865 at Koehler, Saratov, RUS. He died on 3 Nov 1868 at Koehler, Saratov, RUS.

    (6) Sophia[5] Gerk (4084) was born on 24 Aug 1867 at Koehler, Saratov, RUS. She died on 8 Nov 1868 at Koehler, Saratov, RUS, at age 1.

    (7) Magdalena[5] Gerk (4085) was born on 11 Apr 1869 at Koehler, Saratov, RUS. She died on 9 Sep 1869 at Koehler, Saratov, RUS.

    (8) Barbara[5] Gerk (4094) was born on 11 Jul 1870 at Koehler, Saratov, RUS. She married Josef Feit (4095) on 13 Nov 1889 at Hildmann, Saratov, RUS.

        (a) Josef[6] Feit (7737) was born on 1 Aug 1891 at Koehler, Saratov, RUS.

    (9) Adam[5] Gerk (4090) was born on 2 Jul 1872 at Koehler, Saratov, RUS. He died on 5 Jun 1876 at Koehler, Saratov, RUS, at age 3.

    (10) Johannes[5] Gerk (4098) was born on 20 Mar 1874 at Koehler, Saratov, RUS. He married Kristina Heim (4099) on 3 Feb 1897 at Koehler, Saratov, RUS.

        (a) Johannes[6] Gerk (4100) was born on 22 Apr 1899 at Koehler, Saratov, RUS.

        (b) Peter[6] Gerk (4101) was born on 15 Feb 1901 at Koehler, Saratov, RUS.

    (11) Magdalena[5] Gerk (4091) was born on 28 Sep 1876 at Koehler, Saratov, RUS. She died on 25 May 1877 at Koehler, Saratov, RUS.

    (12) Katharina[5] Gerk (6197) was born on 28 Apr 1878 at Pfeifer, Saratov, RUS. She married Peter Ruhl (6198) on 30 Jan 1901 at Koehler, Saratov, RUS.

        (a) Katharina[6] Ruhl (6199) was born on 31 May 1918 at Koehler, Saratov, RUS.

    (13) Peter[5] Gerk (4096) was born on 20 Jun 1880 at Koehler, Saratov, RUS. He married Elisabetha Mueller (4097) on 30 Nov 1901 at Koehler, Saratov, RUS.

    (14) Margareta[5] Gerk (4092) was born on 19 Jan 1884 at Koehler, Saratov, RUS.

    (15) Jakob[5] Gerk (4093) was born on 11 Apr 1887 at Koehler, Saratov, RUS.

i) Elisabeta[4] Gerk (542) was born on 19 Apr 1842 at Koehler, Saratov, RUS. She married Jakob Schechtel (4055) on 8 Nov 1860 at Koehler, Saratov, RUS.

11. Johannes[3] Gerk (531) was born on 16 Apr 1803 at Koehler, Saratov, RUS. He married Katarina Hartwig (543) circa 1826 at Koehler, Saratov, RUS. He died on 30 Apr 1861 at Koehler, Saratov, RUS, at age 58.

a) Jakob[4] Gerk (4103) was born on 16 Aug 1827 at Koehler, Saratov, RUS. He died on 26 Mar 1828 at Koehler, Saratov, RUS.

b) Peter[4] Gerk (544) was born in 1828 at Koehler, Saratov, RUS. He married Anna Maria Klug (550), daughter of Johannes Adam Klug (3321) and Anna Maria Prediger (3322), on 21 Feb 1850 at Koehler, Saratov, RUS. He married Magdalena Geist (4171) on 27 Jan 1864 at Koehler, Saratov, RUS. He married Katarina Freiberger (4173) on 29 Oct 1872 at Koehler, Saratov, RUS. He died on 17 Oct 1883 at Koehler, Saratov, RUS.

(1) Anna[5] Gerk (3107) was born on 3 Apr 1851 at Koehler, Saratov, RUS. She died on 13 Apr 1851 at Koehler, Saratov, RUS.

(2) Valentine[5] Gerk (3055) was born on 30 Dec 1851 at Koehler, Saratov, RUS. He died on 5 Feb 1852 at Koehler, Saratov, RUS.

(3) Katarina[5] Gerk (551) was born on 14 Aug 1853 at Koehler, Saratov, RUS. She married Johannes Heinrich (4248) on 23 Nov 1871 at Koehler, Saratov, RUS. She died on 20 Jan 1899 at Koehler, Saratov, RUS, at age 45.

(4) Anna Maria[5] Gerk (552) was born on 16 Jul 1855 at Koehler, Saratov, RUS. She married Andreas Schneider (4249) on 9 Nov 1876 at Koehler, Saratov, RUS.

(5) Peter[5] Gerk (4174) was born on 25 Oct 1856 at Koehler, Saratov, RUS. He died on 12 Nov 1859 at Koehler, Saratov, RUS, at age 3.

(6) Susanna[5] Gerk (3056) was born on 15 Nov 1858 at Koehler, Saratov, RUS. She married Josef Imker (4242) on 10 Nov 1881 at Koehler, Saratov, RUS.

    (a) Maria[6] Imker (7742) was born on 3 Dec 1891 at Koehler, Saratov, RUS.

(7) Elisabetha[5] Gerk (4251) was born on 5 May 1863 at Koehler, Saratov, RUS. She died on 4 Nov 1866 at Koehler, Saratov, RUS, at age 3.

(8) Sophia[5] Gerk (4245) was born on 4 Nov 1864 at Koehler, Saratov, RUS. She died on 29 May 1865 at Koehler, Saratov, RUS.

(9) Magdalena[5] Gerk (4243) was born on 24 Mar 1866 at Koehler, Saratov, RUS. She married Nikolaus Schmidt (4244) on 30 Jan 1890 at Koehler, Saratov, RUS.

    (a) Josef[6] Schmidt (7757) was born on 6 Feb 1891 at Koehler, Saratov, RUS.

(10) Kristof[5] Gerk (4250) was born on 17 Dec 1867 at Koehler, Saratov, RUS.

(11) Sophia[5] Gerk (4246) was born on 18 Apr 1871 at Koehler, Saratov, RUS. She married Nikolaus Macht (4247) on 12 Feb 1891 at Koehler, Saratov, RUS.

    (a) Johannes[6] Macht (7748) was born on 28 Nov 1891 at Koehler, Saratov, RUS.

c) Susanna[4] Gerk (547) was born on 10 Jan 1832 at Koehler, Saratov, RUS. She married Johannes Reichenborn (3305), son of Johan Peter Reichenborn (3644) and Margareta Schmalz (3645), on 25 Jan 1855 at Koehler, Saratov, RUS. She died on 14 Feb 1861 at Koehler, Saratov, RUS, at age 29.

(1) Barbara[5] Reichenborn (3306) was born on 1 Jun 1856 at Koehler, Saratov, RUS. She married Jakob Seibel (3308) on 8 Nov 1881 at Koehler, Saratov, RUS. She died on 1 Nov 1887 at Koehler, Saratov, RUS, at age 31.

(2) Nicolaus[5] Reichenborn (3307) was born on 10 Aug 1858 at Koehler, Saratov, RUS. He married Katarina Elsenbach (3309) on 12 Jan 1882 at Koehler, Saratov, RUS.

    (a) Katarina[6] Reichenborn (3310) was born on 28 Sep 1882 at Koehler, Saratov, RUS. She died on 4 Jan 1883 at Koehler, Saratov, RUS.

    (b) Johannes[6] Reichenborn (3311) was born on 26 May 1884 at Koehler, Saratov, RUS.

    (c) Teresia[6] Reichenborn (3312) was born on 23 Jul 1887 at Koehler, Saratov, RUS. She died on 16 Jan 1889 at Koehler, Saratov, RUS, at age 1.

    (d) Maria[6] Reichenborn (3313) was born on 10 Nov 1890 at Koehler, Saratov, RUS.

    (e) Leo[6] Reichenborn (3314) was born on 12 May 1893 at Koehler, Saratov, RUS. He died on 2 Jul 1894 at Koehler, Saratov, RUS, at age 1.

    (f) Maria[6] Reichenborn (3315) was born on 9 Jul 1895 at Koehler, Saratov, RUS. She died on 22 Sep 1897 at Koehler, Saratov, RUS, at age 2.

    (g) Nicolaus[6] Reichenborn (3316) was born on 20 Feb 1899 at Koehler, Saratov, RUS.

    (h) Christof[6] Reichenborn (3317) was born on 3 Jan 1902 at Koehler, Saratov, RUS.

d) Maria Margareta[4] Gerk (549) was born on 28 Oct 1834 at Koehler, Saratov, RUS. She married Nikolaus Ruhl (4105) on 27 Jan 1858 at Koehler, Saratov, RUS. She died on 21 Aug 1915 at Crespo, Entre Ríos, ARG, at age 80.

(1) Anna Maria[5] Ruhl (7756) was born on 6 Apr 1874 at Koehler, Saratov, RUS.

e) Anna Maria⁴ Gerk (4104) was born on 13 Oct 1837 at Koehler, Saratov, RUS. She died on 16 Jun 1839 at Koehler, Saratov, RUS, at age 1.

f) Johannes⁴ Gerk (545) was born on 2 Jul 1840 at Koehler, Saratov, RUS. He married Margareta Bauer (4175) on 10 Feb 1859 at Koehler, Saratov, RUS.

    (1) Johann⁵ Gerk (4176) was born on 4 Apr 1860 at Koehler, Saratov, RUS. He died on 19 Jul 1860 at Koehler, Saratov, RUS.

    (2) Sophia⁵ Gerk (4181) was born on 19 Oct 1861 at Koehler, Saratov, RUS.

    (3) Josef⁵ Gerk (4179) was born on 22 Apr 1864 at Koehler, Saratov, RUS. He died on 2 Oct 1866 at Koehler, Saratov, RUS, at age 2.

    (4) Elisabetha⁵ Gerk (4180) was born on 28 Mar 1867 at Koehler, Saratov, RUS. She died on 14 Jan 1868 at Koehler, Saratov, RUS.

    (5) Elisbatha⁵ Gerk (4182) was born on 5 Oct 1869 at Koehler, Saratov, RUS.

    (6) Barbara⁵ Gerk (4177) was born on 8 Jul 1872 at Koehler, Saratov, RUS.

    (7) Maria⁵ Gerk (4178) was born on 18 Apr 1875 at Koehler, Saratov, RUS.

g) Sophia⁴ Gerk (548) was born on 15 Aug 1843 at Koehler, Saratov, RUS. She married Adam Mildenberger (3319) on 9 Nov 1865 at Koehler, Saratov, RUS. She married Johann Adam Bretz (3318) on 12 Sep 1884 at Koehler, Saratov, RUS.

    (1) Alois⁵ Mildenberger (7751) was born on 5 Jun 1872 at Koehler, Saratov, RUS.

    (2) Johannes⁵ Mildenberger (7752) was born on 24 Feb 1875 at Koehler, Saratov, RUS.

    (3) Katharina⁵ Mildenberger (5543) was born on 10 Feb 1877 at Koehler, Saratov, RUS. She married David Ruhl (5544), son of Johannes Ruhl (5545) and Agnesa Gareis (5546), in 1895 at Koehler, Saratov, RUS.

    (4) Magdalena⁵ Bretz (3320) was born on 31 Aug 1900 at Valle Maria, Entre Ríos, ARG.

h) David⁴ Gerk (546) was born on 11 Oct 1847 at Koehler, Saratov, RUS. He married Elisabetha Bellendir (4106) on 9 Nov 1865 at Koehler, Saratov, RUS. He married Katarina Bierwert (839) on 19 Nov 1868 at Leichtling, Saratov, RUS.

    (1) Katarina⁵ Gerk (840) was born on 21 May 1870 at Josefstal, Saratov, RUS. She married Andreas Senger (4111) on 6 Nov 1891 at Leichtling, Saratov, RUS.

        (a) Jakob⁶ Senger (7758) was born on 4 Oct 1892 at Koehler, Saratov, RUS.

    (2) Konrad⁵ Gerk (841) was born on 27 Feb 1872 at Josefstal, Saratov, RUS. He died on 10 Mar 1874 at Josefstal, Saratov, RUS, at age 2.

    (3) Johannes⁵ Gerk (4113) was born on 20 Aug 1873 at Josefstal, Saratov, RUS. He married Elisabetha Anker (4114) on 3 Feb 1897 at Leichtling, Saratov, RUS. He died in 1936 at Koehler, Stalingrad Oblast, USSR.

        (a) Maria⁶ Gerk (4115) was born on 25 Aug 1898 at Koehler, Saratov, RUS. She died on 10 Aug 1899 at Koehler, Saratov, RUS.

        (b) Aleksander⁶ Gerk (5854) was born in 1900 at Koehler, Saratov, RUS.

        (c) Katarina⁶ Gerk (4116) was born on 28 Jun 1901 at Koehler, Saratov, RUS.

        (d) Johannes⁶ Gerk (5853) was born on 13 Oct 1903 at Koehler, Saratov, RUS. He married Bertha Macht (5856) in 1925 at Koehler, Saratov, RUS. He died on 6 May 1983 at Romanowka, Kirghizia, USSR, at age 79.

            i) Waldemar⁷ Gerk (5857) was born on 25 Nov 1927 at Koehler, Stalingrad, USSR.

            ii) Elfrieda⁷ Gerk (5858) was born on 24 Oct 1929 at Koehler, Stalingrad, USSR.

            iii) Robert⁷ Gerk (5859) was born on 16 Nov 1932 at Koehler, Stalingrad, USSR.

            iv) Ernst⁷ Gerk (5860) was born on 8 Nov 1934 at Koehler, Stalingrad, USSR.

            v) Albert⁷ Gerk (5861) was born on 27 Aug 1936 at Koehler, Stalingrad, USSR.

            vi) Alma⁷ Gerk (5862) married (--?--) Schuckmann (5864) at USSR. She was born on 24 Jan 1938 at Koehler, Stalingrad, USSR.

(a) Nikolas[8] Schuckmann (5865) was born in 1962 at USSR.

vii) Konstantin[7] Gerk (5863) was born on 15 Aug 1941 at Koehler, Stalingrad, USSR.

(e) Adam[6] Gerk (5855) was born in 1907 at Vladivostok, RUS.

(4) Anna Marie[5] Gerk (843) was born on 11 Apr 1875 at Josefstal, Saratov, RUS. She married Andreas Klug (4112) on 3 Nov 1891 at Koehler, Saratov, RUS.

(5) Elisabeta Margareta[5] Gerk (844) was born on 4 Apr 1877 at Josefstal, Saratov, RUS.

(6) Adam[5] Gerk (4107) was born on 11 Apr 1879 at Leichtling, Saratov, RUS. He died on 26 Feb 1896 at Leichtling, Saratov, RUS, at age 16.

(7) Peter[5] Gerk (6226) was born on 16 Jan 1882 at Koehler, Saratov, RUS.

(8) Katarina[5] Gerk (4108) was born on 5 Aug 1884 at Leichtling, Saratov, RUS.

(9) Maria[5] Gerk (2962) married Juan Weinbender (2961), son of Amadeo Weinbender (3754) and Elisabeta Gerk (3755). She was born on 1 Nov 1886 at Koehler, Saratov, RUS. She died on 25 Jun 1971 at Pueblo Santa María, Coronel Suárez, Buenos Aires, ARG, at age 84.

(a) Andreas[6] Weinbender (2966) was born in 1915 at ARG. He married Maria Streitenberger (3408), daughter of Juan Streitenberger (3409) and Rosa Dailoff (3410), on 28 Nov 1939 at Pueblo Santa María, Coronel Suárez, Buenos Aires, ARG.

(b) Adam[6] Weinbender (2963) was born on 4 Aug 1916 at Pueblo Santa María, Coronel Suárez, Buenos Aires, ARG.

(c) Catalina[6] Weinbender (2964) was born on 19 Dec 1918 at Pueblo Santa María, Coronel Suárez, Buenos Aires, ARG.

(d) Ines[6] Weinbender (2965) was born on 18 Oct 1920 at Pueblo Santa María, Coronel Suárez, Buenos Aires, ARG.

(e) Serafina[6] Weinbender (2967) was born in 1925 at Coronel Suárez, Buenos Aires, ARG.

(f) Celementa[6] Weinbender (2968) was born in 1927 at Coronel Suárez, Buenos Aires, ARG.

(10) Anna Maria[5] Gerk (4109) was born on 24 Mar 1889 at Leichtling, Saratov, RUS. She married Andreas Ziegler (5539), son of Andreas Ziegler (5540) and Barbara Ruhl (5541), on 16 Nov 1910 at Koehler, Saratov, RUS.

(a) Adam[6] Ziegler (6188) was born on 22 Jul 1925 at Koehler, Saratov, RUS.

(b) Joseph[6] Ziegler (6189) was born on 15 Sep 1927 at Koehler, Saratov, RUS.

(c) Alexander[6] Ziegler (6190) was born on 10 Aug 1929 at Koehler, Saratov, RUS.

(11) Katarina[5] Gerk (4110) was born on 7 Jul 1892 at Leichtling, Saratov, RUS.

12. Anna Maria[3] Gerk (3687) was born on 15 Apr 1805 at Koehler, Saratov, RUS. She married Konrad Leinacker (4047) in 1825.

a) Jakob[4] Leinacker (7812) was born in 1831 at Koehler, Saratov, RUS. He married Barbara Niedermeyer (7813) on 17 Jan 1867 at Rozhdestvenskoye, Stavropol, RUS.

b) Margareta[4] Leinacker (7814) was born in 1840 at Koehler, Saratov, RUS.

13. Kristian[3] Gerk (532) was born on 9 Aug 1807 at Koehler, Saratov, RUS. He married Anna Maria Weisheim (3460) on 2 Nov 1827 at Koehler, Saratov, RUS. He married Maria Elisabetha Bisheimer (3039) on 28 Oct 1840 at Koehler, Saratov, RUS. He died on 23 Dec 1877 at Josefstal, Saratov, RUS, at age 70.

a) Jakob Georg[4] Gerk (554) was born on 4 Mar 1828 at Koehler, Saratov, RUS. He married Margareta Erdle (3560), daughter of Nikolaus Erdle (3561) and Katerina Lambrecht (3562), on 3 Nov 1852 at Josefstal, Saratov, RUS. He married Barbara Rosenbach (624), daughter of Kaspar Rosenbach (654) and Leonora Haberkorn (655), on 25 Oct 1854 at Semenovka, Saratov, RUS. He married Anna Maria Loos (724), daughter of Johannes Loos (2706) and Marianna Schmidt (2707), on 10 Nov 1859 at Josefstal, Saratov, RUS. He died on 4 Sep 1863 at Josefstal, Saratov, RUS, at age 35.

(1) Kristina[5] Gerk (4282) was born on 30 Apr 1854 at Josefstal, Saratov, RUS. She died on 20 May 1854 at Josefstal, Saratov, RUS.

(2) Katarina[5] Gerk (1193) was born on 28 May 1856 at Josefstal, Saratov, RUS. She died on 29 Dec 1857 at Josefstal, Saratov, RUS, at age 1.

(3) Magdalena[5] Gerk (625) was born on 6 Feb 1858 at Josefstal, Saratov, RUS. She died on 8 Dec 1864 at Josefstal, Saratov, RUS, at age 6.

(4) Katarina[5] Gerk (723) was born on 10 Sep 1860 at Josefstal, Saratov, RUS. She married Johann Peter Heinrich (1107), son of Andreas Heinrich (2184) and Katarina Alles (2185), on 20 Oct 1881 at Josefstal, Saratov, RUS.

(a) Anna[6] Heinrich (1104) was born in 1883 at Josefstal, Saratov, RUS. She married Josef Dreser (921), son of Martin Dreser (920) and Elisabeta Gerk (562), in 1902 at Josefstal, Saratov, RUS. She died on 19 May 1962 at Generalovka, Omsk, USSR.

i) Maria[7] Dreser (3091) was born in 1905 at Josefstal, Saratov, RUS. She married Georg Gerk (932), son of Peter Gerk (711) and Anna Marie Breit (2219), in 1925 at Josefstal, Saratov, RUS. She died on 25 Sep 1974 at Petrov Val, Volgograd, USSR.

(a) Maria[8] Gerk (3092) married Marcus Dreser (3127). She was born in 1926 at Josefstal, Stalingrad Oblast, USSR.

i) Waldemar[9] Dreser (3128)

(b) Georg[8] Gerk (3093) married Berta Grizfeld (3129). He was born on 23 Feb 1933 at Josefstal, Stalingrad Oblast, USSR.

i) Katarina[9] Gerk (3130) was born on 3 Aug 1954 at USSR.

ii) Anatolij[9] Gerk (3131) was born on 1 Jan 1956 at USSR.

iii) Waldemar[9] Gerk (3132) was born on 23 Feb 1958 at USSR.

iv) Olga[9] Gerk (3133) was born on 19 Feb 1961 at USSR.

v) Alexander[9] Gerk (3134) was born on 19 Jan 1967 at USSR.

(c) Lydia[8] Gerk (3094) married Theodor Michel (3135). She was born on 28 Jan 1936 at Josefstal, Stalingrad Oblast, USSR.

i) Eugen[9] Michel (3136) **ii)** Alexander[9] Michel (3137) **iii)** Elena[9] Michel (3138)

iv) Andreas[9] Michel (3139)

(d) Frida[8] Gerk (3095) married Theodor Peitsch (3140). She was born on 17 Jun 1938 at Josefstal, Stalingrad Oblast, USSR.

i) Olga[9] Peitsch (3141) **ii)** Eugen[9] Peitsch (3646) **iii)** Aleksander[9] Peitsch (3647)

(e) Alexander[8] Gerk (3096) married Sinaida Wasilewa (3142). He was born on 12 Oct 1940 at Josefstal, Stalingrad Oblast, USSR. He died on 28 Nov 2002 at Germany at age 62.

ii) Georg[7] Dreser (341) married Anna Werner (342), daughter of Johannes Werner (1106). He was born on 18 May 1906 at Josefstal, Saratov, RUS. He died on 4 May 1982 at Generalovka, Omsk Oblast, USSR, at age 75.

(a) Adam[8] Dreser (285) was born on 7 Sep 1929 at Josefstal, Stalingrad Oblast, USSR. He married Anna Heinrich (227), daughter of Alois Heinrich (70) and Ekaterina Dieser (69), on 14 Nov 1949 at Generalovka, Omsk Oblast, USSR. He died on 1 Nov 2005 at Meschede, Germany, at age 76.

i) Adam[9] Dreser (286) married Sinauda Wturena (287). He was born on 21 Sep 1951 at Generalovka, Omsk Oblast, USSR.

(a) Olya[10] Dreser (288) was born in 1977 at Generalovka, Omsk Oblast, USSR.

(b) Ira[10] Dreser (289) was born in 1981 at Generalovka, Omsk Oblast, USSR.

(c) Aleksei[10] Dreser (290) was born in 1988 at Generalovka, Omsk Oblast, USSR.

ii) Maria[9] Dreser (291) married Alexander Ortmann (3156). She was born on 21 Jan 1953 at Generalovka, Omsk Oblast, USSR.

iii) Lyda[9] Dreser (292) married Sergei Poleschuk (3157). She was born on 30 Apr 1954 at Generalovka, Omsk Oblast, USSR.

iv) Anna[9] Dreser (293) married Andrei Weizel (3158). She married Alex Blintschek (3159). She was born on 28 Nov 1955 at Generalovka, Omsk Oblast, USSR.

v) Alexander Josef^9 Dreser (294) was born on 28 Nov 1957 at Generalovka, Omsk Oblast, USSR. He married Lora Singer (295) on 22 Jul 1983 at Generalovka, Omsk Oblast, USSR. He died on 7 Jul 2015 at Meschede, GER, at age 57.

    (a) Edward^{10} Dreser (296) was born on 23 Aug 1988 at Generalovka, Omsk Oblast, USSR.

vi) Katya^9 Dreser (297) was born on 10 Mar 1960 at Generalovka, Omsk Oblast, USSR.

vii) Valya^9 Dreser (298) married Willi Kaftan (3160). She was born on 29 Nov 1961 at Generalovka, Omsk Oblast, USSR.

viii) Paul^9 Dreser (299) was born on 4 Jan 1963 at Generalovka, Omsk Oblast, USSR.

ix) Nina^9 Dreser (300) was born on 20 Jun 1964 at Generalovka, Omsk Oblast, USSR. She married Vladimir Bujak (3161) on 25 Jul 1988 at Generalovka, Omsk Oblast, USSR.

x) Luda^9 Dreser (301) married Andrei Gross (3162) at Generalovka, Omsk Oblast, USSR. She was born on 20 Jun 1964 at Generalovka, Omsk Oblast, USSR.

iii) Peter^7 Dreser (8047) was born on 30 Nov 1912 at Josefstal, Saratov, RUS.

(b) Georg^6 Heinrich (4391) was born on 24 Apr 1888 at Josefstal, Saratov, RUS. He married Katarina Domme (4625), daughter of Mattias Domme (4574) and Anna Maria Blattner (4575), on 3 Nov 1907 at Josefstal, Saratov, RUS. He died on 1 May 1915 at Josefstal, Saratov, RUS, at age 27.

i) Maria^7 Heinrich (4626) (see above) **ii)** Friedrich^7 Heinrich (4627) (see above)

(c) Johann Georg^6 Heinrich (3819) was born on 19 Jul 1890 at Josefstal, Saratov, RUS. He married Elisabeta Kisser (3822), daughter of Wilhelm Kisser (2255) and Anna Marie Haspert (2256), on 7 Oct 1908 at Josefstal, Saratov, RUS. He immigrated on 23 Jun 1911. He died in Nov 1946 at Denver, Colorado, USA, at age 56.

i) Georg^7 Heinrich (3823) married Mary Urban (4660). He was born on 9 Jan 1910 at Josefstal, Saratov, RUS. He died on 25 Mar 2001 at Denver, Colorado, USA, at age 91.

    (a) George^8 Heinrich (4661) **(b)** Mary Ann^8 Heinrich (4662) **(c)** James^8 Heinrich (4663)

    (d) Nancy^8 Heinrich (4664)

ii) Adam J.^{7} Heinrich (4400) married Mary Frank (4665). He was born on 24 Nov 1912 at Kansas, USA. He died on 13 Jan 1996 at Lttleton, Colorado, USA, at age 83.

    (a) Wayne^8 Heinrich (4666) **(b)** Mary Ann^8 Heinrich (4667) **(c)** Joanne^8 Heinrich (4668)

    (d) David^8 Heinrich (4669)

iii) Anna Maria^7 Heinrich (4399) was born on 17 Dec 1914 at Topeka, Kansas, USA.

iv) Rose^7 Heinrich (4402) married Josef Frank (4670). She was born on 29 Apr 1917 at Fort Dodge, Iowa, USA.

    (a) Joseph^8 Frank (4671) **(b)** Rose Mary^8 Frank (4672) **(c)** John^8 Frank (4673)

    (d) Elizabeth^8 Frank (4674) **(e)** Anne^8 Frank (4675)

v) Anna^7 Heinrich (4403) married William Raitz (4676). She married Robert Sherry (4677). She was born on 17 Feb 1919 at Fort Dodge, Iowa, USA. She died on 24 Apr 1989 at USA at age 70.

vi) Clemence^7 Heinrich (4401) married Dorothy Steno (4681). He was born on 22 Dec 1920 at Aurora, Illinois, USA. He died on 14 Aug 1983 at Denver, Colorado, USA, at age 62.

    (a) John^8 Heinrich (4682) **(b)** Michael^8 Heinrich (4683) **(c)** Patrick^8 Heinrich (4684)

vii) Elisabeth^7 Heinrich (4404) married Bud Laird (4678). She married Kenneth Smith (4680). She was born in 1923 at Iowa, USA.

    (a) Patricia^8 Laird (4679)

viii) Sylvania^7 Heinrich (4405) married Dorothy Hankel (4685). He was born on 22 Jan 1925 at Iowa, USA. He died on 6 Jun 2002 at Colorado, USA, at age 77.

    (a) Sherri^8 Heinrich (4686) **(b)** Kathy^8 Heinrich (4687) **(c)** Gerri Ann^8 Heinrich (4688)

ix) Albert P.^{7} Heinrich (4406) married Ruth Teel (4693). He was born in 1927 at Iowa, USA.

(a) Albert[8] Heinrich (4694) **(b)** Richard[8] Heinrich (4695) **(c)** Lori Lynn[8] Heinrich (4696)

x) Peter[7] Heinrich (4407) married Virginia Neville (4689). He was born on 6 May 1929 at Iowa, USA. He died on 22 Feb 1989 at Colorado, USA, at age 59.

(a) Sandra[8] Heinrich (4690) **(b)** Steven[8] Heinrich (4691) **(c)** Cindy[8] Heinrich (4692)

(d) Friedrich[6] Heinrich (3818) was born on 8 Apr 1894 at Josefstal, Saratov, RUS.

(e) Maria[6] Heinrich (2301) was born on 1 May 1895 at Josefstal, Saratov, RUS. She married Josef Schonfeld (4628) circa 1910 at Marienfeld, Saratov, RUS.

i) Katherine[7] Schonfeld (4653) **ii)** Rose[7] Schonfeld (4654) **iii)** Tilly[7] Schonfeld (4655) **iv)** Joseph[7] Schonfeld (4656) **v)** George[7] Schonfeld (4657) **vi)** Helen[7] Schonfeld (4658) **vii)** Robert[7] Schonfeld (4659)

(f) Josef[6] Heinrich (3701) was born on 4 Feb 1898 at Josefstal, Saratov, RUS. He married Anna Gerk (1258), daughter of Valentin Gerk (1253) and Ekaterina Barbara Urich (1254), on 22 May 1916 at Josefstal, Saratov, RUS.

i) Josef[7] Heinrich (8227) (see above)

(g) Johannes[6] Heinrich (2302) was born on 2 Dec 1899 at Josefstal, Saratov, RUS.

(h) Adam[6] Heinrich (3821) was born in 1905 at Josefstal, Saratov, RUS.

(5) Jakob[5] Gerk (725) was born on 26 Jul 1862 at Josefstal, Saratov, RUS. He died on 1 Oct 1863 at Josefstal, Saratov, RUS, at age 1.

b) Nikolaus[4] Gerk (555) was born on 21 Nov 1831 at Koehler, Saratov, RUS. He married Katarina Margareta Ziegler (561) on 24 Nov 1853 at Koehler, Saratov, RUS.

(1) Elisabeta[5] Gerk (562) was born on 14 Jan 1855 at Josefstal, Saratov, RUS. She married Martin Dreser (920), son of Josef Dreser (923) and Magdalena Seitz (924), on 17 Oct 1872 at Josefstal, Saratov, RUS. She died in Nov 1932 at Josefstal, Stalingrad Oblast, USSR, at age 77.

(a) Heinrich[6] Dreser (7409) was born in 1873 at Josefstal, Saratov, RUS. He married Elisabetha Domme (7410), daughter of Jakob Domme (4037) and Margareta Schaeffer (8038), on 8 Nov 1894 at Josefstal, Saratov, RUS. He married Katarina Dieser (159), daughter of Johan Georg Dieser (66) and Katarina Arnold (150), on 20 Oct 1898 at Josefstal, Saratov, RUS.

i) Jakob[7] Dreser (8044) was born in 1906 at Josefstal, Saratov, RUS. He died on 23 Jun 1907 at Josefstal, Saratov, RUS.

ii) Barbara[7] Dreser (8045) was born on 15 Jun 1908 at Josefstal, Saratov, RUS.

iii) Maria[7] Dreser (8046) was born on 20 Jul 1912 at Josefstal, Saratov, RUS.

(b) Martin[6] Dreser (922) was born on 20 May 1874 at Josefstal, Saratov, RUS.

(c) Josef[6] Dreser (921) was born in 1878 at Josefstal, Saratov, RUS. He married Anna Heinrich (1104), daughter of Johann Peter Heinrich (1107) and Katarina Gerk (723), in 1902 at Josefstal, Saratov, RUS. He died on 19 May 1962 at Generalovka, Omsk Oblast, USSR.

i) Maria[7] Dreser (3091) (see above)

(a) Maria[8] Gerk (3092) (see above)

i) Waldemar[9] Dreser (3128) (see above)

(b) Georg[8] Gerk (3093) (see above)

i) Katarina[9] Gerk (3130) (see above) **ii)** Anatolij[9] Gerk (3131) (see above)

iii) Waldemar[9] Gerk (3132) (see above) **iv)** Olga[9] Gerk (3133) (see above)

v) Alexander[9] Gerk (3134) (see above)

(c) Lydia[8] Gerk (3094) (see above)

i) Eugen[9] Michel (3136) (see above) **ii)** Alexander[9] Michel (3137) (see above)

iii) Elena[9] Michel (3138) (see above) **iv)** Andreas[9] Michel (3139) (see above)

(d) Frida[8] Gerk (3095) (see above)

   i) Olga[9] Peitsch (3141) (see above) **ii)** Eugen[9] Peitsch (3646) (see above)

   iii) Aleksander[9] Peitsch (3647) (see above)

(e) Alexander[8] Gerk (3096) (see above)

ii) Georg[7] Dreser (341) (see above)

  (a) Adam[8] Dreser (285) (see above)

   i) Adam[9] Dreser (286) (see above)

     (a) Olya[10] Dreser (288) (see above)

     (b) Ira[10] Dreser (289) (see above)

     (c) Aleksei[10] Dreser (290) (see above)

   ii) Maria[9] Dreser (291) (see above)

   iii) Lyda[9] Dreser (292) (see above)

   iv) Anna[9] Dreser (293) (see above)

   v) Alexander Josef[9] Dreser (294) (see above)

     (a) Edward[10] Dreser (296) (see above)

   vi) Katya[9] Dreser (297) (see above)

   vii) Valya[9] Dreser (298) (see above)

   viii) Paul[9] Dreser (299) (see above)

   ix) Nina[9] Dreser (300) (see above)

   x) Luda[9] Dreser (301) (see above)

  iii) Peter[7] Dreser (8047) (see above)

(d) Georg[6] Dreser (3817) was born on 7 Apr 1884 at Josefstal, Saratov, RUS. He married Eva Benz (6045) in 1903 at Josefstal, Saratov, RUS. He emigrated on 10 Oct 1908 from Bremen, GER.

  i) Barbara[7] Dreser (6046) was born in 1904 at Josefstal, Saratov, RUS.

  ii) Kaspar[7] Dreser (6048) was born in 1906 at Josefstal, Saratov, RUS. He died on 3 Jan 1907 at Josefstal, Saratov, RUS.

  iii) Josef[7] Dreser (6047) was born in 1908 at Josefstal, Saratov, RUS.

  iv) Eva[7] Dreser (8048) was born on 8 Jun 1912 at Josefstal, Saratov, RUS.

(e) Kristof[6] Dreser (8218) was born on 8 Nov 1889 at Josefstal, Saratov, RUS. He married Katharina Barbara Heinrich (8219) on 26 Oct 1909 at Josefstal, Saratov, RUS.

(2) Johann Georg[5] Gerk (890) was born on 13 Jun 1856 at Josefstal, Saratov, RUS. He married Anna Marie Senger (2748), daughter of Johannes Senger (2749) and Anna Marie Kern (2750), on 7 Jun 1877 at Josefstal, Saratov, RUS. He married Margareta Elisabeta Bauer (891), daughter of Johann Adam Bauer (2192) and Maria Eva Sauer (2193), on 7 Nov 1883 at Josefstal, Saratov, RUS. He died in 1933 at Josefstal, Stalingrad Oblast, USSR.

(a) Maria Katarina[6] Gerk (2751) was born on 19 Jul 1877 at Josefstal, Saratov, RUS. She died on 26 Nov 1878 at Josefstal, Saratov, RUS, at age 1.

(b) Konrad[6] Gerk (2321) was born on 4 Oct 1878 at Josefstal, Saratov, RUS. He married Margareta Gerling (2322), daughter of Nikolas Gerling (2323) and Otilie Roskopf (2324), on 11 Oct 1898 at Marienfeld, Saratov, RUS. He died in 1933 at Josefstal, Stalingrad Oblast, USSR.

  i) Maria[7] Gerk (2325) was born on 22 Nov 1899 at Josefstal, Saratov, RUS.

  ii) Katarina[7] Gerk (2326) was born on 18 Feb 1900 at Josefstal, Saratov, RUS.

iii) Peter⁷ Gerk (2327) was born on 9 Sep 1901 at Josefstal, Saratov, RUS.

iv) Anna⁷ Gerk (2328) was born on 29 Jan 1904 at Josefstal, Saratov, RUS. She died on 22 Mar 1907 at Josefstal, Saratov, RUS, at age 3.

v) Georg⁷ Gerk (2332) was born on 14 May 1907 at Josefstal, Saratov, RUS. He died on 9 Dec 1907 at Josefstal, Saratov, RUS.

vi) Jakob⁷ Gerk (2329) was born on 24 Apr 1909 at Josefstal, Saratov, RUS.

vii) Paulina⁷ Gerk (3573) was born on 23 Jul 1911 at Josefstal, Saratov, RUS.

viii) Georg⁷ Gerk (2331) was born on 21 Nov 1913 at Josefstal, Saratov, RUS.

ix) Adam⁷ Gerk (2330) was born on 21 Nov 1913 at Josefstal, Saratov, RUS. He died on 22 Jan 1914 at Josefstal, Saratov, RUS.

x) Anna⁷ Gerk (8224) was born on 24 Jun 1917 at Josefstal, Saratov, RUS.

(c) Josef⁶ Gerk (2752) was born on 16 Aug 1881 at Josefstal, Saratov, RUS. He died on 9 Jun 1891 at Josefstal, Saratov, RUS, at age 9.

(d) Georg⁶ Gerk (889) was born on 27 Sep 1884 at Josefstal, Saratov, RUS. He died on 2 Aug 1888 at Josefstal, Saratov, RUS, at age 3.

(e) Johannes⁶ Gerk (892) was born on 21 Feb 1887 at Josefstal, Saratov, RUS. He died on 19 Jul 1888 at Josefstal, Saratov, RUS, at age 1.

(f) Martin⁶ Gerk (893) was born on 10 Aug 1888 at Josefstal, Saratov, RUS. He married Elisabeta Kisser (898), daughter of Josef Kisser (2246) and Barbara Schmidt (2247), on 22 Oct 1907 at Josefstal, Saratov, RUS. He emigrated on 10 Oct 1908 from Bremen, GER. He died on 8 Oct 1953 at Pueblo Santa María, Coronel Suárez, Buenos Aires, ARG, at age 65.

i) Elisa⁷ Gerk (999) was born on 25 Mar 1910 at Pueblo Santa María, Coronel Suárez, Buenos Aires, ARG. She married Jorge Baier (1867), son of Michael Baier (1868) and Anna Weinman (1869), on 27 Aug 1935 at Pueblo Santa María, Coronel Suárez, Buenos Aires, ARG.

   (a) Miguel⁸ Baier (1954) was born in 1938 at Pueblo Santa María, Coronel Suárez, Buenos Aires, ARG.

ii) Margarita⁷ Gerk (1003) was born on 20 May 1912 at Pueblo Santa María, Coronel Suárez, Buenos Aires, ARG. She married Miguel Schneider (1946), son of Juan Schneider (1958) and Anna Allerborn (1985), on 1 Aug 1931 at Pueblo Santa María, Coronel Suárez, Buenos Aires, ARG. She died on 17 Jun 2001 at Pueblo Santa María, Coronel Suárez, Buenos Airies, ARG, at age 89.

   (a) Andreas⁸ Schneider (1953) was born in 1932 at Pueblo Santa María, Coronel Suárez, Buenos Aires, ARG.

   (b) Juan Marcelo⁸ Schneider (1956) was born in 1943 at Pueblo Santa María, Coronel Suárez, Buenos Aires, ARG.

   (c) José Angel⁸ Schneider (1957) was born in 1948 at Pueblo Santa María, Coronel Suárez, Buenos Aires, ARG.

iii) Andreas⁷ Gerk (996) was born on 11 Jun 1914 at Pueblo Santa María, Coronel Suárez, Buenos Aires, ARG. He married Margareta Schneider (1944) in 1944 at Pueblo Santa María, Coronel Suárez, Buenos Aires, ARG. He died on 3 Apr 1981 at Pueblo Santa María, Coronel Suárez, Buenos Aires, ARG, at age 66.

   (a) Andreas Oscar⁸ Gerk (1948) was born in 1949 at Pueblo Santa María, Coronel Suárez, Buenos Aires, ARG.

   (b) Juan Carlos⁸ Gerk (1949) married Elvira Holzmann (6295). He was born on 10 Apr 1953 at Pueblo Santa María, Coronel Suárez, Buenos Aires, ARG.

      i) Sol⁹ Gerk (6296) was born on 29 Nov 1993 at Coronel Suarez, Buenos Aires, ARG.

   (c) José Amado⁸ Gerk (7391) was born on 10 Jun 1955 at Pueblo Santa María, Coronel Suárez, Buenos Aires, ARG. He married Beatrice Crenz (7392) on 17 Feb 1982 at Pueblo Santa María, Buenos Aires, ARG.

      i) Veronica⁹ Gerk (7393) married Christian Hoff (7394) at Pueblo Santa María, Buenos Aires, ARG. She was born on 10 Jul 1986 at Pueblo Santa María, Buenos Aires, ARG.

(d) Jorge Oscar[8] Gerk (1950) was born on 5 Jun 1957 at Pueblo Santa María, Coronel Suárez, Buenos Aires, ARG. He married Norma Zulema Schenfeld (7389) in 1986 at Pueblo Santa María, Buenos Aires, ARG.

   i) Sofia[9] Gerk (7390) was born on 25 Apr 1990 at Pueblo Santa María, Buenos Aires, ARG.

(e) Miguel Angel[8] Gerk (1951) was born in 1959 at Pueblo Santa María, Coronel Suárez, Buenos Aires, ARG.

iv) Jorge[7] Gerk (998) was born on 18 May 1916 at Pueblo Santa María, Coronel Suárez, Buenos Aires, ARG. He married Sarafina Groh (1945) on 18 Feb 1947 at Pueblo Santa María, Coronel Suárez, Buenos Aires, ARG.

   (a) Miguel Ernesto[8] Gerk (1952) was born in 1957 at Pueblo Santa María, Coronel Suárez, Buenos Aires, ARG.

v) Anastasia[7] Gerk (1001) was born on 13 May 1918 at Pueblo Santa María, Coronel Suárez, Buenos Aires, ARG. She married José Stremel (1870), son of Adam Stremel (1871) and Anna Maria Winter (1872), on 25 Sep 1941 at Pueblo Santa María, Coronel Suárez, Buenos Aires, ARG.

   (a) Anastasia[8] Stremel (1955) was born in 1942 at Pueblo Santa María, Coronel Suárez, Buenos Aires, ARG.

vi) José[7] Gerk (995) was born on 14 Jan 1920 at Pueblo Santa María, Coronel Suárez, Buenos Aires, ARG.

vii) Barbara[7] Gerk (1000) married Martin Maier (3174) at Pueblo Santa María, Buenos Aires, ARG. She was born on 26 Nov 1921 at Pueblo Santa María, Coronel Suárez, Buenos Aires, ARG. She died on 28 May 2006 at Pueblo Santa María, Coronel Suárez, Buenos Aires, ARG, at age 84.

viii) Juan[7] Gerk (997) was born on 31 Mar 1926 at Pueblo Santa María, Coronel Suárez, Buenos Aires, ARG. He married Maria Luisa Roth (1004), daughter of Miguel Roth (3172) and Amalia Jacob (3173), on 12 Feb 1953 at Pueblo Santa María, Coronel Suárez, Buenos Aires, ARG. He died on 28 Jan 1987 at Pueblo Santa María, Coronel Suárez, Buenos Aires, ARG, at age 60.

   (a) Juan Alberta[8] Gerk (1006) was born on 31 May 1956 at Pueblo Santa María, Coronel Suárez, Buenos Aires, ARG. He married Natalia Lima (3175) on 16 Apr 2001 at Pueblo Santa María, Buenos Aires, ARG.

      i) Marina[9] Gerk (3185) was born in 1981 at Pueblo Santa María, Buenos Aires, ARG.

      ii) Anabel[9] Gerk (3186) was born in 1988 at Pueblo Santa María, Buenos Aires, ARG.

   (b) Maria Alicia[8] Gerk (1005) was born on 4 Mar 1958 at Pueblo Santa María, Coronel Suárez, Buenos Aires, ARG. She married Angel Salvador Herr (1010) on 8 Jul 1978 at Pueblo Santa María, Buenos Aires, ARG.

      i) Carolina Ines[9] Herr (1011) was born on 6 Jun 1979 at Coronel Suarez, ARG.

      ii) Diego Fabian[9] Herr (1012) was born on 20 Feb 1983 at Coronel Suarez, Buenos Aires, ARG.

   (c) Angel Oscar[8] Gerk (1007) was born on 25 Oct 1959 at Pueblo Santa María, Coronel Suárez, Buenos Aires, ARG. He married Irma Weiman (3176) on 21 Mar 1981 at Pueblo Santa María, Buenos Aires, ARG.

      i) Ana Ines[9] Gerk (3187) was born on 5 Mar 1982 at Pueblo Santa María, Buenos Aires, ARG.

      ii) Maria Victoria[9] Gerk (3188) was born on 22 Mar 1984 at Pueblo Santa María, Buenos Aires, ARG.

      iii) Lucia Rosario[9] Gerk (3189) was born in 1997 at Pueblo Santa María, Buenos Aires, ARG.

   (d) Liliana Esther[8] Gerk (1008) was born on 24 May 1963 at Pueblo Santa María, Coronel Suárez, Buenos Aires, ARG. She married Gerardo Paredes (1009) on 23 Apr 1993 at Pueblo Santa María, Buenos Aires, ARG.

ix) Martin[7] Gerk (994) was born on 15 Mar 1925 at Pueblo Santa María, Coronel Suárez, Buenos Aires, ARG. He married Ester Guillermina Schamber (1595) in 1954 at Pueblo Santa María, Coronel Suárez, Buenos Aires, ARG.

   (a) Martin Marcelo[8] Gerk (1596) married Marta Escobar (1597). He was born on 23 Dec 1955 at Pueblo Santa María, Coronel Suárez, Buenos Aires, ARG.

(b) Angel Guillermina[8] Gerk (2374) married Ursula de Carmen Pardo Narváez (2379) at ARG. He was born on 28 Aug 1956 at Pueblo Santa María, Coronel Suárez, Buenos Aires, ARG.

    i) Guillermo Sebastián[9] Gerk (2377) was born in 1984 at ARG.

    ii) Daniela Vanesa[9] Gerk (2376) was born in 1987 at ARG.

    iii) Valeria Soledad[9] Gerk (2378) was born in 1990 at ARG.

(c) Daniel Omar[8] Gerk (2375) was born on 9 Aug 1961 at Pueblo Santa María, Coronel Suárez, Buenos Aires, ARG.

x) Maria[7] Gerk (1002) was born in 1928 at Pueblo Santa María, Coronel Suárez, Buenos Aires, ARG. She married José Hergenrader (1947) in 1953 at Pueblo Santa María, Coronel Suárez, Buenos Aires, ARG.

(g) Elisabeta[6] Gerk (894) was born on 24 Oct 1890 at Josefstal, Saratov, RUS. She married Gottfried Winter (952), son of Kristof Winter (953) and Anna Marie Schmidt (2260), on 24 Nov 1909 at Josefstal, Saratov, RUS. She immigrated on 24 Feb 1912 to Philadelphia, USA. She died on 19 Apr 1965 at Fort Dodge, Iowa, USA, at age 74.

i) Catherine Elizabeth[7] Winter (954) was born on 8 Jun 1911 at Josefstal, Saratov, RUS. She married Adam John Kern (955), son of Kaspar Kern (956) and Elisabetha Simon (957), on 28 May 1930 at Garner, Iowa, USA. She died on 4 Mar 2004 at Fort Dodge, Iowa, USA, at age 92.

    (a) Elizabeth Ann[8] Kern (962) was born on 8 Nov 1932 at Mason City, Iowa, USA. She married James Dutcher (963) on 7 Nov 1953 at USA.

    (b) Anna Marie[8] Kern (964) was born on 11 Feb 1934 at Austin, Minnesota, USA. She married Gerald Baker (965) on 11 Sep 1954 at USA. She died on 12 Nov 2018 at Fort Dodge, IA, USA, at age 84.

    (c) Helen Catherine[8] Kern (966) was born on 3 Jan 1936 at Austin, Minnesota, USA. She married Edward Munn (967) on 15 Oct 1960 at USA.

    (d) James Joseph[8] Kern (968) was born on 19 Mar 1941 at Austin, Minnesota, USA. He married Judith Whelchel (969) on 23 Jan 1960.

ii) Anna Maria[7] Winter (2780) died circa 1914 at Topeka, Kansas, USA. She was born on 7 Jul 1914 at Topeka, Kansas, USA.

iii) Elizabeth[7] Winter (6228) was born on 3 Sep 1916 at Fort Dodge, IA, USA. She died on 9 Dec 1918 at Fort Dodge, IA, USA, at age 2.

iv) Anna[7] Winter (960) was born on 17 Jun 1924 at Fort Dodge, Iowa, USA. She married Harold Hanson (961), son of Harry Hanson (2798) and Julia Carlson (2799), on 16 Feb 1946 at Fort Dodge, Iowa, USA.

    (a) Paul[8] Hanson (2800) was born on 10 Mar 1952 at Fort Dodge, Iowa, USA.

    (b) John[8] Hanson (2801) was born on 7 May 1955 at Fort Dodge, Iowa, USA.

(h) Margareta[6] Gerk (895) was born on 25 Sep 1892 at Josefstal, Saratov, RUS. She married Georg Blattner (2387), son of Stephan Blattner (3714) and Barbara Resch (6810), on 23 Nov 1911 at Josefstal, Saratov, RUS. She died circa 1953 at General Roca, Río Negro, ARG.

i) Jorge[7] Blattner (3180) was born at General Roca, Río Negro, ARG.

ii) Serofina[7] Blattner (3181) was born at General Roca, Río Negro, ARG. She married Jorge Kirnbauer (3182).

iii) Clemente[7] Blattner (3179) was born at Villa Larregina, Río Negro, ARG.

iv) Berta[7] Blattner (3184) was born at General Roca, Río Negro, ARG.

v) Anita[7] Blattner (3183) was born at General Roca, Río Negro, ARG.

vi) Barbara[7] Blattner (2388) was born on 11 Jul 1914 at Pueblo Santa María, Coronel Suárez, Buenos Airies, ARG.

vii) Juan[7] Blattner (2389) was born on 11 Nov 1918 at Pueblo Santa María, Coronel Suárez, Buenos Airies, ARG.

(i) Katarina[6] Gerk (896) was born on 28 Oct 1894 at Josefstal, Saratov, RUS. She died on 1 Sep 1896 at Josefstal, Saratov, RUS, at age 1.

(j) Magdalena⁶ Gerk (897) was born on 7 Apr 1896 at Josefstal, Saratov, RUS. She died on 10 Feb 1898 at Josefstal, Saratov, RUS, at age 1.

(k) Katarina⁶ Gerk (2427) was born on 17 Aug 1899 at Josefstal, Saratov, RUS. She died on 5 Mar 1900 at Josefstal, Saratov, RUS.

(l) Anna Maria⁶ Gerk (2357) was born on 13 May 1902 at Josefstal, Saratov, RUS.

(3) Johann⁵ Gerk (1194) was born on 5 Jun 1858 at Josefstal, Saratov, RUS. He died on 1 Oct 1859 at Josefstal, Saratov, RUS, at age 1.

(4) Anna Catharina⁵ Gerk (620) was born on 29 Jul 1860 at Josefstal, Saratov, RUS. She married Georg Gette (621), son of Konrad Gette (622) and Theresia Schaefer (623), on 4 Nov 1886 at Josefstal, Saratov, RUS.

(a) Adam⁶ Gette (835) was born on 5 Apr 1895 at Josefstal, Saratov, RUS.

(b) Elisabeta⁶ Gette (836) was born on 1 Oct 1897 at Josefstal, Saratov, RUS.

(c) Anna⁶ Gette (837) was born on 12 Aug 1899 at Josefstal, Saratov, RUS.

(d) Anna⁶ Gette (838) was born on 28 Apr 1904 at Josefstal, Saratov, RUS.

c) Elisabeta⁴ Gerk (559) was born on 7 Nov 1833 at Koehler, Saratov, RUS. She died before 1852 at Koehler, Saratov, RUS.

d) Peter⁴ Gerk (705) was born on 20 Jan 1836 at Koehler, Saratov, RUS. He married Anna Marie Wagner (706), daughter of Kristof Wagner (3110) and Teresia Tesh (3111), on 10 Nov 1859 at Josefstal, Saratov, RUS.

(1) Konrad⁵ Gerk (704) was born on 16 Sep 1860 at Josefstal, Saratov, RUS. He married Magdalena Heinrich (858), daughter of Johannes Heinrich (2701) and Barbara Klein (2702), on 7 Nov 1878 at Josefstal, Saratov, RUS. He died in 1925 at Josefstal, Saratov, RUS.

(a) Johann Georg⁶ Gerk (859) was born on 14 May 1879 at Josefstal, Saratov, RUS. He married Margareta Schaefer (2207), daughter of Johannes Schaefer (2214) and Barbara Haberkorn (2215), on 7 Oct 1897 at Josefstal, Saratov, RUS. He married Elisabetha Kisser (2216), daughter of Johan Adam Kisser (1986) and Elisabeta Simon (1987), on 17 Sep 1901 at Josefstal, Saratov, RUS.

i) Anna Maria⁷ Gerk (2213) was born on 20 Sep 1899 at Josefstal, Saratov, RUS. She died on 3 Jul 1900 at Josefstal, Saratov, RUS.

ii) Natalia⁷ Gerk (1015) was born on 16 Nov 1908 at Josefstal, Saratov, RUS.

iii) Peter⁷ Gerk (1285) was born on 22 Jun 1902 at Josefstal, Saratov, RUS.

iv) Anna⁷ Gerk (4305) was born in 1904 at Josefstal, Saratov, RUS.

v) Katarina⁷ Gerk (1286) was born on 24 Aug 1906 at Josefstal, Saratov, RUS.

vi) Georg⁷ Gerk (2283) was born on 19 Feb 1911 at Josefstal, Saratov, RUS.

vii) Maria⁷ Gerk (4304) was born on 20 Feb 1912 at Josefstal, Saratov, RUS.

viii) Barbara⁷ Gerk (2294) was born on 15 Aug 1914 at Josefstal, Saratov, RUS.

(b) Magdalena⁶ Gerk (860) was born on 17 May 1882 at Josefstal, Saratov, RUS.

(c) Konrad⁶ Gerk (861) was born on 17 Dec 1883 at Josefstal, Saratov, RUS. He died on 27 Dec 1883 at Josefstal, Saratov, RUS.

(d) Johannes⁶ Gerk (862) was born on 23 Nov 1884 at Josefstal, Saratov, RUS. He married Elisabeta Groh (2232), daughter of Johann Adam Groh (7072) and Katharina Magdalena Schmidt (7079), on 25 Oct 1905 at Josefstal, Saratov, RUS.

i) Susanna⁷ Gerk (2235) was born on 7 Aug 1906 at Josefstal, Saratov, RUS.

ii) Johann⁷ Gerk (2236) was born on 7 Sep 1910 at Josefstal, Saratov, RUS.

iii) Adam⁷ Gerk (2293) was born on 31 Jan 1912 at Josefstal, Saratov, RUS. He died on 15 May 1942 at Krasnoturinsk, Sverdlovsk Oblast, USSR, at age 30.

(e) Georg⁶ Gerk (863) was born on 25 Aug 1887 at Josefstal, Saratov, RUS. He died on 14 Aug 1888 at Josefstal, Saratov, RUS.

(f) Georg[6] Gerk (864) was born on 10 Dec 1889 at Josefstal, Saratov, RUS. He married Anna Margareta Haberkorn (869), daughter of Johannes Haberkorn (1852) and Julia Link (1853), on 9 Nov 1910 at Josefstal, Saratov, RUS. He died on 8 Jun 1943 at Kemerova, USSR, at age 53.

i) Peter[7] Gerk (870) was born on 17 Sep 1911 at Josefstal, Saratov, RUS. He married Rosa Rak (1862) in 1929. He married Maria Blattner (1018), daughter of Anton Andreas Blattner (220) and Margareta Erdle (3163), in 1935? He died in 1946 at Kazakstan, USSR.

(a) Adam[8] Gerk (3145) was born on 11 Sep 1930 at Baku, USSR.

(b) Pius[8] Gerk (3146) was born on 24 Oct 1930 at Baku, USSR.

(c) Georg[8] Gerk (1021) married Margareta (--?--) (1022) at USSR. He was born on 1 Jan 1939 at Kara Jery, Baku, USSR.

i) Maria[9] Gerk (1025) married Vladimir Winterfeld (1026). She was born on 15 Sep 1964 at USSR.

(a) Georg[10] Winterfeld (3147) was born on 28 Apr 1986 at USSR.

(b) Valerie[10] Winterfeld (3148) was born on 4 Nov 1987 at USSR.

(c) Martin[10] Winterfeld (3149) was born on 10 Jul 1990 at USSR.

ii) Viktor[9] Gerk (1023) married Olga Berzuenskaya (3150) at USSR. He was born on 3 Dec 1966 at USSR.

(a) Liza[10] Gerk (3151) was born on 21 May 1999 at USSR.

(b) Elena[10] Gerk (3152) was born on 13 Dec 2000 at USSR.

iii) Anna[9] Gerk (1024) married Viktor Kirchgessner (3153) at USSR. She was born on 9 Aug 1972 at USSR.

(a) Stefan[10] Kirchgessner (3154) was born on 15 Feb 1995 at USSR.

(b) Vanessa[10] Kirchgessner (3155) was born on 17 Feb 1998 at USSR.

ii) Adam[7] Gerk (871) married Maria Vasina (884). He was born on 17 Aug 1916 at Josefstal, Saratov, RUS. He died on 31 May 1999 at Irkutsk, Irkutsk Oblast, USSR, at age 82.

(a) Rosa[8] Gerk (885) was born on 2 Jan 1948 at Irkutsk, Irkutsk Oblast, USSR.

(b) Maria[8] Gerk (886) was born on 17 Aug 1949 at Irkutsk, Irkutsk Oblast, USSR.

(c) Anna[8] Gerk (887) married Vitalii Fominoi (3065) at USSR. She was born on 27 Feb 1952 at Irkutsk, Irkutsk Oblast, USSR.

i) Evgenii[9] Fominoi (3066) married Vera (--?--) (3067) at USSR. He was born in 1973 at Angarsk, Irkutsk Oblast, USSR.

(a) Egorka[10] Fominoi (3068) was born on 1 Aug 2002 at Angarsk, Irkutsk Oblast, USSR.

iii) Georg[7] Gerk (872) married Maria Knaub (876), daughter of Jakob Knaub (1051) and Katarina (--?--) (1052), at USSR. He was born on 22 Apr 1918 at Josefstal, Saratov, RUS. He died on 28 Dec 1998 at Schreibershof, Germany, at age 80.

(a) Erika[8] Gerk (882) married Wilhelm Grezinger (883). She was born on 28 Nov 1946 at Dneproschersinks, Ukraine, USSR.

(b) Viktor[8] Gerk (881) was born on 6 Sep 1948 at Dneproschersinks, Ukraine, USSR.

(c) Valeri[8] Gerk (877) was born on 1 Dec 1953 at Angarsk, USSR. He married Rosa Dippel (878), daughter of Clements Dippel (1053) and Lila Fix (1054), on 23 Apr 1975 at Frunse, USSR. He died on 11 Mar 1996 at Schreibershof, Germany, at age 42.

i) Alexander[9] Gerk (880) was born on 23 Aug 1975 at Frunse, USSR. He married ? ? (1921) in Aug 2001 at Germany.

(a) Maria-Evia[10] Gerk (1922) was born in Jan 2002 at Germany.

ii) Anna[9] Gerk (879) was born on 9 Apr 1980 at Frunse, USSR.

iv) Maria[7] Gerk (874) was born on 14 May 1921 at Josefstal, Saratov, USSR. She married Johannes Maul (888) on 14 May 1948 at USSR. She died in 2005 at Germany.

(a) Waldemar[8] Maul (925) died at Kazakstan, USSR. He was born on 8 Aug 1950 at Bogorogizk, USSR.

(b) Johannes[8] Maul (1850) was born on 28 Jun 1952 at Tula, USSR.

(c) Emma[8] Maul (1851) married ? Bleich (1860). She was born on 8 Dec 1955 at Angarsk, USSR.

v) Ida[7] Gerk (1859) married ? Harahorina (1861). She was born on 22 Oct 1923 at Josefstal, Stalingrad Oblast, USSR.

vi) Ottilia[7] Gerk (875) married Jakob Lehman (1854). She was born on 12 May 1926 at Josefstal, Stalingrad Oblast, USSR.

    (a) Eduard[8] Lehman (2136)

    (b) Alexander[8] Lehman (1855) was born on 4 Feb 1951 at Tula, USSR.

    (c) Lydia[8] Lehman (1856) was born on 11 Sep 1953 at Angarsk, USSR.

    (d) Maria[8] Lehman (2137) married (--?--) Zwillinge (2138). She was born on 19 May 1956 at Angarsk, USSR.

vii) Johannes[7] Gerk (873) married Anna Knaub (1857). He was born on 25 Sep 1928 at Josefstal, Stalingrad Oblast, USSR.

    (a) Waldemar[8] Gerk (1858) was born at USSR.

(g) Anna Margareta[6] Gerk (865) was born on 5 Aug 1892 at Josefstal, Saratov, RUS. She married Johan Georg Holzman (2261), son of Kristof Holzmann (2262) and Anna Margareta Schmidt (2263), on 22 Sep 1910 at Josefstal, Saratov, RUS.

    i) Beata[7] Holzman (3423) was born on 9 Jul 1911 at Josefstal, Saratov, RUS.

    ii) Georg[7] Holzman (3430) was born on 9 Mar 1914 at Josefstal, Saratov, RUS.

    iii) Isabella[7] Holzman (3703) was born on 16 Aug 1915 at Josefstal, Saratov, RUS.

(h) Magdalena[6] Gerk (866) was born on 1 Jun 1895 at Josefstal, Saratov, RUS. She married Georg Holzmann (1989), son of Peter Holzman (1990) and Katarina Arnold (1991), on 29 Oct 1913 at Josefstal, Saratov, RUS.

    i) Maria[7] Holzmann (3433) was born on 29 Oct 1914 at Josefstal, Saratov, RUS.

(i) Katarina[6] Gerk (867) was born on 22 Mar 1899 at Josefstal, Saratov, RUS.

(j) Peter[6] Gerk (3574) was born on 16 Feb 1902 at Josefstal, Saratov, RUS.

(2) Susanna Margareta[5] Gerk (707) was born on 30 Mar 1863 at Josefstal, Saratov, RUS. She married Philip Schaefer (2194), son of Jakob Schaefer (2264) and Elisabtha Bon (2265), on 7 Nov 1883 at Josefstal, Saratov, RUS. She married Peter Schneider (4117) on 28 Jan 1893 at Josefstal, Saratov, RUS.

    (a) Johannes[6] Schneider (4234) was born on 18 Oct 1897 at Marienfeld, Saratov, RUS.

    (b) Susanna[6] Schneider (4235) was born on 3 Jul 1903 at Marienfeld, Saratov, RUS.

(3) Elisabeta[5] Gerk (1326) was born in 1865 at Josefstal, Saratov, RUS. She died on 23 Mar 1866 at Josefstal, Saratov, RUS.

(4) Johann Georg[5] Gerk (708) was born on 5 Feb 1867 at Josefstal, Saratov, RUS. He died on 1 Dec 1869 at Josefstal, Saratov, RUS, at age 2.

(5) Anna Maria[5] Gerk (709) was born on 7 Oct 1869 at Josefstal, Saratov, RUS. She died on 13 Oct 1869 at Josefstal, Saratov, RUS.

(6) Teresia[5] Gerk (710) was born on 13 Feb 1871 at Josefstal, Saratov, RUS. She married Josef Schaefer (770), son of Johann Schaefer (771) and Elisabetha Weigel (772), on 17 Oct 1889 at Josefstal, Saratov, RUS. She died on 13 Mar 1941 at BA, ARG, at age 70.

    (a) Margareta[6] Schaefer (797) was born on 24 Sep 1896 at Josefstal, Saratov, RUS.

    (b) Josef[6] Schaefer (798) was born on 29 Aug 1899 at Josefstal, Saratov, RUS. He married Katalina Heit (2018), daughter of Valentin Heit (2126) and Elisabetha Gallinger (2127), on 11 Nov 1924 at San José, Coronel

Suárez, Buenos Aires, ARG. He died on 5 Sep 1970 at Pueblo San José, Coronel Suárez, Buenos Aires, ARG, at age 71.

(c) Andrew⁶ Schaefer (799) was born on 5 Jul 1902 at Josefstal, Saratov, RUS. He married Rosa Haag (2014), daughter of Johannes Haag (2015) and Magdalena Heit (2016), on 6 Sep 1927 at San José, Coronel Suárez, Buenos Aires, ARG.

(d) Konrad⁶ Schaefer (4808) was born in 1903 at Josefstal, Saratov, RUS.

(e) Katerina⁶ Schaefer (800) was born on 2 Jan 1905 at Josefstal, Saratov, RUS.

(f) Barbara Margareta⁶ Schaefer (8086) was born on 10 Feb 1908 at Pueblo San José, Buenos Aires, ARG.

(g) Catalina⁶ Schaefer (8087) was born on 10 Feb 1908 at Pueblo San José, Buenos Aires, ARG.

(7) Peter⁵ Gerk (711) was born on 4 Oct 1873 at Josefstal, Saratov, RUS. He married Christina Klein (781), daughter of Michael Klein (782) and Magdalena Heinrich (783), on 19 Nov 1891 at Josefstal, Saratov, RUS. He married Anna Marie Breit (2219), daughter of Johannes Breit (2220) and Elenora Berborik (2221), on 17 Sep 1901 at Josefstal, Saratov, RUS. He died in 1932 at Caucasus, USSR.

(a) Augustin⁶ Gerk (868) was born on 11 Jan 1894 at Josefstal, Saratov, RUS.

(b) Magdalena⁶ Gerk (931) was born on 16 Jul 1902 at Josefstal, Saratov, RUS. She died on 7 Nov 1902 at Josefstal, Saratov, RUS.

(c) Georg⁶ Gerk (932) was born on 2 Dec 1903 at Josefstal, Saratov, RUS. He married Maria Dreser (3091), daughter of Josef Dreser (921) and Anna Heinrich (1104), in 1925 at Josefstal, Saratov, RUS. He died on 19 Mar 1965 at Petrov Val, Volgograd, USSR, at age 61.

    i) Maria⁷ Gerk (3092) (see above)

        (a) Waldemar⁸ Dreser (3128) (see above)

    ii) Georg⁷ Gerk (3093) (see above)

        (a) Katarina⁸ Gerk (3130) (see above) **(b)** Anatolij⁸ Gerk (3131) (see above)

        (c) Waldemar⁸ Gerk (3132) (see above) **(d)** Olga⁸ Gerk (3133) (see above)

        (e) Alexander⁸ Gerk (3134) (see above)

    iii) Lydia⁷ Gerk (3094) (see above)

        (a) Eugen⁸ Michel (3136) (see above) **(b)** Alexander⁸ Michel (3137) (see above)

        (c) Elena⁸ Michel (3138) (see above) **(d)** Andreas⁸ Michel (3139) (see above)

    iv) Frida⁷ Gerk (3095) (see above)

        (a) Olga⁸ Peitsch (3141) (see above) **(b)** Eugen⁸ Peitsch (3646) (see above)

        (c) Aleksander⁸ Peitsch (3647) (see above)

    v) Alexander⁷ Gerk (3096) (see above)

(d) Anna⁶ Gerk (3119) married Josef Lambrecht (3120), son of Georg Lambrecht (4621) and Barbara Bellendir (4622), at Josefstal, Stalingrad Oblast, USSR. She was born in 1905 at Josefstal, Saratov, RUS.

    i) Rosa⁷ Lambrecht (3121) was born in 1927 at Josefstal, Stalingrad Oblast, USSR.

    ii) Josef⁷ Lambrecht (3122) was born in 1936 at Josefstal, Stalingrad Oblast, USSR.

    iii) Maria⁷ Lambrecht (3123) was born in 1938 at Josefstal, Stalingrad Oblast, USSR.

    iv) Valentina⁷ Lambrecht (3124) was born in 1941 at Josefstal, Stalingrad Oblast, USSR.

    v) Waldemar⁷ Lambrecht (3125) was born in 1947 at USSR.

    vi) Georg⁷ Lambrecht (3126) was born in 1949 at USSR.

(e) Katarina⁶ Gerk (929) was born on 27 May 1907 at Josefstal, Saratov, RUS. She died on 17 Feb 1908 at Josefstal, Saratov, RUS.

(f) Anton⁶ Gerk (3661) was born on 28 Nov 1908 at Josefstal, Saratov, RUS.

(g) Johannes[6] Gerk (3660) was born on 18 Apr 1910 at Josefstal, Saratov, RUS. He died on 30 Apr 1910 at Josefstal, Saratov, RUS.

(h) Maria[6] Gerk (933) was born on 13 Dec 1911 at Josefstal, Saratov, RUS. She died on 21 Feb 1912 at Josefstal, Saratov, RUS.

(i) Nikodema[6] Gerk (2002) married Paulina Klein (3097). He was born on 6 Apr 1913 at Josefstal, Saratov, RUS.

(8) Anna Margareta[5] Gerk (2199) was born in 1875 at Marienfeld, Saratov, RUS. She married Kaspar Hollmann (2267), son of Peter Hollmann (2201) and Magdalena Gerk (2266), on 21 Feb 1894. She married Franz Gerlinger (4183) on 24 Nov 1898 at Marienfeld, Saratov, RUS.

(a) Magdalena[6] Hollmann (2271) was born on 4 Apr 1895 at Marienfeld, Saratov, RUS. She married Georg Haberkorn (6212), son of Johann Adam Haberkorn (6213), on 3 Feb 1915 at Josefstal, Saratov, RUS.

i) Elisabetha[7] Haberkorn (8225) was born on 25 Jul 1917 at Josefstal, Saratov, RUS.

(b) Johannes[6] Hollmann (2303) was born on 11 Jun 1896 at Marienfeld, Saratov, RUS.

(c) Magdalena[6] Gerlinger (4283) was born on 26 Feb 1901 at Marienfeld, Saratov, RUS.

(d) Elizabeta[6] Gerlinger (4284) was born on 9 Feb 1903 at Marienfeld, Saratov, RUS.

(e) Benedict[6] Gerlinger (4285) was born on 1 Dec 1904 at Marienfeld, Saratov, RUS.

(f) Kristina[6] Gerlinger (4286) was born on 25 Jun 1906 at Marienfeld, Saratov, RUS.

(g) Rosa[6] Gerlinger (4287) was born on 21 Nov 1907 at Marienfeld, Saratov, RUS.

(h) Michael[6] Gerlinger (4288) was born on 21 May 1910 at Marienfeld, Saratov, RUS.

(9) Katarina Barbara[5] Gerk (1843) was born on 8 Mar 1879 at Josefstal, Saratov, RUS. She died on 26 Apr 1896 at Josefstal, Saratov, RUS, at age 17.

e) Konrad[4] Gerk (3040) was born on 30 Oct 1841 at Koehler, Saratov, RUS. He died on 29 Nov 1841 at Koehler, Saratov, RUS.

f) Katarina[4] Gerk (560) was born on 8 Apr 1843 at Koehler, Saratov, RUS. She married Johann Georg Gette (2700), son of Johan Adam Gette (986) and Teresia Schaab (987), on 14 Nov 1861 at Josefstal, Saratov, RUS.

g) Johannes[4] Gerk (743) was born on 4 Mar 1845 at Koehler, Saratov, RUS. He married Barbara Dittler (744), daughter of Heinrich Dittler (2718) and Margareta Heit (2719), on 9 Nov 1865 at Josefstal, Saratov, RUS. He emigrated on 10 Oct 1908 from Bremen, GER.

(1) Margareta Elisabeta[5] Gerk (742) was born on 26 Jun 1866 at Josefstal, Saratov, RUS.

(2) Georg[5] Gerk (745) was born on 7 Jun 1867 at Josefstal, Saratov, RUS. He married Dorothea Hartwig (764), daughter of Konrad Hartwig (765) and Barbara Ditlow (766), on 17 Nov 1887 at Josefstal, Saratov, RUS. He and Dorothea Hartwig (764) emigrated on 10 Oct 1908 from Bremen, GER. He died on 3 Jun 1944 at Santa Anita, Entre Ríos, ARG, at age 76.

(a) Georg[6] Gerk (790) was born on 12 Dec 1888 at Josefstal, Saratov, RUS. He married Margareta Breit (2251), daughter of Josef Breit (2176) and Magdalena Helmert (2177), on 30 Oct 1907 at Josefstal, Saratov, RUS. He emigrated on 10 Oct 1908 from Bremen, GER. He died on 2 May 1967 at Valle Maria, Entre Ríos, ARG, at age 78.

i) Jorge[7] Gerk (7517) was born on 11 Apr 1910 at Lucas González, Entre Ríos, ARG. He married Maria Celestina Gareis (7518) on 19 Sep 1936 at Valle Maria, Entre Ríos, ARG.

ii) Catalina[7] Gerk (2422) was born on 4 May 1912 at Nogoyá, Entre Ríos, ARG. She married José Carelli (2423), son of Benito Carelli (2424) and Carulen Biagi (2425), on 2 Apr 1929 at Valle Maria, Entre Ríos, ARG.

(a) Benito José[8] Carelli (6387) was born on 23 Jul 1936 at ARG.

iii) Gottfried[7] Gerk (2355) died at ARG. He was born on 21 Dec 1913 at Lucas González, Entre Ríos, ARG. He married Azucena Gareis (3033) on 23 Oct 1937 at Valle Maria, Entre Rios, ARG.

(a) Celia Emilia[8] Gerk (3034) was born on 6 Jun 1938 at Valle Maria, Entre Ríos, ARG.

(b) Carlos Humberto[8] Gerk (3035) was born on 3 Feb 1940 at Valle Maria, Entre Ríos, ARG.

(c) Angel Vicente[8] Gerk (3036) married Juana V. Saavedra (3037). He was born on 13 Jul 1945 at Valle Maria, Entre Ríos, ARG.

(d) Rosa Isabel[8] Gerk (3038) was born on 12 Jun 1951 at Valle Maria, Entre Ríos, ARG.

iv) Matias[7] Gerk (2349) was born on 16 May 1916 at Valle Mariá, Entre Ríos, ARG.

v) Aqueda[7] Gerk (2348) was born on 16 May 1916 at Valle Mariá, Entre Ríos, ARG.

vi) José Manuel[7] Gerk (2350) was born on 16 Jun 1917 at Valle Mariá, Entre Ríos, ARG. He died on 18 Feb 1925 at Santa Anita, Entre Ríos, ARG, at age 7.

vii) Emilia[7] Gerk (2351) was born on 24 May 1919 at Valle Mariá, Entre Ríos, ARG. She married Bartolomé Gassmann (2352) on 8 May 1943 at Brasilera, ARG.

viii) Gaspar Wendelin[7] Gerk (2353) was born on 25 Sep 1921 at Valle Mariá, Entre Ríos, ARG. He married Appolonia Strack (2354) on 12 Apr 1947 at ARG.

(a) Maria Ester[8] Gerk (3030) was born on 12 Nov 1950 at Valle Maria, Entre Ríos, ARG.

(b) Ruben Marcelo[8] Gerk (3031) was born on 23 Apr 1954 at Valle Maria, Entre Ríos, ARG.

(c) Ricardo Antonio[8] Gerk (3032) was born on 22 Nov 1955 at Valle Maria, Entre Ríos, ARG.

(b) Anna Katarina[6] Gerk (791) was born on 20 Mar 1891 at Josefstal, Saratov, RUS. She married Juan Georg Haberkorn (2248), son of Josef Haberkorn (6808) and Katarina Wagner (2250), on 30 Oct 1907 at Josefstal, Saratov, RUS. She died on 25 Nov 1916 at Brasilera, Entre Ríos, ARG, at age 25.

i) Juan[7] Haberkorn (6039) was born on 25 Dec 1909 at Crespo, Entre Rios, ARG.

ii) Jorge[7] Haberkorn (6080) was born on 28 Feb 1912 at Crespo, Entre Rios, ARG.

iii) Rosa[7] Haberkorn (2426) was born on 13 Jun 1916 at Valle Maria, Entre Ríos, ARG.

(c) Peter[6] Gerk (792) was born on 5 Jan 1894 at Josefstal, Saratov, RUS. He married Elisa Medina (2616) on 25 Sep 1924 at Santa Anita, Entre Ríos, ARG.

i) Demetrio[7] Gerk (6479) was born at Santa Anita, Entre Ríos, ARG. He married Julia Riedel (6480) on 28 Sep 1957 at Santa Anita, Entre Ríos, ARG.

ii) Enrique[7] Gerk (6486) was born on 18 Jul 1925 at Santa Anita, Entre Ríos, ARG. He married Catalina Regner (6487) on 26 May 1947 at Santa Anita, Entre Ríos, ARG.

(a) Juan Carlos[8] Gerk (6488) was born on 14 Mar 1948 at Santa Anita, Entre Ríos, ARG.

iii) Juan Pedro[7] Gerk (6477) was born on 16 Aug 1927 at Santa Anita, Entre Ríos, ARG. He married Catalina Kessler (6490), daughter of Michael Kessler (6491) and Elisa Hippedinger (6492), on 24 Apr 1965 at Santa Anita, Entre Ríos, ARG.

(a) Gustavo Miguel[8] Gerk (6494) was born on 9 Sep 1966 at Santa Anita, Entre Ríos, ARG.

(b) Carina Elisa[8] Gerk (6493) was born on 24 Oct 1972 at Santa Anita, Entre Ríos, ARG.

iv) Maria Ester[7] Gerk (3004) was born on 24 Feb 1929 at Santa Anita, Entre Ríos, ARG. She married Roberto Honeker (3005) on 26 Aug 1947 at Santa Anita, Entre Ríos, ARG. She died on 29 Jan 1986 at Santa Anita, Entre Ríos, ARG, at age 56.

v) Ana Marie Isabel[7] Gerk (6478) was born on 27 Jun 1939 at Santa Anita, Entre Ríos, ARG.

vi) Leticia Vicario[7] Gerk (6499) was born on 11 Mar 1941 at Santa Anita, Entre Ríos, ARG.

vii) Landelino[7] Gerk (6481) was born on 23 Jul 1943 at Santa Anita, Entre Ríos, ARG.

viii) Irma Celestina[7] Gerk (6482) was born on 7 Sep 1945 at Santa Anita, Entre Ríos, ARG. She died on 14 Feb 1946 at Santa Anita, Entre Ríos, ARG.

ix) Pablo[7] Gerk (6483) was born on 13 Apr 1947 at Santa Anita, Entre Ríos, ARG.

x) Jose[7] Gerk (6484) was born on 30 Aug 1949 at Santa Anita, Entre Ríos, ARG.

xi) Adolfo Emilio[7] Gerk (6485) was born on 20 Nov 1951 at Santa Anita, Entre Ríos, ARG.

(d) David[6] Gerk (1863) was born on 5 Apr 1896 at Josefstal, Saratov, RUS. He died on 4 Jun 1896 at Josefstal, Saratov, RUS.

(e) Elisabeta[6] Gerk (793) was born on 28 Jun 1897 at Josefstal, Saratov, RUS.

(f) Barbara[6] Gerk (796) married Juan Domme (2613) at Santa Anita, Entre Ríos, ARG. She was born on 18 Feb 1899 at Josefstal, Saratov, RUS. She died on 29 Jan 1939 at Santa Anita, Entre Ríos, ARG, at age 39.

    i) Felipe[7] Domme (2617) was born at Santa Anita, Entre Ríos, ARG.

    ii) Juan[7] Domme (2618) was born at Santa Anita, Entre Ríos, ARG.

    iii) Pedro[7] Domme (2619) was born at Santa Anita, Entre Ríos, ARG.

    iv) Brigida[7] Domme (2620) was born at Santa Anita, Entre Ríos, ARG.

    v) Catalina[7] Domme (2621) was born at Santa Anita, Entre Ríos, ARG.

    vi) Luisa[7] Domme (2622) was born at Santa Anita, Entre Ríos, ARG.

    vii) Maria[7] Domme (2623) was born at Santa Anita, Entre Ríos, ARG.

(g) Johann[6] Gerk (794) married Evangelista Rodriguez (6473) at Santa Anita, Entre Ríos, ARG. He was born on 26 Jul 1903 at Josefstal, Saratov, RUS.

    i) Mario[7] Gerk (6475) was born on 4 May 1941 at Santa Anita, Entre Ríos, ARG.

    ii) Julio[7] Gerk (6476) was born on 7 Apr 1946 at Santa Anita, Entre Ríos, ARG.

    iii) Juana Gladys[7] Gerk (6474) was born on 7 May 1948 at Santa Anita, Entre Ríos, ARG.

(h) Anna[6] Gerk (795) was born on 18 Jan 1907 at Josefstal, Saratov, RUS.

(i) Adan[6] Gerk (2120) was born on 18 Jun 1909 at Crespo, Entre Ríos, ARG.

(j) Adan[6] Gerk (2401) was born on 10 Jun 1911 at Racedo, Entre Ríos, ARG. He married Amalia Vertz (2402), daughter of Georg Vertz (2403) and Catalina Jorge (2404), on 7 Aug 1934 at Santa Anita, Entre Ríos, ARG. He died on 9 Nov 1983 at Santa Anita, Entre Ríos, ARG, at age 72.

    i) Nicolas[7] Kerke (2405) was born on 30 Sep 1936 at Santa Anita, Entre Ríos, ARG. He married Veronica Teresita Grenz (2406), daughter of Pedro Grenz (2407) and Ana Schemberger (2408), in 1952 at Santa Anita, Entre Ríos, ARG. He died on 1 Mar 1985 at Santa Anita, Entre Ríos, ARG, at age 48.

        (a) Oscar Enrique[8] Kerke (2409) married Sabina Asselborn (2410). He was born on 29 Jan 1960 at Santa Anita, Entre Ríos, ARG.

            i) Cristian Oscar[9] Kerke (2411) was born on 21 Aug 1980 at Santa Anita, Entre Ríos, ARG. He married Sandra Freitte (6495) on 1 Mar 2003 at ARG.

            ii) Maria Alejandrina[9] Kerke (2412) was born on 11 Nov 1983 at Santa Anita, Entre Ríos, ARG.

        (b) Omar Darío[8] Kerke (2413) married Christina Bolig (2414). He was born on 29 Jan 1970 at Santa Anita, Entre Ríos, ARG.

        (c) Sergio Alberto[8] Kerke (2415) was born on 19 Jun 1971 at Santa Anita, Entre Ríos, ARG. He married Marina Heer (2416) on 12 Apr 1997 at Santa Anita, Entre Ríos, ARG.

        (d) Carina Alicia[8] Kerke (2420) was born on 18 Aug 1975 at Santa Anita, Entre Ríos, ARG.

            i) Alma Anahi Rivero[9] Kerke (4976) was born on 17 Oct 2006 at San Anita, ARG.

            ii) Teo Nicolas[9] Kerke (6187) was born on 6 Jun 2011 at Santa Anita, Entre Ríos, ARG.

        (e) Liliana Noemí[8] Kerke (2417) was born on 13 Mar 1977 at Santa Anita, Entre Ríos, ARG.

        (f) Marcos Miguel[8] Kerke (2418) married Analia Hoffman (2419). He was born on 9 Oct 1981 at Santa Anita, Entre Ríos, ARG.

    ii) Rosa Juana[7] Kerke (2615) was born on 28 Jul 1937 at Santa Anita, Entre Ríos, ARG.

    iii) Isabel[7] Gerk (3571) was born on 25 Oct 1942 at Santa Anita, Entre Ríos, ARG.

    iv) José[7] Kerk (2421) was born on 6 Feb 1952 at Santa Anita, Entre Ríos, ARG.

(3) Katarina[5] Gerk (1271) was born on 27 Feb 1870 at Josefstal, Saratov, RUS. She married Josef Stremel (1272), son of Michael Stremel (1273) and Elisabeth Honecker (1274), on 31 Aug 1887 at Josefstal, Saratov, RUS.

(a) Konrad^6 Stremel (4267) was born on 2 Oct 1888 at Josefstal, Saratov, RUS. He married Anna Margareta Ringelmann (4327) on 11 Feb 1914 at Josefstal, Saratov, RUS.

(b) Georg^6 Stremel (1275) was born on 2 Jul 1896 at Josefstal, Saratov, RUS.

(c) Appolonia^6 Stremel (1276) was born on 27 Oct 1899 at Josefstal, Saratov, RUS.

(d) Peter^6 Stremel (1277) was born on 1 Jul 1902 at Josefstal, Saratov, RUS.

(e) Paul^6 Stremel (1278) was born on 11 Nov 1903 at Josefstal, Saratov, RUS. He died on 2 Mar 1910 at Josefstal, Saratov, RUS, at age 6.

(f) Georg^6 Stremel (1279) was born on 6 Mar 1906 at Josefstal, Saratov, RUS. He died on 25 Apr 1910 at Josefstal, Saratov, RUS, at age 4.

(g) Maria^6 Stremel (1280) was born on 23 Mar 1908 at Josefstal, Saratov, RUS. She died on 15 May 1913 at Josefstal, Saratov, RUS, at age 5.

(h) Georg^6 Stremel (1281) was born on 28 Sep 1911 at Josefstal, Saratov, RUS.

(4) Anton^5 Gerk (746) was born on 18 Jun 1872 at Josefstal, Saratov, RUS. He married Maria Anna Kess (4184) on 7 Oct 1897 at Josefstal, Saratov, RUS.

(5) Barbara^5 Gerk (747) was born on 23 Jan 1877 at Josefstal, Saratov, RUS. She died on 26 Nov 1878 at Josefstal, Saratov, RUS, at age 1.

(6) Elisabeta^5 Gerk (748) was born on 11 Mar 1879 at Josefstal, Saratov, RUS.

(7) Adam^5 Gerk (749) was born on 10 May 1884 at Josefstal, Saratov, RUS. He died on 22 May 1897 at Josefstal, Saratov, RUS, at age 13.

(8) Barbara^5 Gerk (750) was born on 2 Nov 1886 at Josefstal, Saratov, RUS. She died on 14 Aug 1888 at Josefstal, Saratov, RUS, at age 1.

(9) Johannes^5 Gerk (3211) was born on 19 Dec 1890 at Marienfeld, Saratov, RUS.

h) Konrad^4 Gerk (556) was born on 26 Apr 1847 at Koehler, Saratov, RUS. He married Elisabeta Lambrecht (757), daughter of Michael Lambrecht (2721) and Elisabeta Mast (2722), on 9 Nov 1865 at Josefstal, Saratov, RUS. He died on 26 Dec 1877 at Josefstal, Saratov, RUS, at age 30.

(1) Johann Georg^5 Gerk (763) was born on 16 Jul 1867 at Josefstal, Saratov, RUS.

(2) Mattias^5 Gerk (758) married Ekaterina Buss (1243) at Josefstal, Saratov, RUS. He was born on 17 Apr 1869 at Josefstal, Saratov, RUS. He married Anna Maria Ekaterina (Saks) Gette (779), daughter of Elenora Saks (780), on 16 Oct 1890 at Josefstal, Saratov, RUS. He died on 4 Apr 1934 at Josefstal, Stalingrad, USSR, at age 64.

(a) Elisabeta^6 Gerk (2295) was born on 13 Jul 1891 at Josefstal, Saratov, RUS. She married Johann Peter Sommer (2296), son of Friedrich Sommer (2297) and Katerina Holzman (2298), on 21 Oct 1909 at Josefstal, Saratov, RUS.

i) Johann^7 Sommer (2299) was born on 31 Aug 1911 at Josefstal, Saratov, RUS.

ii) Josef^7 Sommer (6906) was born on 25 Sep 1914 at Josefstal, Saratov, RUS.

(b) Josephina^6 Gerk (2300) was born on 19 Mar 1894 at Josefstal, Saratov, RUS. She died on 11 Feb 1906 at Josefstal, Saratov, RUS, at age 11.

(c) Josef^6 Gerk (1244) was born on 31 Jan 1896 at Josefstal, Saratov, RUS. He married Klementine Simon (2333), daughter of Andreas Simon (2334) and Barbara Berg (2335), on 23 Jan 1914 at Josefstal, Saratov, RUS. He died in 1938 at Engels, Saratov, USSR.

i) Maria^7 Gerk (3802) was born at Josefstal, Stalingrad Oblast, USSR.

ii) Adam^7 Gerk (2336) was born on 23 Sep 1914 at Josefstal, Saratov, RUS. He died on 27 Oct 1914 at Josefstal, Saratov, RUS.

iii) Josef^7 Gerk (3751) was born on 25 Sep 1915 at Josefstal, Saratov, RUS.

iv) Ivan^7 Gerk (3801) was born in 1930 at Josefstal, Stalingrad Oblast, USSR. He married Katarina Kuhn (3803) circa 1948 at USSR. He died on 29 Nov 1964 at Pavlogradka, Omsk Oblast, USSR.

(a) Vladimir^8 Gerk (3804) was born on 15 Nov 1950 at Omsk Oblast, USSR.

(b) Elena[8] Gerk (3805) was born on 7 Apr 1952 at Omsk Oblast, USSR.

(c) Viktor[8] Gerk (3806) was born on 22 Nov 1955 at Jitomir, Omsk Oblast, USSR.

(d) Alexander[8] Gerk (3807) was born on 22 Nov 1955 at Jitomir, Omsk Oblast, USSR. He married Vera Putko (3810), daughter of Vladislav Putka (3813) and Nina Woloeva (3814), circa 1982 at USSR.

    i) Svetlena[9] Gerk (3811) was born on 2 Sep 1982 at Omsk, USSR.

    ii) Igor[9] Gerk (3812) was born on 11 Jan 1987 at Omsk, USSR.

(e) Lydia[8] Gerk (3808) was born on 18 Jun 1957 at Omsk Oblast, USSR.

(f) Valentina[8] Gerk (3809) was born on 25 Aug 1961 at Omsk Oblast, USSR.

(d) Georg[6] Gerk (1245) was born on 19 Jan 1898 at Josefstal, Saratov, RUS. He died on 1 Mar 1899 at Josefstal, Saratov, RUS, at age 1.

(e) Johannes[6] Gerk (1246) was born on 10 Jan 1900 at Josefstal, Saratov, RUS.

(f) Anna[6] Gerk (1252) was born on 27 Feb 1902 at Josefstal, Saratov, RUS. She died on 28 Sep 1902 at Josefstal, Saratov, RUS.

(g) Peter[6] Gerk (1247) was born on 2 Jan 1904 at Josefstal, Saratov, RUS.

(h) Friedrich[6] Gerk (1248) died on 21 Jun 1913 at Josefstal, Saratov, RUS, at age 6. He was born on 18 Feb 1907 at Josefstal, Saratov, RUS.

(i) Mattias[6] Gerk (1249) was born on 29 Dec 1908 at Josefstal, Saratov, RUS. He died on 21 Jun 1913 at Josefstal, Saratov, RUS, at age 4.

(j) Josef[6] Gerk (1250) was born on 20 Sep 1910 at Josefstal, Saratov, RUS.

(k) Georg[6] Gerk (1251) was born on 14 Jul 1912 at Josefstal, Saratov, RUS. He married Pia Dieser (123), daughter of Georg Dieser (117) and Elenora Kisser (118), in Nov 1931 at Josefstal, Stalingrad Oblast, USSR. He died on 10 Sep 1997 at Krasnoturinsk, Sverdlovsk, USSR, at age 85.

    i) Eduard[7] Gerk (5551) was born on 29 Jan 1941 at Josefstal, Stalingrad Oblast, USSR.

    ii) Alexander[7] Gerk (5552) was born in Jul 1949 at Krasnoturinsk, Sverdlovsk, USSR.

    iii) Ida[7] Gerk (5553) was born in 1952 at Krasnoturinsk, Sverdlovsk, USSR. She died in 1954 at Krasnoturinsk, Sverdlovsk, USSR.

(l) Barbara[6] Gerk (2342) was born on 8 Apr 1914 at Josefstal, Saratov, RUS.

(3) Elisabeta[5] Gerk (759) was born on 21 Nov 1871 at Josefstal, Saratov, RUS.

(4) David[5] Gerk (760) was born on 6 Nov 1872 at Josefstal, Saratov, RUS. He married Magdalena Seibel (802), daughter of Andreas Seibel (803) and Maria Schmidt (804), on 15 Nov 1895 at Josefstal, Saratov, RUS.

(a) Margareta[6] Gerk (805) was born on 18 Aug 1896 at Josefstal, Saratov, RUS. She died on 11 Jun 1897 at Josefstal, Saratov, RUS.

(b) Margareta[6] Gerk (806) was born on 5 Apr 1898 at Josefstal, Saratov, RUS. She died on 27 Aug 1902 at Marienfeld, Saratov, RUS, at age 4.

(c) Dorothea[6] Gerk (807) was born on 28 Sep 1901 at Josefstal, Saratov, RUS.

(d) Robert[6] Gerk (808) was born on 14 Aug 1903 at Josefstal, Saratov, RUS.

(e) Maria[6] Gerk (809) was born on 10 Jun 1905 at Josefstal, Saratov, RUS. She died on 1 Mar 1907 at Josefstal, Saratov, RUS, at age 1.

(f) Elisabeta[6] Gerk (810) was born on 25 Jun 1907 at Josefstal, Saratov, RUS.

(g) Amalia[6] Gerk (811) was born on 9 Feb 1910 at Josefstal, Saratov, RUS. She died on 13 Jan 1911 at Josefstal, Saratov, RUS.

(h) Andrei[6] Gerk (1031) was born on 24 Mar 1912 at Josefstal, Saratov, RUS.

(i) Gottfried[6] Gerk (1029) was born on 9 Jul 1914 at Josefstal, Saratov, RUS. He died on 8 Feb 1916 at Josefstal, Saratov, RUS, at age 1.

(5) Konrad[5] Gerk (761) was born on 16 Aug 1875 at Josefstal, Saratov, RUS. He died on 23 Nov 1878 at Josefstal, Saratov, RUS, at age 3.

(6) Katarina[5] Gerk (762) was born on 21 Jun 1878 at Josefstal, Saratov, RUS. She married Stephan Schaefer (784), son of Johann Schaefer (771) and Elisabetha Weigel (772), on 5 Nov 1896 at Josefstal, Saratov, RUS. She died on 1 Mar 1905 at Josefstal, Saratov, RUS, at age 26.

    (a) Jakob[6] Schaefer (812) was born on 17 Mar 1898 at Josefstal, Saratov, RUS.

    (b) Katarina[6] Schaefer (813) was born on 14 Dec 1899 at Josefstal, Saratov, RUS. She married Matias Domme (2123), son of Kaspar Domme (4523) and Elisabetha Strack (5922), on 19 Nov 1920 at San José, Coronel Suárez, Buenos Aires, ARG.

    (c) Julianna[6] Schaefer (814) was born on 27 Jul 1902 at Josefstal, Saratov, RUS.

    (d) Peter[6] Schaefer (815) was born on 15 Nov 1903 at Josefstal, Saratov, RUS.

i) Zacharius[4] Gerk (557) was born on 8 Sep 1849 at Koehler, Saratov, RUS. He died in 1855 at Josefstal, Saratov, RUS.

j) Josef[4] Gerk (558) was born on 3 Dec 1851 at Koehler, Saratov, RUS. He died on 28 Jun 1863 at Josefstal, Saratov, RUS, at age 11.

14. Katarina Elisabeta[3] Gerk (3688) was born on 20 Oct 1809 at Koehler, Saratov, RUS.

B. Katarina[2] Gerk (499) was born on 21 Feb 1758 at Müs, Fulda, Hesse, GER. She married Johann Michael Schmidtlein (563), son of Sebastian Schmidtlein (2003), in 1777 at Koehler, Saratov, RUS. She died circa 1835 at Koehler, Saratov, RUS.

1. Maria Katarina[3] Schmidtlein (565) was born in 1778 at Koehler, Saratov, RUS.

2. Maria Margareta[3] Schmidtlein (566) was born in 1783 at Koehler, Saratov, RUS.

3. Maria Elizabeta[3] Schmidtlein (567) was born in 1784 at Koehler, Saratov, RUS.

4. Elizabeth Katarina[3] Schmidtlein (568) was born in 1789 at Koehler, Saratov, RUS.

5. Johann David[3] Schmidtlein (564) married Elisabeta (--?--) (3464) at Koehler, Saratov, RUS. He was born in 1794 at Koehler, Saratov, RUS. He died in 1856 at Koehler, Saratov, RUS.

    a) Peter[4] Schmidtlein (3465) married Katarina (--?--) (3467) at Koehler, Saratov, RUS. He was born in 1829 at Koehler, Saratov, RUS.

        (1) Barbara[5] Schmidtlein (3468) was born in 1848 at Koehler, Saratov, RUS.

        (2) Josef[5] Schmidtlein (3466) was born in 1850 at Koehler, Saratov, RUS.

        (3) Andreas[5] Schmidtlein (3637) was born in 1856 at Koehler, Saratov, RUS.

6. Zacharius[3] Schmidtlein (3627) married Maria Margareta (--?--) (3628) at Koehler, Saratov, RUS. He was born in 1799 at Koehler, Saratov, RUS.

    a) Anna Maria[4] Schmidtlein (3629) was born in 1829 at Koehler, Saratov, RUS. She married Philip Gareis (3630) on 20 Nov 1844 at Koehler, Saratov, RUS.

        (1) Philip[5] Gareis (3631) was born on 9 Aug 1845 at Koehler, Saratov, RUS.

        (2) Johannes[5] Gareis (3632) was born on 1 Dec 1847 at Koehler, Saratov, RUS. He died on 5 Sep 1851 at Koehler, Saratov, RUS, at age 3.

        (3) Anna Maria[5] Gareis (3634) was born on 17 Feb 1850 at Koehler, Saratov, RUS.

        (4) Barbara[5] Gareis (3635) was born on 26 Jul 1852 at Koehler, Saratov, RUS.

        (5) Jakob[5] Gareis (3633) was born on 23 Oct 1854 at Koehler, Saratov, RUS.

        (6) Sophia[5] Gareis (3636) was born on 14 Oct 1856 at Koehler, Saratov, RUS. She died on 22 Mar 1858 at Koehler, Saratov, RUS, at age 1.

C. Zacharius[2] Gerk (500) was born in 1766 at GER. He married (--?--) Hasenhauer (626) circa 1789 at Koehler, Saratov, RUS. He married Anna Maria Brescher (632) circa 1794 at Koehler, Saratov, RUS. He died in 1834 at Koehler, Saratov, RUS.

1. Johann Adam³ Gerk (630) was born in 1789 at Koehler, Saratov, RUS. He married Anna Elisabeth Hock (636) in 1810 at Koehler, Saratov, RUS. He married Anna Elisabetha Rosenbach (638) on 25 Nov 1829 at Koehler, Saratov, RUS. He died in 1843 at Koehler, Saratov, RUS.

a) Katarina⁴ Gerk (3684) was born on 19 Nov 1810 at Koehler, Saratov, RUS. She died on 9 Feb 1812 at Koehler, Saratov, RUS, at age 1.

b) Anna Maria⁴ Gerk (637) was born on 29 Jan 1815 at Koehler, Saratov, RUS.

c) Josef⁴ Gerk (635) was born in 1820 at Koehler, Saratov, RUS. He married Barbara Kissner (1773) on 29 Jan 1845 at Koehler, Saratov, RUS.

(1) Anna Maria⁵ Gerk (3116) was born in 1846 at Koehler, Saratov, RUS.

(2) Katarina⁵ Gerk (3117) was born in 1849 at Koehler, Saratov, RUS.

(3) Barbara⁵ Gerk (1774) was born on 3 Oct 1857 at Pfeifer, Saratov, RUS. She married Jakob Schoenfeld (1775), son of Jakob Schoenfeld (1776) and Maria Ann Sieben (1777), on 19 Nov 1874 at Pfeifer, Saratov, RUS. She immigrated on 15 Jul 1876 to New York, New York, USA. She died on 10 Oct 1937 at Park, Kansas, USA, at age 80.

(a) Barbara⁶ Schoenfeld (1778) was born in 1875 at Pfeifer, Saratov, RUS. She died in Jul 1876.

(b) Marie Ann⁶ Schoenfeld (6248) was born circa 1876 at Pfeifer, Saratov, RUS. She died in 1876.

(c) Georg⁶ Schoenfeld (1779) married Margaret Volmer (1791). He was born on 7 Nov 1877 at Topeka, Kansas, USA. He died on 5 Jan 1951 at Kansas, USA, at age 73.

(d) Peter⁶ Schoenfeld (1780) was born on 3 Sep 1880 at Topeka, Kansas, USA. He died on 28 Feb 1946 at Kansas, USA, at age 65.

(e) Katarina⁶ Schoenfeld (1781) was born on 3 Mar 1883 at Topeka, Kansas, USA. She married Clem Dreher (1792) on 22 Nov 1903 at Hays, Kansas, USA. She died on 2 Jan 1952 at Hays, Kansas, USA, at age 68.

(f) Andreas⁶ Schoenfeld (1782) married Christina Krueger (1793). He was born on 5 Apr 1885 at Topeka, Kansas, USA. He died on 21 Nov 1959 at Kansas, USA, at age 74.

(g) Martin⁶ Schoenfeld (1783) married Mary Ploger (3165). He was born on 15 Nov 1887 at Topeka, Kansas, USA. He died on 3 Jan 1945 at age 57.

(h) Anna Maria⁶ Schoenfeld (1784) was born on 29 Jan 1890 at Topeka, Kansas, USA. She married Andrew Pfeifer (3080), son of Jacob Pfeifer (3081) and Elizabeth Weber (3082), on 18 Nov 1908 at Hays, Kansas, USA. She died on 2 Dec 1977 at Hays, Kansas, USA, at age 87.

i) Lawrence⁷ Pfeifer (2453) **ii)** Eleanor⁷ Pfeifer (2454) **iii)** Florine⁷ Pfeifer (2455)

iv) Barbara⁷ Pfeifer (2457) **v)** Mary⁷ Pfeifer (2456) was born on 6 Feb 1921 at Hays, Kansas, USA. She married John D. Lawler (3083) on 8 Jul 1939 at Hays, Kansas, USA.

(i) Kristina⁶ Schoenfeld (1785) was born on 12 May 1891 at Topeka, Kansas, USA. She died on 23 Aug 1988 at Santa Barbara, California, USA, at age 97.

(j) Barbara⁶ Schoenfeld (1786) was born on 3 Apr 1894 at Topeka, Kansas, USA. She married Joseph Meder (1794) on 16 Aug 1923 at Pfeifer, Kansas, USA. She died on 29 Oct 1986 at Hays, Kansas, USA, at age 92.

(k) Jakob⁶ Schoenfeld (1787) was born on 13 Sep 1896 at Topeka, Kansas, USA. He married Elizabeth Domme (1795) on 7 Aug 1933 at Pfeifer, Kansas, USA. He died on 31 Jan 1965 at Kansas, USA, at age 68.

(l) Adam Joseph⁶ Schoenfeld (1788) was born on 29 Oct 1898 at Topeka, Kansas, USA. He married Lidwina Catherine Graf (1796) on 6 Nov 1940 at Pfeifer, Kansas, USA. He died on 3 Apr 1985 at Collyer, Kansas, USA, at age 86.

i) Donna Louise⁷ Schoenfeld (2781) was born on 13 Jan 1942 at Hays, Kansas, USA. She married Michael Anthony Glora (2782) on 30 Jun 1962 at Grainfield, Kansas, USA. She died on 2 Jun 1998 at Las Vegas, Nevada, USA, at age 56.

(a) Michael Anthony⁸ Glora (2783) was born on 27 Jun 1963 at Albuquerque, New Mexico, USA. He married Regina Ann Carter Rockwood (2784) on 29 Nov 1997 at Las Vegas, Nevada, USA.

i) Jenna Marie⁹ Glora (2785) was born on 23 Dec 1989 at USA.

ii) Kayla Brook⁹ Glora (2786) was born on 7 Jun 1991 at USA.

(b) Patricia Louise[8] Glora (2787) was born on 28 Sep 1966 at Las Vegas, Nevada, USA. She married William Hall Chambers (2788) on 31 Aug 1996 at Hayden Lake, Idaho, USA.

(m) Michael[6] Schoenfeld (1789) married Ella Denning (3166). He was born on 18 Sep 1901 at Topeka, Kansas, USA. He died on 12 Mar 1985 at Grainfeld, Kansas, USA, at age 83.

(n) Edward[6] Schoenfeld (1790) was born on 24 Dec 1906 at Topeka, Kansas, USA. He died on 27 Jun 1994 at Hays, Kansas, USA, at age 87.

(4) Josef[5] Gerk (3675) was born on 11 Feb 1860 at Pfeifer, Saratov, RUS. He married Anna Margareta Schmidt (4124) on 24 Nov 1881 at Pfeifer, Saratov, RUS. He married Katarina Diel (4126) on 29 Jan 1885 at Pfeifer, Saratov, RUS.

(a) Appolonia[6] Gerk (4125) was born on 28 Dec 1883 at Pfeifer, Saratov, RUS.

(b) Margareta[6] Gerk (4127) was born on 10 Sep 1886 at Pfeifer, Saratov, RUS. She died on 5 Dec 1886 at Pfeifer, Saratov, RUS.

(c) Georg[6] Gerk (4128) was born on 26 Sep 1887 at Pfeifer, Saratov, RUS. He died on 27 Sep 1887 at Pfeifer, Saratov, RUS.

(d) Alexander[6] Gerk (4129) was born on 2 Jul 1892 at Pfeifer, Saratov, RUS.

(e) Josef[6] Gerk (4131) was born on 19 Feb 1895 at Pfeifer, Saratov, RUS.

i) Emanuel[7] Gerk (7827) was born in 1923 at Pfeifer, Saratov, USSR.

(f) Ignatius[6] Gerk (4130) was born on 1 Feb 1897 at Pfeifer, Saratov, RUS.

i) Adolf[7] Gerk (7826) was born in 1924 at Pfeifer, Saratov, USSR.

(g) Georg[6] Gerk (4132) was born on 29 Nov 1899 at Pfeifer, Saratov, RUS.

(5) Georg[5] Gerk (3676) was born on 10 Jan 1863 at Pfeifer, Saratov, RUS. He married Katarina Kern (4185) on 30 Oct 1890 at Pfeifer, Saratov, RUS.

(6) Appolonia[5] Gerk (3677) was born on 29 May 1865 at Pfeifer, Saratov, RUS. She died circa 1866 at Pfeifer, Saratov, RUS.

(7) Appolonia[5] Gerk (3678) was born on 2 Oct 1867 at Pfeifer, Saratov, RUS. She married Philipp Jacob (4123) on 24 Nov 1887 at Pfeifer, Saratov, RUS. She died in 1933 at Pfeifer, USSR.

(a) Ignatz[6] Jacob (6508) was born at Pfeifer, Saratov, RUS. He died in 1933 at Pfeifer, Saratov, RUS.

(b) Jehan[6] Jacob (6509) was born at Pfeifer, Saratov, RUS. He died circa 1917.

(c) Marejan[6] Jacob (6510) was born at Pfeifer, Saratov, RUS. She died in 1937 at Pfeifer, Saratov, RUS.

(d) Margaret[6] Jacob (6511) was born at Pfeifer, Saratov, RUS. She died in 1921 at Kamenka, Saratov, USSR.

(e) Barbara[6] Jacob (6512) married Georg Lell (6513) at Pfeifer, Saratov, RUS. She was born in 1888 at Pfeifer, Saratov, USSR. She died in Dec 1973 at Ukrainka, Omsk, USSR.

(f) Georg[6] Jacob (6514) was born in 1906 at Pfeifer, Saratov, RUS. He died in 1988 at Ukraine, USSR.

(g) Phillip[6] Jacob (6515) was born in 1910 at Pfeifer, Saratov, RUS. He died in 1976 at Novosibirsk, USSR.

(h) Adam[6] Jacob (6516) was born in 1916 at Pfeifer, Saratov, RUS. He died in 1933 at Pfeifer, USSR.

(8) Ignatius[5] Gerk (4133) married Elisabetha Conradi (4134) at Pfeifer, Saratov, RUS. He was born on 17 Dec 1869 at Pfeifer, Saratov, RUS.

(a) Maria[6] Gerk (4135) was born on 24 Dec 1897 at Pfeifer, Saratov, RUS.

(b) Appolonia[6] Gerk (4136) was born on 24 Nov 1899 at Pfeifer, Saratov, RUS.

d) Katarina[4] Gerk (639) was born in 1823 at Koehler, Saratov, RUS. She married Georg Mueller (3691), son of Anton Mueller (7719) and Magdalena (--?--) (7728), on 15 Nov 1848 at Koehler, Saratov, RUS.

(1) Jakob[5] Mueller (7722) was born in 1849 at Leichtling, Saratov, RUS.

(2) Elisabetha[5] Mueller (7721) was born in 1853 at Josefstal, Saratov, RUS.

(3) Josef[5] Mueller (7720) was born in 1856 at Josefstal, Saratov, RUS.

e) Johannes[4] Gerk (640) was born on 26 Dec 1830 at Koehler, Saratov, RUS. He married Elisabeta Katarina Heim (641) in 1854 at Koehler, Saratov, RUS. He died on 31 Jan 1861 at Koehler, Saratov, RUS, at age 30.

(1) Georg[5] Gerk (642) was born in 1854 at Koehler, Saratov, RUS. He married Katarina Suppes (4120) on 19 Nov 1873 at Pfeifer, Saratov, RUS. He married Katarina Haag (7798) on 19 May 1887 at Rozhdestvenskoye, Stavropol, RUS.

(a) Elisabetha[6] Gerk (4121) was born on 21 Jul 1875 at Pfeifer, Saratov, RUS.

(b) Johannes[6] Gerk (4122) was born on 6 Sep 1878 at Pfeifer, Saratov, RUS.

f) Johannes[4] Gerk (4118) was born on 26 Mar 1832 at Koehler, Saratov, RUS. He died on 28 Mar 1832 at Koehler, Saratov, RUS.

g) Margareta[4] Gerk (4119) was born on 26 Mar 1832 at Koehler, Saratov, RUS. She died on 28 Mar 1832 at Koehler, Saratov, RUS.

2. Heinrich[3] Gerk (631) was born in 1793 at Koehler, Saratov, RUS. He died on 7 Jan 1841 at Koehler, Saratov, RUS.

3. Anna Maria[3] Gerk (633) was born in 1795 at Koehler, Saratov, RUS.

4. Elisabeta[3] Gerk (634) was born in 1796 at Koehler, Saratov, RUS. She married Philip Kissner (1834) on 25 Apr 1815 at Pfeifer, Saratov, RUS.

a) Anna Marie[4] Kissner (1844) was born on 14 Jul 1816 at Pfeifer, Saratov, RUS.

b) Barbara[4] Kissner (1845) was born on 11 May 1819 at Pfeifer, Saratov, RUS.

c) Maria Barbara[4] Kissner (1846) was born on 7 Sep 1820 at Pfeifer, Saratov, RUS.

d) Mattias[4] Kissner (1847) married Maria Cecilia Berg (1848). He was born on 11 Oct 1822 at Pfeifer, Saratov, RUS.

e) Elisabeta[4] Kissner (1849) was born on 13 Feb 1830 at Pfeifer, Saratov, RUS.

5. Johannes[3] Gerk (3689) was born on 28 Jan 1807 at Koehler, Saratov, RUS.

6. Maria Magdalena[3] Gerk (3682) was born on 8 Oct 1811 at Koehler, Saratov, RUS.

D. Johann Adam[2] Gerk (501) was born in 1768 at Koehler, Saratov, RUS. He married Barbara Schenk (569) in 1788 at Koehler, Saratov, RUS. He died in 1816 at Koehler, Saratov, RUS.

1. Johann Georg[3] Gerk (570) was born in 1792 at Koehler, Saratov, RUS. He married Elisabeta Ruhl (571), daughter of Philip Ruhl (3648) and Anna Margareta Sofle (3649), on 24 Jan 1810 at Koehler, Saratov, RUS. He died in 1831 at Koehler, Saratov, RUS.

a) Andreas[4] Gerk (3681) was born on 29 Nov 1810 at Koehler, Saratov, RUS.

b) Johann Heinrich[4] Gerk (572) was born on 26 Oct 1815 at Koehler, Saratov, RUS. He married Anna Maria Schechtel (1620), daughter of Heinrich Schechtel (3670) and Sophia (--?--) (3671), circa 1837 at Koehler, Saratov, RUS. He died on 18 May 1864 at Marienfeld, Saratov, RUS, at age 48.

(1) Jakob[5] Gerk (713) was born on 24 Mar 1838 at Rothammel, Saratov, RUS. He married Juliana Schoenfeld (714), daughter of Johannes Schoenfeld (3112) and Anna Margareta Jakob (3113), on 17 Nov 1859 at Marienfeld, Saratov, RUS. He died on 2 Jul 1897 at Marienfeld, Saratov, RUS, at age 59.

(a) Elisabeta[6] Gerk (712) was born on 17 Sep 1860 at Marienfeld, Saratov, RUS. She died on 5 May 1864 at Marienfeld, Saratov, RUS, at age 3.

(b) Jakob[6] Gerk (715) was born on 21 Dec 1862 at Marienfeld, Saratov, RUS. He died on 3 Sep 1863 at Marienfeld, Saratov, RUS.

(c) Johannes[6] Gerk (716) was born on 1 May 1864 at Marienfeld, Saratov, RUS. He died on 14 Dec 1865 at Marienfeld, Saratov, RUS, at age 1.

(d) Adam[6] Gerk (718) was born on 2 Aug 1866 at Marienfeld, Saratov, RUS. He married Sophia Reising (773), daughter of Georg Reising (774) and Elisabetha Kloster (775), on 30 Oct 1889 at Marienfeld, Saratov, RUS. He died on 23 May 1893 at Kamyshin, Saratov, RUS, at age 26.

i) Adam[7] Gerk (1841) was born on 25 Aug 1890 at Marienfeld, Saratov, RUS.

ii) Josef[7] Gerk (1842) was born on 22 Feb 1893 at Marienfeld, Saratov, RUS. He died on 24 Jan 1894 at Marienfeld, Saratov, RUS.

(e) Josef⁶ Gerk (717) was born on 11 Nov 1868 at Marienfeld, Saratov, RUS. He died on 10 Jun 1876 at Marienfeld, Saratov, RUS, at age 7.

(f) Johann⁶ Gerk (719) was born on 14 Jan 1871 at Marienfeld, Saratov, RUS. He married Appolonia Stremel (776), daughter of Nikolaus Stremel (777) and Barbara Mildenberger (778), on 30 Oct 1889 at Marienfeld, Saratov, RUS.

i) Elisabeta⁷ Gerk (801) was born on 8 Aug 1890 at Marienfeld, Saratov, RUS. She died on 2 Feb 1893 at Josefstal, Saratov, RUS, at age 2.

ii) Johann⁷ Gerk (2304) was born on 5 Jan 1904 at Marienfeld, Saratov, RUS.

(g) Jakob⁶ Gerk (720) was born on 12 Jan 1873 at Marienfeld, Saratov, RUS. He married Margareta Weigel (2202), daughter of Kaspar Weigel (2203) and Margareta Mitsig (2204), on 29 Sep 1897 at Marienfeld, Saratov, RUS. He died in 1932 at Marienfeld, Stalingrad Oblast, USSR.

i) Magdalena⁷ Gerk (2272) was born on 11 Jul 1898 at Marienfeld, Saratov, RUS.

ii) Johannes⁷ Gerk (2273) was born on 18 Aug 1899 at Marienfeld, Saratov, RUS.

iii) Magdalena⁷ Gerk (2274) married (--?--) Messler (2356). She was born on 2 Aug 1902 at Marienfeld, Saratov, RUS. She died in 1992 at Germany.

(a) Josef⁸ Messler (2062) was born on 15 Dec 1928 at USSR. He married Maria Gerk (2061), daughter of Johann Gerk (910) and Elizabeth Rachschreiba (2060), in 1950 at USSR.

i) Josef⁹ Messler (2063) was born on 20 Jun 1951 at USSR. He died on 5 Jun 1981 at USSR at age 29.

ii) Johannes⁹ Messler (2064) married Elizabeth (--?--) (2070). He was born on 16 Sep 1952 at USSR.

(a) Andreas¹⁰ Messler (2071) was born on 26 May 1973 at USSR.

(b) Waldemar¹⁰ Messler (2072) was born on 24 May 1974 at USSR.

(c) Victor¹⁰ Messler (2073) was born on 30 Sep 1980 at USSR.

iii) Peter⁹ Messler (2065) was born on 29 Apr 1954 at USSR. He died in May 1954 at USSR.

iv) Anna⁹ Messler (2066) married Alexander (--?--) (2074). She was born on 13 Aug 1955 at USSR.

(a) Nina¹⁰ (--?--) (2075) married Waldemar (--?--) (2428). She was born on 27 May 1973 at USSR.

(b) Alvis¹⁰ (--?--) (2076) was born on 31 Jul 1977 at USSR.

v) Maria⁹ Messler (2067) married Alexander Bensch (2069). She was born on 17 May 1957 at USSR.

(a) Natalia¹⁰ Bensch (2077) was born on 25 Sep 1980 at USSR.

(b) Julia¹⁰ Bensch (2078) was born on 21 Oct 1985 at USSR.

(c) Tanya¹⁰ Bensch (2079) was born on 21 Oct 1985 at USSR.

vi) Peter⁹ Messler (2068) married Helena (--?--) (2080). He was born on 27 Jun 1960 at USSR.

(a) Julia¹⁰ Messler (2081) was born on 15 Apr 1983 at USSR.

(b) Natalia¹⁰ Messler (2082) was born on 13 Jul 1987 at USSR.

(c) Waldemar¹⁰ Messler (2083) was born on 14 Jun 1994 at USSR.

iv) Katarina⁷ Gerk (2275) was born on 6 Nov 1904 at Marienfeld, Saratov, RUS. She died on 16 Jul 1905 at Marienfeld, Saratov, RUS.

v) Jakob⁷ Gerk (2276) was born on 6 Mar 1907 at Marienfeld, Saratov, RUS. He died on 13 Apr 1908 at Marienfeld, Saratov, RUS, at age 1.

vi) Katarina⁷ Gerk (2277) was born on 6 Mar 1907 at Marienfeld, Saratov, RUS.

vii) Josef⁷ Gerk (2278) was born on 2 Mar 1909 at Marienfeld, Saratov, RUS.

viii) Susanna[7] Gerk (2279) was born on 2 Mar 1909 at Marienfeld, Saratov, RUS. She died on 29 Dec 1909 at Marienfeld, Saratov, RUS.

ix) Johann[7] Gerk (2280) was born on 12 Mar 1911 at Marienfeld, Saratov, RUS.

x) Jakob[7] Gerk (7570) was born on 22 Jul 1918 at Marienfeld, Saratov, USSR. He died in 1939 at USSR.

(h) Peter Alois[6] Gerk (2308) was born on 2 Dec 1874 at Marienfeld, Saratov, RUS.

(i) Josef[6] Gerk (721) was born on 27 Jan 1877 at Marienfeld, Saratov, RUS. He married Katarina Stang (1013), daughter of Michael Stang (2205) and Magdalena Gette (2206), on 29 Sep 1897 at Marienfeld, Saratov, RUS. He emigrated on 21 Apr 1905. He married Kristina Schmidt (1014), daughter of Georg Schmidt (1874) and Elisabeta Prediger (1873), on 28 Oct 1916 at Crespo, Entre Ríos, ARG. He died on 9 Mar 1958 at Bahía Blanca, Buenos Aires, ARG, at age 81.

i) Katarina[7] Gerk (2281) was born on 31 Dec 1898 at Marienfeld, Saratov, RUS. She died on 20 Dec 1902 at Marienfeld, Saratov, RUS, at age 3.

ii) Josef[7] Gerk (2282) was born on 4 Jul 1903 at Marienfeld, Saratov, RUS. He married Angelika Stork (3213), daughter of Klement Stork (3222) and Margaretha Müller (3223), on 25 Apr 1933 at San Miguel Arcángel, Buenos Aires, ARG. He died on 21 Aug 1973 at Arroyo Corto, Buenos Aires, ARG, at age 70.

(a) Dora[8] Gerk (7572) died in 2014 at ARG. **(b)** Maria Elsa[8] Gerk (7571) was born at ARG.

(c) Inocencia[8] Gerk (7573) was born at ARG. **(d)** Maria Rosa[8] Gerk (7574) was born at ARG.

(e) Josefina[8] Gerk (7575) was born at ARG. **(f)** Clemente[8] Gerk (7576) was born at ARG.

iii) Luisa[7] Gerk (3214) was born on 21 Nov 1906 at San Miguel Arcángel, Buenos Aires, ARG.

iv) Georg[7] Gerk (2773) died at Bahia Blanca, Buenos Aires, ARG.

v) Adan[7] Gerk (2774) died at Bahia Blanca, Buenos Aires, ARG.

vi) Appolonia[7] Gerk (2768) was born at ARG. She died at Bahia Blanca, Buenos Aires, ARG.

vii) Juan Pedro[7] Gerk (2769) was born at La Pampa, ARG. He died at General Manuel Campos, La Pampa, ARG. He married Magdalena Kloster (2770) at ARG.

viii) Juan[7] Gerk (2775) died at Bahia Blanca, Buenos Aires, ARG. He was born on 12 Oct 1909 at San Miguel Arcángel, Buenos Aires, ARG.

ix) Felipe[7] Gerk (2776) married Rosa Kloster (2777). He was born on 5 Jul 1918 at La Pampa, ARG. He died on 2 Jun 1999 at General Manuel Campos, La Pampa, ARG, at age 80.

x) Nicodema[7] Gerk (2771) married Elena Graniery (2772) at ARG. He was born on 23 Dec 1922 at Alpachiri, La Pampa, ARG. He died on 4 Feb 1997 at General Acha, La Pampa, ARG, at age 74.

(a) Marta[8] Gerk (3204) was born at Alpachiri, La Pampa, ARG.

(b) Juan Carlos[8] Gerk (3202) was born at Alpachiri, La Pampa, ARG.

(c) Mária Elena[8] Gerk (3203) was born at Alpachiri, La Pampa, ARG.

(d) Haidee[8] Gerk (3205) was born at Alpachiri, La Pampa, ARG. She married ? Alvarez (3206).

i) Gabriel[9] Alvarez (3208) was born in 1975 at ARG.

ii) Daniel[9] Alvarez (3207) was born in 1983 at ARG.

(e) José Angel[8] Gerk (3197) married Maria Ester Giménez (3198) at General Acha, La Pampa, ARG. He was born on 15 Oct 1951 at Alpachiri, La Pampa, ARG.

i) Marcos Fabián[9] Gerk (3199) was born on 31 Mar 1992 at General Acha, La Pampa, ARG.

ii) Daiana Belén[9] Gerk (3200) was born on 31 May 1999 at General Acha, La Pampa, ARG.

iii) Excel Ramon[9] Gerk (3201) was born on 9 Jun 2003 at General Acha, La Pampa, ARG.

xi) Ana[7] Gerk (2778) married Jorge Viondo (2779). She was born in 1926 at La Pampa, ARG.

(j) Peter Alois[6] Gerk (2228) was born in 1879 at Marienfeld, Saratov, RUS. He married Margarita Lell (2229), daughter of Michael Lell (2230) and Susanna Dietler (2231), on 3 Jul 1905 at Marienfeld, Saratov, RUS. He married Katarina Shiip (2241), daughter of Wilhelm Shiip (2242) and Barbara Hollmann (2243), on 11 Sep 1906 at Marienfeld, Saratov, RUS.

i) Rosa[7] Gerk (2244) was born on 13 Nov 1907 at Marienfeld, Saratov, RUS. She died on 17 Apr 1908 at Marienfeld, Saratov, RUS.

ii) Paulina[7] Gerk (2245) was born on 8 Jul 1913 at Marienfeld, Saratov, RUS.

(k) Maria Katarina[6] Gerk (722) was born on 16 May 1881 at Marienfeld, Saratov, RUS. She married Kristof Hollmann (2208), son of Andriana Hollmann (2209) and Elisabeta Rak (2210), on 27 Oct 1899 at Marienfeld, Saratov, RUS.

i) Peter[7] Hollmann (2290) was born on 4 Sep 1900 at Marienfeld, Saratov, RUS.

ii) Katarina[7] Hollmann (2291) was born on 25 Apr 1902 at Marienfeld, Saratov, RUS.

iii) Katarina[7] Hollmann (2318) was born on 13 Jun 1903 at Marienfeld, Saratov, RUS.

iv) Josef[7] Hollmann (2319) was born on 16 Feb 1908 at Marienfeld, Saratov, RUS.

v) Alois[7] Hollmann (2320) was born on 23 Apr 1909 at Marienfeld, Saratov, RUS.

(2) Magdalena[5] Gerk (2266) was born in 1840 at Koehler, Saratov, RUS. She married Peter Hollmann (2201), son of Michael Hollmann (3170) and Anna Marie Baumgartner (3171), on 17 Nov 1859 at Marienfeld, Saratov, RUS.

(a) Kaspar[6] Hollmann (2267) was born on 23 Mar 1866 at Marienfeld, Saratov, RUS. He married Anna Margareta Gerk (2199), daughter of Peter Gerk (705) and Anna Marie Wagner (706), on 21 Feb 1894. He died on 14 Sep 1896 at Marienfeld, Saratov, RUS, at age 30.

i) Magdalena[7] Hollmann (2271) (see above)

(a) Elisabetha[8] Haberkorn (8225) (see above)

ii) Johannes[7] Hollmann (2303) (see above)

(b) Jakob[6] Hollmann (2200) was born on 22 Jun 1868 at Marienfeld, Saratov, RUS.

(c) Josef[6] Hollmann (2268) was born on 19 Aug 1870 at Marienfeld, Saratov, RUS.

(d) Apolonia[6] Hollmann (2269) was born on 25 Aug 1872 at Marienfeld, Saratov, RUS.

(e) Katarina[6] Hollmann (2270) was born on 1 Dec 1874 at Marienfeld, Saratov, RUS.

(3) Zacharius[5] Gerk (816) was born in 1842 at Koehler, Saratov, RUS. He married Margareta Kloster (2713), daughter of Werngard Kloster (2714) and Marie Eva Kippis (2715), on 18 Nov 1862 at Josefstal, Saratov, RUS. He married Katarina Hergenrater (817), daughter of Johannes Hergenrater (2716) and Kristina Werwert (2717), on 14 Nov 1867 at Marienfeld, Saratov, RUS. He died on 5 Feb 1908 at Marienfeld, Saratov, RUS.

(a) Michael[6] Gerk (818) was born on 26 Oct 1868 at Marienfeld, Saratov, RUS. He married Magdalena Schneider (823), daughter of Johannes Schneider (824) and Barbara Holzmann (825), on 18 Aug 1890 at Marienfeld, Saratov, RUS.

i) Michael[7] Gerk (826) was born on 16 Aug 1891 at Marienfeld, Saratov, RUS. He died on 6 Mar 1899 at Josefstal, Saratov, RUS, at age 7.

ii) Agatha[7] Gerk (827) was born on 26 Dec 1893 at Marienfeld, Saratov, RUS. She died on 4 Oct 1895 at Marienfeld, Saratov, RUS, at age 1.

iii) Jakob[7] Gerk (828) was born on 23 Jun 1896 at Marienfeld, Saratov, RUS. He died on 28 Jun 1974 at Novo Nikolaevka, Volgograd, RUS, at age 78.

iv) Peter[7] Gerk (829) was born on 12 Jan 1898 at Marienfeld, Saratov, RUS.

v) Anna[7] Gerk (830) was born on 7 Jul 1900 at Marienfeld, Saratov, RUS.

vi) Kaspar[7] Gerk (831) was born on 27 Oct 1904 at Marienfeld, Saratov, RUS.

vii) Liberat[7] Gerk (832) was born on 10 Jan 1907 at Marienfeld, Saratov, RUS.

viii) Johann[7] Gerk (833) was born on 4 Aug 1910 at Marienfeld, Saratov, RUS.

(b) Anna Elisabeta[6] Gerk (819) was born on 14 Sep 1870 at Marienfeld, Saratov, RUS. She married Johann Peter Rosskoph (934), son of Konrad Rosskoph (935) and Katarina Stang (936), on 12 Oct 1893 at Marienfeld, Saratov, RUS.

    i) Josef[7] Rosskoph (937) was born on 14 Apr 1895 at Marienfeld, Saratov, RUS.

    ii) Magdalena[7] Rosskoph (938) was born on 5 Apr 1897 at Marienfeld, Saratov, RUS.

    iii) Johannes[7] Rosskoph (939) was born on 31 Dec 1899 at Marienfeld, Saratov, RUS.

    iv) Barbara[7] Rosskoph (940) was born on 5 May 1902 at Marienfeld, Saratov, RUS.

    v) Katarina[7] Rosskoph (941) was born on 8 Oct 1904 at Marienfeld, Saratov, RUS.

    vi) Matvei[7] Rosskoph (942) was born on 24 Feb 1907 at Marienfeld, Saratov, RUS.

(c) Josef[6] Gerk (834) was born on 6 Sep 1871 at Marienfeld, Saratov, RUS. He married Elisabeta Schneider (899), daughter of Johann Schneider (900) and Barbara Holzmann (901), on 11 Oct 1893 at Marienfeld, Saratov, RUS. He died in 1915 at Marienfeld, Saratov, RUS.

    i) Pius[7] Gerk (904) was born on 27 Jun 1894 at Marienfeld, Saratov, RUS. He married Anna Hollmann (1992), daughter of Kaspar Hollmann (1993) and Anna Marie Mai (1994), on 11 Nov 1913 at Marienfeld, Saratov, RUS.

        (a) Marie[8] Gerk (1995) was born on 29 Nov 1914 at Marienfeld, Saratov, RUS.

    ii) Johannes[7] Gerk (905) was born on 11 Apr 1898 at Marienfeld, Saratov, RUS. He died on 8 Feb 1899 at Marienfeld, Saratov, RUS.

    iii) Margareta[7] Gerk (906) was born on 13 Dec 1899 at Marienfeld, Saratov, RUS. She died on 10 Mar 1902 at Marienfeld, Saratov, RUS, at age 2.

    iv) Peter[7] Gerk (907) was born on 15 Aug 1901 at Marienfeld, Saratov, RUS. He married Susanna Schoenfeld (1103), daughter of Josef Schoenfeld (1108) and Anna Margareta Burkhart (1109), on 12 Feb 1920 at Marienfeld, Saratov, RUS. He died on 26 Mar 1975 at Fairview, Alberta, CAN, at age 73.

        (a) Josef[8] Gerk (1110) was born in 1921 at Marienfeld, Saratov, RUS. He died in 1922 at Marienfeld, Saratov, USSR.

        (b) Anne[8] Gerk (1111) was born on 15 May 1923 at Marienfeld, Saratov, USSR. She married Clarence John Sweet (1114) on 28 Nov 1947 at Calgary, Alberta, CAN.

            i) Jacqueline Anne[9] Sweet (1139) was born on 30 Aug 1948 at Calgary, Alberta, CAN. She married Robert Harry Vincent (1143) on 18 Dec 1971 at Calgary, Alberta, CAN.

                (a) Leanne Elizabeth Christine[10] Vincent (1144) was born on 15 Nov 1974 at Ottawa, Ontario, CAN.

                (b) David Stuart[10] Vincent (1145) was born on 17 Aug 1976 at Ottawa, Ontario, CAN.

            ii) Constance Lynn[9] Sweet (1140) was born on 7 Apr 1951 at Calgary, Alberta, CAN. She married William Edward Griffiths (1146) on 29 Apr 1972 at Edmonton, Alberta, CAN.

            iii) Karen Elizabeth[9] Sweet (1141) was born on 24 May 1952 at Calgary, Alberta, CAN. She married Frederick John Bassie (1147) on 7 Jun 1973 at Calgary, Alberta, CAN.

                (a) Elizabeth Anne[10] Bassie (1148) was born on 19 Nov 1994 at Calgary, Alberta, CAN.

            iv) Catherine Joy[9] Sweet (1142) was born on 22 Dec 1958 at Calgary, Alberta, CAN. She married Alfred James Kincaid (1149) on 7 Nov 1983 at San Francisco, California, USA.

                (a) William James Jesse[10] Kincaid (1150) was born on 21 May 1991 at Edmonton, Alberta, CAN.

        (c) Matilda[8] Gerk (1112) was born on 31 Dec 1924 at Marienfeld, Stalingrad Oblast, USSR. She married Henry Edward Rice (1115) on 3 Feb 1947 at Peace River, Alberta, CAN. She died on 18 Jul 2018 at Red Deer, AB, CAN, at age 93.

            i) Larry Edward[9] Rice (2008) was born on 29 Aug 1948 at Berwyn, Alberta, CAN. He married Connie Ann Sands (2009) on 25 Apr 1975 at Rocky Mountain House, Alberta, CAN. He died on 16 Oct 1976 at Rocky Mountain House, Alberta, CAN, at age 28.

                (a) Michelle[10] Meniuer-Mason (2113) was born on 27 May 1972 at Edmonton, Alberta, CAN. She married Tom Marius Halsan (2114) on 22 May 1988 at Steinkjer, Norway.

i) Hailey Diane[11] Halsan (2115) was born on 22 Jan 2000 at Levanger, Norway.

(b) Sheldon Larry Samuel[10] Rice (2010) was born on 20 Oct 1975 at Rocky Mountain House, Alberta, CAN.

(c) Kelsey Donald[10] Rice (2011) married Michelle (--?--) (2112). He was born on 31 May 1977 at Rocky Mountain House, Alberta, CAN.

ii) Cynthia[9] Rice (1938) was born on 19 Feb 1955 at Berwyn, Alberta, CAN. She married Albert Lacoursiere (1939) on 12 Oct 1975 at Rocky Mountain House, Alberta, CAN.

(a) Robin Anthony[10] Lacoursiere (1940) was born on 9 Jul 1974 at Rocky Mtn. House, Alberta, CAN. He married Jennifer Clayton (1941) on 12 Oct 1996 at CAN.

i) Hayden[11] Lacoursiere (1942) was born on 15 Mar 2000 at CAN.

(b) Guy Christopher[10] Lacoursiere (1943) was born on 9 Oct 1980 at Edmonton, Alberta, CAN.

iii) Bernadette[9] Rice (2020) was born on 13 May 1966 at Valleyview, Alberta, CAN.

(d) Barbara[8] Gerk (1113) was born on 26 Dec 1927 at Marienfeld, Stalingrad Oblast, USSR. She married William Benjamin Rice (1116) on 6 Jan 1946 at Peace River, Alberta, CAN. She married Joseph Bespflug (1117) on 5 Dec 1965 at Valleyview, Alberta, CAN.

(e) Peter[8] Gerk (1118) was born on 4 Oct 1928 at Compeer, Alberta, CAN. He married Sylvia Margaret Lee (1129), daughter of Henry George Lee (1151) and Ivy Elsie Young (1152), on 24 Dec 1950 at Berwyn, Alberta, CAN. He died on 28 Nov 2001 at Grande Prairie, Alberta, CAN, at age 73.

i) Peter Edward[9] Gerk (1153) was born on 24 Dec 1951 at Kelowna, B.C., CAN. He died on 26 Nov 1996 at Grande Prairie, Alberta, CAN, at age 44.

ii) Conrad Wayne[9] Gerk (1154) was born on 21 Nov 1952 at Kelowna, B.C., CAN. He married Ellen Nora Schur (1155), daughter of John Schur (1156) and Frances Habura (1157), on 9 Nov 1974 at Peace River, Alberta, CAN.

(a) Charmaine Samantha[10] Gerk (1158) was born on 15 Jun 1977 at Peace River, Alberta, CAN. She married Mark Henry Moeller (4522) on 12 Nov 2005 at Grande Prairie, Alta., CAN.

i) Kevin Henry[11] Moeller (6349) was born on 20 Apr 2008 at Dawson Creek, BC, CAN.

(b) Dallas John[10] Gerk (1159) was born on 30 Mar 1979 at Peace River, Alberta, CAN. He died on 11 Nov 2016 at Calgary, AB, CAN, at age 37.

iii) Wanda June[9] Gerk (1160) was born on 24 Aug 1955 at Kelowna, B.C., CAN. She married Leonard Leslie Brown (1163), son of Terrance Leslie Brown (2051) and Bertha Virginia Nice (2052), on 14 Aug 1976 at Grande Prairie, Alberta, CAN.

(a) Crystal Anne[10] Brown (1164) was born on 25 Oct 1978 at Peace River, Alberta, CAN.

(b) Garrett Matthew[10] Brown (1165) was born on 1 Apr 1981 at Peace River, Alberta, CAN. He married Angela Renee Wolsey (6388) on 20 Feb 2010 at Grande Prairie, AB, CAN.

iv) Barbara Kathaleen[9] Gerk (1161) was born on 3 Aug 1958 at Kelowna, B.C., CAN. She married Edward Lee Dunn (1166), son of William Lee Dunn (2053) and Greta Mae Pauline Proctor (2054), on 28 Sep 1985 at Grande Prairie, Alberta, CAN.

(a) Terrell Lee[10] Dunn (1167) was born on 8 Jul 1986 at Peace River, Alberta, CAN. She married Paul Daniel Wedman (6386) on 20 Oct 2007 at Grande Prairie, AB, CAN.

i) Elliot Hunter[11] Wedman (6395) was born on 11 May 2012 at Grande Prairie, AB, CAN.

(b) Brandi Mae[10] Dunn (1168) was born on 19 Nov 1987 at Peace River, Alberta, CAN.

v) Sheldon Mark[9] Gerk (1162) was born on 16 Jul 1962 at Fairview, Alberta, CAN. He married Carlene Ellen Wald (1169), daughter of Jack Wald (1170) and Patricia Stone (1171), on 15 Aug 1981 at Brownvale, Alberta, CAN.

(a) Chance Anthony[10] Gerk (1172) was born on 12 Jan 1984 at Grande Prairie, Alberta, CAN. He married Carolyn Peetso (6385) on 4 Sep 2010 at Peace River, AB, CAN.

(b) Cody Joseph[10] Gerk (1173) was born on 18 Dec 1985 at Peace River, Alberta, CAN. He married Amanda Joan Banack (6389) on 28 Jun 2008 at Grimshaw, AB, CAN.

i) Corey Amanda[11] Gerk (6390) was born on 23 Nov 2006 at Peace River, AB, CAN.

ii) Natalie Lee[11] Gerk (6391) was born on 11 Jun 2009 at Peace River, AB, CAN.

iii) Holly May[11] Gerk (6392) was born on 18 Jun 2010 at Peace River, AB, CAN.

(c) Kaytee Carlene[10] Gerk (1174) was born on 17 Dec 1989 at Peace River, Alberta, CAN.

(f) Susanne Pauline[8] Gerk (1119) was born on 7 Dec 1929 at Altario, Alberta, CAN. She married Stewart William Wilson (1130) circa 1948 at Peace River, Alberta, CAN. She died on 12 Sep 1989 at Valleyview, Alberta, CAN, at age 59.

i) Richard John[9] Gerk (1931) was born on 14 Apr 1946 at Calgary, Alberta, CAN.

ii) Linda Susan[9] Wilson (2021) was born on 28 May 1949 at Berwyn, Alberta, CAN. She married David Leo Coogan (2025) on 18 Oct 1965 at Beaverlodge, Alberta, CAN.

    (a) Robert Edward[10] Coogan (2026) was born on 25 Dec 1965 at Grande Prairie, Alberta, CAN. He married Kathy Arlene Posein (2028) on 13 May 1995 at Edmonton, Alberta, CAN.

    i) Joshua David[11] Coogan (2029) was born on 21 May 1997 at Edmonton, Alberta, CAN.

    ii) Mattew Robert[11] Coogan (2030) was born on 10 Jan 2000 at Edmonton, Alberta, CAN.

    (b) Donna Lynn[10] Coogan (2027) was born on 19 Jan 1967 at Valleyview, Alberta, CAN. She married Luke Joseph Gamache (2031) on 12 Oct 1993 at Valleyview, Alberta, CAN.

    i) Kelsey Adrien[11] Gamache (2032) was born on 18 Oct 1995 at High Level, Alberta, CAN.

iii) David Terrance[9] Wilson (2022) was born on 1 May 1950 at Berwyn, Alberta, CAN. He married Carol Lorraine Holmen (2033) on 6 Mar 1971 at Valleyview, Alberta, CAN.

    (a) James Stuart[10] Wilson (2034) was born on 13 Jul 1971 at Grande Prairie, Alberta, CAN.

    (b) Marty Edward[10] Wilson (2035) married Kathy Irene Keyes-Leach (2038). He was born on 23 Aug 1972 at Fairview, Alberta, CAN.

    i) Adam Wesley[11] Wilson (2039) was born on 11 Feb 1999 at Alberta, CAN.

    ii) Kourtney Sandra[11] Wilson (2040) was born on 2 Feb 2000 at Alberta, CAN.

    (c) Clay Terrance[10] Wilson (2036) was born on 6 Jun 1974 at Fairview, Alberta, CAN.

    (d) Sandra Lorraine[10] Wilson (2037) was born on 25 Sep 1978 at Valleyview, Alberta, CAN.

iv) Kenneth William[9] Wilson (2023) was born on 25 Nov 1951 at Berwyn, Alberta, CAN. He married Mary Brenda Giebelhaus (2041) on 21 Apr 1972 at Grande Prairie, Alberta, CAN.

    (a) Joanne Marie[10] Wilson (2042) was born on 5 Apr 1972 at Grande Prairie, Alberta, CAN. She married Troy Robert Gordon (2045) on 9 Apr 1994 at Valleyview, Alberta, CAN.

    i) Kevin Robert[11] Gordon (2046) was born on 27 Apr 1989 at Grande Prairie, Alberta, CAN.

    ii) Kyle Kenneth[11] Gordon (2047) was born on 7 Apr 1995 at Grande Prairie, Alberta, CAN.

    (b) Keith William[10] Wilson (2043) was born on 13 Sep 1973 at Valleyview, Alberta, CAN.

    (c) Brian George[10] Wilson (2044) was born on 22 Mar 1979 at Valleyview, Alberta, CAN.

v) Patricia Ann[9] Wilson (2024) was born on 26 Dec 1952 at Berwyn, Alberta, CAN. She married Richard Allan Hopkin (2048) on 10 Sep 1971 at Valleyview, Alberta, CAN.

    (a) Brent[10] Hopkin (2049) was born on 29 Dec 1973 at Valleyview, Alberta, CAN.

    (b) Amy Vera[10] Hopkin (2050) was born on 8 Apr 1986 at Valleyview, Alberta, CAN.

(g) Joseph Adam[8] Gerk (1120) was born on 5 Apr 1931 at Altario, Alberta, CAN. He married Katherine Kronewitt (1131), daughter of Peter Kronewitt (2139) and Franscisca Kirschner (2140), on 2 Jun 1959 at Sexsmith, Alberta, CAN. He died on 16 Jun 1982 at St. Paul, Alberta, CAN, at age 51.

i) Michael Rodney[9] Gerk (2141) was born on 8 Feb 1960 at Berwyn, Alberta, CAN. He married Kathleen Mary McKenzie (2142) in 1981. He married Deana Marie Lucas (2148), daughter of William George Lucas (2149) and Patricia Ellen Kandel (2150), on 20 Dec 1996 at Lethbridge, Alberta, CAN.

(a) Gregory Allan[10] Gerk (2143) was born on 2 May 1982 at Medicine Hat, Alberta, CAN.

(b) Jessica Marie[10] Gerk (2144) was born on 4 Sep 1985 at Medicine Hat, Alberta, CAN.

(c) Andrew Cole[10] Gerk (2151) was born on 15 Jun 1994 at Lethbridge, Alberta, CAN.

ii) Karen Ann[9] Gerk (2145) was born on 14 Mar 1961 at Grande Prairie, Alberta, CAN. She married Timmothy William Goodrich (2152), son of Erwin Kermit Goodrich (2153) and Thelma Larraine Garbutt (2154), on 31 Dec 1984 at Lethbridge, Alberta, CAN.

(a) Barent Adam[10] Goodrich (2155) was born on 7 Jul 1987 at Lethbridge, Alberta, CAN.

iii) Patrick Quinn[9] Gerk (2146) was born on 1 Oct 1963 at Grande Prairie, Alberta, CAN. He married Allison Jean Seebeck (2156), daughter of Calvin Windfred Seebeck (2157) and Margaret Bernice Winch (2158), on 30 Nov 1990 at Lethbridge, Alberta, CAN.

(a) Aaron Quinn[10] Gerk (2159) was born on 21 Jan 1994 at Lethbridge, Alberta, CAN.

(b) Kaylee Katherine[10] Gerk (2160) was born on 16 Apr 1997 at Lethbridge, Alberta, CAN.

iv) Jo-Ann[9] Gerk (2147) was born on 17 Oct 1966 at Valleyview, Alberta, CAN.

(h) John Henry[8] Gerk (1121) was born on 6 Mar 1933 at Compeer, Alberta, CAN. He married Kathaleen Lee (1132) in Jul 1958 at Kelowna, B.C., CAN. He married Dorothy Alexander (1133) on 13 Apr 1964 at Brownvale, Alberta, CAN. He died on 6 Feb 2014 at Grimshaw, AB, CAN, at age 80.

i) Maxine Marie[9] Gerk (2116) was born on 25 Feb 1965 at Berwyn, Alberta, CAN. She died on 15 Nov 1978 at Griffin Creek, Alberta, CAN, at age 13.

ii) Christine Dianne[9] Gerk (2117) was born on 29 Apr 1967 at Berwyn, Alberta, CAN. She died on 15 Nov 1978 at Griffin Creek, Alberta, CAN, at age 11.

iii) Troy Ernest[9] Gerk (2118) was born on 6 Nov 1969 at Fairview, Alberta, CAN.

iv) Trevor John[9] Gerk (2119) was born on 1 Jul 1971 at Fairview, Alberta, CAN.

(i) Amelia Elizabeth[8] Gerk (1122) married Ron Radke (1134) at Calgary, Alberta, CAN. She was born on 5 May 1934 at Compeer, Alberta, CAN.

(j) Wendlin Gabriel[8] Gerk (1123) was born on 15 May 1935 at Brownvale, Alberta, CAN. He married Anne Halerewich (1135), daughter of John Halerewich (2624) and Emily Lewichy (2625), on 11 Jul 1959 at Berwyn, Alberta, CAN.

i) Wendy Marie[9] Gerk (2626) was born on 10 Mar 1960 at Berwyn, Alberta, CAN. She married Melvin Victor Wald (2629), son of John George Wald (2630) and Mary Ann Osowetski (2631), on 25 Apr 1980 at Peace River, Alberta, CAN.

(a) Corey Douglas[10] Wald (2632) was born on 4 Aug 1985 at Peace River, Alberta, CAN.

(b) Randi Sue[10] Wald (2633) was born on 28 Apr 1989 at Peace River, Alberta, CAN.

ii) Lynne Anne[9] Gerk (2627) was born on 11 Feb 1961 at Fairview, Alberta, CAN. She married Robert Glen Gair (2634), son of David Glen Gair (2635) and Miriam Elizabeth Gould (2636), on 23 May 1976 at Berwyn, Alberta, CAN.

(a) Richie Dean[10] Gair (2637) was born on 12 Jul 1976 at Peace River, Alberta, CAN.

(b) Derrick Robert[10] Gair (2638) was born on 30 Jun 1981 at Peace River, Alberta, CAN.

iii) Sandra Rose[9] Gerk (2628) was born on 11 Oct 1963 at Fairview, Alberta, CAN. She married Bradley John Friesen (2639), son of Martin Friesen (2640) and Doris Elsie Newell (2641), on 27 Jun 1981 at Berwyn, Alberta, CAN.

(a) Kelly Brad[10] Friesen (2642) was born on 15 Dec 1984 at Peace River, Alberta, CAN.

(b) Terry Gordon[10] Friesen (2643) was born on 5 May 1989 at Peace River, Alberta, CAN.

(c) Lonny Gabriel[10] Friesen (2644) was born on 14 Jun 1991 at Peace River, Alberta, CAN.

iv) Helen Michelle[9] Gerk (1836) was born on 26 Apr 1968 at Peace River, Alberta, CAN. She married Brian Andrew Campbell (1837), son of Marvin Campbell (2645) and Mary Novak (2646), on 8 Nov 1986 at Grimshaw, Alberta, CAN.

(a) Brett Clinton[10] Campbell (1838) was born on 18 Jun 1987 at Peace River, Alberta, CAN.

(b) Trina Suzanne[10] Campbell (1839) was born on 13 Dec 1991 at Peace River, Alberta, CAN.

(c) Hannah Marie[10] Campbell (1840) was born on 5 Aug 1992 at Peace River, Alberta, CAN.

(k) Aloysius (Alex)[8] Gerk (1124) was born on 24 Oct 1936 at Berwyn, Alberta, CAN. He married Charlotte Ann Bettenson (1136), daughter of Lloyd Elwood Bettenson (2055) and Olive Ann Somers (2056), on 1 Jun 1961 at Whitelaw, Alberta, CAN. He died on 24 Jan 2001 at Grande Prairie, Alberta, CAN, at age 64.

i) Rosalie Kay[9] Gerk (2057) was born on 15 Sep 1962 at Berwyn, Alberta, CAN.

ii) Kenneth Lloyd[9] Gerk (2058) was born on 31 Jul 1963 at Berwyn, Alberta, CAN.

iii) Tracey Lynne[9] Gerk (2059) was born on 22 Aug 1967 at Berwyn, Alberta, CAN.

(l) Marie Anne[8] Gerk (1125) was born on 27 Feb 1938 at Griffin Creek, Alberta, CAN. She married Herbert Sweet (1137) on 26 Nov 1956 at Calgary, Alberta, CAN. She died on 20 Aug 2006 at Calgary, AB, CAN, at age 68.

i) Randall[9] Sweet (7836) was born at AB, CAN.

ii) Kevin[9] Sweet (7837) was born at AB, CAN.

iii) Donna[9] Sweet (7838) was born at AB, CAN.

iv) Darcy[9] Sweet (7839) was born in 1957 at AB, CAN. He died in 1957 at AB, CAN.

(m) Francis[8] Gerk (1126) was born on 15 Aug 1939 at Brownvale, Alberta, CAN. He married Rose Violet Obrigewich (1176) circa 1959. He married Jean Marie Dukart (1177), daughter of Francis Joseph Dukart (2647) and Marie Eloise Woodward (2648), on 4 Aug 1979 at Peace River, Alberta, CAN.

i) Roseanne Marie[9] Gerk (2649) was born on 31 Jan 1960 at High Prairie, Alberta, CAN.

(a) Ryan Ashley[10] Callan (2794) was born on 30 May 1979 at Peace River, Alberta, CAN.

(b) Shawn MIchael[10] Callan (2795) was born on 15 Feb 1981 at Fairview, Alberta, CAN.

(c) Bradley James[10] Boomer (2796) was born on 4 Jul 1985 at Peace River, Alberta, CAN.

ii) Lorne Frank[9] Gerk (2650) was born on 26 Feb 1961 at Fairview, Alberta, CAN. He married Janice Marie McLaughlin (2789) on 6 Dec 1989 at Grande Prairie, Alberta, CAN.

(a) Brandon Frankie[10] Gerk (2790) was born on 11 Dec 1983 at Fairview, Alberta, CAN. He died on 30 Oct 2010 at Fairview, AB, Canada, at age 26.

(b) Duncan Lorne[10] Gerk (2791) was born on 27 Jan 1989 at Fairview, Alberta, CAN. He died on 30 Oct 2010 at Fairview, AB, CAN, at age 21.

(c) Colby Donald[10] Gerk (2792) was born on 6 Mar 1991 at Fairview, Alberta, CAN.

iii) Cheryl Loreli[9] Gerk (2651) was born on 27 May 1963 at Fairview, Alberta, CAN.

(a) Darcy John[10] Danyshchuk (2797) was born on 27 Sep 1989 at Spirit River, Alberta, CAN.

iv) Coreena Christina[9] Gerk (2793) was born on 25 Oct 1964 at Fairview, Alberta, CAN. She died on 10 Jan 1965 at Fairview, Alberta, CAN.

(n) George Edward[8] Gerk (1127) married Marlene Goselen (1175). He was born on 11 Jul 1941 at Griffin Creek, Alberta, CAN. He died on 9 May 2019 at Peace River, AB, CAN, at age 77.

(o) Dennis James[8] Gerk (1128) was born on 13 Aug 1945 at Berwyn, Alberta, CAN. He married Sharon Ann Lyons (1138), daughter of Clarence Melvin Lyons (2652) and Marguerite Victor (2653), on 25 Jan 1969 at Calgary, Alberta, CAN. He died on 26 Sep 1989 at Calgary, Alberta, CAN, at age 44.

i) Daryne John[9] Gerk (1198) was born on 9 Apr 1970 at Calgary, Alberta, CAN.

ii) Dennis James[9] Gerk (1199) was born on 12 Apr 1973 at Calgary, Alberta, CAN.

iii) Colin Christopher David[9] Gerk (1200) married Julie Marie Pelland (1201). He was born on 1 Jul 1976 at Calgary, Alberta, CAN.

(a) Shayleen Kristen[10] Gerk (1202) was born on 4 May 1996 at Calgary, Alberta, CAN.

(b) Brandon Michael Dennis[10] Gerk (1203) was born on 8 Jun 1998 at Calgary, Alberta, CAN.

v) Kaspar[7] Gerk (908) was born on 28 Aug 1903 at Marienfeld, Saratov, RUS. He married Margaret Schoenfeld (1102) in Nov 1925 at Marienfeld, Saratov, USSR. He died in 1985 at USSR.

(a) Waldemar[8] Gerk (1184)

(b) Peter[8] Gerk (1182)

(c) Magdalena[8] Gerk (1183)

(d) Susanna[8] Gerk (1178) was born on 12 Nov 1926 at Marienfeld, Stalingrad Oblast, USSR. She married Adolf Haus (2097) on 10 Feb 1957 at USSR.

i) Lilli[9] Haus (2098) was born on 27 May 1959 at USSR. She married Peter Penner (2099) in 1982 at USSR.

(a) Anna[10] Penner (2100) was born on 19 May 1983 at USSR.

(b) Irina[10] Penner (2101) was born on 23 Mar 1985 at USSR.

ii) Anna[9] Haus (2102) was born on 23 Aug 1961 at USSR. She died in 1980 at USSR.

(e) Elizabeth[8] Gerk (1179) was born on 10 Jul 1929 at Marienfeld, Stalingrad Oblast, USSR. She married Heinrich Schlitt (2103) in 1950 at USSR. She died on 14 Jul 1998 at age 69.

i) Lydia[9] Schlitt (2109) married (--?--) Mulaewa (2433). She was born at USSR.

(a) Lisa[10] Mulaewa (2434) **(b)** Arthur[10] Mulaewa (2435)

ii) Elvira[9] Schlitt (2104) married Victor Chochrina (2105). She was born on 13 Mar 1955 at USSR.

(a) Heinrich[10] Chochrina (2106) was born at USSR.

(b) Alexander[10] Chochrina (2107) was born at USSR.

(c) Anton[10] Chochrina (2108) was born at USSR.

(f) Dominic[8] Gerk (1180) married Maria (--?--) (2110). He was born in 1935 at Marienfeld, Stalingrad Oblast, USSR.

i) Waldemar[9] Gerk (2429) **ii)** Lena[9] Gerk (2430) **iii)** Nadia[9] Gerk (2111) was born in 1960 at USSR.

(g) Elvira[8] Gerk (1181) married Alexander Haus (1185) at USSR. She was born on 25 Jun 1937 at Marienfeld, Stalingrad Oblast, USSR.

i) Alexander[9] Haus (1186) was born on 25 Aug 1964 at USSR.

(a) Maria[10] Haus (2431) was born on 1 Oct 1993.

ii) Olga[9] Haus (1187) was born on 21 Feb 1968 at USSR.

(a) Johannes[10] (--?--) (2432) was born on 27 Aug 1993.

vi) Josef[7] Gerk (909) was born on 5 Sep 1906 at Marienfeld, Saratov, RUS. He died on 25 Oct 1906 at Marienfeld, Saratov, RUS.

vii) Johann[7] Gerk (910) was born on 25 Jan 1908 at Marienfeld, Saratov, RUS. He married Elizabeth Rachschreiba (2060) in 1929 at Marienfeld, Stalingrad Oblast, USSR.

(a) Maria[8] Gerk (2061) was born on 20 Jul 1930 at Marienfeld, Stalingrad Oblast, USSR. She married Josef Messler (2062), son of (--?--) Messler (2356) and Magdalena Gerk (2274), in 1950 at USSR.

i) Josef[9] Messler (2063) (see above)

ii) Johannes[9] Messler (2064) (see above)

(a) Andreas[10] Messler (2071) (see above)

(b) Waldemar[10] Messler (2072) (see above)

(c) Victor[10] Messler (2073) (see above)

iii) Peter[9] Messler (2065) (see above)

iv) Anna[9] Messler (2066) (see above)

    (a) Nina[10] (--?--) (2075) (see above) **(b)** Alvis[10] (--?--) (2076) (see above)

v) Maria[9] Messler (2067) (see above)

    (a) Natalia[10] Bensch (2077) (see above) **(b)** Julia[10] Bensch (2078) (see above)

    (c) Tanya[10] Bensch (2079) (see above)

vi) Peter[9] Messler (2068) (see above)

    (a) Julia[10] Messler (2081) (see above) **(b)** Natalia[10] Messler (2082) (see above)

    (c) Waldemar[10] Messler (2083) (see above)

(b) Johannes[8] Gerk (2084) was born in 1932 at Marienfeld, Stalingrad Oblast, USSR. He died in 1932 at USSR.

(c) Josef[8] Gerk (2085) was born on 6 Mar 1935 at Marienfeld, Stalingrad Oblast, USSR.

(d) Peter[8] Gerk (2086) was born on 4 Dec 1937 at Marienfeld, Stalingrad Oblast, USSR. He died on 4 Jan 2005 at GER at age 67.

(e) Waldemar[8] Gerk (2087) was born on 29 Feb 1940 at Marienfeld, Stalingrad Oblast, USSR.

(f) Johannes[8] Gerk (2088) was born in 1942 at USSR.

(g) Edward[8] Gerk (2089) married Galina (--?--) (2090). He was born on 28 May 1950 at USSR.

    i) Elizabeth[9] Gerk (2091) was born on 25 Jul 1975 at USSR.

    ii) Galina[9] Gerk (2092) was born on 23 Aug 1976 at USSR.

    iii) Alexander[9] Gerk (2093) was born on 23 Feb 1978 at USSR.

    iv) Alisha[9] Gerk (2094) was born on 27 May 1982 at USSR.

    v) Maria[9] Gerk (2095) was born on 24 Apr 1985 at USSR.

    vi) Edward[9] Gerk (2096) was born on 26 Jun 1988 at USSR.

viii) Maria[7] Gerk (911) was born on 8 Apr 1910 at Marienfeld, Saratov, RUS. She died on 31 Jan 1914 at Marienfeld, Saratov, RUS, at age 3.

ix) Alois[7] Gerk (1996) was born on 19 May 1912 at Marienfeld, Saratov, RUS. He died on 16 Feb 1914 at Marienfeld, Saratov, RUS, at age 1.

(d) Peter[6] Gerk (820) was born on 6 Oct 1872 at Marienfeld, Saratov, RUS. He married Elisabeta Schoenfeld (902), daughter of Adam Schoenfeld (903), on 9 Oct 1895 at Marienfeld, Saratov, RUS.

i) Dorothea[7] Gerk (912) was born on 5 Jun 1896 at Marienfeld, Saratov, RUS. She married Konstantin Herling (1997), son of Johann Peter Herling (1998) and Elisabeta Holzman (1999), on 19 Nov 1912 at Marienfeld, Saratov, RUS.

ii) Marianna[7] Gerk (913) was born on 19 Jul 1898 at Marienfeld, Saratov, RUS. She died on 20 Jul 1898 at Marienfeld, Saratov, RUS.

iii) Peter[7] Gerk (1988) was born on 30 Oct 1899 at Marienfeld, Saratov, RUS. He died on 20 Nov 1902 at Marienfeld, Saratov, RUS, at age 3.

iv) Adam[7] Gerk (914) was born on 9 Mar 1902 at Marienfeld, Saratov, RUS.

v) Josef[7] Gerk (915) was born on 21 Jun 1904 at Marienfeld, Saratov, RUS.

vi) Jakob[7] Gerk (916) was born on 1 Feb 1907 at Marienfeld, Saratov, RUS. He died on 1 May 1907 at Marienfeld, Saratov, RUS.

vii) Georg[7] Gerk (2343) was born on 1 Feb 1907 at Marienfeld, Saratov, RUS.

viii) Johann[7] Gerk (917) was born on 27 Aug 1910 at Marienfeld, Saratov, RUS.

ix) Elisabeta^7 Gerk (2000) was born on 24 Mar 1913 at Marienfeld, Saratov, RUS.

(e) Johann Adam^6 Gerk (821) was born on 27 Mar 1877 at Marienfeld, Saratov, RUS. He married Anna Maria Gette (1923), daughter of Andreas Gette (2211) and Anna Marie Schaab (2212), on 28 Nov 1900 at Marienfeld, Saratov, RUS. He died on 10 Jul 1949 at Bahía Blanca, Buenos Aires, ARG, at age 72.

i) Margareta^7 Gerk (1924) married José Elsempaj (2865) at San Miguel Arcángel, Buenos Aires, ARG. She died at San Miguel Arcángel, Buenos Aires, ARG. She was born on 26 Oct 1901 at Marienfeld, Saratov, RUS.

(a) Adán^8 Elsempaj (2879) was born at San Miguel Arcángel, Buenos Aires, ARG.

(b) Juan^8 Elsempaj (2880) was born at San Miguel Arcángel, Buenos Aires, ARG.

(c) José^8 Elsempaj (2881) was born at San Miguel Arcángel, Buenos Aires, ARG.

(d) Norberto^8 Elsempaj (2882) was born at San Miguel Arcángel, Buenos Aires, ARG.

(e) Maria^8 Elsempaj (2883) was born at San Miguel Arcángel, Buenos Aires, ARG.

(f) Bárbara^8 Elsempaj (2884) was born at San Miguel Arcángel, Buenos Aires, ARG.

ii) Adam^7 Gerk (1287) died at La Colina, ARG. He was born on 17 Sep 1903 at Marienfeld, Saratov, RUS. He married Anna Margarita Ringelmann (1925), daughter of Philipp Ringelmann (3215) and Anna Mariá Koenig (3216), on 9 Sep 1924 at San Miguel Arcángel, Buenos Aires, ARG.

(a) Tomás^8 Gerk (1926) was born at ARG. He married Elda Destefano (1927) at ARG.

i) Margarita^9 Gerk (1928) was born in 1956 at Buenos Aires, ARG.

ii) Estela^9 Gerk (1929) was born in 1960 at Buenos Aires, ARG.

iii) Cesar^9 Gerk (1930) was born in 1962 at Buenos Aires, ARG.

(b) Frederico^8 Gerk (3217) was born on 29 Jan 1927 at San Miguel Arcángel, Buenos Aires, ARG.

(c) Lutgero^8 Gerk (3218) was born on 5 Aug 1928 at San Miguel Arcángel, Buenos Aires, ARG.

iii) Alexander^7 Gerk (2390) married Margarita Bockemeier (2866) at Hinjo, Buenos Aires, ARG. He was born in 1905 at Liverpool, England. He died on 7 Jun 1976 at San Miguel Arcángel, Buenos Aires, ARG.

(a) Margarita^8 Gerk (2885)

(b) Juan^8 Gerk (3221) was born on 13 Aug 1928 at San Miguel Arcángel, Buenos Aires, ARG. He died on 29 Apr 1929 at San Miguel Arcángel, Buenos Aires, ARG.

(c) Felipe^8 Gerk (2886) was born on 1 Nov 1929 at San Miguel Arcángel, Buenos Aires, ARG. He died in 1996 at ARG.

(d) Luisa^8 Gerk (2887) was born on 27 Sep 1932 at San Miguel Arcangel, Buenos Aires, ARG.

(e) Alejandro^8 Gerk (2888) was born in 1937 at ARG. He died on 11 Mar 1990 at ARG.

iv) Pedro^7 Gerk (2392) married Maria Orozco (2889). He was born on 22 Aug 1908 at San Miguel Arcángel, Buenos Aires, ARG. He married Eva Denk (2867), daughter of Johann Peter Denk (3219) and Barbara Heiland (3220), on 25 Apr 1933 at San Miguel Arcángel, Buenos Aires, ARG. He died on 4 Jun 1968 at Río Colorado, ARG, at age 59.

(a) Susana^8 Gerk (2891)

(b) Maria^8 Gerk (2892)

(c) Elisa^8 Gerk (2890) was born on 30 Jan 1934 at Partido de Adolfo Alsina, ARG.

v) Maria^7 Gerk (2877) was born at San Miguel Arcángel, Buenos Aires, ARG. She died at Lamadríd, ARG. She married Jacobo Tome (2878) at San Miguel Arcángel, Buenos Aires, ARG.

vi) Ana^7 Gerk (2391) was born on 5 Mar 1912 at San Miguel Arcángel, Buenos Aires, ARG. She married Teodora Redel (2868) circa 1933 at San Miguel Arcángel, Buenos Aires, ARG. She died on 7 Mar 1998 at Bahia Blanca, Buenos Aires, ARG, at age 86.

(a) Teodora^8 Redel (2893) was born on 2 Feb 1934 at San Miguel Arcángel, Buenos Aires, ARG.

(b) Ester[8] Redel (2894) was born on 28 Feb 1936 at San Miguel Arcángel, Buenos Aires, ARG.

(c) Maria Petronila[8] Redel (2895) was born on 30 May 1937 at San Miguel Arcángel, Buenos Aires, ARG.

(d) Ariel[8] Redel (2896) was born on 19 Jan 1939 at Bahia Blanca, Buenos Aires, ARG.

(e) Alicia Olga[8] Redel (2897) was born on 12 Jul 1941 at Bahia Blanca, Buenos Aires, ARG.

(f) Clemente[8] Redel (2898) was born on 2 Dec 1943 at Bahia Blanca, Buenos Aires, ARG.

(g) Teresa[8] Redel (2899) married Clemente Ramírez (3415). She was born on 10 May 1947 at Bahia Blanca, Buenos Aires, ARG.

    i) César Clemente[9] Ramírez (3416) was born on 26 Jan 1964 at Bahía Blanca, Buenos Aires, ARG. He died on 17 Feb 1986 at Corrientes, ARG, at age 22.

    ii) Diana[9] Ramírez (3417) was born on 17 Dec 1965 at Bahía Blanca, Buenos Aires, ARG. She died on 24 Dec 2017 at Resistencia, Chaco, ARG, at age 52.

    iii) Nidia[9] Ramírez (3418) was born on 7 Aug 1970 at Bahía Blanca, Buenos Aires, ARG.

    iv) Diego[9] Ramírez (3419) was born on 31 Mar 1973 at Puerto Belgrano, Buenos Aires, ARG. He died on 4 Oct 1976 at Resistencia, Chaco, ARG, at age 3.

    v) Silvia[9] Ramírez (3420) was born on 25 Feb 1975 at Puerto Belgrano, Buenos Aires, ARG.

    vi) Malvina[9] Ramírez (3421) was born on 2 Oct 1979 at Puerto Belgrano, Buenos Aires, ARG.

    vii) Apolo Mario Bautista[9] Ramírez (3422) was born on 28 Oct 1986 at Resistencia, Chaco, ARG.

(h) Irma Beatriz[8] Redel (2900) was born on 7 Feb 1950 at Bahia Blanca, Buenos Aires, ARG.

vii) Manuel[7] Gerk (2869) married Delia Montenegro (2870) at Bahía Blanca, Buenos Aires, ARG. He was born on 27 Mar 1915 at San Miguel Arcángel, Buenos Aires, ARG. He died on 3 Oct 1978 at Bahía Blanca, Buenos Aires, ARG, at age 63.

(a) Ana[8] Gerk (2901) **(b)** Margarita[8] Gerk (2902) **(c)** Manuel[8] Gerk (2903) **(d)** Cuchipe[8] Gerk (2904)

viii) Rosa[7] Gerk (2393) married Tomas Fanjak (2905). She married Federico Siberd (2871) at San Miguel Arcángel, Buenos Aires, ARG. She was born on 15 Jul 1916 at San Miguel Arcángel, Buenos Aires, ARG. She died on 3 Jun 1988 at Bahía Blanca, Buenos Aires, ARG, at age 71.

ix) Juan[7] Gerk (2394) died at San Miguel Arcángel, Buenos Aires, ARG. He married Bárbara Koler (2872) at San Miguel Arcángel, Buenos Aires, ARG. He was born on 1 Dec 1918 at San Miguel Arcángel, Buenos Aires, ARG.

(a) Juana[8] Gerk (2906) was born at San Miguel Arcángel, Buenos Aires, ARG.

(b) Pita[8] Gerk (2907) was born at San Miguel Arcángel, Buenos Aires, ARG.

(c) Raúl Oscar[8] Gerk (4652) was born at San Miguel Arcángel, Buenos Aires, ARG.

(d) José[8] Gerk (2909) was born at San Miguel Arcángel, Buenos Aires, ARG.

(e) Feliciano[8] Gerk (2910) was born at San Miguel Arcángel, Buenos Aires, ARG.

(f) Marta[8] Gerk (2911) was born at San Miguel Arcángel, Buenos Aires, ARG.

(g) Delia[8] Gerk (2919) was born in 1947 at ARG.

(h) Juan[8] Gerk (2908) was born on 23 Mar 1950 at San Miguel Arcángel, Buenos Aires, ARG.

x) Nicolás[7] Gerk (2395) was born on 20 Apr 1921 at San Miguel Arcángel, Buenos Aires, ARG. He married Haydee Pelandrini (2873) in 1948 at Bahía Blanca, Buenos Aires, ARG. He died on 17 May 1975 at Bahía Blanca, Buenos Aires, ARG, at age 54.

(a) Nicolás[8] Gerk (2912) was born at San Miguel Arcángel, Buenos Aires, ARG.

(b) Isabel[8] Gerk (2913) was born at San Miguel Arcángel, Buenos Aires, ARG.

(c) Ana Esther[8] Gerk (2914) was born at San Miguel Arcángel, Buenos Aires, ARG.

xi) Clemente[7] Gerk (2396) died at Pigue, Buenos Aires, ARG. He was born in 1923 at San Miguel Arcángel, Buenos Aires, ARG. He married María Geist (2874), daughter of Juan Geist (6210) and Rosa Stegmann (6211), on 7 Feb 1946 at San Miguel Arcángel, Buenos Aires, ARG.

xii) Bárbara[7] Gerk (2397) married Juan Carrasco (2876) at San Miguel Arcángel, Buenos Aires, ARG. She was born on 6 Dec 1924 at San Miguel Arcángel, Buenos Aires, ARG.

    (a) Natividad[8] Carrasco (2915)

    (b) Teresa[8] Carrasco (2916) was born in 1944 at Punta Alta, Santa Fe, ARG.

xiii) Catalina[7] Gerk (2398) was born on 20 Jul 1926 at San Miguel Arcángel, Buenos Aires, ARG. She married José Gallinger (2875) on 4 Nov 1946 at San Miguel Arcángel, Buenos Aires, ARG. She died on 14 Mar 2013 at Puan, ARG, at age 86.

    (a) José[8] Gallinger (2917)

    (b) Mírta[8] Gallinger (2918) married (--?--) González (2982) at ARG.

        i) Hernán[9] González (2983) was born at ARG.

(f) Barbara[6] Gerk (822) was born on 7 Jun 1884 at Marienfeld, Saratov, RUS. She married Johann Burgardt (2225), son of Peter Burgardt (2226) and Magdalena Schneider (2227), on 11 Nov 1903 at Marienfeld, Saratov, RUS.

    i) Peter[7] Burgardt (2337) was born on 30 Apr 1904 at Marienfeld, Saratov, RUS.

    ii) Josef[7] Burgardt (2338) was born on 5 May 1906 at Marienfeld, Saratov, RUS.

    iii) Katarina[7] Burgardt (2339) was born on 16 Feb 1908 at Marienfeld, Saratov, RUS. She died on 21 Aug 1910 at Marienfeld, Saratov, RUS, at age 2.

    iv) Josef[7] Burgardt (2340) was born on 20 Sep 1909 at Marienfeld, Saratov, RUS.

    v) Elisabeta[7] Burgardt (2341) was born on 20 Sep 1911 at Marienfeld, Saratov, RUS.

(4) Anna Maria[5] Gerk (2725) was born in 1844 at Koehler, Saratov, RUS. She married Jakob Alles (2726), son of Matias Alles (2727) and Marianna Wachmeister (2728), on 25 Jan 1866 at Marienfeld, Saratov, RUS.

    (a) Jakob[6] Alles (2764) was born on 28 Sep 1869 at Marienfeld, Saratov, RUS.

    (b) Anna Elisabeta[6] Alles (3090) was born on 7 Jul 1875 at Marienfeld, Saratov, RUS.

    (c) Adam[6] Alles (8092) was born in 1880 at Marienfeld, Saratov, RUS.

    (d) Andreas[6] Alles (8091) was born on 2 Nov 1884 at Marienfeld, Saratov, RUS.

(5) Elisabeta[5] Gerk (1621) was born on 16 Jun 1847 at Schuck, Saratov, RUS. She died on 1 Apr 1854 at Marienfeld, Saratov, RUS, at age 6.

(6) Barbara[5] Gerk (2732) was born in 1849 at Koehler, Saratov, RUS. She married Georg Hartwig (2733), son of Philip Hartwig (2734) and Kristina Frey (2735), on 19 Nov 1868 at Marienfeld, Saratov, RUS.

    (a) Kaspar[6] Hartwig (2757) was born on 16 Oct 1871 at Marienfeld, Saratov, RUS.

    (b) Katarina[6] Hartwig (2758) was born on 11 May 1874 at Marienfeld, Saratov, RUS.

c) Zacharius[4] Gerk (575) was born in 1821 at Koehler, Saratov, RUS. He married Katarina Schoenberger (577) circa 1845 at Koehler, Saratov, RUS. He died on 28 Feb 1890 at Josefstal, Saratov, RUS.

(1) Florian[5] Gerk (578) was born in 1845 at Koehler, Saratov, RUS. He married Katarina Wagner (1700), daughter of Johannes Wagner (2741) and Katarina Biehn (2742), on 26 Jun 1870 at Josefstal, Saratov, RUS.

    (a) Rosalia[6] Gerk (4187) was born on 4 Aug 1871 at Josefstal, Saratov, RUS.

    (b) Adolf[6] Gerk (4801) was born on 4 May 1873 at Josefstal, Saratov, RUS.

    (c) Rosalia[6] Gerk (1701) was born on 12 Jun 1882 at Josefstal, Saratov, RUS.

    (d) Elisabeta[6] Gerk (1702) was born on 22 May 1884 at Josefstal, Saratov, RUS.

(2) Katarina[5] Gerk (580) was born in 1847 at Koehler, Saratov, RUS. She married Johannes Lambrecht (2703), son of Johannes Lambrecht (2704) and Kristina Delov (2705), on 24 Nov 1864 at Josefstal, Saratov, RUS.

(a) Johannes[6] Lambrecht (2711) was born on 3 Mar 1867 at Josefstal, Saratov, RUS.

(b) Elisabeta Barbara[6] Lambrecht (2712) was born on 14 Feb 1869 at Josefstal, Saratov, RUS.

(3) Kristina Barbara[5] Gerk (3685) was born on 23 Mar 1850 at Koehler, Saratov, RUS. She died on 25 Jul 1851 at Koehler, Saratov, RUS, at age 1.

(4) Anna Maria[5] Gerk (581) was born in 1851 at Koehler, Saratov, RUS. She married Kristof Helmer (2736), son of Peter Helmer (2737) and Katarina Gerk (2738), on 30 Aug 1869 at Josefstal, Saratov, RUS.

(a) Ann Maria[6] Helmer (2753) (see above)**(b)** Johann Peter[6] Helmer (2754) (see above)

(c) Nikolai Kristof[6] Helmer (2755) (see above)

(5) Maria Magdalena[5] Gerk (4186) was born on 18 Feb 1852 at Schuck, Saratov, RUS.

(6) Barbara[5] Gerk (582) was born in 1853 at Koehler, Saratov, RUS. She married Gabriel Rolheiser (5096), son of Anton Rolheiser (5097) and Barbara Krever (5098), on 25 Oct 1871 at Rothammel, Saratov, RUS.

(a) Florian[6] Rolheiser (5099) was born on 23 Nov 1872 at Husaren, Saratov, RUS.

(b) Maria[6] Rolheiser (5100) was born on 21 Dec 1873 at Husaren, Saratov, RUS.

(7) Johannes[5] Gerk (579) was born in 1855 at Koehler, Saratov, RUS.

(8) Margareta[5] Gerk (583) was born in 1856 at Koehler, Saratov, RUS.

(9) Georg Josef[5] Gerk (730) was born on 25 Nov 1863 at Josefstal, Saratov, RUS. He died on 18 Nov 1864 at Josefstal, Saratov, RUS.

(10) Peter Andreas[5] Gerk (731) was born on 5 Jan 1866 at Josefstal, Saratov, RUS.

(11) Anna Elisabeta[5] Gerk (732) was born on 27 Aug 1868 at Josefstal, Saratov, RUS.

d) Magdalena[4] Gerk (576) was born in 1824 at Koehler, Saratov, RUS.

2. Peter[3] Gerk (573) was born in 1796 at Koehler, Saratov, RUS. He married Anna Elizabeta Leonard (584) circa 1817 at Koehler, Saratov, RUS. He died on 28 May 1854 at Marienfeld, Saratov, RUS.

a) Katarina[4] Gerk (585) was born in 1818 at Koehler, Saratov, RUS. She married Johannes Schamberger (3683) on 20 Jan 1836 at Koehler, Saratov, RUS.

b) Margareta[4] Gerk (587) was born in 1825 at Koehler, Saratov, RUS. She married Adam Haberkorn (4189) on 9 Nov 1844 at Koehler, Saratov, RUS. She died on 22 Jan 1893 at Marienfeld, Saratov, RUS.

(1) Peter[5] Haberkorn (4256) was born in 1847 at Semenovka, Saratov, RUS.

(2) Johannes[5] Haberkorn (4257) was born in 1850 at Semenovka, Saratov, RUS.

(3) Margareta[5] Haberkorn (4254) was born in 1853 at Marienfeld, Saratov, RUS.

(4) Agnesia[5] Haberkorn (4255) was born in 1856 at Marienfeld, Saratov, RUS. She married Kaspar Schoenfeld (7365), son of Jakob Schoenfeld (2187) and Dorothea Klein (2188), on 9 Nov 1876 at Marienfeld, Saratov, RUS.

(5) Anna Maria[5] Haberkorn (4233) was born on 6 Mar 1870 at Marienfeld, Saratov, RUS.

c) Kristof[4] Gerk (4188) was born on 21 Feb 1828 at Koehler, Saratov, RUS. He died on 4 May 1828 at Koehler, Saratov, RUS.

d) Katarina[4] Gerk (586) was born on 14 Jan 1829 at Koehler, Saratov, RUS.

e) Margareta[4] Gerk (588) was born on 27 Feb 1831 at Koehler, Saratov, RUS.

f) Peter[4] Gerk (589) was born on 27 May 1833 at Koehler, Saratov, RUS. He married Anna Maria Ringelmann (3069), daughter of Johannes Ringelmann (3521) and Katarina (--?--) (3522), on 20 Nov 1851 at Marienfeld, Saratov, RUS. He died on 4 Nov 1857 at Marienfeld, Saratov, RUS, at age 24.

(1) Adam[5] Gerk (3070) was born on 8 Jul 1857 at Marienfeld, Saratov, RUS. He died on 18 Aug 1857 at Marienfeld, Saratov, RUS.

g) Johannes[4] Gerk (734) was born on 25 Nov 1836 at Koehler, Saratov, RUS. He married Maria Anna Eckermann (735), daughter of Leonard Eckermann (3108) and Barbara Heffner (3109), on 10 Feb 1857 at Marienfeld, Saratov, RUS. He married Margareta Schneider (2932), daughter of Gottfried Schneider (2933) and Anna Marie Mischik (2934), on 7 Feb 1883 at Marienfeld, Saratov, RUS. He died on 21 Nov 1902 at Marienfeld, Saratov, RUS, at age 65.

(1) Michael[5] Gerk (1204) was born on 2 Sep 1856 at Marienfeld, Saratov, RUS. He married Anna Maria Ditler (4190) in 1876 at Marienfeld, Saratov, RUS. He married Katarina Kloster (1205), daughter of Johan Kloster (3475) and Barbara Ditler (3476), on 7 Jun 1882 at Semenovka, Saratov, RUS. He emigrated on 11 Nov 1886 from Hamburg, GER. He died on 4 Sep 1943 at Iliff, Colorado, USA, at age 87.

    (a) Peter[6] Gerk (2465) was born on 15 Dec 1878 at Marienfeld, Saratov, RUS. He died on 4 Dec 1879 at Marienfeld, Saratov, RUS.

    (b) Johan Paul[6] Gerk (4191) was born on 13 Sep 1881 at Semenovka, Saratov, RUS.

    (c) Barbara[6] Gerk (1206) married Lawrence Acevado (1337). She was born on 19 Feb 1884 at Marienfeld, Saratov, RUS.

        i) Miguel[7] Acevado (7599) was born on 20 Nov 1912 at General Acha, La Pampa, ARG.

    (d) Rosa[6] Gerk (1207) was born on 27 Jan 1886 at Marienfeld, Saratov, RUS. She married Kaspar Stremel (1208), son of Josef Stremel (2006) and Anna Margareta Wilberger (2007), on 15 Nov 1905 at Crespo, Entre Ríos, ARG. She died on 5 Nov 1964 at Crespo, Entre Ríos, ARG, at age 78.

        i) Ana[7] Stremel (6222) was born in 1906 at Entre Rios, ARG.

        ii) Adan[7] Stremel (7604) was born on 3 May 1908 at Crespo, Entre Ríos, ARG.

        iii) Kaspar[7] Stremel (1338) was born on 7 Mar 1910 at Crespo, Entre Ríos, ARG. He married Maria Jacob (2130), daughter of Georg Jacob (3008) and Elisabeta Gette (3009), on 18 Apr 1933 at Crespo, Entre Ríos, ARG. He married Maria Luisa Schmidt (2131) on 14 Oct 1954 at Crespo, Entre Ríos, ARG. He died on 5 Jun 1961 at Buenos Aires, Buenos Aires, ARG, at age 51.

            (a) Josef[8] Stremel (3010) was born in Aug 1935 at Crespo, Entre Ríos, ARG.

            (b) John[8] Stremel (3011) was born in Nov 1936 at Crespo, Entre Ríos, ARG.

            (c) Kaspar[8] Stremel (1339) was born on 30 Aug 1940 at ARG. He died on 18 Jun 1957 at ARG at age 16.

        iv) Juliana[7] Stremel (7605) was born on 5 Nov 1911 at Crespo, Entre Ríos, ARG.

        v) Amalia[7] Stremel (2013) was born on 21 Mar 1916 at Crespo, Entre Ríos, ARG.

        vi) Guillermo[7] Stremel (7602) was born on 3 Mar 1920 at Crespo, Entre Ríos, ARG. He married Ermendo Fuchs (7603) on 7 Nov 1946 at Crespo, Entre Ríos, ARG.

        vii) Maria Luisa[7] Stremel (7601) was born on 3 Mar 1920 at Crespo, Entre Ríos, ARG.

        viii) Filomena[7] Stremel (7600) was born on 27 Oct 1921 at Crespo, Entre Ríos, ARG. She died on 31 Dec 1921 at Crespo, Entre Ríos, ARG.

    (e) Katalina[6] Gerk (1214) was born on 15 Jul 1888 at Crespo, Entre Ríos, ARG. She married Pedro Lell (1215), son of Johannes Lell (2004) and Anna Margareta Herrlein (2005), on 18 Sep 1907 at Crespo, Entre Ríos, ARG. She died on 1 Nov 1918 at Sterling, Colorado, USA, at age 30.

        i) John Alois[7] Lell (7867) was born on 23 May 1910 at Sterling, CO, USA. He died on 16 Apr 2004 at Tigard, OR, USA, at age 93.

        ii) Rose Veronica[7] Lell (7868) was born on 29 Jul 1912 at Sterling, CO, USA. She died on 6 Sep 2006 at Denver, CO, USA, at age 94.

        iii) Joseph[7] Lell (7866) was born on 27 Aug 1914 at Sterling, CO, USA. He died on 31 Dec 1937 at Sterling, CO, USA, at age 23.

        iv) Alexander Alois[7] Lell (7869) was born on 21 Oct 1916 at Sterling, CO, USA. He died on 4 Sep 2013 at Luling, LA, USA, at age 96.

    (f) John[6] Gerk (1209) was born on 16 May 1891 at Valle Maria, Entre Ríos, ARG. He married Katarina Dillie (1210) on 29 Dec 1915 at Sterling, CO, USA. He married Mary E. Roskopf (3672) on 4 Sep 1944 at Logan, Colorado, USA. He died on 5 Oct 1979 at Sterling, Colorado, USA, at age 88.

        i) Mary Catherine[7] Gerk (2694) was born on 7 Jul 1917 at Iliff, Colorado, USA. She married John Kaiser (3242), son of Johan Henry Peter Kaiser (3551) and Emma Margaret Mollendor (3552), on 29 Dec 1935 at Iliff, Colorado, USA. She died on 15 Jun 2012 at Lakewood, CO, USA, at age 94.

            (a) John Edward[8] Kaiser (3243)

(b) Leroy[8] Kaiser (3244)

(c) James[8] Kaiser (3245)

(d) Bonnie[8] Kaiser (3246) was born on 23 Feb 1953 at Sterling, Colorado, USA. She died on 14 Jul 1981 at Sterling, Colorado, USA, at age 28.

ii) Anna[7] Gerk (2695) was born on 5 Sep 1918 at Iliff, Colorado, USA. She married Glen Ertle (3247) on 25 Nov 1937 at CO, USA. She died on 2 Nov 2012 at Sterling, CO, USA, at age 94.

(a) Glenda[8] Ertle (3248) **(b)** Jerry[8] Ertle (3249) **(c)** Mary[8] Ertle (3250) **(d)** Glen[8] Ertle (3251)

(e) Larry[8] Ertle (3252) **(f)** Paulette[8] Ertle (3253) **(g)** Bill[8] Ertle (3254) **(h)** Diana[8] Ertle (3255)

(i) Alan[8] Ertle (3256) **(j)** Kenneth[8] Ertle (3257) **(k)** Dennis[8] Ertle (3258)

iii) Josephine[7] Gerk (2696) was born on 7 Feb 1922 at Iliff, Colorado, USA. She married Herbert Krietzer (3259) on 21 Nov 1940 at Logan, Colorado, USA.

(a) Larry[8] Krietzer (3260) **(b)** Donald[8] Krietzer (3261) **(c)** Allan[8] Krietzer (3262)

(d) Robert[8] Krietzer (3263)

iv) Albert[7] Gerk (2697) was born on 16 Aug 1923 at Iliff, Colorado, USA. He married Pauline Mildenberger (3264) on 9 May 1949 at Sterling, Colorado, USA. He died on 23 Dec 2004 at Greeley, Colorado, USA, at age 81.

(a) Patricia[8] Gerk (3265)

(b) Barbara[8] Gerk (3266) married Gary Warden (3615).

(c) Ronald D.[8] Gerk (3267) was born on 13 Jun 1955 at Holyoke, Colorado, USA. He married Lois Taylor (3616) on 28 Jun 1980 at Douglas, Wyoming, USA. He died on 26 Aug 2004 at Denver, Colorado, USA, at age 49.

  i) Shandi[9] Gerk (3617) was born on 27 Jun 1982 at Sterling, Colorado, USA.

  ii) Grant[9] Gerk (3618) was born on 13 Feb 1985 at Sterling, Colorado, USA.

v) John[7] Gerk (2698) was born on 16 Aug 1925 at Iliff, Colorado, USA. He married Shirley Clark (3268) on 24 Nov 1949 at Colorado, USA. He died on 21 Sep 2015 at Richmond, CA, USA, at age 90.

(a) Galen Thomas (Tom)[8] Gerk (7828) was born on 7 Sep 1950 at Denver, CO, USA.

(b) Katherine Anita[8] Gerk (3270) was born on 27 Feb 1952 at Oakland, CA, USA.

(c) Karen Lee[8] Gerk (3272) was born on 19 Apr 1953 at Richmond, CA, USA.

(d) Sharon Marie[8] Gerk (3271) was born on 19 Apr 1953 at Richmond, CA, USA.

(e) David[8] Gerk (7830) was born on 12 Jan 1954 at Richmond, CA, USA.

(f) Theresa Sue[8] Gerk (3273) was born on 7 Aug 1957 at Richmond, CA, USA.

(g) Timothy John[8] Gerk (7829) was born on 20 Jun 1959 at Richmond, CA, USA.

(h) Patrick Allen[8] Gerk (3274) was born on 17 Mar 1963 at Richmond, CA, USA. He died on 3 Apr 1998 at CA, USA, at age 35.

(i) Anthony[8] Gerk (3275) was born on 12 Oct 1964 at Richmond, CA, USA. He died on 1 Jun 1992 at CA, USA, at age 27.

(j) Thomas[8] Gerk (3269) was born on 12 Sep 1969 at USA.

vi) Raymond Benedict[7] Gerk (1211) was born on 18 Jan 1928 at Sterling, Colorado, USA. He married Dorothy Louise Applehans (1212), daughter of Jacob James Applehans (3240) and Mary Ann Sommers (3241), on 10 Jan 1950 at Colorado, USA. He died on 6 Nov 2016 at Sterling, CO, USA, at age 88.

(a) Julie Ann[8] Gerk (3293) was born on 14 Jul 1950 at Sterling, Colorado, USA.

(b) Janice Marie[8] Gerk (3294) was born on 12 Jan 1953 at Sterling, Colorado, USA.

(c) James[8] Gerk (3295) was born on 10 Dec 1956 at Sterling, Colorado, USA. He married Marilyn K Schaefer (3296) on 9 Oct 1976 at Sterling, Colorado, USA.

i) Troy James[9] Gerk (3297) was born on 28 May 1978 at Sterling, Colorado, USA.

ii) Kristin Marie[9] Gerk (3298) was born on 21 Nov 1980 at Sterling, Colorado, USA.

iii) Jermey Ray[9] Gerk (3299) was born on 16 Jul 1984 at Sterling, Colorado, USA.

(d) Daniel[8] Gerk (3300) was born on 10 Jan 1963 at Sterling, Colorado, USA. He married JoAnn Vorce (3301) on 9 Jan 1990 at Sterling, Colorado, USA.

vii) Edward William[7] Gerk (2699) was born on 3 Jun 1929 at Iliff, Colorado, USA. He married Rose Kippes (3060) on 27 Nov 1947 at Iliff, CO, USA. He died on 6 Aug 2003 at Brighton, Colorado, USA, at age 74.

(a) Edward[8] Gerk (3061) **(b)** Daniel John[8] Gerk (3062) **(c)** Glori Ann[8] Gerk (3277)

(d) Randall John[8] Gerk (3064) **(e)** Roselyn[8] Gerk (3276) **(f)** Jolene[8] Gerk (3278)

(g) Dennis Joseph[8] Gerk (7577) was born on 30 Mar 1950 at Sterling, CO, USA. He died on 23 May 2015 at Aurora, CO, USA, at age 65.

i) Amanda[9] Gerk (7578) was born in 1993 at CO, USA.

(h) Gerald Peter[8] Gerk (3063) was born on 6 Nov 1953 at CO, USA.

viii) Pauline[7] Gerk (3279) was born on 14 May 1932 at Iliff, Colorado, USA. She married Edward Lauer (3280) on 21 Nov 1951 at Logan, CO, USA. She died on 8 Sep 1972 at Iliff, Colorado, USA, at age 40.

(a) Terrince[8] Lauer (3281) **(b)** Sherilia[8] Lauer (3282) **(c)** Cindy[8] Lauer (3283)

(d) Kenneth[8] Lauer (3284) **(e)** Timothy[8] Lauer (3285)

ix) Dolores Irene[7] Gerk (3286) was born on 8 Oct 1933 at Iliff, Colorado, USA. She married Peter A. Klug (3287) in 1956. She died on 10 Sep 2003 at Iliff, Colorado, USA, at age 69.

(a) Michael[8] Klug (3400) **(b)** Laura[8] Klug (3401)

x) Elizabeth[7] Gerk (3288) was born on 13 Dec 1936 at Iliff, Colorado, USA. She married George Klug (3289) in 1955 at Sterling, CO, USA. She died on 12 Aug 2008 at Sterling, CO, USA, at age 71.

(a) Daniel[8] Klug (3290)

(b) Denise[8] Klug (3291)

(c) Peter[8] Klug (3292) was born on 4 Feb 1961 at Sterling, CO, USA. He died on 31 Oct 1986 at Gig Harbor, WA, USA, at age 25.

(g) Elizabeth Laura[6] Gerk (1340) was born on 19 Oct 1893 at Entre Ríos, ARG. She married Jakob Helbert (1344) on 11 Sep 1918 at Sterling, CO, USA. She died on 6 Jun 1975 at Sterling, Colorado, USA, at age 81.

i) Joseph Edward[7] Helbert (7619) was born on 17 Jul 1919 at Green, CO, USA. He died on 16 May 1985 at Las Vegas, NV, USA, at age 65.

ii) Edward[7] Helbert (7616) was born on 4 Nov 1920 at Sterling, CO, USA. He died on 27 May 1972 at Sterling, CO, USA, at age 51.

iii) Eulalia Mae[7] Helbert (3545) married William E. Duperrieu (3546). She was born on 9 May 1922 at Sterling, CO, USA. She died on 28 Sep 2005 at Centralia, IL, USA, at age 83.

iv) Raymond John[7] Helbert (7615) was born on 11 Feb 1925 at Sterling, CO, USA. He died on 23 Nov 1991 at El Paso, TX, USA, at age 66.

v) Francis Raymond[7] Helbert (7617) was born on 14 Sep 1926 at Elwood, Nebraska, USA. He died on 21 Dec 2009 at Tonopah, NV, USA, at age 83.

vi) Dorothy Mae[7] Helbert (7618) was born in 1930 at USA.

(h) Mary Elizabeth[6] Gerk (1239) was born on 19 May 1895 at San Juan, Entre Ríos, ARG. She married Jakob Schwerdt (1240), son of Gottfried Schwerdt (7622) and Barbara Simon (3626), on 27 Dec 1915 at Sterling, CO, USA. She died on 3 Oct 1978 at Santa Clara, California, USA, at age 83.

i) Joseph Aloysius[7] Schwerdt (1241) was born on 18 Oct 1916 at Sterling, Colorado, USA. He died on 12 Jan 1992 at Los Angeles, California, USA, at age 75.

ii) Edward Michael[7] Schwerdt (7623) was born on 22 Sep 1918 at Sterling, CO, USA. He died on 15 Nov 2004 at age 86.

iii) Raymond Luke[7] Schwerdt (1242) was born on 14 Jun 1922 at Sterling, Colorado, USA. He died on 17 Feb 1994 at Shasta, California, USA, at age 71.

iv) Mary Josephine[7] Schwerdt (7621) married Marvin Dale Goforth (7624). She was born on 23 Oct 1928 at Bend, OR, USA. She died on 19 Dec 2010 at Paradise, CA, USA, at age 82.

(i) Jakob[6] Gerk (1213) was born on 3 May 1899 at Buenos Aires, ARG. He married Margaret Sommer (1216), daughter of Josef Sommer (3673) and Anna Jakobs (3674), on 1 Feb 1926 at Iliff, Colorado, USA. He died on 11 Oct 1986 at Sterling, Colorado, USA, at age 87.

i) Joseph Gregory[7] Gerk (1217) was born on 9 May 1927 at Iliff, Colorado, USA. He married Corinne Mae DeSoto (1231), daughter of Domenic DeSoto (7883) and Frances (--?--) (7884), on 5 Jun 1948 at Iliff, Colorado, USA. He died on 12 May 2003 at Iliff, Colorado, USA, at age 76.

(a) Ken[8] Gerk (1345) was born on 25 Sep 1950 at Iliff, Colorado, USA. He married Peggy Yahn (3619) on 10 Jun 1972 at Sterling, Colorado, USA.

i) Beth[9] Gerk (3620) was born on 12 Feb 1976 at Greeley, Colorado, USA.

ii) Kelly A.[9] Gerk (3621) was born on 13 Feb 1977 at Greeley, Colorado, USA. She married Jason Bush (3623) on 19 Jun 1999 at Greeley, Colorado, USA.

(a) Mackenzie[10] Bush (3624) was born on 12 Jun 2001 at Greeley, Colorado, USA.

(b) Abby[10] Bush (3625) was born on 4 Feb 2004 at Greeley, Colorado, USA.

iii) Kendra[9] Gerk (3622) was born on 23 Feb 1990 at Greeley, Colorado, USA. She married Alex Balsiger (7844) on 11 Jun 2016 at Greeley, CO, USA.

(b) Peggy[8] Gerk (1346) was born on 31 Jul 1951 at Sterling, Colorado, USA. She married James Lueck (1347) on 28 Sep 1974 at Iliff, Colorado, USA.

i) Nicholas[9] Lueck (3650) was born on 1 May 1980 at Sterling, Colorado, USA.

ii) Alison[9] Lueck (3651) was born on 3 Apr 1985 at Sterling, Colorado, USA.

(c) James (Jim)[8] Gerk (1348) was born on 28 Oct 1952 at Sterling, Colorado, USA. He married Mary DalPonte (3652) on 1 Jul 1978 at Iliff, Colorado, USA.

i) Paul[9] Gerk (3653) was born on 2 Jan 1984 at Ft. Morgan, Colorado, USA. He married Erica Korrey (7870) on 6 Nov 2010 at Illif, CO, USA.

(a) Evelyn Grace[10] Gerk (7871) was born on 9 May 2018 at Fort Morgan, CO, USA.

ii) Adam[9] Gerk (3654) was born on 23 Apr 1985 at Ft. Morgan, Colorado, USA.

iii) Matthew[9] Gerk (3655) was born on 16 Apr 1990 at Ft. Morgan, Colorado, USA.

(d) Charles (Chas)[8] Gerk (1349) was born on 6 Aug 1954 at Sterling, Colorado, USA. He married Debra Loos (3656) on 6 Sep 1975 at Iliff, Colorado, USA.

i) Charles (Tony)[9] Gerk (3657) was born on 26 Sep 1979 at Sterling, Colorado, USA. He married Lauren Stecik (7840) on 10 Apr 2011 at Fort Worth, TX, USA.

(a) Catherine[10] Gerk (7842) was born at Sterling, CO, USA.

(b) Charles[10] Gerk (7843) was born at Sterling, CO, USA.

(c) Lydia Frances[10] Gerk (7841) was born on 3 Mar 2018 at Sterling, CO, USA.

ii) Andrew Joseph[9] Gerk (3658) was born on 8 Sep 1984 at Sterling, Colorado, USA. He married Lauren Beecher Yost (7845) on 12 Jun 2010 at Greeley, CO, USA.

iii) Ashley Elizabeth[9] Gerk (3659) was born on 8 Sep 1984 at Sterling, Colorado, USA. She married Nicholas Rusler (7846) on 17 Jan 2009 at Pueblo, CO, USA.

(e) Geoff[8] Gerk (1232) was born on 7 Jan 1960 at Iliff, Colorado, USA. He married Peggy C. Murphy (3018) on 6 Jul 1986 at Colorado, USA.

i) Tyler[9] Gerk (3547) was born on 19 Feb 1988 at Salida, Colorado, USA.

ii) Sam[9] Gerk (3548) was born on 9 Apr 1990 at Salida, Colorado, USA.

iii) Mitch[9] Gerk (3549) was born on 5 Jun 1994 at Salida, Colorado, USA.

(f) David[8] Gerk (1350) was born on 29 Jan 1962 at Sterling, Colorado, USA. He died on 20 May 2014 at Greeley, CO, USA, at age 52.

(g) Richard[8] Gerk (1351) was born on 9 Sep 1968 at Sterling, Colorado, USA. He married Dena K. Huss (3021) on 7 Nov 1992 at Iliff, Colorado, USA.

i) Jake[9] Gerk (3662) was born on 26 Jun 1995 at Haxton, Colorado, USA.

ii) Megan[9] Gerk (3663) was born on 2 May 1997 at Haxton, Colorado, USA.

iii) Joe[9] Gerk (3664) was born on 13 Mar 2001 at Haxton, Colorado, USA.

iv) Michael[9] Gerk (3550) was born on 20 Dec 2004 at Haxton, Colorado, USA.

ii) Lawrence Edward[7] Gerk (1218) was born on 8 Jun 1928 at Iliff, Colorado, USA. He married Jane Marie Cantonwine (1352), daughter of Milton Cantonwine (1353) and Melba Neer (1354), on 28 Apr 1957 at Longmont, Colorado, USA. He died on 21 Jan 2013 at Greeley, CO, USA, at age 84.

(a) Lawrence Edward[8] Gerk (1355) was born on 28 Jun 1958 at Denver, Colorado, USA.

(b) Regina Marie[8] Gerk (1356) was born on 2 Apr 1960 at Denver, Colorado, USA. She married Jeffery LaVerne Andrew (1362) on 26 Sep 1985 at Steamboat Springs, Colorado, USA.

i) Samel Lawrence[9] Andrew (1363) was born on 2 Aug 1991 at Steamboat Springs, Colorado, USA.

(c) Andrew Joseph[8] Gerk (1357) was born on 7 Aug 1962 at Denver, Colorado, USA. He married Leigh Ann Frank (1364) on 7 Aug 1987 at Loveland, Colorado, USA.

i) Heidi Leigh[9] Gerk (1365) was born on 13 Dec 1990 at Greeley, Colorado, USA.

ii) Heather[9] Gerk (1366) was born on 13 Dec 1990 at Greeley, Colorado, USA.

(d) Catherine Mary[8] Gerk (1358) was born on 17 Jan 1964 at Greeley, Colorado, USA. She married Thomas Rock Roche (1367) on 21 Dec 1989 at Fort Collins, Colorado, USA.

i) Keli Thomas[9] Roche (1368) was born on 17 Aug 1990 at Greeley, Colorado, USA.

ii) Cassidy Marie[9] Roche (1369) was born on 27 May 1996 at Greeley, Colorado, USA.

(e) Elizabeth Ann[8] Gerk (1359) was born on 9 Mar 1965 at Greeley, Colorado, USA. She married Dean Allen Lauterback (1370) on 29 Oct 1988 at Greeley, Colorado, USA. She married John Fisher (1371) on 3 Jul 1996 at Fort Collins, Colorado, USA.

(f) Teresa Lynn[8] Gerk (1360) was born on 14 Apr 1967 at Greeley, Colorado, USA. She married Steven David Baker (1372) on 15 Sep 1990 at Greeley, Colorado, USA.

i) Seth David[9] Baker (1373) was born on 13 Feb 1997.

(g) John Robert[8] Gerk (1361) was born on 29 Jan 1970 at Greeley, Colorado, USA. He married Anna Robinson (1374) on 7 May 1994 at Colorado, USA.

i) Madison Jane[9] Gerk (1375) was born on 23 Jul 1997 at USA.

iii) Rosemary[7] Gerk (1219) was born on 24 Apr 1931 at Iliff, Colorado, USA. She married James F. Rizzolo (1376), son of Antonio Rizzolo (1377) and Margaret Conti (1378), on 22 Nov 1958 at Sterling, Colorado, USA. She died on 29 Mar 2012 at Sterling, CO, USA, at age 80.

(a) Daniel James[8] Rizzolo (1379) was born on 18 Apr 1962 at Denver, Colorado, USA. He married Norma Garcia Jones (1380) on 3 Sep 1983 at Sterling, Colorado, USA.

i) Danielle Rene[9] Rizzolo (1381) was born on 4 Jul 1984 at Sterling, Colorado, USA.

(b) Darell Alan[8] Rizzolo (1382) was born on 27 Sep 1963 at Sterling, Colorado, USA.

(c) Melissa Rose[8] Rizzolo (1383) was born on 23 May 1966 at Sterling, Colorado, USA. She married Mark Steven Hess (1384) on 8 Aug 1987 at Sterling, Colorado, USA.

i) Kinsey[9] Hess (1385) was born on 4 Jun 1992 at Brush, Colorado, USA.

ii) Zachary James[9] Hess (1386) was born on 24 Apr 1998 at Colorado Springs, Colorado, USA.

iv) Margaret Ann[7] Gerk (1220) was born on 29 Oct 1932 at Iliff, Colorado, USA. She married Vincent Schmitt (1387) on 15 May 1954 at Iliff, Colorado, USA.

(a) Stephanie Jo[8] Schmitt (1388) was born on 16 Nov 1955.

(b) Wayne Allen[8] Schmitt (1389) was born on 26 Jan 1958.

(c) Thomas Jay[8] Schmitt (1390) was born on 7 Feb 1960.

(d) Carolyn Jane[8] Schmitt (1391) was born on 23 Feb 1962.

v) Stanley Raymond[7] Gerk (1221) was born on 22 Jul 1934 at Iliff, Colorado, USA. He married Rhodene Raye Petit (7620) on 5 Oct 1959 at Logan, CO, USA.

vi) Regina[7] Gerk (1223) was born in Dec 1935 at Iliff, Colorado, USA. She died on 13 Jun 1936 at Iliff, Colorado, USA.

vii) Dorothy[7] Gerk (1222) was born on 18 Jun 1937 at Iliff, Colorado, USA. She married Linus J. Fehringer (1392) on 28 Aug 1965 at Colorado, USA.

(a) Gerard William[8] Fehringer (1393) was born on 5 Apr 1968.

(b) Nathan Alan[8] Fehringer (1394) was born on 22 Nov 1970.

viii) Regina Ann[7] Gerk (1225) was born on 15 Feb 1939 at Iliff, Colorado, USA. She married James Allen Sande (1395) on 21 Jul 1974 at Arvada, Colorado, USA.

ix) Agnes[7] Gerk (1224) was born on 9 Oct 1940 at Iliff, Colorado, USA.

x) Rita Marie[7] Gerk (1396) was born on 19 Dec 1942 at Sterling, Colorado, USA. She married Robert Fehringer (1397) on 28 Aug 1965 at Sterling, Colorado, USA. She died on 6 Jun 2012 at Greeley, CO, USA, at age 69.

(a) Kristie[8] Fehringer (1398) married (--?--) Burns (6423) at USA. She was born on 9 Jun 1966.

i) Jarrod[9] Burns (6424) **ii)** Nicole[9] Burns (6425) **iii)** Morgan[9] Burns (6426)

iv) Jennifer[9] Burns (6427)

(b) Matthew[8] Fehringer (1399) married Kris (--?--) (6428). He was born on 27 May 1967.

i) Kyle[9] Fehringer (6429) **ii)** Cody[9] Fehringer (6430) **iii)** Jamison[9] Fehringer (6431)

(c) Michael[8] Fehringer (1400) married Kerri (--?--) (6432). He was born on 17 Aug 1968.

i) Maxwell[9] Fehringer (6433) **ii)** Braeden[9] Fehringer (6434) **iii)** Kaleigh[9] Fehringer (6435)

iv) Maddi[9] Fehringer (6436)

(d) Carrie[8] Fehringer (1401) was born on 9 Sep 1972.

xi) Herman[7] Gerk (1226) was born on 27 Apr 1944 at Sterling, Colorado, USA. He married Linda Lock (3585) on 6 Dec 1969 at Sterling, Colorado, USA.

(a) Jennifer[8] Gerk (3587) was born on 10 Jan 1971 at Sterling, Colorado, USA. She married Jeff Dollerschell (3588) on 18 Sep 1993 at Iliff, Colorado, USA.

i) Ryan[9] Dollerschell (3589) was born on 18 Aug 1995 at Iliff, Colorado, USA.

ii) Haley[9] Dollerschell (3590) was born on 13 Aug 1997 at Iliff, Colorado, USA.

iii) Mitch[9] Dollerschell (3591) was born on 29 Sep 2002 at Iliff, Colorado, USA.

(b) Alan[8] Gerk (3586) was born on 12 May 1972 at Sterling, Colorado, USA. He married Michele Deroo (3592) on 7 Oct 2000 at Sterling, Colorado, USA.

i) Raegan[9] Gerk (3593) was born on 14 Jan 2003 at Sterling, Colorado, USA.

(c) Randal[8] Gerk (3594) was born on 28 Jul 1973 at Sterling, Colorado, USA. He married Jaclyn Knaub (3595) on 12 Jun 2004 at Iliff, Colorado, USA.

i) Jordan Ann Marie[9] Gerk (4697) was born on 4 Oct 2006 at Iliff, Colorado, USA.

(d) Jonna[8] Gerk (3596) was born on 25 Nov 1975 at Sterling, Colorado, USA. She married Brad Stromberger (3597) on 11 Jul 1998 at Iliff, Colorado, USA.

    i) Brooke[9] Stromberger (3598) was born on 13 Nov 2000 at Iliff, Colorado, USA.

    ii) Alli[9] Stromberger (3599) was born on 23 Feb 2004 at Iliff, Colorado, USA.

(e) Janell[8] Gerk (3600) was born on 16 Aug 1978 at Sterling, Colorado, USA.

(f) Janise[8] Gerk (3601) was born on 19 Apr 1983 at Sterling, Colorado, USA.

(g) Jolene[8] Gerk (3602) was born on 17 Aug 1985 at Sterling, Colorado, USA.

(h) Jessica[8] Gerk (3603) was born on 3 Jan 1988 at Sterling, Colorado, USA.

xii) Loretta[7] Gerk (1227) was born on 8 Jun 1946 at Sterling, Colorado, USA.

xiii) William[7] Gerk (1228) was born on 11 Sep 1948 at Sterling, Colorado, USA.

(j) Michael[6] Gerk (1229) was born on 3 Jul 1901 at San Juan, Entre Ríos, ARG. He married Mary Sommer (1230) on 4 Feb 1930 at Iliff, Colorado, USA. He died on 20 Jun 1957 at Sterling, Colorado, USA, at age 55.

i) Mary Elizabeth[7] Gerk (1233) was born on 23 Mar 1931 at Iliff, Colorado, USA. She married Clarence Peter Kippes (2132) on 1 Dec 1951 at Colorado, USA.

    (a) Michael Eugene[8] Kippes (2133) married Jane L. Veith (6519) at USA. He was born on 30 Sep 1952 at Greeley, Colorado, USA.

    (b) Robert[8] Kippes (2134) was born on 31 Jul 1954 at Greeley, Colorado, USA.

    (c) Mary Jeanne[8] Kippes (2135) was born on 17 Apr 1959 at Greeley, Colorado, USA.

ii) George Eugene[7] Gerk (1234) married Eleanor Tixier (6520) at USA. He was born on 24 Aug 1932 at Iliff, Colorado, USA.

    (a) Christopher[8] Tixier Gerk (6521) was born on 23 Feb 1967 at Denver, CO, USA.

    (b) Stephanie Miriam[8] Tixier Gerk (6522) was born on 14 Sep 1968 at Denver, CO, USA. She died on 14 Sep 1968 at Denver, CO, USA.

    (c) Michelle[8] Tixier Gerk (6523) was born on 18 May 1971 at Denver, CO, USA.

iii) Jerome John[7] Gerk (1235) was born on 30 Nov 1934 at Iliff, Colorado, USA. He died on 27 Jun 1938 at Iliff, Colorado, USA, at age 3.

iv) Irene Anette[7] Gerk (1236) was born on 30 Mar 1937 at Iliff, Colorado, USA. She married Gordon Francis Wos (6524) on 17 Aug 1957 at Greeley, CO, USA. She died on 23 May 2005 at Tempe, Arizona, USA, at age 68.

    (a) Susan Marie[8] Wos (6525) married Robert Matteson (6528) at Hawaii, USA. She was born on 10 May 1958 at McNary, AZ, USA. She married Donald Lashier (6526) on 1 May 1979 at Mesa, AZ, USA. She died on 26 Nov 2007 at USA at age 49.

        i) Jonathan Sheridan[9] Lashier (6527) was born on 11 Sep 1982 at Salt Lake City, UT, USA.

    (b) Thomas Gordon[8] Wos (6529) was born on 13 May 1959 at McNary, AZ, USA. He married Nancy Supersynski (6530) on 14 Jul 1984 at Aurora, CO, USA.

        i) Vanessa Mae[9] Wos (6531) was born on 23 May 1989 at Aurora, CO, USA.

        ii) Bryan Thomas[9] Wos (6532) was born on 12 Feb 1991 at Aurora, CO, USA.

    (c) David Michael[8] Wos (6537) married Michelle Bracy (6538) at Las Vegas, NV, USA. He was born on 15 Oct 1960 at McNary, AZ, USA.

    (d) Annette Mary[8] Wos (6533) was born on 8 Mar 1962 at Westminister, CO, USA. She married Ben Berg (6534) on 10 Aug 1991 at Westminister, CO, USA.

        i) Ryan[9] Berg (6535) was born on 18 Sep 1993 at Denver, CO, USA.

        ii) Nathaniel[9] Berg (6536) was born on 21 Aug 1995 at Denver, CO, USA.

v) Joseph Wayne[7] Gerk (1237) was born on 4 Sep 1939 at Iliff, Colorado, USA. He married Margaret Denise Dixon (6539) on 15 Jul 1967 at Sterling, CO, USA.

(a) Brain Joseph[8] Gerk (6540) was born on 12 Apr 1968 at Denver, CO, USA. He married Ann Danielle Doran (6541) on 27 May 2000 at Ventura, CA, USA.

> i) Amelia Judith[9] Gerk (6543) ii) Shawn Hogan[9] Gerk (6542) was born on 22 Jul 2005.

> iii) Charles Dixon[9] Gerk (6544) was born in Nov 2011.

(b) Shannon Rene[8] Gerk (6547) was born on 1 Jun 1970. She married Michael Karicher (6548) on 15 Jul 1994 at Ventura, CA, USA.

> i) Harrison[9] Karicher (6549) was born on 3 Dec 2002 at Wisconsin.

> ii) Heidi Elizabeth[9] Karicher (6550) was born on 18 Dec 2006 at AK, USA.

(c) Heather Denise[8] Gerk (6545) married Hussain Chinoy (6546) at Chicago, IL, USA. She was born on 28 Aug 1972.

vi) Julia Ann[7] Gerk (1238) was born on 30 Sep 1942 at Sterling, Colorado, USA. She married Robert Leighton Campbell (2458) on 15 Jun 1968 at Greeley, Colorado, USA.

(a) Scott Leighton[8] Campbell (2459) was born on 7 Sep 1969 at Denver, Colorado, USA.

(b) Gary Robert[8] Campbell (2460) was born on 30 Aug 1972 at Denver, Colorado, USA. He married Victoria Catherine Smith (6553) on 19 May 2012 at San Diego, CA, USA.

vii) Jerome[7] Gerk (1288) was born on 24 Apr 1945 at Sterling, Colorado, USA. He married Joyce Riphenberg (6551) on 2 Aug 1975 at Trempealeau, Wisconsin, USA.

(a) Nicholas Beau[8] Gerk (6552) was born on 30 Jun 1981 at Denver, CO, USA. He died on 19 Dec 2007 at Denver, CO, USA, at age 26.

(2) Margareta[5] Gerk (1197) was born on 25 Nov 1858 at Marienfeld, Saratov, RUS. She died on 17 Dec 1859 at Marienfeld, Saratov, RUS, at age 1.

(3) Maria Anna Margareta[5] Gerk (733) was born on 23 May 1861 at Marienfeld, Saratov, RUS. She married Nikolai Schoenfeld (2186), son of Jakob Schoenfeld (2187) and Dorothea Klein (2188), on 2 Feb 1882 at Marienfeld, Saratov, RUS.

(a) Nicolás[6] Schoenfeld (7563) was born in 1890 at ARG. He married Barbara Regner (7564) on 18 Jan 1910 at Lucas González, Entre Ríos, ARG.

(b) Barbara[6] Schoenfeld (7516) was born on 17 Sep 1892 at San José, Entre Ríos, ARG.

(c) Juan Pedro[6] Schoenfeld (8104) was born on 26 Apr 1897 at Crespo, Entre Ríos, ARG.

(d) Regina[6] Schoenfeld (7512) was born on 10 Jun 1903 at Nogoyá, Entre Ríos, ARG. She married Andrés Rudel (7513) on 4 Apr 1923 at Lucas González, Nogoyá, Entre Ríos, ARG.

(e) José[6] Schoenfeld (7514) was born on 8 Jul 1905 at Lucas González, Nogoyá, Entre Ríos, ARG. He married Ángela Bequer (7515) on 19 Nov 1929 at Lucas González, Nogoyá, Entre Ríos, ARG.

(4) Katarina[5] Gerk (736) was born on 18 Sep 1863 at Marienfeld, Saratov, RUS. She married Jakob Haberkorn (4192) on 6 Feb 1884 at Gobel, Saratov, RUS.

(a) Anna Margareta[6] Haberkorn (4794) was born in 1893 at Saratov, RUS. She died on 7 Apr 1896 at Semenovka, Saratov, RUS.

(5) Zacharius[5] Gerk (737) was born on 16 Aug 1866 at Marienfeld, Saratov, RUS. He died on 26 Nov 1870 at Marienfeld, Saratov, RUS, at age 4.

(6) Anna Maria[5] Gerk (1327) was born in Sep 1869 at Marienfeld, Saratov, RUS. She died on 8 Nov 1869 at Marienfeld, Saratov, RUS.

(7) Anna Margareta[5] Gerk (738) was born on 26 Nov 1870 at Marienfeld, Saratov, RUS.

(8) Josef[5] Gerk (739) was born on 14 Apr 1873 at Marienfeld, Saratov, RUS.

(9) Margareta[5] Gerk (4193) was born in 1875 at Marienfeld, Saratov, RUS. She married Adam Gobel (4194) on 21 Nov 1895 at Gobel, Saratov, RUS.

(10) Peter John[5] Gerk (740) was born on 30 Jan 1876 at Marienfeld, Saratov, RUS. He married Catherine Dittler (1328), daughter of Stephan Dittler (1329) and Anna Marie Haberkorn (1330), on 7 Nov 1900 at Marienfeld, Saratov, RUS. He immigrated on 26 Apr 1910. He married Catherine Burgardt (1593) in 1927? He married

Catherine Kuehn (1594) on 23 Sep 1943 at Julesburg, Colorado, USA. He died on 29 Oct 1957 at Julesburg, Colorado, USA, at age 81.

(a) Barbara Katherine[6] Gerk (1335) was born on 29 Oct 1901 at Marienfeld, Saratov, RUS. She married Alexander Lambrecht (1402) on 19 May 1919 at Sterling, Colorado, USA. She died on 21 Dec 1985 at Julesburg, Colorado, USA, at age 84.

i) Sally[7] Lambrecht (1405) married Roy Luke (1443).

ii) Irene[7] Lambrecht (1403) married Gene Armstrong (1440) before 1960. She married Thomas Ward (1441) after 1960.

iii) Mary[7] Lambrecht (1404) married (--?--) Plagman (1442).

iv) Peter[7] Lambrecht (3029) was born on 13 Nov 1920 at Topeka, Kansas, USA.

v) Alexander J.[7] Lambrecht (1406) was born on 2 Jul 1922 at Iliff, Colorado, USA. He married Joletta May McArtor (1444) on 25 Jun 1944 at Julesburg, Colorado, USA. He married Joanne Petterson (1470) on 2 Feb 1976. He died on 25 Jul 1999 at Ovid, Colorado, USA, at age 77.

(a) Richard Lee[8] Lambrecht (1445) married Georgia Adele Ross (1446). He was born on 11 Dec 1944 at Sterling, Colorado, USA.

i) Christopher[9] Lambrecht (1447) ii) Richard[9] Lambrecht (1448)

(b) Patricia Ann[8] Lambrecht (1449) married James Mark Hodges (1450). She married Delbert Deckard (1455). She was born on 22 Nov 1947 at Ovid, Colorado, USA.

i) Troy[9] Hodges (1451) was born on 11 Jun 1968. He married Nikki Lynn Owings (1452) on 16 Oct 1994.

(a) Kelsey Ann[10] Hodges (1453) was born on 23 May 1995 at Sterling, Colorado, USA.

(b) Todd Logan[10] Hodges (1454) was born on 18 Dec 1997 at Sterling, Colorado, USA.

(c) Cynthia Louise[8] Lambrecht (1456) married Kenneth Harold Brown (1457). She was born on 16 Nov 1948 at Ovid, Colorado, USA. She married William Dale Wilber (1461) in Dec 1985.

i) William Brian[9] Wilber (1458) was born on 22 Apr 1966 at Julesburg, Colorado, USA.

ii) Robert Rhine[9] Wilber (1459) was born on 27 Aug 1968 at Great Lakes Naval Hospital, Illinois, USA.

iii) Aaron Matthew[9] Brown (1460) was born on 2 Jun 1975.

(d) James William[8] Lambrecht (1462) was born on 5 May 1950 at Ovid, Colorado, USA. He married Glenda Kay Myers (1463) in May 1971. He married Terry Diane Dusterhoff (1465) in Apr 1977. He married Katherine Ann Sandquist (1468) on 12 Mar 1992 at Julesburg, Colorado, USA.

i) Bradley Steven[9] Lambrecht (1464) was born on 18 Feb 1973 at Fullerton, California, USA.

ii) Jessica Diane[9] Lambrecht (1466) was born on 10 Oct 1979 at Orange, California, USA.

iii) Jennifer Diane[9] Lambrecht (1467) was born on 9 Feb 1982 at Julesburg, Colorado, USA.

iv) Abigail Lea[9] Lambrecht (1469) was born on 16 Jul 1986 at Ogallala, Nebraska, USA.

vi) Betty Jane[7] Lambrecht (1471) was born on 26 Dec 1933 at Julesburg, Colorado, USA. She married Bernard A. Powell (1472) on 24 Oct 1952.

(a) Deborah Ann[8] Powell (1473) was born on 21 Apr 1953 at Julesburg, Colorado, USA. She married Kent Inouye (1474) on 30 Dec 1971 at Fort Collins, Colorado, USA.

i) Melissa Ann[9] Inouye (1475) was born on 18 Jul 1972 at Fort Collins, Colorado, USA.

ii) Matthew Ruchi[9] Inouye (1476) was born on 1 Apr 1977 at Sterling, Colorado, USA.

iii) Mason Akio[9] Inouye (1477) was born on 1 Nov 1979 at Sterling, Colorado, USA.

iv) Megan I.[9] Inouye (1478) was born on 28 Oct 1981 at Sterling, Colorado, USA.

(b) Denise Jane[8] Powell (1479) was born on 14 May 1955 at Julesburg, Colorado, USA. She married Jim Blake (1480) on 6 May 1979.

i) Joseph Paul[9] Blake (1481) was born on 29 May 1983 at Greeley, Colorado, USA.

(c) David Bernard[8] Powell (1482) was born on 3 Oct 1956 at Julesburg, Colorado, USA. He married Pat Schwynoch (1483), daughter of Isidore Stang (1484) and Mildred Little (1485), on 11 Jun 1977 at Julesburg, Colorado, USA.

    i) Natasha Lea[9] Powell (1486) was born on 30 Dec 1978 at Julesburg, Colorado, USA.

    ii) Nicole Amie[9] Powell (1487) was born on 24 Mar 1981 at Holyoke, Colorado, USA.

    iii) Tiffany Ann[9] Powell (1488) was born on 19 May 1983 at Holyoke, Colorado, USA.

(b) Katarina Barbara[6] Gerk (1331) was born on 2 Aug 1903 at Marienfeld, Saratov, RUS. She married Josef Francis Stremel (1341), son of Jakob Stremel (1342) and Katarina Kisser (1343), in Sep 1922 at Colorado, USA. She died on 1 Aug 1997 at Fort Collins, Colorado, USA, at age 93.

i) Joseph Francis[7] Stremel (1407) was born on 7 Nov 1922. He died on 13 Dec 1922.

ii) John[7] Stremel (1408) was born on 10 May 1924. He died on 3 Apr 1926 at age 1.

iii) Edward Peter[7] Stremel (1409) was born on 7 Jul 1926 at Denver, Colorado, USA. He married Roseann Pintarelli (1410) on 7 Jan 1950 at Denver, Colorado, USA.

    (a) Luann[8] Stremel (1411) married Allen Jackson (1489). She married Bryon Benton (1491). She was born on 6 Feb 1955 at Denver, Colorado, USA.

        i) Belinda[9] Jackson (1490) was born on 20 Jan 1986 at Denver, Colorado, USA.

    (b) Kristine[8] Stremel (1412) was born on 25 Jun 1957 at Denver, Colorado, USA.

    (c) Joann[8] Stremel (1413) was born on 31 May 1958 at Denver, Colorado, USA. She married Ronald Fredrick Bauer (1492) on 24 Aug 1982 at Denver, Colorado, USA.

        i) Angela Rose[9] Bauer (1493) was born on 19 Oct 1988 at Denver, Colorado, USA.

    (d) Rosemary[8] Stremel (1414) was born on 3 May 1961 at Brighton, Colorado, USA. She married Tim Healion (1494) on 28 Sep 1991 at Reno, Nevada, USA.

    (e) Joseph Edward[8] Stremel (1415) was born on 5 Jul 1962 at Brighton, Colorado, USA. He married Donna Jean Finney (1416), daughter of William Dallas Finney (1417) and Mary Eileen Houston (1418), on 18 Aug 1990.

        i) Katherine Diane[9] Stremel (1419) was born on 3 Apr 1992 at Thornton, Colorado, USA.

        ii) Alec Edward[9] Stremel (1420) was born on 11 Jul 1995 at Thornton, Colorado, USA.

iv) Catherine[7] Stremel (1421) married Joseph Piro (1422). She was born on 30 Jan 1929.

    (a) Theresa[8] Piro (1423) **(b)** Gena[8] Piro (1424)

v) Rosellia[7] Stremel (1425) married Jerry Cavanah (1426). She was born on 15 May 1932.

    (a) Kathleen[8] Cavanah (1427)

vi) Mary[7] Stremel (1428) was born on 14 Feb 1934 at Colorado, USA. She died on 28 Oct 1936 at Colorado, USA, at age 2.

vii) Gerald J.[7] Stremel (1429) was born on 29 Jul 1937. He married Sherillene Hardy (1430) on 31 Dec 1974 at Denver, Colorado, USA.

viii) Elaine[7] Stremel (1431) married Ray McCallon (1432). She was born on 29 Aug 1939.

    (a) Jeanette[8] McCallon (1433) **(b)** Kelly[8] McCallon (1434) **(c)** Carol[8] McCallon (1435)

(c) Paulina[6] Gerk (1332) was born on 1 Nov 1905 at Marienfeld, Saratov, RUS. She died in 1906 at Marienfeld, Saratov, RUS.

(d) Maria[6] Gerk (1333) was born on 6 Jun 1907 at Marienfeld, Saratov, RUS. She died on 16 Oct 1910 at Marienfeld, Saratov, RUS, at age 3.

(e) Johann[6] Gerk (1334) was born on 13 Nov 1909 at Marienfeld, Saratov, RUS. He died on 27 Jun 1924 at Sterling, Colorado, USA, at age 14.

(f) Peter John[6] Gerk (1336) was born on 22 Apr 1912 at Atwood, Colorado, USA. He married Lena Catherine Shank (1436), daughter of Jakob Shank (1437) and Julia Bellendir (1438), on 16 Jan 1934 at Julesburg, Colorado, USA. He died on 28 Jan 1991 at Holyoke, Colorado, USA, at age 78.

i) Delores Marie[7] Gerk (1439) was born on 24 Jul 1934 at Ovid, Colorado, USA. She married Delvin L. Schulz (1499) on 8 Jun 1952 at Julesburg, Colorado, USA.

(a) Marcine Lynette[8] Schulz (1500) was born on 10 Jul 1953 at Julesburg, Colorado, USA. She married Hugh Ebert (1501) on 14 Jun 1974 at Manhattan, Kansas, USA. She married William Dale Russey (1503) in 1980 at Hugo, Oklahoma, USA. She married David Earl Estep (1505) on 28 Feb 1993.

i) Karis Danielle[9] Ebert (1502) was born on 29 May 1976 at Denver, Colorado, USA.

ii) Kameron Dale[9] Russey (1504) was born on 28 Sep 1982 at Durant, Oklahoma, USA.

(b) Curtis Lawton[8] Schulz (1506) was born on 27 Sep 1954 at Julesburg, Colorado, USA. He married Karen Smith (1507), daughter of Rayburn C. Smith Smith (1508) and Glenna Tipon (1509), on 31 Dec 1977 at Hugo, Oklahoma, USA. He married Brenda Kay Secrest (1511) on 23 Dec 1983 at Holly, Colorado, USA.

i) Kylee Nicole[9] Schulz (1510) was born on 28 Mar 1979 at Paris, Texas, USA.

(c) Peggy Annette[8] Schulz (1512) was born on 13 Oct 1955 at Julesburg, Colorado, USA. She married Kevin Rolfe Yorks (1513) on 12 Jan 1980.

i) Kelsey Angeline[9] Yorks (1514) was born on 25 Mar 1984 at Everett, Washington, USA.

ii) Kalen Marie[9] Yorks (1515) was born on 4 Nov 1985 at Everett, Washington, USA.

(d) Clayton Leniel[8] Schulz (1516) was born on 3 Nov 1960 at Julesburg, Colorado, USA. He married Denise Rachelle Cooley (1517), daughter of Jackie Lee Cooley (1520) and Shirley Boone (1521), on 2 Feb 1980.

i) Jason Leniel[9] Schulz (1518) was born on 28 Aug 1980 at Hugo, Oklahoma, USA.

ii) Nathan Curtis[9] Schulz (1519) was born on 29 May 1982 at Hugo, Oklahoma, USA.

ii) Raymond Peter[7] Gerk (1495) was born in Mar 1936 at Ovid, Colorado, USA. He married Carolella K. Fender (1527) on 3 Feb 1962.

(a) Shelley Ray[8] Gerk (1528) was born on 29 Nov 1962 at Julesburg, Colorado, USA. She married Burt Augustine Heinrich (1529), son of Roy Lee Thomas Heinrich (1618) and Therese Mathilda Bacak (1619), on 14 Feb 1989 at Las Vegas, Nevada, USA.

i) Heath Thomas[9] Heinrich (1616) was born on 4 Oct 1989 at Lubbock, Texas, USA.

ii) Lauren Reed[9] Heinrich (1617) was born on 20 May 1994 at Lubbock, Texas, USA.

(b) Shannon Renee[8] Gerk (1530) was born on 11 Jul 1965 at Hereford, Texas, USA.

(c) Shyla Reed[8] Gerk (1531) was born on 13 Jan 1969 at Hereford, Texas, USA.

iii) Robert Lee[7] Gerk (1496) was born on 11 Dec 1938 at Ovid, Colorado, USA. He married Elaine Loralie Rethmeier (1532) on 19 Jan 1963 at Julesburg, Colorado, USA. He died on 20 Nov 2002 at Holyoke, Colorado, USA, at age 63.

(a) Mark Robert[8] Gerk (1533) was born on 20 Apr 1964 at Hereford, Texas, USA. He married Edwina Jean Voth (7579) on 26 Aug 1989 at Phillips, CO, USA.

(b) Casey Scott[8] Gerk (1534) was born on 18 Jun 1966 at Hereford, Texas, USA. He married Hollie Lynn Eurich (3016) on 15 Nov 1986 at Colorado, USA.

(c) Brad Lee[8] Gerk (1535) was born on 8 Mar 1968 at Hereford, Texas, USA. He married Christina L. Mayhugh (3017) on 23 Aug 1993 at Colorado, USA.

iv) James Edward[7] Gerk (1497) was born on 23 Nov 1940 at Julesburg, Colorado, USA. He married Carolyn Ruth Blochowitz (1536), daughter of George Frederick Blochowitz (1537) and Julia Helen Lanckriet (1538), on 29 Aug 1964 at Julesburg, Colorado, USA. He died on 15 Aug 2017 at Julesburg, CO, USA, at age 76.

(a) Brian James[8] Gerk (1539) was born on 12 Aug 1965 at Hereford, Texas, USA. He married Cindy L Bennett (3020) on 6 Feb 1990 at Denver, Colorado, USA.

(b) Stephanie Sue[8] Gerk (1540) was born on 8 Sep 1966 at Hereford, Texas, USA. She married Richard Sanger (1541) on 20 Aug 1988 at Julesburg, Colorado, USA.

   i) Collin[9] Sanger (1542)

v) Judith Ann[7] Gerk (1498) married John Grahl (1543). She was born on 6 Dec 1944 at Julesburg, Colorado, USA.

   (a) Matthew[8] Grahl (1544) **(b)** Nancy[8] Grahl (1545)

vi) Penny Janelle[7] Gerk (1522) was born on 16 Jan 1962 at Julesburg, Colorado, USA. She married Stacy Lee Bennett (1523) on 5 Mar 1983. She married Shawn Kirk Spurlin (1526) on 3 Jan 1997.

   (a) Tanner Lee[8] Bennett (1524) was born on 10 Mar 1987.

   (b) Will Lucas[8] Bennett (1525) was born on 12 Jun 1990.

(g) Infant Boy[6] Gerk (1546) was born on 11 Dec 1914 at Julesburg, Colorado, USA. He died on 11 Dec 1914 at Julesburg, Colorado, USA.

(h) Isidore John[6] Gerk (1295) was born on 31 Oct 1915 at Sterling, Colorado, USA. He married Mary Catherine Lechman (1296), daughter of Joseph Lechman (1297) and Anna Catherine Bieber (1298), on 20 Jan 1941 at Julesburg, Colorado, USA. He married Darlien Marie Lyons (1560), daughter of Lloyd Harry Lyons (1561) and Anna Marie Niewohner (1562), on 26 Jun 1982 at Julesburg, Colorado, USA. He died on 28 Dec 2004 at Julesburg, Colorado, USA, at age 89.

i) Leonard[7] Gerk (1299) was born on 7 Nov 1941 at Ovid, Colorado, USA. He married Jo Beth Gass (1300) on 24 Oct 1966 at Big Spring, Texas, USA.

   (a) Melissa Elizabeth[8] Gerk (1547) was born on 21 Mar 1969 at Big Spring, Texas, USA. She died on 21 Mar 1969 at Big Spring, Texas, USA.

   (b) Kimberly Dione[8] Gerk (1301) was born on 9 Apr 1971 at Denver, Colorado, USA. She married Damon R. Lona (1302) on 16 Sep 1995 at Las Vegas, Nevada, USA.

      i) Danac R[9] Lona (1548) was born on 26 Feb 2000 at Wheat Ridge, Colorado, USA.

ii) Marilyn Anne[7] Gerk (1303) was born on 3 Feb 1944 at Ovid, Colorado, USA. She married James Frank Fender (1304) on 26 Jan 1963 at Julesburg, Colorado, USA.

   (a) Carla Kay[8] Fender (1312) was born on 24 Jun 1963 at Julesburg, Colorado, USA. She married Scott Charles Weiss (1313) on 29 Aug 1988 at Aurora, Colorado, USA.

   (b) Ronda Kay[8] Fender (1314) was born on 4 Jan 1965 at Julesburg, Colorado, USA. She married James Stutzman (1315) on 24 Aug 1985 at Julesburg, Colorado, USA.

      i) Emily Anne[9] Stutzman (1549) was born on 29 Aug 1994 at Las Vegas, Nevada, USA.

   (c) Julia Ann[8] Fender (1316) was born on 19 Apr 1966 at Julesburg, Colorado, USA. She married Paul Sharp (1317) on 3 Jun 1989 at Greeley, Colorado, USA.

      i) Alllison Michelle[9] Sharp (1550) was born on 26 Sep 1995 at Fort Morgan, Colorado, USA.

      ii) Trevor Ryan[9] Sharp (1551) was born on 27 Jan 1998 at Fort Collins, Colorado, USA.

   (d) Tricia Ann[8] Fender (1318) was born on 15 May 1970 at Julesburg, Colorado, USA. She married John J. Haggerty (1552) on 29 Aug 1993 at Fort Collins, Colorado, USA. She married Geoffrey Sean Webb (1553) on 10 Dec 1998 at Las Vegas, Nevada, USA.

iii) Rose Mary[7] Gerk (1305) was born on 20 Mar 1947 at Julesburg, Colorado, USA. She married Charles Terrance Lankford (1306) on 3 Jul 1970 at Lubbock, Colorado, USA.

   (a) John[8] Lankford (1319) was born on 20 Jan 1971 at Lubbock, Texas, USA. He died on 17 Feb 1973 at Dallas, Texas, USA, at age 2.

   (b) Lisa Christine[8] Lankford (1320) was born on 23 May 1975 at Corsicana, Texas, USA. She married Daniel James Robillard (1554) on 13 Sep 1997 at Davis, California, USA.

iv) Allan John[7] Gerk (1307) was born on 11 Mar 1949 at Julesburg, Colorado, USA. He married Carol Jean Carson (1555) on 1 Jan 1996.

v) Catherine Anne[7] Gerk (1308) was born on 17 Feb 1954 at Julesburg, Colorado, USA. She married Lonnie Ray Wegman (1309) on 8 Mar 1975 at Julesburg, Colorado, USA.

(a) Robert Ray^8 Wegman (1323) was born on 28 Oct 1975 at Julesburg, Colorado, USA.

(b) Michael James^8 Wegman (1324) was born on 21 Jan 1977 at Julesburg, Colorado, USA.

(c) Elizabeth Anne^8 Wegman (1325) was born on 20 Jul 1978 at Julesburg, Colorado, USA.

vi) Isidore John^7 Gerk (1310) was born on 14 Jan 1956 at Julesburg, Colorado, USA. He married Delberta Harris (1311), daughter of Delbert Alan Harris (1556) and Alice Mae Haag (1557), on 14 Sep 1974 at North Platte, Nebraska, USA. He married Darlien M Rewinkee (3019) on 26 Jun 1982 at Colorado, USA.

(a) Johanna^8 Gerk (1321) was born on 11 Feb 1975 at North Platte, Nebraska, USA. She married Neil Brian Davis (1322) on 2 Jul 1995 at Julesburg, Colorado, USA.

i) Justin Brian^9 Davis (1558) was born on 30 May 1996 at Lawton, Oklahoma, USA.

ii) Brianna Mae^9 Davis (1559) was born on 6 Nov 1999 at Lawton, Oklahoma, USA.

(i) Rose Margaret^6 Gerk (1563) was born on 17 Nov 1917 at Iliff, Colorado, USA. She married Frank Anthony Byers (1564) on 11 Oct 1976 at Honolulu, Hawaii, USA.

(j) Alexander John^6 Gerk (1565) was born on 27 Aug 1919 at Iliff, Colorado, USA. He married Dorothy Ann Weems (1566) on 8 Jul 1951 at Julesburg, Colorado, USA. He died on 14 Apr 1992 at Greeley, Colorado, USA, at age 72.

i) John Kent^7 Gerk (1567) was born on 18 May 1952 at Julesburg, Colorado, USA. He married Patricia Ann Sanger (1568) on 7 Dec 1975 at Colorado, USA. He married Tracy Ann Bennett (1569) on 8 Aug 1985 at Kauai, Hawaii, USA. He died on 25 Feb 2015 at Julesburg, CO, USA, at age 62.

(a) Jack Bradley Loyal^8 Gerk (1570) was born at Julesburg, Colorado, USA.

(b) Alexander Dakota^8 Gerk (1571) was born on 26 Nov 1989 at Julesburg, Colorado, USA.

(c) Haley Virginia^8 Gerk (1572) was born on 25 Apr 1991 at Julesburg, Colorado, USA.

(d) John Stryder^8 Gerk (1573) was born on 19 Sep 1996 at Julesburg, Colorado, USA.

ii) Stephen Alexander^7 Gerk (1574) was born on 15 Feb 1954 at Denver, Colorado, USA. He married Denise JoDean Weitzel (1575) on 8 Aug 1981 at Sterling, Colorado, USA.

(a) Cristopher Ryan^8 Gerk (1576) was born on 3 Mar 1982 at Sterling, Colorado, USA.

(b) Tyler Stephan^8 Gerk (1577) was born on 23 Oct 1983 at Sterling, Colorado, USA.

(c) Lynlee Kay^8 Gerk (1578) was born on 13 Apr 1988 at Sterling, Colorado, USA.

(d) Jeromy^8 Gerk (1579) was born on 8 Sep 1990 at Sterling, Colorado, USA.

(e) Spencer Morgan^8 Gerk (1580) was born on 14 Jul 1993 at Sterling, Colorado, USA.

(f) Kyle Joseph^8 Gerk (1581) was born on 19 Jan 1995 at Sterling, Colorado, USA.

iii) Kathleen Sue^7 Gerk (1582) was born on 2 Mar 1955 at Julesburg, Colorado, USA. She married Danny Emerald Orcutt (1583) on 29 Mar 1974 at Big Springs, Nebraska, USA.

(a) Heidi Ann^8 Orcutt (1584) was born on 23 Mar 1975 at Longmont, Colorado, USA. She married Armondo Figaroa (1585) on 27 Dec 1996 at Las Vegas, Nevada, USA.

i) Isaac Michael^9 Figaroa (1586) was born on 13 Sep 1996 at Greeley, Colorado, USA.

(b) Jeffrey Dan^8 Orcutt (1587) was born on 26 Nov 1977 at Longmont, Colorado, USA.

(c) Katie Sue^8 Orcutt (1588) was born on 21 Mar 1978 at Longmont, Colorado, USA.

(k) Twin Girls^6 Gerk (1589) was born in 1920 at Iliff, Colorado, USA. She died in 1920 at Iliff, Colorado, USA.

(l) Sylvester Michael^6 Gerk (1590) was born on 27 Jul 1922 at Iliff, Colorado, USA. He married Louis Pidgeon (5810) in 1946 at Julesburg, CO, USA. He died on 19 Apr 2009 at Julesburg, CO, USA, at age 86.

i) Jennifer^7 Gerk (5811) **ii)** Bruce^7 Gerk (5812) **iii)** Carol^7 Gerk (5813)

iv) Greg^7 Gerk (5815) **v)** Kenneth Michael^7 Gerk (5814) was born on 29 Dec 1953 at CO, USA. He died on 28 Dec 2014 at Julesberg, CO, USA, at age 60.

(m) Beatrice Ann^6 Gerk (1591) was born on 20 Jul 1924 at Red Lion, Colorado, USA.

(n) Baby Girl[6] Gerk (1592) was born on 18 Jan 1926 at Sedgwick, Colorado, USA. She died on 24 Jan 1926 at Sedgwick, Colorado, USA.

(11) Josef[5] Gerk (741) was born on 27 Jul 1878 at Marienfeld, Saratov, RUS. He married Katarina Naab (2222), daughter of Kaspar Naab (2223) and Magdalena Hollmann (2224), on 29 Oct 1902 at Marienfeld, Saratov, RUS. He immigrated on 15 Apr 1908. He died on 25 Jan 1935 at Marienfeld, Stalingrad Oblast, USSR, at age 56.

(a) Rosa[6] Gerk (2284) was born on 18 Aug 1903 at Marienfeld, Saratov, RUS. She died on 12 Aug 1910 at Marienfeld, Saratov, RUS, at age 6.

(b) Rosalia[6] Gerk (2285) was born on 14 Oct 1905 at Marienfeld, Saratov, RUS. She married Adam Hollmann (3469) in 1926 at Marienfeld, Stalingrad Oblast, USSR. She died in 1983 at Omsk Oblast, USSR.

   i) Katarina[7] Hollmann (3477) was born in 1929 at Marienfeld, Stalingrad Oblast, USSR.

   ii) Maria[7] Hollmann (3478) was born in 1933 at Marienfeld, Stalingrad Oblast, USSR.

   iii) Rosa[7] Hollmann (3479) was born in 1935 at Marienfeld, Stalingrad Oblast, USSR.

   iv) Irma[7] Hollmann (3480) was born in 1941 at Marienfeld, Stalingrad Oblast, USSR.

   v) Emma[7] Hollmann (3481) was born in 1947 at Omsk Oblast, USSR.

   vi) Johann[7] Hollmann (3482) was born in 1950 at Omsk Oblast, USSR. He married Alexandra (--?--) (6437) in 1972 at USSR.

      (a) Wjatscheslav[8] Hollmann (6438) was born in 1973 at USSR.

      (b) Oleg[8] Hollmann (6439) was born in 1977 at USSR.

      (c) Valentin[8] Hollmann (6440) was born in 1986 at USSR.

(c) Georg[6] Gerk (2286) married Natalia Kissner (3226). He was born on 19 Aug 1907 at Marienfeld, Saratov, RUS. He died in 1989 at Doguschaivka, Kazakstan, USSR.

   i) Rosa[7] Gerk (3483) married (--?--) Koval (3513). She was born in 1937 at Balzer, Saratov, USSR.

      (a) Natalia[8] Koval (3514) was born in 1959 at Odessa, USSR.

   ii) Erna[7] Gerk (3484) married (--?--) Wiede (3515). She was born in 1939 at Balzer, Saratov, USSR.

      (a) Paulus[8] Wiede (3517) was born at USSR.

      (b) Viktor[8] Wiede (3516) was born in 1960 at USSR.

   iii) Ivan[7] Gerk (3485) was born in Nov 1941 at Kazakstan, USSR. He died in 1987 at Kazakstan, USSR.

      (a) Valeri[8] Gerk (3518) was born in 1966 at Kazakstan, USSR.

      (b) Natalia[8] Gerk (3519) was born in 1975 at Kazakstan, USSR.

   iv) Nelli[7] Gerk (3486) married (--?--) Boltach (3520). She was born in 1951 at Kazakstan, USSR.

   v) Maria[7] Gerk (3487) was born in 1954 at Kazakstan, USSR.

(d) Josef[6] Gerk (2287) was born on 3 Oct 1911 at Marienfeld, Saratov, RUS. He died in 1961 at Kazakstan, USSR.

   i) Viktor[7] Gerk (3488) was born on 14 Sep 1939 at Marienfeld, Stalingrad Oblast, USSR. He married Ella Gomer (6872) in 1961 at USSR. He died on 26 Aug 2009 at age 69.

(e) Augustine[6] Gerk (2288) married Georg Prediger (3489). She was born on 10 Feb 1913 at Marienfeld, Saratov, RUS. She died in 1990 at Omsk Oblast, USSR.

   i) Augustine[7] Prediger (3490) was born in 1938 at Marienfeld, Stalingrad Oblast, USSR.

   ii) Valentina[7] Prediger (3491) was born in 1948 at Omsk Oblast, USSR.

   iii) Viktor[7] Prediger (3492) was born in 1950 at Omsk Oblast, USSR.

   iv) Waldemar[7] Prediger (3493) was born in 1952 at Omsk Oblast, USSR.

(f) Katarina[6] Gerk (2289) married Anatoli Reznichenko (7815) at USSR. She was born on 4 Jul 1914 at Marienfeld, Saratov, RUS. She died on 16 May 1984 at Moskalevka, Kazakstan, USSR, at age 69.

    i) Ivan[7] Gerk (7816) was born on 21 May 1955 at Moscalaevka, USSR.

(g) Florian[6] Gerk (3494) was born on 12 Jun 1918 at Marienfeld, Saratov, RUS. He married Elena Sitzmann (3495) in 1941 at USSR. He died in Sep 1995 at Kopishenka, Kazakstan, USSR, at age 77.

    i) Maria[7] Gerk (3497) married Viktor Nolde (6353) at USSR. She was born on 5 Apr 1942 at Kazakstan, USSR.

        (a) Alexander[8] Nolde (6354) was born at USSR. He married Natalie (--?--) (6355) at USSR.

            i) Maria[9] Nolde (6356) was born at USSR. **ii)** Dimitri[9] Nolde (6357) was born at USSR.

        (b) Elena[8] Nolde (6358) was born at USSR. **(c)** Vladimir[8] Nolde (6359) was born at USSR.

        (d) Eduard[8] Nolde (6360) was born at USSR.

    ii) Irina[7] Gerk (3498) was born on 1 Feb 1948 at Kazakstan, USSR.

    iii) Waldemar[7] Gerk (3499) married Lili Stern (4020). He was born on 7 Jan 1952 at Kazakstan, USSR. He died on 13 Sep 2010 at Semiozerny, RUS, at age 58.

        (a) Natali[8] Gerk (4021) was born on 23 Aug 1977 at Kazakstan, USSR. She married Vladimir Schäfer (6350) circa 1998.

            i) Alina[9] Schäfer (6351) was born on 27 Jan 1999.

            ii) Hanna-Sofie[9] Schäfer (6352) was born on 17 Nov 2001.

    iv) Alexander[7] Gerk (3500) was born on 11 May 1954 at Kazakstan, USSR. He married Marina Schust (4015) in 1973.

        (a) Irina[8] Gerk (4016) was born in 1973 at Kazakstan, USSR.

        (b) Natalia[8] Gerk (4017) was born in 1974 at Kazakstan, USSR.

        (c) Svetlana[8] Gerk (4018) was born in 1978 at Kazakstan, USSR.

        (d) Alexander[8] Gerk (4019) was born on 27 Apr 1981 at Kazakstan, USSR.

    v) Viktor[7] Gerk (3501) married Lidia Rube (4022). He was born on 25 Mar 1957 at Moskalovka, Kustanai, Kazakstan, USSR.

        (a) Stefan[8] Gerk (4023) was born on 31 May 1985 at Kazakstan, USSR.

        (b) Eduard[8] Gerk (4024) was born on 2 Apr 1988 at Kazakstan, USSR.

(h) Johannes[6] Gerk (3502) married Elena (--?--) (3503) at USSR. He was born in 1921 at Marienfeld, Saratov, USSR. He died in 1991 at Rudni, Kustanai, Kazakstan, USSR.

    i) Valeri[7] Gerk (3496) was born in 1945 at Kazakstan, USSR. He died in 1988 at Kazakstan, USSR.

    ii) Galina[7] Gerk (3504) was born in 1948 at Kazakstan, USSR.

    iii) Olga[7] Gerk (3505) was born in 1958 at Kazakstan, USSR.

(i) Anna[6] Gerk (3506) was born on 29 Sep 1924 at Marienfeld, Stalingrad Oblast, USSR. She married Andreas Reich (3507) circa 1945 at USSR. She died on 16 Sep 1989 at USSR at age 64.

    i) Viktor[7] Gerk (3508) was born on 24 May 1946 at Kazakstan, USSR. He married Eugenia Konichina (4025) in 1969 at USSR.

        (a) Tatjana[8] Gerk (4026) married Marat Migal (6361). She was born in 1970 at Aschchabad, Turkmenistan, USSR.

            i) Viktor[9] Migal (6362) **ii)** Michael[9] Migal (6363) **iii)** Mark[9] Migal (6364)

        (b) Andrej[8] Gerk (4027) was born in 1972 at Aschchabad, Turkmenistan, USSR.

        (c) Alexej[8] Gerk (4028) was born in 1976 at Aschchabad, Turkmenistan, USSR.

        (d) Dmitri[8] Gerk (4029) was born in 1986 at Aschchabad, Turkmenistan, USSR.

ii) Irina[7] Reich (3509) married Viktor Gobel (6365) at USSR. She was born on 19 May 1948 at Kazakstan, USSR. She died in Jul 2011 at age 63.

   (a) Valentina[8] Gobel (6366) was born at USSR.

   (b) Alexander[8] Gobel (6367) was born at USSR.

   (c) Anna[8] Gobel (7825) was born on 14 May 1990 at USSR. She died on 19 Jul 2013 at age 23.

iii) Waldemar[7] Reich (3510) married Valentina Sanina (6368). He was born on 27 May 1951 at Kazakstan, USSR. He died on 14 Dec 2016 at Flensberg, GER, at age 65.

   (a) Anton[8] Reich (6369) was born at USSR.

   (b) Dimitri[8] Reich (6370) was born at USSR.

iv) Alexander[7] Reich (3511) was born on 1 Sep 1952 at Kazakstan, USSR. He married Galina Antimonova (6371) circa 1975 at USSR.

   (a) Anna[8] Reich (6372) was born on 23 Jan 1976 at USSR.

   (b) Laura[8] Reich (6373) married Dominique Schneider (6374). She was born on 4 Feb 1979 at USSR.

   (c) Viktoria[8] Reich (6375) was born on 8 Mar 1988 at USSR.

v) Maria[7] Reich (3512) was born on 21 Oct 1954 at Kazakstan, USSR. She married Rafael Hammel (6376) in 1976 at USSR.

   (a) Eugenia[8] Hammel (6382) married Juri Will (6383).

   (b) Andreas[8] Hammel (6377) was born on 23 Aug 1977 at USSR. He married Xenia (--?--) (6378) on 16 Nov 2002.

      i) Daniel[9] Hammel (6379) was born on 5 Dec 2005.

      ii) Adrian[9] Hammel (6380) was born on 28 Jan 2011.

   (c) Viktor[8] Hammel (6381) was born on 11 Aug 1988 at USSR.

(12) Adam[5] Gerk (2936) was born on 26 Sep 1883 at Marienfeld, Saratov, RUS.

(13) Anna[5] Gerk (2937) was born on 13 Aug 1886 at Marienfeld, Saratov, RUS. She died on 19 Dec 1887 at Marienfeld, Saratov, RUS, at age 1.

(14) Anna Maria[5] Gerk (2938) was born on 22 Dec 1888 at Marienfeld, Saratov, RUS. She married Peter Leichtling (2941), son of Adam Leichtling (2942) and Margareta Holman (2943), on 23 Jan 1906 at Marienfeld, Saratov, RUS.

   (a) Adam[6] Leichtling (2944) was born on 7 Nov 1908 at Marienfeld, Saratov, RUS.

(15) Johannes[5] Gerk (2940) was born on 7 Feb 1892 at Marienfeld, Saratov, RUS. He died on 6 Sep 1895 at Marienfeld, Saratov, RUS, at age 3.

(16) Dorothea[5] Gerk (2939) was born on 15 Mar 1895 at Marienfeld, Saratov, RUS.

(17) Johannes[5] Gerk (4195) was born on 12 May 1899 at Marienfeld, Saratov, RUS.

3. Heinrich[3] Gerk (574) was born in 1799 at Koehler, Saratov, RUS. He married Kristina Ziegler (590) in 1819 at Koehler, Saratov, RUS. He married Elisabetha Rupp (4196) on 24 May 1843 at Koehler, Saratov, RUS. He died on 10 Sep 1848 at Koehler, Saratov, RUS.

   a) Katarina[4] Gerk (592) was born in 1819 at Koehler, Saratov, RUS. She married Peter Bellendir (4203), son of Johan Georg Bellendir (5577), on 31 Jan 1839 at Koehler, Saratov, RUS.

   (1) Peter[5] Bellendir (4258) was born in 1842 at Koehler, Saratov, RUS.

   (2) Johannes[5] Bellendir (4259) was born in 1846 at Koehler, Saratov, RUS.

   (3) Josef[5] Bellendir (6739) was born in 1872 at Koehler, Saratov, RUS. He married Eva Rohwein (6709), daughter of Johann Adam Rohwein (618) and Susanna Benz (972), on 3 Nov 1892 at Josefstal, Saratov, RUS.

b) Valentin⁴ Gerk (591) was born in 1821 at Koehler, Saratov, RUS. He married Katarina Mildenberger (595) in 1841 at Koehler, Saratov, RUS. He married Maria Eva Graf (650), daughter of Heinrich Graf (7801) and Anna Maria Plaz (7802), on 26 Nov 1846 at Semenovka, Saratov, RUS. He died circa 1885 at Rozhdestvenskoye, Stavropol, RUS.

(1) Peter⁵ Gerk (3049) was born on 11 Oct 1842 at Koehler, Saratov, RUS. He died on 29 Jul 1848 at Koehler, Saratov, RUS, at age 5.

(2) Anna Maria⁵ Gerk (3050) was born on 20 Nov 1843 at Koehler, Saratov, RUS.

(3) Peter⁵ Gerk (596) was born in 1848 at Koehler, Saratov, RUS.

(4) Jacob⁵ Gerk (1959) was born on 12 Aug 1850 at Koehler, Saratov, RUS. He married Anastasia Roth (3414), daughter of Nikolaus Roth (7796) and Marie Anna Schaeffer (7797), on 6 Oct 1873 at Ekaterinodar, Stavropol, RUS. He married Otilia Koehler (1960), daughter of Andreas Koehler (1983) and Anna Koch (1984), on 3 Nov 1882 at Semenovka, Stavropol, RUS. He died on 2 Dec 1935 at Yankton, South Dakota, USA, at age 85.

(a) Jacob⁶ Gerk (1961) married Mabel Estelle Eaton (3402) at USA. He was born on 12 Nov 1880 at Stavropol, RUS. He died on 27 Nov 1941 at San Diego, California, USA, at age 61.

(b) Anna Elisabeth⁶ Gerk (1962) was born on 7 Jun 1883 at Stavropol, RUS. She married John Joseph McInerney (1963) on 9 Oct 1899 at Yankton, South Dakota, USA. She married John Baptiste Brigel (8081) on 8 Apr 1911 at Toronto, ON, CAN. She died on 14 Apr 1963 at Los Angeles, California, USA, at age 79.

(c) Peter James⁶ Gerk (1964) was born on 16 Sep 1888 at Tres Arroyos, Buenos Aires, ARG. He married Agnes Eleanore Knutson (1980) in 1919. He died on 16 Nov 1960 at Minneapolis, Minnesota, USA, at age 72.

i) Donald James⁷ Gerk (1981) was born on 23 Mar 1923 at Minneapolis, Minnesota, USA. He married Elaine Naomi Stennes (3604) on 21 May 1949 at MN, USA.

(a) Richard Bruce⁸ Gerk (3605) was born on 17 Nov 1950 at Mineapolis, Minnesota, USA.

(b) Barbara Lorraine⁸ Gerk (3606) was born on 29 Aug 1952 at Mineapolis, Minnesota, USA.

(c) Nancy Joyce⁸ Gerk (3608) was born on 9 Mar 1955 at Mineapolis, Minnesota, USA.

(d) Carolyn Jean⁸ Gerk (3607) was born on 26 Feb 1958 at Mineapolis, Minnesota, USA. She died on 21 Dec 1980 at Mineapolis, Minnesota, USA, at age 22.

ii) Robert Eugene⁷ Gerk (1982) was born on 19 Feb 1928 at Minneapolis, Minnesota, USA. He married Gloria Marie Carpentier (3167), daughter of Peter Lucien J. Carpentier (3190) and Nellie Delia Durand (3191), in 1950 at Minneapolis, Minnesota, USA. He died on 22 Aug 2007 at Green Valley, AZ, USA, at age 79.

(a) Cheryl Diane⁸ Gerk (3192) was born on 6 Sep 1950 at Mineapolis, Minnesota, USA. She married Robert Dingle (3194) in Jul 1971 at USA.

i) Christopher⁹ Dingle (3195) **ii)** Johnathan⁹ Dingle (3196)

(b) Cathy Marie⁸ Gerk (3193) was born on 1 May 1952 at Mineapolis, Minnesota, USA.

(d) Charles Valentine⁶ Gerk (1965) was born on 5 Mar 1890 at Tres Arroyos, Buenos Aires, ARG. He married Anna Stella Pesek (1966), daughter of Frank Pesek (3399), on 4 Sep 1911 at Yankton, South Dakota, USA. He died on 2 Jan 1967 at Spokane, Washington, USA, at age 76.

i) Corma Ethel⁷ Gerk (2679) was born on 17 Aug 1914 at Miles City, Montana, USA. She married Robert A. Schick (3413) on 8 May 1943 at Seattle, WA, USA. She died on 26 Sep 2011 at Seattle, WA, USA, at age 97.

ii) Lorna Anastasia⁷ Gerk (2680) was born on 21 Jun 1916 at Miles City, Montana, USA. She married William Elberson (3411) on 21 May 1941 at Deer Lodge, Montana, USA. She died on 3 Nov 2016 at Sandy, OR, USA, at age 100.

(a) Lynette Anne⁸ Elberson (3457) was born on 16 Jan 1941 at Deer Lodge, Montana, USA.

(b) Leslie Rosa⁸ Elberson (3458) was born on 5 Oct 1945 at Spokane, Washington, USA.

(c) William⁸ Elberson (3459) was born on 18 Jul 1946 at Deer Lodge, Montana, USA.

(e) William Philip⁶ Gerk (1967) was born on 5 Aug 1892 at Liverpool, England. He married Alice Shay (3463) on 4 Nov 1923 at Yankton, South Dakota, USA. He died on 18 Jan 1941 at South Sioux City, Nebraska, USA, at age 48.

(f) Christine Katherine[6] Gerk (1968) was born on 31 Jan 1894 at Yankton, South Dakota, USA. She married George Davies (1969), son of Carl Davies (1970) and Anna Meier (1971), on 5 May 1917 at Yankton, South Dakota, USA.

    i) Nadine[7] Davies (3397) was born in 1915 at Yankton, South Dakota, USA.

    ii) Anton P.[7] Davies (1972) was born on 8 Apr 1915 at Yankton, South Dakota, USA. He married Delora A Peterson (6393) on 26 Oct 1935 at Yankton, SD, USA. He died on 24 Apr 1950 at age 35.

        (a) Terrell Lee[8] Davies (3437) was born at USA.

        (b) Robert Allen[8] Davies (3438) was born at USA.

    iii) Harold[7] Davies (2656) was born on 20 Mar 1918 at Yankton, South Dakota, USA. He died on 2 May 1967 at Los Angeles, California, USA, at age 49.

        (a) Todd Wesley[8] Davies (3436) was born on 12 Jun 1948 at USA.

    iv) Ethel[7] Davies (2657) was born on 8 Jan 1920 at Rouse, South Dakota, USA. She married John E. Meyers (6394) on 21 Sep 1938 at Yankton, SD, USA. She died on 12 Apr 2009 at Santa Rosa, CA, USA, at age 89.

    v) Carl[7] Davies (3398) was born on 15 Aug 1922 at Yankton, South Dakota, USA. He died on 28 Jan 1983 at Los Angeles, CA, USA, at age 60.

(g) Maria[6] Gerk (1973) was born on 9 Mar 1897 at Yankton, South Dakota, USA. She married Maurice Koontz (2658) in 1915. She died in 1969 at Littleton, Colorado, USA.

(h) Clara[6] Gerk (1974) was born on 15 Jan 1899 at Yankton, South Dakota, USA. She married Fred Moderegger (1975), son of Frank Moderegger (1976) and Maria Hotzsinger (1977), on 2 Nov 1913 at Yankton, South Dakota, USA.

    i) Blanche Madonna[7] Moderegger (2691) was born on 20 Apr 1916 at Sioux City, IA, USA. She died on 2 Dec 1997 at USA at age 81.

    ii) Marguerite Blanche[7] Moderegger (2692) was born on 1 Aug 1918 at Sioux City, Iowa, USA. She married Don Lynberg (7606) on 5 Jun 1937 at Union, SD, USA. She died on 7 Mar 1989 at Benton, OR, USA, at age 70.

    iii) Lucile Clara Lucille[7] Moderegger (2693) was born on 15 Aug 1920 at Sioux City, Iowa, USA. She married Francis Knutson (7882) on 18 Dec 1937 at Onawa, IA, USA. She died on 24 Oct 2007 at Costa Mesa, CA, USA, at age 87.

(i) John Arthur[6] Gerk (1978) was born on 9 Jul 1901 at Yankton, South Dakota, USA. He married Rose Dost (2659), daughter of Ottomar Bruno Dost (7597), on 10 Sep 1923 at Chicago, Illinois, USA. He died on 22 May 1979 at Garland, Arkansas, USA, at age 77.

    i) Richard[7] Gerk (2660) was born on 5 Jul 1924 at Columet, Illinois, USA. He died on 3 May 1995 at Garland, Arkansas, USA, at age 70.

(j) Joseph Casper[6] Gerk (1979) was born on 24 Jun 1905 at Yankton, South Dakota, USA. He married Ila Goyler (3396) circa 1926 at USA. He married Sally Siporin (7808) on 18 Sep 1945 at Los Angeles, CA, USA. He married Dorothy June Armsbury (2675), daughter of Isaac Newton Armsbury (3177) and Rosena Susan Mason (3178), on 22 Mar 1955 at Jackson, MO, USA. He died on 14 Jun 1982 at Denver, Colorado, USA, at age 76.

    i) Jack[7] Gerk (2676) was born on 27 Jul 1926 at Iowa, USA. He died on 6 Dec 1982 at Denver, Colorado, USA, at age 56.

    ii) Colleen Nora[7] Gerk (2677) was born on 15 Jan 1928 at Nebraska, USA. She married Norman Bumgardner (3389) on 21 May 1971 at Orange, CA, USA. She died on 15 May 1993 at Riverside, California, USA, at age 65.

    iii) Bonnie Lou[7] Gerk (2678) was born on 7 Oct 1929 at Auburn City, Nebraska, USA. She married Albert Vigneau (7614) on 31 Jan 1964 at Imperial, CA, USA. She died on 31 Mar 1988 at Huntington Beach, CA, USA, at age 58.

    iv) Gaylord N.[7] Gerk (3386) was born on 24 Nov 1930 at Denver, Colorado, USA. He married Mary ? (3388) in 1970 at Denver, Colorado, USA. He married Margaret A. Tricamo (3387) on 22 Aug 1980 at Arapahoe, Colorado, USA.

(5) Katarina[5] Gerk (1196) was born on 6 Apr 1852 at Marienfeld, Saratov, RUS. She died on 15 Oct 1852 at Josefstal, Saratov, RUS.

(6) Elisabeta[5] Gerk (1191) was born on 30 Oct 1853 at Marienfeld, Saratov, RUS. She married Anton Konrad (7811) on 6 Oct 1873 at Ekaterinodar, Stavropol, RUS.

(7) Katarina[5] Gerk (1192) was born on 6 Mar 1856 at Marienfeld, Saratov, RUS. She married Johannes Roth (7795), son of Nikolaus Roth (7796) and Marie Anna Schaeffer (7797), on 20 Jan 1875 at Stavropol, Stavropol, USSR.

(8) Johann[5] Gerk (1195) was born on 11 Feb 1858 at Marienfeld, Saratov, RUS.

(9) Elisabeta[5] Gerk (651) was born on 15 Aug 1860 at Marienfeld, Saratov, RUS. She married Valentin Schmidtlein (7763) on 31 Oct 1882 at Stavropol, Stavropol, RU.

    (a) Josef[6] Schmidtlein (7764) was born on 6 Feb 1902 at Rozhdestvenskoye, Stavropol, RU.

(10) Nikolaus[5] Gerk (652) was born on 15 Dec 1862 at Marienfeld, Saratov, RUS.

(11) Phillip[5] Gerk (653) was born on 22 Sep 1868 at Marienfeld, Saratov, RUS. He married Katarina Hirschfeld (7799) on 7 Oct 1893 at Rozhdestvenskoye, Stavropol, RUS.

c) Johannes[4] Gerk (1703) was born in 1826 at Koehler, Saratov, RUS. He married Katarina Schaefer (1704), daughter of Johannes Schaefer (3103) and Katarina Haberkorn (3104), on 1 Nov 1848 at Koehler, Saratov, RUS. He died on 27 May 1886 at Marienfeld, Saratov, RUS.

(1) Elisabeta[5] Gerk (1711) was born on 17 Sep 1849 at Koehler, Saratov, RUS. She married Kristof Mueller (1712), son of Andreas Mueller (2723) and Elisabeta Weigel (2724), on 15 Nov 1865 at Marienfeld, Saratov, RUS.

    (a) Johannes Peter[6] Mueller (1713) was born on 7 Aug 1866 at Marienfeld, Saratov, RUS.

    (b) Elisabeta[6] Mueller (1714) was born on 22 Jun 1868 at Marienfeld, Saratov, RUS.

    (c) Johan[6] Mueller (1715) was born on 3 Jul 1870 at Marienfeld, Saratov, RUS.

    (d) Magdalena[6] Mueller (1716) was born on 3 Sep 1872 at Marienfeld, Saratov, RUS.

    (e) Susana[6] Mueller (1717) was born on 25 Jun 1874 at Marienfeld, Saratov, RUS.

    (f) Kristina[6] Mueller (7684) was born in 1875 at Marienfeld, Saratov, RUS. She married Josef Schiefelbein (7686) in 1895 at Marienfeld, Saratov, RUS. She married Santiago Berberich (7685) on 7 Apr 1910 at Paraná, Entre Ríos, ARG. She died on 3 Sep 1929 at Valle María, Entre Ríos, ARG.

    (g) Anna Margareta[6] Mueller (1048) was born on 15 Oct 1884 at Marienfeld, Saratov, RUS. She married Jakob Mildenberger (1036), son of Jakob Mildenberger (1037) and Margaret Leichtling (1038), on 6 Dec 1900 at Marienfeld, Saratov, RUS. She died in Jul 1910 at Marienfeld, Saratov, RUS, at age 25.

      i) Rosalie[7] Mildenberger (1802) was born in 1902 at Marienfeld, Saratov, RUS. She died in 1902 at Marienfeld, Saratov, RUS.

      ii) Adam[7] Mildenberger (1718) married Anna Schoenfeld (1722), daughter of Josef Schoenfeld (1108) and Anna Margareta Burkhart (1109). He was born on 30 Sep 1903 at Marienfeld, Saratov, RUS. He died on 3 Sep 1964 at age 60.

        (a) Josef[8] Mildenberger (1732) was born on 6 May 1930. He died on 15 Jun 1995 at age 65.

        (b) Raymond[8] Mildenberger (1733) was born on 6 Nov 1936 at Brownvale, Alberta, CAN. He died in 1991.

      iii) Barbara[7] Mildenberger (1719) was born on 20 May 1905 at Marienfeld, Saratov, RUS. She married Felix Schamber (1734), son of Johannes Peter Schamber (1735) and Anna Maria Mosmann (1736), on 12 Oct 1922 at Minsk, USSR. She died on 1 Jun 1995 at Aurora, Colorado, USA, at age 90.

        (a) Baby Boy[8] Schamber (1737) was born on 2 May 1924 at Minsk, USSR. He died on 7 May 1924 at Minsk, USSR.

        (b) Josef[8] Schamber (1738) was born on 19 Mar 1925 at Minsk, USSR. He died on 27 Apr 1988 at Denver, Colorado, USA, at age 63.

        (c) Elisabeth[8] Schamber (1739) was born in Jan 1931 at Minsk, USSR. She died in Jun 1932 at Minsk, USSR, at age 1.

        (d) Elisabeth[8] Schamber (1740) was born on 22 Mar 1933 at Minsk, USSR. She died on 22 Mar 1951 at Dinkelsbuhl, Germany, at age 18.

        (e) Rosalia[8] Schamber (1741) was born on 20 Apr 1938 at Minsk, USSR. She died on 18 Jan 1980 at Georgia, USA, at age 41.

iv) Angelina^7 Mildenberger (1803) was born in 1907 at Marienfeld, Saratov, RUS. She died in 1907 at Marienfeld, Saratov, RUS.

v) Raymond^7 Mildenberger (1720) was born on 3 Sep 1908 at Marienfeld, Saratov, RUS. He married Magdalena Werner (1721) in 1932 at CAN. He died on 23 Sep 1953 at Salvador, Sask, CAN, at age 45.

  (a) Agatha^8 Mildenberger (1823) was born on 18 Aug 1932 at Primate, Sask, CAN. She married John Schreiber (1824) on 16 Apr 1952 at Denzil, Sask, CAN.

  (b) Alex^8 Mildenberger (1811) was born on 23 Dec 1933 at Primate, Sask, CAN. He married Monica Winterhault (1812) on 29 Nov 1956.

  (c) Henry^8 Mildenberger (1825) was born on 28 Jul 1935 at Primate, Sask, CAN. He married Shirley Kirwer (1826) on 6 Oct 1958 at Primate, Sask, CAN.

  (d) Mary^8 Mildenberger (1827) was born on 2 Nov 1936 at Macklin, Sask, CAN. She married Nelson Klotz (1828) on 25 Aug 1956. She married Stan Hanna (1829) on 14 Apr 1984.

  (e) Leo^8 Mildenberger (1813) was born on 22 Feb 1939 at Macklin, Sask, CAN. He married Jenny Galick (1814) on 20 Nov 1965.

    i) Jim^9 Mildenberger (1815) married Melody Cordoviz (1816) on 15 Jul 1995.

  (f) Ida^8 Mildenberger (1830) was born on 15 Aug 1941 at Macklin, Sask, CAN. She married Adolph Winterhault (1831) in 1957.

  (g) Richard^8 Mildenberger (1818) married Jean Lee (1819). He married Audrey Mayguard (1822). He was born in 1944 at Macklin, Sask, CAN.

    i) Warren^9 Mildenberger (1820) **ii)** Karen^9 Mildenberger (1821)

  (h) Ron^8 Mildenberger (1817) was born on 21 Jul 1946 at Macklin, Sask, CAN.

  (i) Rita^8 Mildenberger (1832) was born on 7 Jul 1951 at Macklin, Sask, CAN. She married Leonard Havens (1833) on 16 Aug 1969.

(h) Katarina^6 Mueller (1723) married Josef Mildenberger (1724), son of Jakob Mildenberger (1037) and Margaret Leichtling (1038), on 10 Nov 1905 at Marienfeld, Saratov, RUS. She was born on 12 Aug 1886 at Marienfeld, Saratov, RUS. She died in 1969 at Colorado, USA.

i) Katarina^7 Mildenberger (1727) was born on 16 Jul 1906 at Marienfeld, Saratov, RUS. She died on 7 Sep 1983 at age 77.

ii) Michael^7 Mildenberger (1725) was born on 12 Apr 1910 at Marienfeld, Saratov, RUS. He married Marcella Younger (1726) on 21 Nov 1932 at Iliff, Colorado, USA. He died on 27 Aug 2000 at Iliff, Colorado, USA, at age 90.

(a) Norma^8 Mildenberger (1742) **(b)** Dorothy^8 Mildenberger (1743) **(c)** Mary^8 Mildenberger (1744)

(d) Gerry^8 Mildenberger (1745) **(e)** Kenneth^8 Mildenberger (1746) **(f)** JoAnn^8 Mildenberger (1747)

 (g) Robert^8 Mildenberger (1748)

        iii) John Jakob^7 Mildenberger (1728) was born on 1 Jun 1926. He died on 23 May 1976 at age 49.

(2) Agnes^5 Gerk (1708) was born on 18 Jun 1851 at Marienfeld, Saratov, RUS. She died on 13 Oct 1852 at Marienfeld, Saratov, RUS, at age 1.

(3) Elisabeta Katarina^5 Gerk (1705) was born on 1 Sep 1853 at Marienfeld, Saratov, RUS. She married Georg Alles (2743), son of Matthew Alles (2744) and Marie Anna Millendor (2745), on 11 Apr 1875 at Marienfeld, Saratov, RUS.

  (a) Marie Anna^6 Alles (6702) was born in 1876 at Marienfeld, Saratov, RUS. She married Friedrich Holzmann (6701), son of Franz Holzmann (6699) and Katarina Elisabetha Leonardt (6700), on 20 Nov 1895 at Josefstal, Saratov, RUS. She and Friedrich Holzmann (6701) emigrated on 6 Nov 1908.

  i) Jakob^7 Holzmann (6704) was born in 1900 at Josefstal, Saratov, RUS.

  ii) Georg^7 Holzmann (6705) was born in 1902 at Josefstal, Saratov, RUS.

  iii) Josef^7 Holzmann (6706) was born in 1904 at Josefstal, Saratov, RUS.

  iv) Katarina^7 Holzmann (6703) was born on 27 Aug 1907 at Josefstal, Saratov, RUS. She died on 24 Jul 1908 at Josefstal, Saratov, RUS.

(b) Elisabeta[6] Alles (2756) was born on 1 Mar 1896 at Marienfeld, Saratov, RUS.

(4) Johannes[5] Gerk (1707) was born on 6 Aug 1855 at Marienfeld, Saratov, RUS. He died on 6 Jul 1858 at Marienfeld, Saratov, RUS, at age 2.

(5) Peter[5] Gerk (2436) was born on 17 Apr 1857 at Marienfeld, Saratov, RUS. He married Elisabeta Dietler (2461), daughter of Heinrich Dittler (2746) and Katarina Leonardt (2747), on 26 May 1877 at Marienfeld, Saratov, RUS. He married Leonora Gareis (2437), daughter of Joseph Gareis (2438) and Margareta Haspert (2439), on 18 Aug 1887 at Valle María, Entre Ríos, ARG. He died on 11 Sep 1923 at Santa Anita, Entre Ríos, ARG, at age 66.

(a) Elisabeta[6] Gerk (2462) was born on 17 Jun 1880 at Marienfeld, Saratov, RUS.

(b) Anna Maria[6] Gerk (2463) was born on 17 Sep 1882 at Marienfeld, Saratov, RUS.

(c) Johannes[6] Gerk (2464) was born on 1 Feb 1885 at Marienfeld, Saratov, RUS.

(d) Catalina[6] Gerk (2440) was born on 29 May 1888 at Colonia Gral Alvear, Entre Ríos, ARG.

(e) Adán[6] Gerk (2441) was born on 5 Feb 1890 at Valle Maria, Entre Ríos, ARG. He married Margareta Glassmann (2447), daughter of Casimiro Glassmann (6471) and Catalina Kessler (6472), on 8 Oct 1912 at Santa Anita, Entre Ríos, ARG. He died on 27 May 1959 at Santa Anita, Entre Ríos, ARG, at age 69.

i) Catalina[7] Gerk (2494) married Antonio Egel (6441) at ARG. She was born on 17 Jul 1913 at Santa Anita, Entre Ríos, ARG.

ii) Pedro[7] Gerk (2496) was born on 7 Jan 1916 at Santa Anita, Entre Ríos, ARG. He married Paulina Holzmann (2508) circa 1937 at Santa Anita, Entre Ríos, ARG. He died on 24 Aug 1976 at Santa Anita, Entre Ríos, ARG, at age 60.

(a) Celso Oscar[8] Gerk (2518) was born at Santa Anita, Entre Ríos, ARG.

(b) Hector Orlando[8] Gerk (2521) married Elisa Bach (2522) at Santa Anita, Entre Ríos, ARG. He was born on 30 Nov 1939 at Hererra, Entre Ríos, ARG.

i) Orlando Maria[9] Gerk (2546) was born at Santa Anita, Entre Ríos, ARG. He died at Santa Anita, Entre Ríos, ARG. He married Daniela Kesler (2547) at Santa Anita, Entre Ríos, ARG.

(a) Florencia[10] Gerk (2548) was born at ARG. **(b)** Agustín[10] Gerk (2549) was born at ARG.

ii) Ricardo Maria[9] Gerk (2550) was born at Santa Anita, Entre Ríos, ARG. He married Karina (--?--) (2551).

(a) Josefina[10] Gerk (2552) was born at ARG. **(b)** Catalina[10] Gerk (2553) was born at ARG.

(c) Delfina[10] Gerk (2554) was born at ARG.

(c) Hugo[8] Gerk (2519) married Ana Herlein (2520) at Santa Anita, Entre Ríos, ARG. He was born on 11 Mar 1941 at Hererra, Entre Ríos, ARG. He died on 8 Sep 1987 at Sunchales, Santa Fe, ARG, at age 46.

i) Norma[9] Gerk (2542) was born at ARG. She married Enrique (--?--) (2543) at ARG.

(a) Matias[10] (--?--) (2544) was born at ARG. **(b)** Ezequiel[10] (--?--) (2545) was born at ARG.

ii) Marcelo[9] Gerk (2541) was born in 1971 at Sunchales, Santa Fe, ARG.

(d) José Roberto[8] Gerk (2523) was born in 1942 at Hererra, Entre Ríos, ARG. He married Lucia Josefa Kloster (2524) on 22 May 1971 at Entre Ríos, ARG.

i) Mariana[9] Gerk (2555) married Marcelo Barrios (2556). She was born on 21 Aug 1976 at Buenos Airies, ARG.

(a) Maria Sol[10] Barrios (2557) was born on 6 Oct 2001 at Buenos Airies, ARG.

ii) Silvina[9] Gerk (2558) was born on 7 Dec 1978 at Buenos Airies, ARG.

(e) Blas Horacio[8] Gerk (2516) was born on 10 Sep 1944 at Santa Anita, Entre Ríos, ARG.

(f) Mario Ismael[8] Gerk (2513) was born on 20 Aug 1945 at Santa Anita, Entre Ríos, ARG. He married María Inmaculada Kloster (2514) on 7 Feb 1970 at Santa Anita, Entre Ríos, ARG.

i) Hernon Mario[9] Gerk (2536) was born on 15 Nov 1970 at Santa Anita, Entre Ríos, ARG. He married Lorena Cecilia Basgall (2537) on 1 May 1999 at Santa Anita, Entre Ríos, ARG.

(a) Santiago[10] Gerk (2538) was born on 8 Oct 1999 at Santa Anita, Entre Ríos, ARG.

(b) Emiliano[10] Gerk (2539) was born on 2 Jul 2001 at Santa Anita, Entre Ríos, ARG.

ii) Cristian Ismael[9] Gerk (2540) was born on 14 Nov 1977 at José C. Paz, Buenos Airies, ARG.

(g) Delia Maria[8] Gerk (2525) married Eugenio Jacob (2526) at Santa Anita, Entre Ríos, ARG. She was born on 16 Feb 1947 at Santa Anita, Entre Ríos, ARG.

i) Gerardo Ignacio[9] Jacob (2559) married Carina (--?--) (2560). He was born on 23 Jul 1970 at Santa Anita, Entre Ríos, ARG.

ii) Hugo Ernesto[9] Jacob (2561) married Gisela (--?--) (2562) at ARG. He was born on 14 Nov 1974 at Santa Anita, Entre Ríos, ARG.

(h) Ruben[8] Gerk (3007) was born on 30 Mar 1947 at Santa Anita, Entre Ríos, ARG. He died on 21 Aug 1993 at Santa Anita, Entre Ríos, ARG, at age 46.

(i) Arsenio Ruben[8] Gerk (2515) was born on 30 Apr 1948 at Santa Anita, Entre Ríos, ARG. He died on 21 Aug 1993 at Las Piur, Córdoba, ARG, at age 45.

(j) Father Carlos Eugenio[8] Gerk (2517) was born on 23 Jul 1949 at Santa Anita, Entre Ríos, ARG.

iii) Luisa[7] Gerk (2493) married Agustin Holzman (2507) at Santa Anita, Entre Ríos, ARG. She was born on 26 Nov 1917 at Santa Anita, Entre Ríos, ARG.

iv) Matilde Serafina[7] Gerk (2499) was born on 8 Aug 1924 at Santa Anita, Entre Ríos, ARG. She married Cipriano Gerstner (2510) on 17 Jun 1945 at Santa Anita, Entre Ríos, ARG. She died on 22 Feb 2005 at Santa Anita, Entre Ríos, ARG, at age 80.

(a) Horacio Cipriano[8] Gerstner (3564) married Antonia Catalina Perticaro (6442). He was born on 27 Aug 1946 at Buenos Aires, ARG.

i) Silvia Alejandra[9] Gerstner (6443) married Fernando Suárez (6444). She was born on 2 Nov 1969 at S. Fernando.

ii) Luis Alberto[9] Gerstner (6445) married Natalia Chiariano (6446). He was born on 24 Nov 1974 at S. Fernando.

(a) Guillermo Gabriel[10] Gerstner (6447) was born on 7 Oct 2002 at S. Isidro, Buenos Aires, ARG.

(b) Plácido[8] Gerstner (3565) married Ana Antonia Real (6448). He was born on 15 Mar 1948 at Buenos Aires, ARG.

i) Vanina Pamela[9] Gerstner (6449) married Fabián Goñi (6450). She was born on 14 Jan 1975 at V. López, Buenos Aires, ARG.

ii) Jésica Romina[9] Gerstner (6451) was born on 16 Mar 1979 at ARG.

iii) Fernando Esteban[9] Gerstner (6452) was born on 2 Oct 1980 at ARG.

iv) Plácido Federico[9] Gerstner (6453) was born on 3 Feb 1984 at ARG.

(c) Nélida María[8] Gerstner (3566) married Juan Carlos Naimo (6454). She was born on 11 Sep 1949 at Buenos Aires, ARG.

i) Gustavo Javier[9] Naimo (6455) married Leda de los Santos Márquez (6456). He was born on 26 Mar 1944 at ARG.

(a) Pedro Manuel[10] Naimo (6457) was born on 27 Sep 2000 at ARG.

ii) Cintia Carina[9] Naimo (6458) married Gerardo Mayer (6459). She was born on 9 Apr 1975 at Buenos Aires, ARG.

(d) Elsa Ofelia[8] Gerstner (3567) married Néstor Alberto Silva (6460). She was born on 22 Aug 1951 at S. Fernando, Buenos Aires, ARG.

i) Diego Martín[9] Silva (6461) was born on 10 Jan 1976 at S. Fernando, Buenos Aires, ARG.

ii) Cristian Gonzalo[9] Silva (6462) was born on 16 Oct 1980 at S. Fernando, Buenos Aires, ARG.

(e) Oscar Ernesto[8] Gerstner (3568) married Liliana Marta Fanego (6463) at ARG. He was born on 11 May 1953 at Buenos Aires, ARG. He died on 12 Mar 2004 at S. Fernando, Buenos Aires, ARG, at age 50.

    i) Romina Soledad[9] Gerstner (6464) was born on 15 Aug 1982 at S. Fernando, Buenos Aires, ARG.

    ii) Camilia[9] Gerstner (6465) was born on 12 Aug 1997 at S. Fernando, Buenos Aires, ARG.

    iii) Valentín Ignacio[9] Gerstner (6466) was born on 7 Mar 2000 at S. Fernando, Buenos Aires, ARG.

(f) Carlos Ricardo[8] Gerstner (3569) married Mónica Fanego (6467). He was born on 11 Mar 1955 at San Fernando, Buenos Aires, ARG.

    i) Rodrigo Sebastián[9] Gerstner (6468) was born on 7 Jun 1982 at ARG.

(g) Margarita Catalina[8] Gerstner (3570) married Pascual Ernesto Thomas (6469) at ARG. She was born on 17 Feb 1962 at San Fernando, Buenos Aires, ARG.

    i) Julieta Yanina[9] Thomas (6470) was born on 14 Jul 1986 at Gral. Pacheco, Buenos Aires, ARG.

v) Angela[7] Gerk (2501) was born on 15 Feb 1928 at Santa Anita, Entre Ríos, ARG. She married Abel Gerstner (2511) circa 1948 at Santa Anita, Entre Ríos, ARG.

(a) Héctor[8] Gerstner (3470) married Cristina Gómez (6402). He was born on 26 Mar 1949 at Buenos Aires, ARG.

    i) Martín[9] Gerstner (6403) was born on 5 Apr 1975 at Buenos Aires, ARG.

    ii) Marcelo[9] Gerstner (6404) was born on 9 Apr 1976 at Buenos Aires, ARG.

    iii) Cristian[9] Gerstner (6405) was born on 8 Aug 1978 at Buenos Aires, ARG.

    iv) Elizabeth[9] Gerstner (6406) was born on 24 Sep 1985 at Buenos Aires, ARG.

(b) Hugo[8] Gerstner (3471) was born on 19 Nov 1950 at Buenos Aires, ARG. He married Ana Ledesma (6407) in 1984 at ARG.

    i) Santiago Hugo[9] Gerstner (6408) was born on 18 Jan 1985 at Buenos Aires, ARG.

    ii) Pablo[9] Gerstner (6409) was born on 14 Jan 1986 at Buenos Aires, ARG.

    iii) Belén[9] Gerstner (6410) was born on 15 Dec 1987 at Buenos Aires, ARG.

    iv) Federico[9] Gerstner (6411) was born on 6 Jul 1990 at Buenos Aires, ARG.

(c) Olga[8] Gerstner (3472) was born on 8 Apr 1954 at Buenos Aires, ARG. She married Igancio Ábalo (6412) in 1976 at ARG.

    i) Alfredo Jose[9] Ábalo (6413) was born on 22 Aug 1976 at Buenos Aires, ARG.

    ii) Hugo Ignacio[9] Ábalo (6414) was born on 8 Sep 1978 at Buenos Aires, ARG.

    iii) Natalia Soledad[9] Ábalo (6415) was born on 4 Sep 1983 at Buenos Aires, ARG.

(d) Estela[8] Gerstner (3473) was born on 7 Oct 1958 at Buenos Aires, ARG. She married Eduardo González (6416) in 1989 at ARG.

    i) Mariel[9] González (6417) was born on 6 Sep 1989 at Buenos Aires, ARG.

    ii) Mauricio[9] González (6418) was born on 28 Nov 1990 at Buenos Aires, ARG.

(e) Fernando[8] Gerstner (3474) married Cecilia Soledad Schmitt (6419) at ARG. He was born on 14 Jan 1970 at Buenos Aires, ARG.

vi) Rosa Estela[7] Gerk (2500) was born on 18 Apr 1926 at Santa Anita, Entre Ríos, ARG. She died on 29 Sep 1982 at Santa Anita, Entre Ríos, ARG, at age 56.

vii) Ema[7] Gerk (2502) was born at Santa Anita, Entre Ríos, ARG.

viii) Vilvaldo[7] Gerk (2505) was born on 4 Sep 1919 at Santa Anita, Entre Ríos, ARG. He married Cunigunda Rohr (2506) on 8 Sep 1942 at Santa Anita, Entre Ríos, ARG. He died on 1 Jul 1987 at Santa Anita, Entre Ríos, ARG, at age 67.

(a) Imelda[8] Gerk (2527) was born at Santa Anita, Entre Ríos, ARG. She married Vicente Ekardt (2528) at Santa Anita, Entre Ríos, ARG.

(b) Hector[8] Gerk (2530) was born on 27 Mar 1945 at Santa Anita, Entre Ríos, ARG.

(c) Elsa Alicia[8] Gerk (2529) was born on 15 Feb 1947 at Santa Anita, Entre Ríos, ARG. She died on 30 May 1979 at Santa Anita, Entre Ríos, ARG, at age 32.

(d) Elva Maria[8] Gerk (2531) married Mario Herlein (2532) at Santa Anita, Entre Ríos, ARG. She was born on 3 Jul 1950 at Santa Anita, Entre Ríos, ARG.

(e) Rosita Estela[8] Gerk (2533) was born on 20 Apr 1952 at Santa Anita, Entre Ríos, ARG. She died on 11 Dec 1954 at Santa Anita, Entre Ríos, ARG, at age 2.

(f) Olga[8] Gerk (2534) was born on 19 Jul 1957 at Santa Anita, Entre Ríos, ARG. She married Juan Sommer (2535) on 9 Feb 1980 at Santa Anita, Entre Ríos, ARG.

ix) Josefina[7] Gerk (2495) was born on 10 Nov 1921 at Santa Anita, Entre Ríos, ARG.

x) Magdalena[7] Gerk (2503) was born on 2 Aug 1936 at Santa Anita, Entre Ríos, ARG. She died on 15 Apr 1978 at Santa Anita, Entre Ríos, ARG, at age 41.

xi) Antonia[7] Gerk (2497) was born at Santa Anita, Entre Ríos, ARG. She married Ernesto Klug (2509) at Santa Anita, Entre Ríos, ARG.

xii) Margarita[7] Gerk (2504) was born at Santa Anita, Entre Ríos, ARG. She married Remigio Klug (2512) at Santa Anita, Entre Ríos, ARG.

(f) Annamaria[6] Gerk (6225) was born on 3 May 1892 at Valle Maria, Entre Ríos, ARG.

(g) Margarita[6] Gerk (2442) was born on 19 Oct 1893 at Colonia Gral Alvear, Entre Ríos, ARG. She married José Glassmann (2448) on 8 Oct 1912 at Santa Anita, Entre Ríos, ARG. She died on 11 Feb 1968 at Santa Anita, Entre Ríos, ARG, at age 74.

i) Juana[7] Glassmann (6505) was born at Santa Anita, Entre Ríos, ARG. She died on 19 May 1923 at Santa Anita, Entre Ríos, ARG.

(h) Ana Maria[6] Gerk (6496) was born on 8 Apr 1895 at Valle Maria, Entre Ríos, ARG.

(i) Catalina[6] Gerk (2443) was born on 24 May 1896 at Colonia Gral Alvear, Entre Ríos, ARG. She married Santiago Schaefer (2444) on 15 Feb 1916 at Santa Anita, Entre Ríos, ARG. She died on 26 Sep 1970 at Santa Anita, Entre Ríos, ARG, at age 74.

(j) Juan[6] Gerk (2563) was born on 26 Jun 1898 at Santa Anita, Entre Ríos, ARG. He married Catalina Becher (2564) on 28 Jul 1920 at Santa Anita, Entre Ríos, ARG. He died on 8 Apr 1954 at Santa Anita, Entre Ríos, ARG, at age 55.

i) Maria[7] Gerk (2565) married José Egel (2566) at Santa Anita, Entre Ríos, ARG. She was born on 5 Sep 1921 at Santa Anita, Entre Ríos, ARG.

ii) Crecencia[7] Gerk (2567) married Eduardo Holzman (2568) at Santa Anita, Entre Ríos, ARG. She was born on 30 Nov 1922 at Santa Anita, Entre Ríos, ARG.

iii) Juan Pedro[7] Gerk (2583) married Ana Riedel (2584) at Santa Anita, Entre Ríos, ARG. He was born on 5 Mar 1924 at Santa Anita, Entre Ríos, ARG. He died on 4 May 1998 at Santa Anita, Entre Ríos, ARG, at age 74.

(a) Leonilda[8] Gerk (2588) married Luis Kranevitter (2589) at Santa Anita, Entre Ríos, ARG. She was born on 16 Jul 1947 at Santa Anita, Entre Ríos, ARG.

(b) Delia[8] Gerk (2590) was born on 14 Jul 1951 at Santa Anita, Entre Ríos, ARG. She married Narcizo Honeker (2591) on 29 Apr 1972 at Santa Anita, Entre Ríos, ARG.

i) Pablo[9] Honeker (2592) was born at Santa Anita, Entre Ríos, ARG.

ii) Martin[9] Honeker (2593) was born at Santa Anita, Entre Ríos, ARG.

(c) Elba[8] Gerk (2594) married (--?--) Basgall (2595) at Santa Anita, Entre Ríos, ARG. She was born on 15 Sep 1952 at Santa Anita, Entre Ríos, ARG.

(d) Roque[8] Gerk (2596) married Lucia Sacks (2597) at Santa Anita, Entre Ríos, ARG. He was born on 20 May 1954 at Santa Anita, Entre Ríos, ARG.

i) Walter[9] Gerk (2598) was born on 22 May 1983 at Santa Anita, Entre Ríos, ARG.

ii) Erika[9] Gerk (2599) was born on 16 Oct 1986 at Santa Anita, Entre Ríos, ARG.

iv) Regina[7] Gerk (2569) married Jorge Holzman (2570) at Santa Anita, Entre Ríos, ARG. She was born on 24 Jun 1925 at Santa Anita, Entre Ríos, ARG.

v) Dolores[7] Gerk (2571) married (--?--) Riedell (2572) at Santa Anita, Entre Ríos, ARG. She was born on 13 Aug 1926 at Santa Anita, Entre Ríos, ARG.

vi) Margareta[7] Gerk (2573) married (--?--) Bailman (2574) at Santa Anita, Entre Ríos, ARG. She was born on 25 Jun 1928 at Santa Anita, Entre Ríos, ARG.

vii) Elisa[7] Gerk (2575) married (--?--) Bailman (2576) at Santa Anita, Entre Ríos, ARG. She was born on 7 Jan 1930 at Santa Anita, Entre Ríos, ARG.

viii) Catalina[7] Gerk (2577) married (--?--) Bailman (2578) at Santa Anita, Entre Ríos, ARG. She was born on 1 Sep 1931 at Santa Anita, Entre Ríos, ARG.

ix) Apolonia[7] Gerk (2579) married Tuto Gerber (2580) at Santa Anita, Entre Ríos, ARG. She was born on 23 Sep 1933 at Santa Anita, Entre Ríos, ARG.

x) Juan Miguel[7] Gerk (2585) was born on 4 May 1935 at Santa Anita, Entre Ríos, ARG. He married Flora Herlein (2586) on 4 Apr 1959 at Santa Anita, Entre Ríos, ARG. He died on 8 Nov 1977 at Santa Anita, Entre Ríos, ARG, at age 42.

   (a) Hector Omar[8] Gerk (2600) was born on 11 Apr 1962 at Santa Anita, Entre Ríos, ARG. He married Maria Kloster (2601) on 9 May 1992 at Santa Anita, Entre Ríos, ARG.

   i) Nancy Vanesa[9] Gerk (2605) was born on 17 Sep 1993 at Santa Anita, Entre Ríos, ARG.

   ii) Dario Miguel[9] Gerk (2602) was born on 12 Feb 1995 at Santa Anita, Entre Ríos, ARG.

   iii) Diego Martin[9] Gerk (2604) was born on 17 Aug 1996 at Santa Anita, Entre Ríos, ARG.

   iv) Danilo Manuel[9] Gerk (2603) was born on 13 Jan 1998 at Santa Anita, Entre Ríos, ARG.

   (b) Ismael[8] Gerk (2606) was born on 27 Dec 1967 at Santa Anita, Entre Ríos, ARG. He died on 18 Apr 1969 at Santa Anita, Entre Ríos, ARG, at age 1.

xi) Adan Agustin[7] Gerk (2587) was born on 21 Nov 1936 at Santa Anita, Entre Ríos, ARG. He died on 9 Jul 2001 at Santa Anita, Entre Ríos, ARG, at age 64.

xii) Amalia[7] Gerk (2581) married Martin Jacob (2582) at Santa Anita, Entre Ríos, ARG. She was born on 26 Jun 1938 at Santa Anita, Entre Ríos, ARG.

(k) Ana[6] Gerk (2445) was born on 20 Jan 1900 at Valle Maria, Entre Ríos, ARG. She married Benedicto Mohr (2446) on 12 Nov 1918 at Santa Anita, Entre Ríos, ARG.

(l) Anna Margareta[6] Gerk (2491) was born on 7 Jul 1901 at Santa Anita, Entre Ríos, ARG. She married Adan Holzmann (2492) circa 1921 at Santa Anita, Entre Ríos, ARG.

   i) Gaspar[7] Holzmann (6504) was born in Aug 1921 at Santa Anita, Entre Ríos, ARG. He died on 17 Aug 1921 at Santa Anita, Entre Ríos, ARG.

(m) Helena[6] Gerk (6497) was born on 20 Dec 1902 at Santa Anita, Entre Ríos, ARG.

(n) Barbara[6] Gerk (6498) was born on 30 Jul 1904 at Santa Anita, Entre Ríos, ARG.

(o) Nicolas[6] Gerk (2466) was born on 7 Jul 1905 at Santa Anita, Entre Ríos, ARG. He married Catalina Schaab (2467) on 21 Oct 1930 at Santa Anita, Entre Ríos, ARG. He died on 9 Aug 1943 at Santa Anita, Entre Ríos, ARG, at age 38.

   i) José Nicolas[7] Gerk (2468) was born on 4 Dec 1931 at Santa Anita, Entre Ríos, ARG. He married Clara Bach (2469) on 21 Apr 1956. He died on 7 Mar 1966 at Santa Anita, Entre Ríos, ARG, at age 34.

   (a) Graciela[8] Gerk (2482) was born on 21 Oct 1963 at Santa Anita, Entre Ríos, ARG. She married Esteban Gomez (2483) on 10 Nov 1984 at ARG.

   ii) Leonilda[7] Gerk (2470) married Juan Kloster (2471). She was born on 15 Apr 1935 at Santa Anita, Entre Ríos, ARG.

   iii) Josefa[7] Gerk (2472) married Adan Bach (2473) at Santa Anita, Entre Ríos, ARG. She was born on 29 Nov 1936 at Santa Anita, Entre Ríos, ARG.

iv) Antonio[7] Gerk (2474) was born on 24 Jul 1939 at Santa Anita, Entre Ríos, ARG. He married Irma Weinzentel (2475) on 21 Apr 1965 at Santa Anita, Entre Ríos, ARG.

(a) Ernesto[8] Gerk (2484) married Silvano Risposi (2487). He was born on 17 Jun 1968 at Santa Anita, Entre Ríos, ARG.

i) Augustino[9] Gerk (2607) was born at Basavilbaso, Entre Ríos, ARG.

ii) Gonzalo[9] Gerk (2608) was born at Basavilbaso, Entre Ríos, ARG.

(b) Marcelo[8] Gerk (2486) married Debora Kadrel (2489). He was born on 6 Apr 1973 at Santa Anita, Entre Ríos, ARG.

(c) Maria del Carmen[8] Gerk (2485) married Claudio Gomez (2488). He was born on 1 Apr 1976 at Santa Anita, Entre Ríos, ARG.

i) Gaston[9] Gerk (2609) **ii)** Candela[9] Gerk (2610) **iii)** Felipe[9] Gerk (2611)

v) Oscar Carlos[7] Gerk (2476) was born on 6 Jan 1942 at Santa Anita, Entre Ríos, ARG. He married Ofelia Kloster (2477) on 17 Feb 1968 at Santa Anita, Entre Ríos, ARG.

(a) Sonia María[8] Gerk (2478) was born on 20 Oct 1969 at Santa Anita, Entre Ríos, ARG. She married Alberto Kloster (2479) on 18 Dec 1993 at Santa Anita, Entre Ríos, ARG.

(b) Miriam Elizabeth[8] Gerk (2480) married Fabian Reidel (2481) at Santa Anita, Entre Ríos, ARG. She was born on 24 Mar 1972 at Santa Anita, Entre Ríos, ARG.

(p) Rosa[6] Gerk (3572) was born on 12 Mar 1907 at Santa Anita, Entre Ríos, ARG.

(q) Barbara[6] Gerk (2490) was born on 6 Mar 1909 at Santa Anita, Entre Ríos, ARG.

(r) Elisa[6] Gerk (2612) was born on 14 Jan 1911 at Santa Anita, Entre Ríos, ARG. She died in 2001 at Chile.

(6) Klara[5] Gerk (1706) was born on 27 Mar 1859 at Marienfeld, Saratov, RUS. She married Jakob Greber (2189), son of Jakob Greber (2190) and Marianne Lell (2191), on 17 Jan 1883 at Marienfeld, Saratov, RUS.

(a) Magdalena[6] Greber (2307) was born on 6 Jan 1896 at Marienfeld, Saratov, RUS.

(b) Katarina[6] Greber (2305) was born on 12 Sep 1898 at Marienfeld, Saratov, RUS.

(c) Katarina[6] Greber (2306) was born on 12 May 1900 at Marienfeld, Saratov, RUS.

(7) Katarina[5] Gerk (1709) was born on 7 Mar 1867 at Marienfeld, Saratov, RUS.

d) Anna Margareta[4] Gerk (593) was born on 30 Sep 1828 at Koehler, Saratov, RUS. She married Johannes Alles (4199), son of Matias Alles (2727) and Marianna Wachmeister (2728), on 9 Nov 1848 at Koehler, Saratov, RUS.

(1) Margareta[5] Alles (4252) was born in 1853 at Pfeifer, Saratov, RUS.

(2) Katarina[5] Alles (7708) died at Josefstal, Saratov, RUS. She was born in 1857 at Marienfeld, Saratov, RUS. She married Jakob Wagner (4651), son of Valentin Wagner (4645) and Dorothea Dreser (4646), on 6 Nov 1878 at Josefstal, Saratov, RUS.

(a) Marianna[6] Wagner (7706) was born in 1883 at Josefstal, Saratov, RUS. She married Jorge Jacob (7707) on 16 Aug 1916 at Crespo, Entre Ríos, ARG.

(b) Anna Maria[6] Wagner (4737) was born in 1885 at Josefstal, Saratov, RUS. She married Josef Blattner (4736), son of Johan Georg Blattner (3707) and Anna Elisabeta Burghardt (4345), on 27 Oct 1902 at Josefstal, Saratov, RUS.

i) Andreas[7] Blattner (5920) was born in 1903 at Josefstal, Saratov, RUS.

ii) Katharina[7] Blattner (5921) was born in 1905 at Josefstal, Saratov, RUS. She married Ignacio Jacob (7703) on 21 Feb 1922 at Crespo, Entre Ríos, ARG.

iii) Josef[7] Blattner (5401) was born on 28 Sep 1907 at Josefstal, Saratov, RUS. He died on 31 Dec 1908 at Crespo, Entre Ríos, ARG, at age 1.

iv) Juliana[7] Blattner (7704) was born on 25 Jan 1909 at Crespo, Entre Ríos, ARG. She married J Jacob (7983) on 24 Apr 1931 at Crespo, Entre Ríos, ARG.

(c) Kaspar[6] Wagner (4825) was born on 2 Oct 1887 at Josefstal, Saratov, RUS. He married Anna Maria Reising (4837) on 27 Oct 1908 at Josefstal, Saratov, RUS. He immigrated on 2 Feb 1909.

(3) Johannes[5] Alles (7761) was born in 1859 at Marienfeld, Saratov, RUS. He married Susanna Stremel (7762), daughter of Nikolaus Stremel (777) and Barbara Mildenberger (778), on 6 Nov 1878 at Marienfeld, Saratov, RUS.

e) Barbara[4] Gerk (4198) was born on 27 Jan 1831 at Koehler, Saratov, RUS.

f) Maria Katarina[4] Gerk (594) was born on 26 May 1833 at Koehler, Saratov, RUS. She married Josef Buss (3563), son of Johannes Buss (3529) and Ekaterina Seibert (3530), on 28 Nov 1851 at Koehler, Saratov, RUS.

    (1) Teresa[5] Buss (3580) was born in 1855 at Semenovka, Saratov, RUS.

    (2) Jakob[5] Buss (4633) was born on 26 Jul 1860 at Semenovka, Saratov, RUS.

g) Margareta[4] Gerk (4200) was born in 1835 at Koehler, Saratov, RUS.

h) Teresia[4] Gerk (3686) was born on 3 Sep 1837 at Koehler, Saratov, RUS. She married Johann Leonardt (4204), son of Franz Leonardt (8172) and Konstansia Kloster (8173), on 11 Oct 1855 at Koehler, Saratov, RUS.

    (1) Josef[5] Leonardt (4895) was born on 18 Mar 1861 at Semenowka, Saratov, RUS. He married Anna Margareta Zink (4896), daughter of Peter Zink (5366) and Barbara Lell (5367), on 13 Nov 1884 at Josefstal, Saratov, RUS. He died in 1941 at USSR.

        (a) Julia Elisabeth[6] Leonardt (4360) was born on 10 Feb 1885 at Marienfeld, Saratov, RUS. She married Kristof Weigel (4358), son of Kaspar Weigel (2203) and Margareta Mitsig (2204), on 17 Jun 1908 at Josefstal, Saratov, RUS. She died on 5 Mar 1953 at Albert lea, Minn, USA, at age 68.

            i) Ida[7] Weigel (4370) was born on 22 Mar 1909 at Josefstal, Saratov, RUS. He died on 25 Mar 1909 at Josefstal, Saratov, RUS.

            ii) Juliana[7] Weigel (4380) was born on 27 Jul 1910 at Josefstal, Saratov, RUS.

            iii) Nikolaus[7] Weigel (4381) was born on 16 Apr 1911 at Josefstal, Saratov, RUS. He died on 30 May 1912 at Topeka, Kansas, USA, at age 1.

            iv) Anna Margaret[7] Weigel (4904) was born on 2 Jul 1913 at Topeka, KS, USA.

            v) Joseph[7] Weigel (4905) was born on 12 May 1915 at Topeka, KS, USA. He died on 9 Dec 1994 at Albuquerque, NM, USA, at age 79.

            vi) John James[7] Weigel (4906) was born on 19 Apr 1917 at Topeka, KS, USA. He died on 7 May 1973 at USA at age 56.

            vii) Joseph Sylvester[7] Weigel (4907) was born on 30 Apr 1919 at Topeka, KS, USA.

            viii) Francis James[7] Weigel (4908) was born on 15 Jul 1921 at Topeka, KS, USA.

            ix) Dominic Joseph[7] Weigel (4909) was born on 4 Nov 1922 at Topeka, KS, USA.

            x) Paul Francis[7] Weigel (4910) was born on 20 Nov 1924 at Topeka, KS, USA.

            xi) Catherine Francis[7] Weigel (4911) was born on 1 Jan 1927 at Albert Lea, MN, USA.

            xii) Marie Rose[7] Weigel (4912) was born on 18 Mar 1928 at Albert Lea, MN, USA.

            xiii) Adam Joseph[7] Weigel (4913) was born on 14 Nov 1930 at Albert Lea, MN, USA.

        (b) Johannes[6] Leonardt (424) was born in 1890 at Josefstal, Saratov, RUS. He married Maria Gerk (412), daughter of Johann Georg Gerk (404) and Anna Margareta Rohwein (405), in Jan 1923 at Josefstal, Saratov, RUS. He died in 1932 at Josefstal, Saratov, USSR.

            i) Anna[7] Leonardt (474) (see above)

            ii) Palina[7] Leonardt (475) (see above)

        (c) Adam[6] Leonardt (5549) was born in 1892 at Josefstal, Saratov, RUS.

        (d) Anna[6] Leonardt (5550) was born in 1894 at Josefstal, Saratov, RUS.

        (e) Susanna[6] Leonardt (5548) was born in 1896 at Josefstal, Saratov, RUS.

        (f) Josef[6] Leonardt (4897) was born on 30 Apr 1897 at Josefstal, Saratov, RUS. He married Katarina Sachs (4898) in 1923 at Josefstal, Stalingrad, USSR. He married Juliana Urich (4900), daughter of Andrei Urich (4914) and Barbara Wagner (4915), in 1934 at Josefstal, Stalingrad, USSR. He died in 1954 at USSR.

            i) Paul[7] Leonardt (4899) was born on 24 Jun 1925 at Josefstal, Stalingrad, USSR.

ii) Leo[7] Leonardt (4901) was born in 1938 at Josefstal, Stalingrad, USSR. He died in 2007.

iii) Ida[7] Leonardt (4902) was born in 1941 at Josefstal, Stalingrad, USSR.

iv) Eduard[7] Leonardt (4903) married Nina Fadeeva (5371). He was born in 1947 at USSR. He died in 2007.

    (a) Swetlana[8] Leonardt (5372) was born in 1969 at USSR.

    (b) Julia[8] Leonardt (5373) was born in 1974 at USSR.

(2) Agatha[5] Leonardt (6757) was born in 1866 at Semenovka, Saratov, RUS. She married Michael Adam Rohwein (5041), son of Michael Adam Rohwein (6735) and Katarina Schaefer (6736), on 26 May 1886 at Josefstal, Saratov, RUS. She married Peter Alois Ringelmann (6781), son of Johannes Ringelmann (6782) and Agnes Berg (6783), on 8 Jan 1893 at Josefstal, Saratov, RUS.

    (a) Peter[6] Rohwein (6761) was born on 25 Aug 1887 at Josefstal, Saratov, RUS.

    (b) Jakob[6] Rohwein (5043) was born on 30 May 1890 at Josefstal, Saratov, RUS.

(3) Johannes[5] Leonardt (6914) was born in 1875 at Semenowka, Saratov, RUS. He married Anna Margareta Dieser (6083), daughter of Anton Dieser (5960) and Anna Marie Reising (5961), on 17 Jan 1906 at Semenowka, Saratov, RUS.

i) Johannes[4] Gerk (727) was born on 26 Aug 1839 at Koehler, Saratov, RUS. He married Marianna Rosskoph (728), daughter of Peter Rosskoph (3072) and Anna Maria Bretiger (3073), on 17 Nov 1859 at Marienfeld, Saratov, RUS. He died on 12 Jul 1866 at Marienfeld, Saratov, RUS, at age 26.

    (1) Heinrich[5] Gerk (726) was born on 3 Nov 1860 at Marienfeld, Saratov, RUS. He married Christina Bahl (787), daughter of Johannes Bahl (788) and Ottilia Stremel (789), on 26 Jan 1887 at Marienfeld, Saratov, RUS.

    (2) Maria Anna[5] Gerk (729) was born on 26 Apr 1864 at Marienfeld, Saratov, RUS. She married Adam Weinbinder (767), son of Johannes Weinbinder (768) and Elisabetha Groh (769), on 24 Nov 1888 at Marienfeld, Saratov, RUS.

j) Maria Margareta[4] Gerk (4201) was born on 29 Nov 1844 at Koehler, Saratov, RUS.

k) Eva Elisabetha[4] Gerk (4202) was born on 9 Feb 1846 at Semenovka, Saratov, RUS.

4. Zacharius[3] Gerk (1690) was born in 1812 at Koehler, Saratov, RUS. He married Barbara Helmer (1691) on 30 Jan 1834 at Koehler, Saratov, RUS. He died on 30 Sep 1882 at Koehler, Saratov, RUS.

a) Elisabeta[4] Gerk (1692) was born on 9 Nov 1834 at Koehler, Saratov, RUS. She married Anton Haspert (4137) on 31 Jan 1855 at Koehler, Saratov, RUS. She died on 21 Jan 1856 at Koehler, Saratov, RUS, at age 21.

b) Katarina[4] Gerk (4138) was born on 4 Oct 1836 at Koehler, Saratov, RUS. She married Jakob Schmidt (4139) on 31 Jan 1855 at Koehler, Saratov, RUS. She died on 28 Oct 1863 at Koehler, Saratov, RUS, at age 27.

c) Anna Maria[4] Gerk (4205) was born on 1 Feb 1839 at Koehler, Saratov, RUS. She married Johann Koehler (4206) on 18 Jan 1860 at Koehler, Saratov, RUS.

d) Anna Maria[4] Gerk (1694) was born on 12 Dec 1840 at Koehler, Saratov, RUS. She married Peter Koehler (4140) on 29 Jan 1863 at Koehler, Saratov, RUS.

e) Heinrich[4] Gerk (1695) was born on 7 Apr 1846 at Koehler, Saratov, RUS. He married Anna Margareta Schectel (3704) on 29 Jan 1863 at Koehler, Saratov, RUS.

    (1) Peter[5] Gerk (4209) was born in 1864 at Koehler, Saratov, RUS. He died on 22 Jul 1865 at Koehler, Saratov, RUS.

    (2) Johann[5] Gerk (4221) was born on 8 May 1866 at Koehler, Saratov, RUS. He married Barbara Leinacker (4222) on 27 Nov 1884 at Koehler, Saratov, RUS.

        (a) Barbara[6] Gerk (4227) was born on 17 Apr 1885 at Koehler, Saratov, RUS. She died on 18 Jul 1885 at Koehler, Saratov, RUS.

        (b) Susana[6] Gerk (2946) was born on 24 May 1886 at Koehler, Saratov, RUS. She married Adam Schmidt (2945), son of Nikolaus Schmidt (3752) and Elisabeta Reimer (3753), circa 1906. She died on 17 Jun 1962 at Pueblo Santa María, Coronel Suárez, Buenos Aires, ARG, at age 76.

            i) Adam[7] Schmidt (2947) was born on 22 May 1908 at Pueblo Santa María, Coronel Suárez, Buenos Aires, ARG.

ii) Juan Jorge[7] Schmidt (2948) was born on 11 Nov 1909 at Pueblo Santa María, Coronel Suárez, Buenos Aires, ARG. He married Maria Schiefelbein (2955) on 17 Sep 1953 at Pueblo Santa María, Coronel Suárez, Buenos Aires, ARG.

iii) Juan Pedro[7] Schmidt (2949) was born on 12 Nov 1911 at Pueblo Santa María, Coronel Suárez, Buenos Aires, ARG.

iv) José[7] Schmidt (2950) was born on 26 Oct 1913 at Pueblo Santa María, Coronel Suárez, Buenos Aires, ARG.

v) Pedro[7] Schmidt (2951) was born on 5 Nov 1915 at Pueblo Santa María, Coronel Suárez, Buenos Aires, ARG. He married Rose Roth (2956) on 11 Jun 1946 at Pueblo Santa María, Coronel Suárez, Buenos Aires, ARG.

vi) Luis[7] Schmidt (2952) was born on 17 Mar 1917 at Pueblo Santa María, Coronel Suárez, Buenos Aires, ARG.

vii) Miguel[7] Schmidt (2953) was born on 24 Aug 1919 at Pueblo Santa María, Coronel Suárez, Buenos Aires, ARG. He married Luisa Elvira Eberle (2957) on 23 Jan 1951 at Pueblo Santa María, Coronel Suárez, Buenos Aires, ARG.

viii) Maria[7] Schmidt (2954) was born on 18 Nov 1921 at Pueblo Santa María, Coronel Suárez, Buenos Aires, ARG.

ix) Josefina[7] Schmidt (2958) was born in 1924 at Coronel Suárez, Buenos Aires, ARG.

x) Jeronineo[7] Schmidt (2960) was born in 1925 at Coronel Suárez, Buenos Aires, ARG.

xi) Catalina[7] Schmidt (2959) was born in 1927 at Pueblo Santa María, Coronel Suárez, Buenos Aires, ARG.

(c) Johann[6] Gerk (4228) was born on 18 Dec 1887 at Koehler, Saratov, RUS. He died on 23 Dec 1887 at Koehler, Saratov, RUS.

(d) Johannes[6] Gerk (4223) was born on 30 Jul 1889 at Koehler, Saratov, RUS. He married Magdalena (--?--) (4239) circa 1910 at Koehler, Saratov, RUS.

i) Rosa[7] Gerk (4240) was born in 1913 at Koehler, Saratov, RUS.

ii) Peter[7] Gerk (4241) was born in 1915 at Koehler, Saratov, RUS.

(e) Anna[6] Gerk (3864) was born on 8 Sep 1891 at Koehler, Saratov, RUS. She married Nikolaus Dietrich (3865), son of Andreas Dietrich (6554) and Klara Hasenhauer (6555), on 25 Jan 1911 at Koehler, Saratov, RUS.

(f) Peter[6] Gerk (4224) was born on 18 Oct 1893 at Koehler, Saratov, RUS. He died on 4 Aug 1895 at Koehler, Saratov, RUS, at age 1.

(g) Adam[6] Gerk (4225) was born on 25 Dec 1895 at Koehler, Saratov, RUS. He died on 10 May 1896 at Koehler, Saratov, RUS.

(h) Margareta[6] Gerk (4229) was born on 9 Aug 1897 at Koehler, Saratov, RUS.

(i) Maria[6] Gerk (4226) was born on 24 Mar 1900 at Koehler, Saratov, RUS.

(3) Sophia[5] Gerk (4208) was born in May 1868 at Koehler, Saratov, RUS. She died on 13 May 1868 at Koehler, Saratov, RUS.

(4) Josef[5] Gerk (4214) was born in 1870 at Koehler, Saratov, RUS. He married Anna Maria Senger (4215) on 5 Feb 1891 at Koehler, Saratov, RUS.

(a) Maria[6] Gerk (4216) was born on 21 Sep 1893 at Koehler, Saratov, RUS.

(b) Josef[6] Gerk (4217) was born on 28 Dec 1895 at Koehler, Saratov, RUS. He died on 8 May 1896 at Koehler, Saratov, RUS.

(c) Anna[6] Gerk (4218) was born on 1 Apr 1897 at Koehler, Saratov, RUS.

(d) Barbara[6] Gerk (4219) was born on 8 Jan 1899 at Koehler, Saratov, RUS.

(e) Alexander[6] Gerk (4220) was born on 24 May 1901 at Koehler, Saratov, RUS.

(f) Rosa[6] Gerk (5542) was born on 17 Dec 1916 at Koehler, Saratov, RUS. She married Johannes Schabanow (6191), son of Gawrili Schabanow (6192) and Maria Nupri (6193), on 2 Jun 1934 at Sasergje, USSR.

    i) Klara[7] Schabanow (6194) was born on 16 May 1935 at Sasergje, USSR.

    ii) Lydia[7] Schabanow (6195) was born on 23 Nov 1937 at Polos, USSR.

    iii) Rudolf[7] Schabanow (6196) was born on 26 Nov 1941 at Dserschinsk, USSR.

(5) Andreas[5] Gerk (4210) was born on 5 Mar 1873 at Koehler, Saratov, RUS. He died on 5 Jul 1873 at Koehler, Saratov, RUS.

(6) Jakob[5] Gerk (4211) was born on 25 May 1874 at Koehler, Saratov, RUS. He died on 12 Sep 1876 at Koehler, Saratov, RUS, at age 2.

(7) Peter[5] Gerk (4212) was born on 7 Apr 1877 at Koehler, Saratov, RUS. He married Magdalena Leonardt (4213) on 26 Nov 1891 at Koehler, Saratov, RUS.

(8) Anna Margareta[5] Gerk (4207) was born on 19 Sep 1878 at Koehler, Saratov, RUS.

(9) Gustav[5] Gerk (3705) was born on 6 Oct 1882 at Koehler, Saratov, RUS. He married Katarina Senger (3706), daughter of Jakob Senger (6556) and Katharina Schmidt (6557), on 5 Oct 1910 at Koehler, Saratov, RUS.

    (a) Gustav[6] Gerk (7810) was born in 1923 at Koehler, Saratov, RUS.

f) Barbara[4] Gerk (3051) was born on 7 Apr 1846 at Koehler, Saratov, RUS. She died on 17 Nov 1846 at Koehler, Saratov, RUS.

g) Johannes[4] Gerk (1696) was born on 30 May 1848 at Koehler, Saratov, RUS. He died on 26 Dec 1858 at Koehler, Saratov, RUS, at age 10.

h) Jakob[4] Gerk (1697) was born on 19 Sep 1850 at Koehler, Saratov, RUS. He died on 14 Apr 1851 at Koehler, Saratov, RUS.

i) Marianna Magdalena[4] Gerk (3052) was born on 8 May 1852 at Koehler, Saratov, RUS. She died on 29 Aug 1855 at Koehler, Saratov, RUS, at age 3.

j) Magdalena[4] Gerk (3439) was born on 4 Oct 1854 at Koehler, Saratov, RUS.

k) Elisabeta[4] Gerk (1698) was born on 23 Nov 1855 at Koehler, Saratov, RUS.

l) Margareta[4] Gerk (3053) was born on 4 Jul 1858 at Koehler, Saratov, RUS.

E. Johannes[2] Gerk (7831) was born on 7 Feb 1761 at Müs, Fulda, Hesse, GER. He died on 22 Sep 1763 at Müs, Fulda, Hesse, GER, at age 2.

F. Johannes[2] Gerk (7832) was born on 4 Nov 1763 at Müs, Hesse, GER. He died circa 1765 at Fulda, Hesse, GER..

As of 19 Feb 2020

Right Photo: Cross in abandoned cemetery in Josefstal, Russia. Many Gerk's are buried there.

Soviet officials ripped the names off most such crosses, in attempt to obliterate evidence of the Volga Germans.

September, 2009

www.ingramcontent.com/pod-product-compliance
Lightning Source LLC
Chambersburg PA
CBHW080605270326
41928CB00016B/2927

9780987814913